W9-BTP-901

Making Things Happen
Mastering Project Management

Other resources from O'Reilly

Related titles
Applied Software Process Management
The Art of Agile Development
The Art of SQL

Beautiful Code
The Myths of Innovation
Prefactoring
Process Improvement Essentials

oreilly.com
oreilly.com is more than a complete catalog of O'Reilly books. You'll also find links to news, events, articles, weblogs, sample chapters, and code examples.

oreillynet.com is the essential portal for developers interested in open and emerging technologies, including new platforms, programming languages, and operating systems.

Conferences
O'Reilly brings diverse innovators together to nurture the ideas that spark revolutionary industries. We specialize in documenting the latest tools and systems, translating the innovator's knowledge into useful skills for those in the trenches. Visit *conferences.oreilly.com* for our upcoming events.

Safari Bookshelf (*safari.oreilly.com*) is the premier online reference library for programmers and IT professionals. Conduct searches across more than 1,000 books. Subscribers can zero in on answers to time-critical questions in a matter of seconds. Read the books on your Bookshelf from cover to cover or simply flip to the page you need. Try it today for free.

Making Things Happen

Mastering Project Management

Scott Berkun

O'REILLY®

Beijing • Cambridge • Farnham • Köln • Sebastopol • Tokyo

Making Things Happen
by Scott Berkun

Published by O'Reilly Media, Inc. 1005 Gravenstein Highway North, Sebastopol, CA 95472

O'Reilly books may be purchased for educational, business, or sales promotional use. Online editions are also available for most titles (*safari.oreilly.com*). For more information, contact our corporate/institutional sales department: (800) 998-9938 or *corporate@oreilly.com*.

Editor: Mary Treseler	**Indexer:** Ellen Troutman Zaig
Production Editor: Marlowe Shaeffer	**Cover Designer:** Mark Paglietti
Copyeditor: Marlowe Shaeffer	**Interior Designers:** Marcia Friedman and
Proofreader: Audrey Doyle	Ron Bilodeau
	Illustrator: Robert Romano

Printing History:

March 2008:	First Edition. (A revised edition of the work previously published as *The Art of Project Management*.)

ISBN: 978-0-596-51771-7
[LSI]   [2011-02-25]

TABLE OF CONTENTS

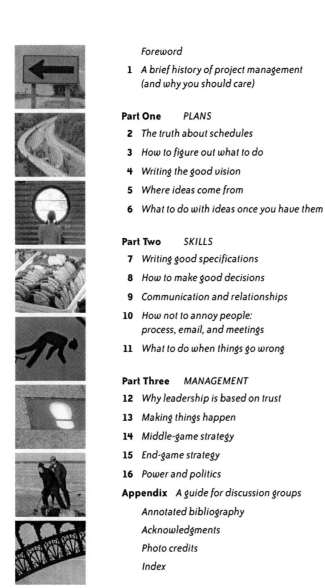

26.24

FOREWORD

Something crazy happened with the first edition of this book. It sold lots of copies. It made several bestseller lists, was nominated for awards, and earned enough attention to send its author around the world to talk about ideas from the book. Then something crazier happened: the book's title needed to change.

Taking this as an opportunity, the folks at O'Reilly and I agreed we should add more value to the book if it was going to have a second life with a new name. First published as *The Art of Project Management*, this text has been cleaned-up, enhanced, updated, and expanded for your pleasure. You may wonder why the title was changed. Here are some possibilities:

1. The Department of Homeland Security discovered a terrorist threat in the old title.
2. Tim O'Reilly realized his media empire could achieve instant world domination if he could just get owners of the first book to buy it a second time, under the ruse of a title change.
3. <Insert motive from your own imagination here.>

Whatever the reason, here we are. I've done my best to improve this book without pulling a George Lucas *Star Wars* fiasco. Here's the bird's-eye view of what has changed:

- The text is revised for clarity and concision. It's a more confident, fluff-free book.
- The addition of more than 120 thought-provoking exercises, appearing at the end of every chapter.
- By popular demand, endnotes were promoted to footnotes, appearing within the chapter texts.
- There is a new discussion guide to help you form groups to keep learning.

If you are new to this book in any form, the Preface will fill you in on everything you need to know.

Since the first edition was published two years ago, I've been busy. I wrote another book called *The Myths of Innovation*; created various essays, podcasts, and videos; and I continue to run a popular blog on creativity and management. It's all up at *www.scottberkun.com*; I hope you'll stop by, as your purchase of this book helps make the many free things I produce possible.

Cheers and best wishes,

Scott Berkun
Redmond, WA
March 2008

PREFACE

My favorite word in the English language is how. How does this work? How was this made? How did they do this? Whenever I see something interesting happen, I'm filled with questions that involve this small but powerful little word. And most of the answers I find center on how people apply their own intelligence and wisdom, rather than their knowledge of specific technologies or theories.

Over years of building things and comparing my experiences to those of other managers, programmers, and designers, I've learned how to manage projects well. This book is a summation of those ideas. It includes approaches for leading teams, working with ideas, organizing projects, managing schedules, dealing with politics, and making things happen—even in the face of great challenges and unfair situations.

Despite the broad title of this book, most of my working experience comes from the tech sector, and in particular, Microsoft Corporation. I worked there from 1994 to 2003, leading teams of people on projects such as Internet Explorer, Microsoft Windows, and MSN. For a few years I worked in Microsoft's engineering excellence group. While there, I was responsible for teaching and consulting with teams across the company, and was often asked to lecture at public conferences, corporations, and universities. Most of the advice, lessons, and stories in this book come from those experiences.

Although I come from a software and web development background, I've written this book broadly and inclusively, calling on references and techniques from outside the engineering and management domains. There is great value here for people in the general business world. I'm convinced that the challenges of organizing, leading, designing, and delivering work have much in common, regardless of the domain. The processes involved in making toaster ovens, skyscrapers, automobiles, web sites, and software products share many of the same challenges, and this book is primarily about overcoming those challenges.

Unlike some other books on how to lead projects, this book doesn't ascribe to any grand theory or presumptively innovative philosophy. Instead, I've placed my bet on practicality and diversity. Projects result in good things when the right combination of people, skills, attitudes, and tactics is applied, regardless of their origin or (lack of) pedigree. The structure of this book is the most sensible one I found: focus on the core situations and provide advice on how to handle them well. I've wagered heavily on picking the right topics and giving good advice over all other considerations. I hope you find that I've made the right choice.

Who should read this book

To see if this book is for you, I suggest flipping back to the Table of Contents, picking a topic you're interested in, and skimming through what I have to say. I don't trust prefaces much, and I recommend you don't either; they rarely have the same style or voice as the rest of the book. But here goes anyway.

The book will be most valuable for people who fit themselves into one or more of the following categories:

- **Experienced team leaders and managers.** This book is well suited for anyone playing a leadership role on any kind of project. The examples are from software development, but many concepts apply easily to other kinds of work. You might be the official team leader, or simply one of the more experienced people on the team. While some topics may be very familiar, the direct approach the book takes will help you clarify and refine your opinions. Even if you disagree with points I make, you will have a clear foundation to work against in refining your own point of view.

- **New team leaders and managers.** If you look at the topics listed in the Table of Contents, you'll find a solid overview of everything project leaders and managers actually do. Each chapter provides coverage of the common mistakes even experienced people make, with explanations as to why they happen and what tactics can be used to avoid them. This book provides you with a broader view of the new responsibilities you've taken on and the smartest ways to go about managing them. Because most chapters cover big topics, they often include annotated references to deeper sources.

- **Individual programmers and testers, or other contributors to projects.** This book will improve your understanding of what you're contributing to, and what approaches you can use to be effective in doing so. If you've ever wondered why projects change directions so often or seem to be poorly managed, this book will help you understand the causes and remedies. If nothing else, reading this book will help you increase the odds your work will make a difference (and that you will stay sane while doing it). If you are interested in eventually leading teams yourself, this book will help you explore what that will really be like and whether you are cut out for it.

- **Students of business management, product design, or software engineering.** I use the word *students* in the broadest sense: if you have a personal interest in these topics or are formally studying them, this book should be appealing. Unlike textbook coverage of these topics, this book is heavily situation- and narrative-focused. The experiences and stories are real, and they are the basis for the lessons and tactics—not the other way around. I deliberately avoid drawing lines between different academic subjects because, in my experience, those lines neither help projects nor contribute to understanding reality (the universe is not divided in the same way universities tend to be). Instead, this book combines business theory, psychology, management tactics, design processes, and software engineering in whatever way necessary to offer advice on the outlined topics.

Assumptions I've made about you in writing this book

- **You are not stupid.** I assume that if I've chosen the right chapters and written them well, you won't need me to spend time slowly constructing elaborate frameworks of information. Instead, I will get to the point and spend time there. I assume you're a peer—perhaps with more, less, or different experience—who has dropped by for some advice.

- **You are curious and pragmatic.** I draw on examples from many disciplines, and I assume you'll find value in lessons from outside of web and software development. This won't get in the way, but pointers for curious minds will surface, sometimes just in footnotes. I assume you want to learn, are open to different ideas, and will recognize the value of well-considered opinions—even if you don't agree with them.

- **You do not like jargon or big theories.** I don't think jargon and big theories help in learning and applying new information. I avoid them, except where they provide a path to useful information that will be helpful later on.

- **You don't take yourself, software, or management too seriously.** Software development and project management can be boring. While this book won't be a comical romp (although a book by Mark Twain or David Sedaris on software engineering has potential), I won't hesitate to make jokes at my expense (or someone else's expense), or use examples that make points through comedic means.

How to use this book

If at any point you get bored, or find the examples distracting, skip ahead. I wrote this book with consideration for people who skim or have a specific problem they need advice on right away. The chapters stand up well on their own, particularly those on human nature (Chapters 8–13 and Chapter 16). However, there is some benefit to reading it straight through; some later concepts build on earlier ones, and the book roughly follows the chronology of most projects. The first chapter is the broadest in the book and has a deeper tone than the rest. If you're curious about why you should care about project management, or what other important people have said about it, then you should give it a shot. If you try it and hate it, I definitely recommend giving another chapter a try before abandoning ship.

All of the references and URLs listed in the book, as well as additional notes and commentary, are online at *www.makingthingshappen.org*. If you're interested in discussion groups about the book, make sure to peek at the Appendix in the back. It explains what groups exist and gives you advice on how to start your own.

And now, because you were smart and patient enough to read this entire introduction, I'll assume you're up to speed on the other mechanics of book reading (page numbers, footnotes, and all that) and just get out of your way.

How to contact us

Please address comments and questions concerning this book to the publisher:

O'Reilly Media, Inc.
1005 Gravenstein Highway North
Sebastopol, CA 95472
800-998-9938 (in the United States or Canada)
707-829-0515 (international or local)
707-829-0104 (fax)

We have a web page for this book, where we list errata, examples, and any additional information. You can access this page at:

http://www.oreilly.com/catalog/9780596517717

To comment or ask technical questions about this book, send email to:

bookquestions@oreilly.com

For more information about our books, conferences, Resource Centers, and the O'Reilly Network, see our web site at:

http://www.oreilly.com

Safari® Books Online

 When you see a Safari® Books Online icon on the cover of your favorite technology book, that means the book is available online through the O'Reilly Network Safari Bookshelf.

Safari offers a solution that's better than e-books. It's a virtual library that lets you easily search thousands of top tech books, cut and paste code samples, download chapters, and find quick answers when you need the most accurate, current information. Try it for free at *http://safari.oreilly.com*.

CHAPTER ONE

**A brief history of project management
(and why you should care)**

In many organizations, the person leading a project doesn't have the job title *project manager*. That's OK. Everyone manages projects in their daily work, whether they are working alone or leading a team. For the moment, these distinctions are not important. My intent is to capture what makes projects successful, and how the people who lead successful projects do it. These strategies don't require specific hierarchies, job titles, or methods. So, if you work on a project and have at least some responsibility for its outcome, what follows will apply to you. And should your business card happen to say *project manager* on it, all the better.

This book is useful in three ways: as a collection of individual topic-focused essays, as a single extended narrative, and as a reference for common situations. Each chapter takes on a different high-level task, provides a basic framework, and offers tactics for successfully completing the task. However, in this opening chapter, I need to take a different approach: there are three broader topics that will make the rest of the book easier to follow, and I will present them now.

The first is a short history of projects and why we should learn from what others have done. The second is some background on the different flavors of project management, including some notes from my experience working at Microsoft. And the third is a look at the underlying challenges involved in project management and how they can be overcome. Although these points will be useful later on, they are not required to understand the following chapters. So, if you find the approach in this first chapter too wide for your liking, feel free to move on to Chapter 2 and the core of this book.

Using history

Project management, as an idea, goes back a very long way. If you think about all of the things that have been built in the history of civilization, we have thousands of years of project experience to learn from. A dotted line can be drawn from the software developers of today back through time to the builders of the Egyptian pyramids or the architects of the Roman aqueducts. For their respective eras, project managers have played similar roles, applying technology to the relevant problems of the times. Yet today, when most people try to improve how their web and software development projects are managed, it's rare that they pay attention to lessons learned from the past. The timeline we use as the scope for useful knowledge is much closer to present day than it should be.

The history of engineering projects reveals that most projects have strong similarities. They have requirements, designs, and constraints. They depend on communication, decision making, and combinations of creative and logical thought. Projects usually involve a schedule, a budget, and a customer. Most importantly, the central task of projects is to combine the works of different people into a singular, coherent whole that will be useful to people or customers. Whether a project is built out of HTML, C++, or cement and steel, there's an undeniable core set of concepts that most projects share.

Curious about better ways to lead web and software development efforts, I've taken a serious interest in that core. I studied other fields to see how they solved the central challenges to their projects. I wondered how projects like the Hubble Space Telescope and the Boeing 777 were designed and constructed. Could I reuse anything from their complex specifications and planning processes? Or when the Chrysler Building was built in New York City and the Parthenon in Athens, did the project leaders plan and estimate their construction in the same way my programmers did? What were the interesting differences, and what can be gained by examining those differences?

How about newspaper editors, who organize and plan for daily production of information? They were doing multimedia (pictures and words) long before the first dreams of web publishing. What about feature film production? The *Apollo 13* launch? By examining these questions, I was able to look at how I went about leading project teams in a new way.

However, these inquiries didn't always provide obvious answers. I can't promise that you'll ship sooner or plan better specifically because the advice in this book was influenced by these sources. But I do know that when I returned to the software world after looking elsewhere, my own processes and tools looked different to me. I found ways to change them that I hadn't considered before. On the whole, I realized that many of the useful approaches and comparisons I found were never mentioned during my computer science studies in college. They were never discussed at tech-sector conferences or written about in trade magazines.

The key lessons from my inquiries into the past are the following three points:

1. **Project management and software development are not sacred arts.** Any modern engineering work is one new entry in the long history of making things. The technologies and skills may change, but many of the core challenges that make engineering difficult remain. All things, whether programming languages or development methodologies, are unique in some ways but derivative in others. But if we want to reuse as much knowledge as we can from the past, we need to make sure we're open to examining both aspects—the unique and the derivative—in comparing with what has come before.

2. **The simpler your view of what you do, the more power and focus you will have in doing it.** If we keep a simple view of our work, we can find useful comparisons to other ways to make things that exist all around us. There will be more examples and lessons from history and modern industries that can be pulled from,

compared with, and contrasted against. This is similar to the concept defined by the Japanese word *shoshin*—which means beginner's mind,[1] or open mind—an essential part of many martial arts disciplines. Staying curious and open is what makes growth possible, and it requires practice to maintain that mindset. To keep learning, we have to avoid the temptation to slide into narrow, safe views of what we do.

3. **Simple doesn't mean easy.** The best athletes, writers, programmers, and managers tend to be the ones who always see what they do as simple in nature but simultaneously difficult. Remember that simple is not the same thing as easy. For example, it's a simple thing to run a marathon. You start running and don't stop until you've reached 26.2 miles. What could be simpler? The fact that it's difficult doesn't negate its simplicity. Leadership and management are also difficult, but their nature—getting things done in a specific way toward a specific goal—is simple.

I'll allude to these concepts in many chapters. So, if I make references that are out of the stereotypical bounds of software development, I hope you'll understand why. And when I suggest that decision making or scheduling are simple management functions, I'll assume you'll know that this in no way suggests these things are easy to do.

Learning from failure

"Human beings, who are almost unique [among animals] in having the ability to learn from the experience of others, are also remarkable for their apparent disinclination to do so."

—*Douglas Adams*

One simple question that arises in studying the history of projects is this: why would anyone willingly suffer through mistakes and disappointments if they could be avoided? If the history of both ancient and modern engineering is public, and we get paid for doing smart things regardless of where the inspiration came from, why do so few organizations reward people for harvesting lessons from the past? As projects are completed or are canceled (and many development projects end this way[2]) every day, little is done to learn from what happened. It seems that managers in most organizations rarely reward people for seeking out this kind of knowledge. Perhaps it's fear of what they'll find (and the fear of being held accountable for it). Or maybe it's just a lack of interest on anyone's part to review painful or frustrating experiences when time could be spent moving on to the next new thing instead.

---

1   Beginner's mind is an introductory concept of Zen Buddhism. The canonical story is that of the empty cup: if you hold on tightly to what your cup is filled with, your cup will never have room for new knowledge. See Shunryu Suzuki's *Zen Mind, Beginner's Mind* (Weatherhill, 1972).

2   *The CHAOS Report* (The Standish Group) is a commonly referenced paper on budget, schedule, and general failures of software projects. See *http://standishgroup.com/sample_research/*.

In Henry Petroski's book *To Engineer Is Human: The Role of Failure in Successful Design* (Vintage Books, 1992), he explains how many breakthroughs in engineering took place as a result of failure. In part, this happens because failures force us to pay attention. They demand us to re-examine assumptions we'd forgotten were there (it's hard to pretend everything's OK when the prototype has burst into flames). As Karl Popper[3] suggested, there are only two kinds of theories: those that are wrong and those that are incomplete. Without failure, we forget, in arrogance, that our understanding of things is never as complete as we think it is.

The trick then is to learn as much as possible from other people's failures. We should use their experiences to leverage against the future. While the superficial details of failure might differ dramatically from project to project, the root causes or team actions that led to them might be entirely transferable (and avoidable). Even on our own projects, we need to avoid the habit of running away and hiding from failures. Instead, we should see them as opportunities to learn something. What factors contributed to it happening? Which ones might be easy to minimize or eliminate? According to Petroski, real knowledge from real failure is the most powerful source of progress we have, provided we have the courage to carefully examine what happened.

Perhaps this is why The Boeing Company, one of the largest airplane design and engineering firms in the world, keeps a black book of lessons it has learned from design and engineering failures.[4] Boeing has kept this document since the company was formed, and it uses it to help modern designers learn from past attempts. Any organization that manages to do this not only increases its chances for successful projects, but also helps create an environment that can discuss and confront failure openly, instead of denying and hiding from it. It seems that software developers need to keep black books of their own.

Web development, kitchens, and emergency rooms

One problem with history is that it's not always relatable. It can be hard to apply lessons across decades and sustain empathy for things that seem so different from how work is done today. One alternative is to make comparisons with interesting kinds of modern projects. While this doesn't have the gravitas of engineering history, it does allow for first-person experiences and observations. Often, seeing things firsthand is the only way to give people enough information to make connections among diverse ideas.

---

3 Karl Popper was a prominent philosopher of science in the 20th century. See *http://en.wikipedia. org/wiki/Karl_Popper*.

4 From James R. Chiles, *Inviting Disaster: Lessons from the Edge of Technology* (HarperBusiness, 2002).

As an example, I know a web developer who believes that his work is unlike anything else in the history of the universe. He feels that because web development requires him to make complex engineering decisions—designing and coordinating as he goes, verifying changes in a matter of hours or even minutes, and then publishing it all to the world—his project and task management is unlike anything ever seen before. He is proud to rattle off CSS, XHTML, Flash, Ajax, and other technologies he has mastered, claiming that they would have baffled the greatest minds 50 years ago. I'm sure that in your experience, you've met people like him. Or perhaps you have worked in situations where it seemed improbable that anyone else in the universe ever managed anything as complex as what you were doing.

I suggested to this developer friend that he wander into the back of his favorite lunch establishment on a busy day. For a variety of reasons, it's interesting to step foot into kitchens (see Anthony Bourdain's excellent book, *Kitchen Confidential*, Ecco, 2001), but my specific point was about productivity. The first time anyone sees the quick task management and coordination that occur in a busy professional kitchen, he's likely to reconsider how difficult his own job is. Cooks are often juggling frying pans with different orders at different states of completion, and scrambling between multiple sets of burners in opposite corners of the kitchen, while waiters run in and out, delivering news of new adjustments and problems from customers.

All of this happens in small, cramped rooms, well over 90 degrees, with bright fluorescent lights glaring above. And despite how many orders go out every few seconds, new ones come in just as fast. Sometimes orders get sent back, or, much like software projects, require custom and last-minute modifications (table 1 is lactose intolerant; table 2 needs the sauce on the side, etc.). Large, busy kitchens are amazing to watch. As chaotic as they may seem at first, great kitchens run with a level of intensity and precision that blows most development teams away.

Working chefs and line cooks are culinary project managers, or as Bourdain refers to them, air traffic controllers (another profession for the introspective to consider). Even though kitchen staff works on a scale smaller and less celebrated than a manager of a software development team, there's no comparison for daily intensity. If you doubt me, next time you're at that busy lunch place, ask your server if you can peek inside the kitchen. He might not let you, but if he does, you will not be disappointed. (Some trendier restaurants and bars have open kitchens. If you find one, sit as close to the kitchen as you can. Then follow one person for a few minutes. Watch how orders are placed, tracked, constructed, and delivered. If you go on a busy day, you'll think differently about how software bugs are opened, tracked, and fixed.)

Another interesting field lesson in project management comes from hospital emergency rooms. I've watched on the Discovery Channel and PBS how small teams of expert doctors, nurses, and specialists work together as a project team to treat the diverse and sometimes bizarre medical situations that come through the hospital doors. It's not surprising that this is the profession that invented the process of triage, a term commonly used on software projects to prioritize issues and defects (discussed in Chapter 15).

The medical environment, especially trauma situations, offers a fascinating comparison for team-based work, high-stress decision making, and project outcomes that affect many people every day (see Figure 1-1 for a rough comparison of this and other work environments). As Atul Gawande wrote in his excellent book, *Complications: A Surgeon's Notes on an Imperfect Science* (Picador USA, 2003):

> We look for medicine to be an orderly field of knowledge and procedure. But it is not. It is an imperfect science, an enterprise of constantly changing knowledge, uncertain information, fallible individuals, and at the same time lives on the line. There is science in what we do, yes, but also habit, intuition, and sometimes plain old guessing. The gap between what we know and we aim for persists. And this gap complicates everything we do.

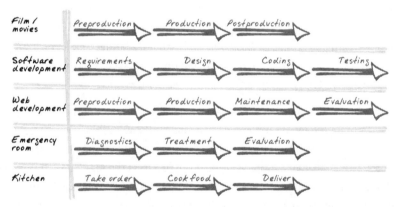

FIGURE 1-1. *In the abstract, many disciplines have similar processes. They all dedicate time to planning, executing, and refining. (However, you should never go to a kitchen for medical treatment or eat in an emergency room.)*

This point, and many others in Gawande's enlightening book, holds true for software development. Fred Brooks, in the classic book on software engineering, *The Mythical Man-Month* (Addison-Wesley Professional, 1995), makes similar comparisons between teams of surgeons and teams of programmers. Even though lives are rarely at stake when working on web sites or databases, there are many valid similarities in the challenges these different teams of people must face.

The role of project management

Project management can be a profession, a job, a role, or an activity. Some companies have project managers whose job is to oversee entire 200-person projects. Others use the title for line-level junior managers, each responsible for a small area of a large project. Depending on how an organization is structured, what its culture is, and what the goals of the project are, project management can be an informal role ("it's done by whomever, whenever necessary") or highly defined ("Vincent, Claude, and Raphael are full-time project managers").

In this book, I'll primarily use the phrase *project manager*, or *PM*, to refer to whoever is involved in project leadership and management activity. By *project management activity* I mean leading the team in figuring out what the project is (planning, scheduling, and requirements gathering), shepherding the project through design and development work (communication, decision making, and mid-game strategy), and driving the project through to completion (leadership, crisis management, and end-game strategy).

If this sort of work is structured less formally in your world, just translate project manager or PM to mean "person doing project management tasks, even though it's not her primary job" or "person thinking about the project at large." I've encountered many different ways for these activities to be distributed across teams, and the advice in this book is largely indifferent to them. This book is less about job titles and formalizations, and more about how to get things done and make things happen. But to keep my writing as simple as possible, I'll rely on the phrase *project manager*, or *PM*.

Sometimes the absence of a dedicated project manager works fine. Programmers and their bosses maintain schedules and engineering plans (if any), and a business analyst or marketing person does the planning or requirements work. Anything else that might qualify as project management simply gets distributed across the team. Perhaps people on the team have been hired for their interest beyond writing code. They might not mind early planning, user interface design, or business strategy. There can be significant optimizations in working this way. As long as everyone is willing to pay the tax of responsibility for keeping things together, and distributing the burden that a dedicated project manager would carry for the team, there's one less employee that the team needs. Efficiency and simplicity are good things.

But other times, the absence of a project manager creates dysfunction. Without a person whose primary job is to shepherd the overall effort, individual biases and interests can derail the directions of the team. Strong adversarial factions may develop around engineering and business roles, slowing progress and frustrating everyone involved.

Consider that in hospital emergency rooms, one doctor takes the lead in deciding the course of action for a patient. This expedites many decisions and gives clarity to the roles that everyone on the trauma team is expected to play. Without that kind of clear authority for project management-type issues, development teams can run into trouble. If there is no clear owner for leading bug triage, or no one is dedicated to tracking the schedule and flagging problems, those tasks might lag dangerously behind individual, programming-centric activities.

While I think many of the best programmers understand enough about project management to do it themselves, they also recognize the unique value of a good, dedicated person playing the role of manager.

Program and project management at Microsoft

Microsoft had a problem in the late 1980s regarding how to coordinate engineering efforts with the marketing and business side of each division (some might say this is still a problem for Microsoft and many other companies). A wise man named Jabe Blumenthal realized that there could be a special job where an individual would be involved with these two functions, playing a role of both leadership and coordination. He'd be involved in the project from day one of planning, all the way through the last day of testing. It had to be someone who was at least technical enough to work with and earn the respect of programmers, but also someone who had talents and interests for broader participation in how products were made.

For this role to work, he'd have to enjoy spending his days performing tasks as varied as writing specifications, reviewing marketing plans, generating project schedules, leading teams, doing strategic planning, running bug/defect triage, cultivating team morale, and doing anything else that needed to be done that no one else was doing (well). This new role at Microsoft was called *program manager*. Not everyone on the team would report directly to him, but the program manager would be granted significant authority to lead and drive the project. (In management theory, this is roughly the idea of a matrix organization,[5] where there are two lines of reporting structure for individuals: one based on function and the other based on project. So, an individual programmer or tester might have two reporting relationships—a primary one for her functional role and a secondary, but strong, one for the project she works on.)

---

5 A good summary of matrix and other organization types can be found in Steven A. Silbiger's *The Ten-Day MBA* (William Morrow and Company, 1993), pp. 139–145. But almost any book on management theory covers this topic.

Jabe played this role on a product called Multiplan (later to become Microsoft Excel), and it worked. The engineering and development process improved along with the quality of coordination with the business team, and throughout the hallways at Microsoft there was much rejoicing. After many memos and meetings, most teams within the company slowly adopted the role. Say what you will, good or bad, about the resulting products, but the idea makes sense. By defining a role for a line-level generalist who was not a gofer or a lackey, but a leader and a driver, the dynamics of how development teams worked at Microsoft changed forever. This role of program manager was what I did through most of my career at Microsoft, and I worked on product teams that included Internet Explorer, MSN, and Windows. Eventually, I even managed teams of people who played this role.

To this day, I don't know of many companies that have gone as far in redefining and formalizing a specialized form of project management. It was rare in my many interactions with other web and software development firms to encounter someone who played a similar kind of role (either they were engineers or business types, or on rare occasions, designers). Many companies use team structures for organizing work, but few define roles that cross over engineering and business hierarchies deliberately. Today, there are more than 5,000 program managers at Microsoft (out of more than 80,000 total employees), and although the power of the idea has been diluted and abused, the core spirit of it can be found in many teams within the company.

But regardless of what it said on my business card, or what Microsoft lore you choose to believe or ignore, my daily functions as a program manager were project management functions. In the simplest terms, this meant that I was responsible for making the project—and whoever was contributing to it—as successful as possible. All of the chapters in this book reflect the core tasks involved in doing this, from early planning (Chapters 3 and 4), to spec writing (Chapter 7), to decision making (Chapter 8), to implementation management and release (Chapters 14 and 15).

Beneath these skills, certain attitudes and personality traits come into play. Without awareness of them, anyone leading or managing a project is at a serious disadvantage.

The balancing act of project management

It is hard to find good project managers because they need to maintain a balance of attitudes. In his essay "Pursuing the Perfect Project Manager,"[6] Tom Peters calls these conflicting attitudes paradoxes or dilemmas. This name is appropriate because different situations require different behavior. This means that a project manager needs not only to be aware of these traits, but also to develop instincts for which ones are appropriate at

---

6   Visit *http://www.tompeters.com/col_entries.php?note=005297&year=1991.*

which times. This contributes to the idea of project management as an art: it requires intuition, judgment, and experience to use these forces effectively. The following list of traits is roughly derived from Peters' essay:

- **Ego/no-ego.** Because of how much responsibility project managers have, they often derive great personal satisfaction from their work. It's understandable that they'd have a high emotional investment in what they're doing, and for many, this emotional connection is what enables them to maintain the intensity needed to be effective. But at the same time, project managers must avoid placing their own interests ahead of the project. They must be willing to delegate important or fun tasks and share rewards with the entire team. As much as ego can be a fuel, a good project manager has to recognize when his ego is getting in the way.

- **Autocrat/delegator.** In some situations, the most important things are a clear line of authority and a quick response time. A project manager has to be confident and willful enough to take control and force certain actions onto a team. However, the general goal should be to avoid the need for these extreme situations. A well-managed project should create an environment where work can be delegated and collaborated on effectively.

- **Tolerate ambiguity/pursue perfection.** The early phases of any project are highly open and fluid experiences where the unknown heavily outweighs the known. As we'll discuss in Chapters 5 and 6, controlled ambiguity is essential for good ideas to surface, and a project manager must respect it, if not manage it. But at other moments, particularly in the later phases of a project, discipline and precision are paramount. It requires wisdom to discern when the quest for perfection is worthwhile, versus when a mediocre or quick-and-dirty solution is sufficient. (See the section "Finding and weighing options" in Chapter 8.)

- **Oral/written.** Despite how email centric most software development organizations are, oral skills are critically important to project management. There will always be meetings, negotiations, hallway discussions, and brainstorming sessions, and the project manager must be effective at both understanding and communicating ideas face to face. The larger the organization or the project is, the more important written skills become. Despite her personal preferences, a project manager needs to recognize when written or oral communication will be more effective.

- **Acknowledge complexity/champion simplicity.** Many people fall victim to complexity. When they face a complex organizational or engineering challenge, they get lost in the details and forget the big picture. Others stay in denial about complexity and make bad decisions because they don't fully understand the subtleties of what's involved. The balancing act here is to recognize which view of the project is most useful for the problem or decision at hand, and to comfortably switch between them or keep them both in mind at the same time (without your head exploding). Project managers must be persuasive in getting the team to strive for simplicity in the work they do, without minimizing the complexities involved in writing good, reliable code.

- **Impatient/patient.** Most of the time, the project manager is the person pushing for action, forcing others to keep work lean and focused. But in some situations, impatience works against the project. Some political, cross-organizational, or bureaucratic activities are unavoidable time sinks: someone has to be in the room, or be on the conference call, and they have to be patient. So, knowing when to force an issue, and when to back off and let things happen, is a sense project managers need to develop.

- **Courage/fear.** One of the great misnomers of American culture is that the brave are people who feel no fear. This is a lie. The brave are those who feel fear but choose to take action anyway. A project manager must have a healthy respect for all the things that can go wrong and see them as entirely possible. But a project manager needs to match this respect with the courage necessary to take on big challenges.

- **Believer/skeptic.** There is nothing more powerful for team morale than a respected leader who believes in what she is doing. It's important for a project manager to have confidence in the work being done and see true value in the goals that will be achieved. At the same time, there is a need for skepticism (not cynicism) about how things are going and the ways in which they are being done. Someone has to probe and question, exposing assumptions and bringing difficult issues to light. The balancing act is to somehow vigorously ask questions and challenge the assumptions of others without shaking the team's belief in what they are doing.

As Peters points out in his essay, it's very rare to find people capable of all of these skills, much less with the capacity to balance them properly. Many of the mistakes that any PM will make involve miscalculations in balancing one or more of these conflicting forces. However, anyone can get better at improving his own ability to keep these forces balanced. So, while I won't focus on this list of paradoxes heavily again (although it comes up a few times later on), it is a worthy reference. Looking at this list of conflicting but necessary forces can help you step back, reconsider what you're doing and why, and make smarter decisions.

Pressure and distraction

One fear of those new to project management is that success requires change. New projects are created with the intent to change the state of the world by modifying, building, or destroying something. Maintaining the status quo—unless that's the explicit goal, for some strange reason—is not a successful outcome. The world is changing all the time and if a project is not as good today as it was last year, it means that it's fallen behind because the goals were misguided or the execution of the project failed in some way.

It's hard to ignore the underlying pressure this implies for project managers, but it comes with the territory. Don't just sit there—make it better. There is always a new way to think, a new topic to learn and apply, or a new process that makes work more fun or more effective. Perhaps this is a responsibility more akin to leadership than to management, but the distinction between the two is subtle. No matter how much you try to separate them, managing well requires leadership skills, and leading well requires management skills. Anyone involved in project management will be responsible for some of both, no matter what his job description says.

But getting back to the issue of pressure, I've seen many managers who shy away from leadership moments (e.g., any moment where the team/project needs someone to take decisive action) and retreat to tracking the efforts of others instead of facilitating or even participating in them. If all someone does is keep score and watch from the sidelines, he might be better suited for the accounting department. When someone in a leadership role consistently responds to pressure by getting out of the fray, he's not leading—he's hiding. Ineffective or pressure-adverse PMs tend to fade into the periphery of the project, where they add little value.

Confusing process with goals

Some PMs in this situation resort to quantifying things that don't need to be quantified. Unsure of what else to do, or afraid to do what most needs to be done, they occupy their time with secondary things. And as the gap between the PM and the project grows, the amount of unnecessary attention paid to charts, tables, checklists, and reports increases. It's possible that at some point the PMs begin to believe that the data and the process *are* the project. They focus on the less-important things that are easy to work with (spreadsheets or reports), rather than the important things that are challenging to work with (the programming effort or the schedule). They may develop the belief that if they just follow a certain procedure to perfection and check the right things off the checklist, the project is guaranteed to succeed (or, more cynically, any failure that might happen won't technically be their fault).

To minimize the possibility of confusion, good project managers resist defining strict boundaries around kinds of work they are willing or not willing to do. They avoid bright yellow lines between project management tasks and the project itself. Adherence to checklists implies that there is a definitive process that guarantees a particular outcome, which is never the case. In reality, there are always just three things: a goal, a pile of work, and a bunch of people. Well-defined roles (see Chapter 9) might help those people to organize around the work, but the formation of roles is not the goal. A checklist might help those people do the work in a way that meets the goal, but the checklist is not the goal either. Confusing processes with the goals is one of the great sins of management. I should know: I've committed it myself.

Years ago, working on the Internet Explorer 4.0 project, I was the PM for several large areas of the user interface. I felt significant pressure: it was the largest assignment I'd ever had. In response, I developed the belief that if I could write everything down into checklists, I'd never fail. While things do need to be tracked carefully on a project, I'd taken it too far. I'd built an elaborate spreadsheet to show multiple data views, and the large whiteboards in my office were covered with tables and lists (and extra whiteboards were on the way).

My boss let me run with it because things were going well. That is, until he saw me spending more time with my checklists and processes than I did with my team—a big red flag (warning sign). He came into my office one day, and seeing the comically large matrix of checklists and tables I'd written on every flat surface in my office, sat me down and closed the door. He said, "Scott, this stuff is nice, but your project is your team. Manage the team, not the checklists. If the checklists help you manage the team, great. But the way you're going, soon you'll be using your team to help you manage your checklists."

So, instead of focusing on processes and methods, project managers should be focused on their teams. Simple planning or tracking systems should certainly be used, but they must match the complexity of the project and the culture of the team. More precisely, planning and tracking should support the team in reaching project goals—not inhibit them. I'm confident that as long as the PM is paying attention and has earned the team's trust, any missing tasks, processes, reports, checklists, or other needed project management machinery will become clear before the problems they might solve become serious.

As we'll discuss in Chapter 10, just because a book or an executive says to do something, or because a technique was employed last month or last year, doesn't mean it applies today. Every team and project is different, and there are often good reasons to question old judgments. The reason to be conservative with methods and processes is that the unnecessary ones tend to snowball, dragging teams down into the tar pit of difficult projects, as described in Fred Brooks' *The Mythical Man-Month*. When processes are required to manage processes, it's hard to know where the actual work is being done. It's often the team leader or project manager who has the greatest ability to steer the team clear of bureaucracy, or more cynically, to send the team full throttle into endless circles of procedures and committee-driven thinking.

The right kind of involvement

All managers—from Fortune 500 executives to coaches of sports teams—are vulnerable to over-involving themselves. They know that they are potential overhead, and compulsive involvement is one convenient (though negative) way to try and compensate for it. This partially explains the endless supply of micromanagers; the easiest move for a weak manager is to abuse her power over her subordinates (and in extreme cases, simultaneously blame the subordinates for being incompetent enough to need so much attention). The insecurities managers have stem from the fact that, in industrial revolution terms, managers are not in the line of production. They don't make things with their hands, and they are not the same kind of asset as those who do.

Managers are not hired to contribute a linear amount of work like a worker or programmer is expected to do. Instead, leaders and managers are hired to amplify the value of everyone around them. The methods for adding this kind of value are different from working on the line. But because many managers are former programmers and were promoted into management from the line, odds are good that they have more confidence and skills at writing code than they do leading and managing people who are writing code.

Like a coach for a baseball team, the presence of a manager is supposed to contribute something different in nature from adding another individual contributor. Sometimes this is done by settling arguments or shielding the team from politics. Other times, it's providing good, high-level plans or finding clever workarounds for unexpected situations. Because these contributions are harder to measure, many PMs struggle with the ambiguity of their role. As managers, they are easy targets for blame and have few places to hide. It takes a combination of conviction, confidence, and awareness to be effective and happy as a leader of a team.

Take advantage of your perspective

The best way to find the points of leverage is to make use of the difference in psychology gained from being off the line. A PM will, in the course of his duties, naturally spend more time working with different people on the team than others do, thereby gaining more sources of information and a wider perspective of the project. The PM will understand the business view of the project as well as the technical view, and he'll help the team translate between them when necessary. That wider perspective makes it possible to deliver critical nuggets of information to the right people at the right time. Though this power can have broad effects, what follows is a simple story that helps illustrate this point in a comprehensive way.

As a habit, I've always walked the halls and dropped in on programmers who had their doors open. I'd usually just make small talk, try to get them to laugh about something, and ask them to show me what they were working on. If they offered, I'd watch a demo of whatever they'd show me. Doing this every few days, even for a few minutes, often gave me a good idea of the real status of the project (in Chapter 9, we'll discuss this practice of management by walking around).

For example, one morning during the IE 5.0 project, I dropped by Fred's office. He was arguing with Steve, another programmer, about how they were going to get the new List View control to work properly—an unforeseen compatibility issue had been discovered that morning. Neither one of them wanted to do the work. And from what I could hear, it would take a half-day or more to fix. I poked my nose in and confirmed what they were talking about. They nodded their heads, as if to say, "Yeah, why should you care?" I then told them to go talk to Bill down the hall. They again asked why, thinking this was a very specific architectural issue that I couldn't easily understand. I smiled and said, "Because I just left his office, and he has the new tree control working perfectly on his machine. He came across the problem last night and fixed it as part of another work item."

Now, of course, in this little story I didn't save the world or avert a major disaster. If I hadn't made this connection for them, only a few hours or a half-day would have been wasted (although, as we'll discuss later in Chapter 8, schedules generally slip a little at a time). But that's not the point. Good project managers make it their business to know all kinds of useful things about the state of the team—and the state of the world—and then apply that knowledge to help people get stuff done. It's all of the small bits of timely information transfer, like the one in this story, that make mediocre teams good and good teams great. No project- or bug-tracking system completely replaces the need for people to talk to each other about what's going on because social networks are always stronger (and sometimes faster) than technological ones. The big challenges like project vision, feature lists, and schedules always come down to lots of little challenges that are positively influenced by how easily good knowledge and information flow through a team. Project managers play a critical role in making that flow active and healthy.

But whether it's little or big things, the actions and decisions managers make should have clear benefits for the entire team. It might take a week or a month to become visible, but a good project manager will create a positive impact on the quality of the work produced, and often the quality of life experienced by everyone involved. People will feel differently about their work, will say openly that they have a better understanding of what they're doing and why, and feel better about what's coming next than they did before. This kind of change only happens one meeting, decision, or discussion at a time, but over the course of a project, that vibe and energy can shift and improve dramatically.

Project managers create unique value

As a result, good managers and leaders often earn a special kind of respect from the programmers, testers, designers, marketers, and documentation people who come into contact with them. The PM should be able to perform feats of thinking, strategy, and leadership that positively impact the team in ways few others can. Often this involves finding shortcuts and clever optimizations in the daily workflow, or giving a boost of enthusiasm or encouragement in the right way and at the right time. They don't have to be superhuman, or even particularly bright, to do this (as I've no doubt discovered). They just have to understand the advantage of their perspective and choose to make use of it.

There is one simple incontrovertible fact: project managers or leaders spend more time with each person on the team than anyone else. They are in more meetings, drop by more offices, and talk to more individual contributors than any other person. They may make or influence more decisions than anyone else in the organization. If the project manager is happy, sad, motivated, or depressed, some of that is going to rub off on everyone she encounters. What PMs bring to the project, good or bad, will be contagious for the rest of the team.

So, if the project manager is focused on, committed to, excited about, and capable of succeeding, the odds increase that everyone else will behave the same way. Managers of any kind are in similar positions of potential power, and there are few leverage points of as much value in most working environments. This means that if it is at all possible to cultivate the attitudes and ideas I've described so far, there is no greater place to make those investments than in leaders and managers. This isn't to say that a project manager has to be a charismatic hero figure who, with barely a shrug, can lead armies of programmers into battle (see the section "The hero complex" in Chapter 11). Instead, he just needs to be genuinely interested in helping his teammates' reports and be successful at it more often than not.

In the end, the core idea I believe in is that as long as no one gets hurt (except perhaps competitors), and you involved people in the right way, nothing else matters but the fact that good stuff is made. It doesn't matter how many ideas came from you or someone else, as long as the outcome is positive. Project management is about using any means necessary to increase the probability and speed of positive outcomes. A useful daily mantra I've used is "Make good stuff happen." People would see me in the hallway or working with a programmer at a whiteboard and ask, "Hey Scott, what'cha doing?" And I'd smile and say, "Making good stuff happen." It became a dominant part of how I approached each and every day, and when I managed others, this attitude extended out and across the team through them. As this book moves on to topic-focused chapters, I hope you'll feel this attitude, and the core ideas of this opening chapter, come through.

Summary

Each chapter in this book will end with a short summary of key points to help you review later:

- Project management is everywhere, and it's been around for a long time.
- If you keep a beginner's mind, you'll have more opportunities to learn.
- Project management can be a job, a role, or an activity (the advice in this book applies well no matter how you define it).
- Program management is Microsoft's strongly defined project management role. It is derived from the idea of a matrix organization.
- Leadership and management require an understanding of, and intuition for, several common paradoxes. These include ego/no-ego, autocracy/delegation, and courage/fear.

- Watch out for pretension and over-involvement in your management activity. The process should support the team, not the other way around.

- If you are a dedicated manager, look for ways to capitalize on your unique perspective of the team and project.

Exercises

A. Pick your favorite friend who works in or studies a field other than yours. How does he manage his projects? Is there a special job for the project leader, or is the work of project management distributed across different people?

B. If being a good PM requires a balancing act of attitudes, how can a PM make sure she is not going too far in one direction or another? How can a PM enlist the help of people she works with to keep her in balance?

C. Make up a reason and throw a party. (You survived Chapter 1, isn't that reason enough?) After you've recovered from your hangover, and bailed your friends out of jail, consider the following: how is a party different from a project? Compare the challenges and rewards of being a party organizer to being a project manager on a work-related project. What's different and what's the same?

D. Think of a project you worked on that failed. What did you learn and how did you learn it? List the mistakes you made and what you can do differently next time to prevent them from happening again. The process of writing about it will force you to think more carefully and gain more insight from the experience.

E. Can you think of a kind of work that doesn't involve project management? If so, how do those in that field organize and plan how the work gets done? What limitations does a lack of organization create? What opportunities does it create?

F. Can you create leadership moments, or are they events that happen for reasons out of your control? If you wanted to increase the number of possibilities to demonstrate leadership, what could you do?

G. Imagine a team where people are rewarded exclusively for how well they follow processes and rules, instead of for reaching goals. What would happen to the quality of work? What would the role of project manager be like? What does this say about the potential dangers project managers can create?

H. Middle managers, or people who manage managers, are particularly prone to over-involving themselves, and creating unnecessary processes, because they are in the middle of the organization. How can a smart middle manager avoid the temptation to micromanage and create too many rules?

CHAPTER TWO

The truth about schedules

People tend to be late. It might be only a few minutes, or just a couple of times a week, but people are often behind on their daily schedules. (However, because denial is another great skill humans have, I'll understand if you refuse to admit this applies to you.) High school students are late for class, adults are late for meetings at work, and friends arrive 10 minutes late at the bar for drinks. We believe that being on time isn't about targeting a specific moment but instead is about being within a range of moments. And for some that range is wider than for others. Restaurant hosts are an interesting example. They claim a table will be ready soon,[1] but often we're made to wait much longer than they said it would be. It's these experiences of delayed schedules, being put on hold on the telephone, or waiting in the doctor's office, that have made us cynical about schedules—we have so much experience with life not happening on time.

It shouldn't be a surprise then that so many projects come in late. Most of us arrive at the task of scheduling projects with a poor track record for delivering or receiving things on time. We tend to estimate based on weak assumptions, predict outcomes based on the best possible circumstances, and—given our prior experiences—simultaneously avoid placing confidence in schedules we see or create. Why we do this, how it impacts project schedules, and what can be done to avoid these problems is the subject of this chapter.

But before we can figure out how to make better schedules, we first have to understand what problems schedules solve. If they are so unreliable, why bother with them at all? Schedules serve several different purposes—only some of which are focused on measuring the use of time.

Schedules have three purposes

All schedules, whether for planning a party or updating a web site, serve three purposes. The first is to make commitments about when things will be done. The schedule provides a contract between every person involved, confirming what each person is going to deliver over a particular period of time. Generally, when people think about project schedules, it's this first purpose that they're thinking about. Schedules are often focused externally, outside the project team rather than within, because they are used to help close a deal or comply with a customer's timeline. Often, the customer is explicitly paying for the timeline as well as for the service provided (think UPS or FedEx). In order to allow customers or partners to make plans based on a given project, a time has to be agreed upon for when specific things will happen.

---

1   Once, while dining at Pizzeria Uno in Pittsburgh, my friends and I were told a table would be ready in 10 minutes. Exactly 10 minutes later, my friend Chad McDaniel asked about our table. The hostess said, again, it would be ready in 10 minutes. Chad asked, "Is this the same 10 minutes or a different 10 minutes?" She didn't appreciate the joke.

The second purpose of a schedule is to encourage everyone to see her efforts as part of a whole, and to invest in making her pieces work with the others. Until there is a draft schedule suggesting specific dates and times for when things have to be ready, it's unlikely that connections and dependencies will be noticed. Without a schedule, everyone will focus on her own tasks and not think about how her work will impact others.

It's only when the details are written down, with people's names next to them, that real calculations can be made and assumptions examined. This is true even for small teams or for individuals working alone. There is psychological power in a schedule because it publicizes the commitments being made. It is not as easy to forget or ignore something when it's posted on a whiteboard in the hallway, reminding the team of what needs to be done. And specific to PMs: with a draft schedule in place, questions about how realistic certain things are can be raised, and comparisons can be made between what the project is being asked to do and what is even possible.

This psychological shift is called a forcing function. A *forcing function* is anything that— when put in place—naturally forces a change in perspective, attitude, or behavior. So, schedules are important forcing functions for projects. If used properly by a PM, schedules force everyone to carefully think through the work they need to do. This forcing function is a critical step toward realizing the project's potential. Even if the schedule slips, is doubled, or is halved, the commitments and connections everyone has made as a result of drafting the schedule can be maintained. So, this second purpose of a schedule can be achieved and can be entirely worthwhile even if the schedule itself turns out to be seriously inaccurate. For example, if the project comes in very late, the existence of a schedule will still enable the project to be completed.

The third purpose of schedules is to provide a tool to track progress and break work into manageable chunks. Breaking things down into a one- or two-day size helps people understand what they need to do. Imagine if, when building a house, the builder gave one line item: "House: 120 days." With such low granularity, it's difficult for anyone, including the builder himself, to understand the work. But if the builder can provide a week-by-week breakdown of activities, everyone can understand what tasks will be done when, what the priorities are, and ask meaningful questions and clarify assumptions. From the PM's perspective, a good schedule gives a clearer view of the project, flushes out challenges and oversights early, and increases the odds that good things will happen.

The larger and more complex the project, the more important schedules are. On larger projects, there are more dependencies between people, and decisions and timings have greater odds of impacting others. When you have a handful of people working on a small team, the odds of people recognizing problems in each other's work are much higher.

Schedule slips on small teams aren't good news, but, in such a case, a half-day slip represents an additional half-day of energy for three people only, so recovery is possible. Someone can stay late one night, or, if necessary, the team can all come in together and help make up the time. On a larger project, with dozens or hundreds of people and components, a one-day slip can quickly cascade and create problems in all sorts of unforeseen ways, which is often beyond a team's point of recovery. Either way, big team or small, schedules give managers and bean counters the opportunity to ask questions, make adjustments, and help the team by surfacing and responding to issues as they arise.

With these three purposes in mind, it's easy to see that perfect schedules don't solve all of the problems that projects have. A schedule cannot remedy bad design or engineering practices, nor can it protect a project from weak leadership, unclear goals, and poor communication. So, for as much time as it takes to create schedules, they are still just lists of words and numbers. It's up to someone to use them as a tool for managing and driving the project. With this in mind, it's time to bring out the big vocabulary and explore software methodologies—the heavy machinery of project management.

Silver bullets and methodologies

There are many different systems for how to plan and manage the development of software. These systems are often called *methodologies*, which means a body of practices aimed at achieving a certain kind of result. Common software methods include the waterfall model, spiral model, Rapid Applications development, Extreme Programming, and Feature-driven development. All of these methods attempt to solve similar organization and project management problems. They each have strengths and weaknesses, and it takes knowledge and experience to decide which one is right for what kind of project.

But my goal in this chapter, and in this book, isn't to compare different methodologies. Instead, I believe there are concepts that underlie them all that need to be mastered in order to succeed with any methodology. In all cases, methodologies need to be adjusted and adapted to fit the specifics of a team and a project, which is only possible with knowledge that is deeper than the methodologies themselves. So, if you can follow the underlying ideas in this chapter and book, your odds of being effective will increase, independent of which methodology you're using. I'll explain aspects of certain methods as needed to clarify points, but you'll have to look elsewhere if you're methodology shopping.[2]

---

2   You can find a good comparative discussion of traditional and agile methods for software development in *Balancing Agility and Discipline: A Guide for the Perplexed,* by Barry Boehm and Richard Turner (Addison-Wesley, 2003).

Although methods for software development are important, they are not silver bullets. The worst thing is to blindly follow a set of rules that are clearly not working, simply because they show up in some famous book or are promoted by a well-respected guru. Often, obsessing over the process is a warning sign of leadership trouble: it can be an attempt to offload the natural challenges and responsibilities managers face in bureaucratic procedures that cloud the need for real leadership action. Perhaps more devastating to a team is that methodology fixation can signal what is truly important to the organization. As Tom DeMarco writes in *Peopleware* (Dorset House, 1999):

> The obsession with methodologies in the workplace is another instance of the high-tech illusion. It stems from the belief that what really matters is the technology.... Whatever the technological advantage may be, it may come only at the price of a significant worsening of the team's sociology.

By focusing on method and procedure, instead of building procedures to support people, projects start the scheduling process by limiting the contributions of individuals. They can set a tone of rules and rule following, rather than thinking and rule adjusting or rule improving. So, be very careful of how you apply whatever methodology you use: it shouldn't be something inflicted on the team.[3] Instead, it should be something that supports, encourages, and assists the team in doing good work (see Chapter 10 for advice on process).

The use of a particular methodology is never the sole reason for a project making or missing its dates. Instead, there are factors that impact all projects, and project managers have to understand them before any scheduling work is ever done. But before we talk about that, we need to cover the components of a schedule.

What schedules look like

There is one basic rule for all schedules: the rule of thirds. It's a rough estimation and back-of-the-envelope thing, but it's the simplest way to understand schedules. If you are experienced with scheduling, prepare to cringe—I'm oversimplifying the entire process. I'm doing this to provide the simplest footing to explain what tends to go wrong, why it happens, and what can be done about it.

Here's how the rule of thirds works. Break the available time into three parts—one for design, one for implementation, and one for testing. Depending on the methodologies you use, these kinds of work will be called different things, but all methodologies have time dedicated to these three activities. On any given day, or any given hour, you're

---

3   See Watts S. Humphrey's *Managing the Software Process* (Addison-Wesley Professional, 1989) for coverage of defining, understanding, and managing software process change.

figuring out what should be done (designing), actually doing it (implementing production code), or verifying, analyzing, and refining what's been done (testing).

As the rule goes, for every day you expect to write production code, a day should be spent planning and designing the work, and a day should be planned to test and refine that work (see Figure 2-1). It's the simplest thing in the world, and it's an easy way to examine any existing schedule or to start a new one from scratch. If the total amount of time isn't roughly divided into the three kinds of work, there should be well-understood reasons why the project demands an uneven distribution of effort. Imbalances in the rule of thirds—say, 20% more time dedicated to testing than implementation—are fine as long as they are deliberate.

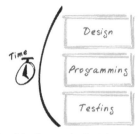

FIGURE 2-1. *The plain-vanilla rule-of-thirds project schedule.*

Consider a hypothetical web development project: if you're given six weeks to launch it, the first step should be to divide that time roughly into thirds, and, using those divisions, make calculations about when work can be completed. If this doesn't provide enough time to do the work expected at a high level, something is fundamentally wrong. Either the schedule needs to change, or the amount of work expected to be completed needs to be reduced (or any expectations of quality need to be lowered). Trimming from the testing time will only increase the odds that the time spent actually writing code will be misguided or will result in code that is harder to manage and maintain. The rule of thirds is useful in that it forces the zero-sum nature of projects to surface. Adding new features requires more than just a programmer implementing them—there are unavoidable design and testing costs that someone has to pay. When schedules slip, it's because there were hidden or ignored costs that were never accounted for.

Piecemeal development (the anti-project project)

It's worth considering the simplest case possible: there is no project. All work is done on a piecemeal basis—requests come in, they are evaluated against other work, and then they are put into the next available slot on the schedule. Some development teams, web site developers, or IT programming departments work in much this way. These organizations rarely make investments or commitments in large increments. Agile methods (discussed shortly) are often recommended to these teams as the most natural system for organizing work because these methods stress flexibility, simplicity, and expectations of change. If you work on several small assignments (not projects) at a time, you will have to extrapolate from the project-centric examples I use in this book.

However, the rule of thirds still applies to these situations. Even if each programmer is working alone on small tasks, he is probably spending about one-third of his total time figuring out what needs to be done, one-third of his time doing it, and one-third making sure it works properly. He might jump back and forth between those uses of time every few minutes, but as a rough way to understand any kind of work, the rule of thirds applies at any scale.

Divide and conquer (big schedules = many little schedules)

If you examine most software development methodologies, you can see the outlines of the rule of thirds. The specific goals and approaches used to design or implement things may be very different, but at the highest level, the desired results are similar.

Where it gets complex is on larger or longer projects, where schedules are divided into smaller pieces, with each piece having its own design, implementation, and testing time. Extreme Programming (known as XP) calls these pieces iterations; the spiral model calls them phases; and some organizations call them milestones. While XP implies that these chunks of time are only a few weeks, and the spiral model implies that they are months, the fundamental idea is the same: create detailed schedules for limited periods of time.

The more change and project volatility that is expected, the shorter each milestone should be. This lowers the amount of overall risk in the schedule because the master plan has been divided into manageable pieces. Those breaks between chunks of the schedule provide natural opportunities to make adjustments and improve the chances that the next milestone will more accurately direct its work. (We'll discuss how to do this in Chapter 14.)

Agile and traditional methods

XP and other agile methods assume the future is always volatile, so they bet on processes that incorporate easy direction changes. Projects that have very high production costs (say, building a skyscraper, a video game console, or an embedded operating system) go the other way and invest heavily in planning and designing activities. It can be done, but everyone has to commit to the decisions made during planning, and the prohibitive cost for changes tends to be the only way that happens.

Most software development projects are somewhere in the middle. They have some initial planning, but to help manage future volatility of requirements and customer demands, the work is divided into phases that have allocated time for design, implementation, and quality assurance. If a new issue arises, it can be considered for the current phase or put in the bucket of work to be properly investigated and understood during the next phase.

For most projects, that initial planning time is used to capture enough information from customers and business folks to define how many phases are needed and what the focus should be for each one (see Figure 2-2). Depending on the larger plan, each phase might dedicate more time to design or test. A phase could be divided into two smaller phases (approaching a more agile style of development), or two phases could be combined together (approaching more monolithic development). But in all cases, time should be allocated between phases to take advantage of what has changed. This includes responding to problems that arose during the previous phase, which couldn't be addressed fully during that phase.

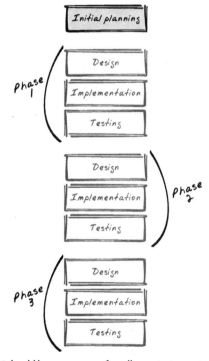

FIGURE 2-2. *A big project should be a sequence of smaller projects.*

That's as far as I'm going to go into high-level scheduling methodology. Chapters 14 and 15 will cover how to manage a project through the entire schedule, but they will focus on management and leadership perspectives—not on the details of how you've applied a particular methodology. If you could follow the last few paragraphs (even if you don't completely agree with the points made in them), then the advice in Chapters 14 and 15 should be relevant and useful, regardless of how you've organized or planned your project.

Anyway, I apologize to any development veterans who passed out or became ill during this section. Now that it's over, I promise that this lightweight and simple view of scheduling is almost all you'll need in order to understand the concepts in the rest of the chapter.

Why schedules fail

Project schedules are the easy scapegoats for everything that can possibly go wrong. If someone fudges an estimate, misses a requirement, or gets hit by a bus, it's the schedule (and the person responsible for it) that catches the blame. If the nation's power supply were to go out for 10 days, or the team's best programmers were to catch the plague, invariably someone would say, "See, I told you the schedule would slip" and wag her finger in the schedule master's face. It's completely unfair, but it happens all the time. As much as people loathe schedules, they still hold them up to an unachievable standard. Even the best schedulers in the world, with the smartest minds and best tools at their disposal, are still attempting to predict the future—something our species rarely does well.

But if a team starts a project fully aware of the likely reasons schedules fall apart and takes some action to minimize those risks, the schedule can become a more useful and accurate tool in the development process.

Shooting blind from very, very far away

If a schedule is created during initial planning, hundreds of decisions that may impact the schedule have yet to be made. There will be issues and challenges, which no one can foresee, and there is no way an early speculative plan can possibly account for them. Until requirements are understood and high-level design is well underway, a project manager has too little information to make realistic predictions. Yet, often a rough-cut schedule is created with made-up numbers and wild speculations, and this straw man is handed to the team under the guise of a believable project plan. Often, people fall victim to the precision versus accuracy trap: an impressive-looking schedule with specific dates and times (precision) isn't necessarily close to reflecting reality (accuracy). Precision is easy, but accuracy is very difficult.

However, it is true that all projects and schedules have to start somewhere. A shot in the dark can be used to energize a team and put some boundaries in place. It can begin a process of investigation to flesh out schedules and raise and answer important questions. But if an unverified and unexamined sweeping speculation is used as the basis for a schedule—without further refinement—great risks await. There is strong evidence that it is difficult for anyone to estimate the amount of time required early on in a project.

Barry Boehm, in his 1988 essay on software engineering,[4] found that schedule errors scale in relation to how early in the project schedule estimation is done (as shown in Figure 2-3). If total schedule estimates are made early, they can be off by as much as 400%, in either direction (I suspect the errors are skewed against us, tending to take more time than we expect, although his data didn't show this). During design, as more decisions become clear, the variance narrows, but it's still large. It's only when the project is in implementation that the range of schedule estimation becomes reasonable, but even then, there is still a 20% swing in how accurate scheduling decisions are likely to be.

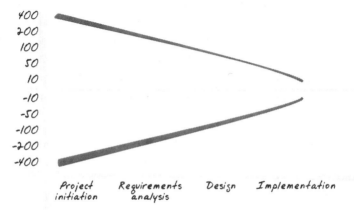

FIGURE 2-3. *The range of estimation errors during projects (adapted from Boehm's Software Engineering Economics).*

This means that project managers need to understand that schedule estimation grows in accuracy over time. Schedules demand that attention is paid to them as progress is made, and that adjustments are made as the project moves forward.

A schedule is a probability

When I was fresh out of college and working on my first few large projects (Windows and Internet Explorer), high-level schedules would be handed down to my team by someone much more important than I. Being too junior to have much involvement in

---

4   "Understanding and Controlling Software Costs," *IEEE Transactions on Software Engineering*, vol. 14, no. 10, October 1988, pp.1462–77; also in Barry Boehm's *Software Engineering Economics* (Prentice Hall, 1991).

the process, the schedule would be presented one day, and it was my job to apply that master schedule to the small number of programmers and testers that I worked with.

While we did negotiate on differences between that master schedule and the schedule generated by my team based on work items,[5] that high-level schedule always seemed to appear out of nowhere. It would descend from above, carefully formatted, broken down into nice columns of dates and numbers. It was like some artifact stolen from the future.

No matter how cynical we were, for the most part we followed those schedules faithfully. Despite the mystery of their origins, we had good reason to trust our team leads, and we were busy enough with our own work not to worry too much about theirs. (In fact, they often provided basic explanations for those initial top-down schedules, but we were too busy and too trusting to pay much attention.)

Later on, when scheduling became something I was responsible for, I realized the unspoken truth about schedules. They are not gifts from the future. There is no magic formula or science for creating perfect schedules. Despite my youthful perceptions, scheduling is not an isolated task: it always represents and encompasses many different aspects of what the project is now and will be later. Schedules are simply a kind of prediction. No matter how precisely they are drafted or how convincing they appear, they are just a summation of lots of little estimations, each one unavoidably prone to different kinds of unforeseeable oversights and problems. Good schedules come only from a leader or a team that relentlessly pursues and achieves good judgment in many different aspects of software development. You can't be an expert in one narrow part of the making of things and ever expect to schedule well.

So, if everyone on the team can agree that the schedule is a set of probabilities, the problem isn't in the schedule itself—it's in how the schedule is used. If ever a schedule is shown in a team meeting, or sent around in email, a valid question is this: how probable is the defined timeline? If no probability is offered (e.g., what the five most likely risks are and a speculation on the probability of their occurrence), and whoever made the schedule can't offer explanations as to the assumptions she is making, it should always be assumed that the schedule is possible, but improbable.[6] It should be open to the team to make suggestions as to what considerations or information can be added or changed in the schedule to make it more probable.

---

5 Schedules based on programmer work items are called bottom-up schedules. Schedules based on management are called top-down schedules. Typically the difference between them is negotiated.

6 Any given schedule is only one of many possible schedules. Depending on which contingencies (design failures, political revolution, space alien attack, etc.) are included, the timeline is different. If no possible failures are considered, the schedule cannot be credible. Its creator hasn't been creative or skeptical enough.

The secret here is that a schedule doesn't have to be perfect (which is a relief, of course, because there are no perfect schedules). Schedules need to be good enough for the team and the leaders to believe in, provide a basis for tracking and making adjustments, and have a probability of success that satisfies the client, the business, or the overall project sponsor.

Estimating is difficult

During the design process (covered in Chapters 5 and 6), part of the work for designers, programmers, and testers is to break down the design into small chunks of work that can be built. These chunks, often called work items or a work breakdown structure (WBS[7]), become the line items in the master schedule for the project. The work items are (fingers crossed) intelligently distributed[8] across the programming team, and by tallying them up, a schedule is created. Each of these work items has to have an amount of time assigned to it by the programmer, and on the basis of those estimates, the schedule is built.

By the simplest definition, good work estimates have a high probability of being accurate, and bad work estimates have a low probability. I don't expect to win any awards for these definitions, but they do imply at least one useful thing: it's the judgment of team leaders that defines the bar for a given project. It requires an active process of reviewing estimates and pushing, leading, and nudging others to get them to the level they need to be. I think it's smart to openly involve the test/QA team in the estimation process, letting them participate in the design discussions and ask questions or offer commentary. At a minimum, this will help them with their own estimates for testing work, which may not correlate to programming work estimates. Often, QA has the best insight into design oversights and potential failure cases that others will overlook.

The world is based on estimation

One thing that makes scheduling difficult is that few people enjoy estimating complex things that they will be held accountable for. It's always fun to brag and make bets about our skills ("This book/movie/web site stinks: I could make one *soooo* much better"), but when we're pressed to step up and deliver—signing our names on a contract detailing our responsibility—things change. We know that it's entirely possible that whatever we commit to doing today might be impossible or undesirable to do when that time comes. It

---

7 Most texts describe how to create work breakdown structures. I'll touch on this in Chapter 14, but if you want more, start with *http://en.wikipedia.org/wiki/Work_breakdown_structure* or *Total Project Control*, by Stephen Devaux (Wiley, 1999).

8 Kent Beck's *Extreme Programming Explained* (Addison-Wesley, 1999) offers a programmer-directed model for distributing work, where programmers self-select work items. Ideally these decisions are a compromise between what's best for the project and what's best for the individuals on the team.

just might turn out to be more difficult than we thought. Programmers are just like everyone else and have good reasons to have estimation anxiety. By saying that something can be done in a certain amount of time, they risk being very wrong.

In my experience, even programmers who understand the estimation process and believe in it, don't like to do it. Part of it is the mismatch of imagination ("How will this work, given the very limited information I have?") with temporal precision ("Tell me exactly how many hours this will take to do."). But sympathy here should be limited: everyone who works in engineering and construction has the same kind of challenge, whether it's building skyscrapers, remodeling a kitchen, or launching spacecraft to land on other planets. From reading about how these folks estimate things, it doesn't seem that their challenges or techniques are fundamentally different from what web developers and software engineers face. The primary difference is in how much time they are given to generate estimates and how disciplined they are in the use of that time (Chapters 5 and 6 will discuss this in detail).

Good estimates come from good designs

To the credit of programmers everywhere, the most important thing I've learned about good estimates is that they only come from credible designs and requirements. Good engineering estimates are possible only if you have two things: good information and good engineers. If the specs are crap, and a programmer is asked to conjure up a number based on an incomprehensible whiteboard scribbling, everyone should know exactly what they're getting: a fuzzy scribble of an estimate. This means that good estimates are everyone's business, and it should be the work of the entire team—project managers and designers in particular—to do what they can to support engineers in making credible estimates. If estimating feels like a chore, or if team leaders aren't invested in the process, don't expect reliable or probable estimates.

If leaders acknowledge weak estimates in the schedule and are comfortable with greater schedule risk, there's nothing wrong with weak estimates. On smaller, faster projects, rough estimates may be all that the project needs. Requirements may change often, and the nature of the business might demand more flexibility. There's nothing wrong with low-quality estimates, provided no one is confusing them with high-quality ones.

A handy technique I found was that whenever a programmer balked at giving an estimate, I'd ask, "What questions can I answer that would make you more confident about giving an estimate?" By getting him to be specific, I gave him the opportunity to confront the fear or frustration he might feel, which allowed me to help solve his problem. Of course, I'd have to help find answers to his questions, and possibly debate the issues I felt it was his job to investigate, but at least we'd be talking about getting better estimates.

Here are some additional ways to ensure good estimates:

- **Establish baseline confidence intervals for estimates.** A guess = 40% confidence in accuracy. A good estimate = 70%. A detailed and thorough analysis = 90%. Team leaders need to agree on how accurate they want estimates to be, as well as the amount of time programmers will have in order to make them and how the risks of missed estimates will be managed. Don't fixate on the numbers: just use them to help make the quality of estimates concrete. A 90% estimate should be on the nose 9 times out of 10. If you decide to ask your team to improve the quality of estimates, you must match this request with more time for them to do so.

- **Lead programmers must set the bar for quality estimations by asking good questions and taking wise approaches that the team can emulate.** Do whatever is necessary to kill the motivation for snide comments or backpedaling (e.g., "Don't hold me to this," "It's just a guess," etc.). Find out the legitimate needs they have for delivering good estimates, and back it up with the time needed to match the estimate-quality goals.

- **Programmers should be trusted.** If your brain surgeon told you the operation you need takes five hours, would you pressure him to do it in three? I doubt it. Sometimes, pressure has to be applied to keep people honest—but only as a balancing measure (the canonical need for this is a programmer who gives high estimates for things she doesn't like, and low ones for things she does). On occasion, obtaining multiple estimates (from two different developers) can be one way to do a sanity check.

- **Estimates depend on the programmer's understanding of the project goals.** Estimates are based on a programmer's interpretation of not only the design specifications (if they exist), but also the project's goals and objectives. In Gerald Weinberg's *The Psychology of Computer Programming* (Dorset House, 1971), he records how lack of clarity about higher-level objectives has a direct influence on the low-level assumptions programmers make. As clear as the technological problem might be, the programmer's approach to solving it might change dramatically depending on the high-level intentions of the entire project.

- **Estimates should be based on previous performance.** It's a good habit for programmers to track their estimates over projects. It should be part of their discussions with their manager, who should be interested in understanding who on their team is better at estimating what. Extreme Programming uses the term *velocity* to refer to a programmer's (or team's) probable performance, based on previous performance.[9]

- **Specification or design quality should be to whatever point engineering needs to make good estimates.** This is a negotiation between project management and programmers. The higher the quality of estimates desired, the higher the quality the specifications should be. We'll talk more about good specifications in Chapter 7.

9   See Kent Beck and Martin Fowler's *Planning Extreme Programming* (Addison-Wesley, 2002), pp. 60–62.

- **There are known techniques for making better estimates.** The most well-known technique is PERT,[10] which tries to minimize risks by averaging out high, medium, and low estimates for work. This is good for two reasons. First, it forces everyone to realize estimates are predictions, and that there is a range of possible outcomes. Second, it gives project managers a chance to throttle how aggressive or conservative the schedules are (more weight can be applied toward the low or high estimates).

The common oversights

While good estimates go a long way toward improving schedules, many factors that impact schedules cut across line items. The trap this creates is that despite how perfect all the estimates for work items are, the real schedule risks are the things not written down. While it's true that the odds of contracting the plague are slim in most parts of the world, the probability of an important engineer getting the flu or going on vacation is pretty high. There is a common set of these schedule oversights that all project managers need to be familiar with. The trouble is that it's often only after you've been burned by one oversight that you're willing to look out for it in the future. This is why project management, and schedule management in particular, requires experience to become proficient. There are too many different ways to fail, and no way to practice looking for them, without being responsible for their consequences.

Here's my pet list of questions that have helped me to catch potential schedule problems early on. Most of these came from asking questions about what went wrong after a project was completed, and trying to find a question someone could have asked early on that would have avoided the problem. (What was missing? What wasn't accounted for? What would have made a difference or would have enabled me to take corrective action?)

- Were sick days and vacation time for all contributors included in some form in the schedule?

- Were holiday seasons, or other times of year with major distractions, factored in (e.g., from Thanksgiving to Christmas in the U.S., summers in Europe)? Major deadlines are extremely hard to hit during these times.

- Did individuals have access to the schedule, and were they asked to report regular progress (in a non-annoying way)?

- Was someone watching the overall schedule on a daily or weekly basis? Did this person have enough authority to ask good questions and make adjustments?

---

10 PERT stands for Program Evaluation and Review Technique. The standard formula is: (best estimate + (4 × most likely) + worst estimate) / 6. However, there are zillions of variations and theories for how best to compute weighted estimates.

- Did the team feel ownership and commitment to the schedule? If not, why? Did the team contribute to the definition of the schedule and the work to be done, or was it handed down to them?

- Did team leaders add more feature requests than they helped eliminate? Did team leaders ever say *no* to new work and provide a reasonable philosophy to the team for how to respond to new (late) requests?

- Were people on the team encouraged to and supported in saying *no* to new work requests that didn't fit the goals and the vision?

- What probabilities were used in making estimates? 90%? 70%? 50%? Was this expressed in the master high-level schedule? Was the client/VP/customer aware of this? Was there discussion of another proposal that took more time but came with a higher probability?

- Were there periodic moments in the schedule when schedule adjustments and renegotiations could take place by leaders and management?

- Did the schedule assume fewer working hours over holiday seasons? (In the U.S., Thanksgiving to Christmas is often a low productivity time.) Are any highly probable disruptive weather events weighed into the schedule (for example, blizzards in Chicago, tornados in Kansas, sun in Seattle)?

- Were the specifications or design plans good enough for engineering to make good work estimates?

- Was engineering trained or experienced in making good work estimates?

The snowball effect

The most depressing thing about the previous list is that even if you get most of it right, because of how interdependent each contribution is to a schedule, it's still easy for schedules to slip. Each decision the team makes, from design choices to estimations, is the basis for many of the decisions that follow. An oversight early on in the process that is discovered later on will have an amplified impact on the project. This compounding behavior of schedules is easy to underestimate because the cause and effect aren't often visible at the same time (you may see the effect way after the cause occurred). In the worst cases, when several major oversights occur, the odds of a schedule holding together are slim to none (see Figure 2-4).

And of course, this gets even harder. The way probability works is that the likelihood of a series of independent events occurring is the multiplication of the likelihood of each individual event (also known as *compound probability*). So, if the probability of you finishing this chapter is 9 out of 10 (9/10), and the probability of you finishing the next one is 9/10, the total probability of you finishing both chapters isn't 9/10: it's 81/100.

Weak or no vision document

✗

Poorly written or no specs

✗

Poor or aggressive work estimates

✗

No budget for integration

✗

No budget for UI iterations

＝

A prayer of a schedule

FIGURE 2-4. *The snowball effect.*

This means that if your team is 90% probable to makes its dates each week, over time the odds of a slip happening continually increase. Probability is cold and heartless, and it helps to remind us that entropy is everywhere and is not the friend of projects or their managers.

What must happen for schedules to work

Now that we understand why schedules are so difficult to maintain, I can offer advice on how to minimize the risks and maximize the benefits of any project schedule. These approaches and behaviors cut across traditional roles or backgrounds, which I think reflects the true nature of scheduling. Because the schedule represents the totality of the project, the only way to use schedules effectively is to understand something about all of the things that must happen in order to make the project successful. It's an interdisciplinary task, not just an engineering or management activity.

- **Milestone length should match project volatility.** The more change that is expected, the shorter the milestones should be. Small milestones set the team up for easier mid-game adjustments. This gives management shorter intervals between reviews, and it reduces the risks of making changes. The team can be prepped to expect change at milestone crossovers, so they will expect change instead of resist it.

- **Be optimistic in the vision and skeptical in the schedule.** A major psychological challenge for scheduling is to make use of proper skepticism, without deflating the passion and motivation of the team. Unlike the creation of a vision document, where optimism about the future must reign, a schedule has to come from the opposite per-spective. The numbers that are written down to estimate how long things should take require a brutal and honest respect for Murphy's Law ("What can go wrong will go wrong"). Schedules should not reflect what might happen under optimal conditions. Instead, a good schedule declares what will happen—despite several important things not going as expected. It's important to have the test/QA team involved in scheduling because they lend a naturally skeptical and critical eye to engineering work.

- **Bet on design.** The process of design is the best insurance against ignorance and unexpected challenges. Better design practices are the only way to improve the ride of the team through implementation and other phases. Design skills are not the same as implementation skills, and the strongest or fastest coder won't necessarily be the best design thinker or problem solver. Good design process isn't taught in many computer science programs, despite how essential it is to thinking about and approaching engineering projects. See Chapters 5 and 6 for more on this topic.

- **Plan checkpoints for add/cut discussions.** Schedules should include short periods of review where leaders can review current progress and account for new information or customer feedback. This should be built into the master schedule and be an explicit part of any project contract. In these reviews, existing work items can be cut, or new ones added, as dictated by leadership's analysis of the current situation. Natural points for these reviews are in between phases, or on a limited basis, at the end of each design or implementation phase, but they can take place anytime there are serious concerns or obvious discrepancies between plan and reality. The goals of these discussions should be to return the project to sanity, refresh the schedule, reprioritize items, and start the next part of the schedule with clarity and belief in what comes next (see Chapters 14 and 15).

- **Inform the team about planning philosophy.** Whatever schedule approach or technique is used, it should be common knowledge to the team. If each programmer and tester has a basic understanding of how schedules work and the particular strategy project management is using for the current project, they'll be able to ask better questions and be more likely to understand and believe in what's being planned.

- **Gauge the team's experience with the problem space.** One of the magic variables in scheduling is how experienced the team is with the kind of problems it is being asked to solve. If the team is building a database-driven web site, and five of the six programmers have done this kind of work several times before, it's fair to assume they'll be better at designing and estimating work than a team that has never done it before. This should factor heavily into how aggressive or conservative a schedule can be.

- **Gauge the team's confidence and experience in working together.** Even though estimates come from individual programmers, the programmers are working together as a unit to build one complete thing. Even a team of veteran superstar programmers will not be as efficient as expected if they haven't worked with each other before (or faced difficult challenges together). It should be a red flag if ever a newly formed team is asked to work on a large, risky project or is asked to commit to an aggressive schedule.

- **Take on risks early.** If you know that Sally has the most complex component, deal with those challenges up front in the schedule. The bigger the risk, the more time you'll want on your side in dealing with it. If you don't address risks until later on in the schedule, you'll have fewer degrees of freedom in responding to them. The same goes for political, organizational, or resource-related risks. We'll talk about work item management, at the development pipeline, in Chapter 14.

Summary

- Schedules serve three functions: allowing for commitments to be made, encouraging everyone to see her work as a contribution to a whole, and enabling the tracking of progress. Even when schedules slip, they still have value.

- Big schedules should be divided into small schedules to minimize risks and increase the frequency of adjustments.

- All estimates are probabilities. Because schedules are a collection of estimates, they are also probabilities. This works against schedule accuracy because probabilities accumulate ($80\% \times 80\% = 64\%$).

- The earlier that estimates are made, the less accurate they are. However, rough estimates are the only way to provide a starting point for better ones.

- Schedules should be made with skepticism, not optimism. Invest in design to shed light on assumptions and generate reliable confidence.

Exercises

A. If you use a daily planner, take a look at yesterday's schedule. How many of the events started on time? Of the ones that started late, how many were your fault ?

B. Who do you know that is always late? How does this change how people perceive him? Would you prefer he were less optimistic about how long it will take him to do things? Does he suffer in any way for being late? What motivations are there for him to change his habits?

C. Dig up the original schedule from your last project. Compare it to what actually happened. What would you have done differently knowing what you know now? How can you use this information on your next project?

D. Spend a day where you start and finish everything exactly on time. Afterward, ask if it was worth the effort. Why or why not?

E. Find a friend who works in a different field than you. How does she schedule her projects? What tools does she use to estimate how long work will take? What mistakes are common in her field, and what can you learn from how she handles them? (If you have no friends, building construction, filmmaking, and wedding planning all make for interesting comparisons to study.)

F. The rule of thirds is a rough guideline, and there are exceptions. What kinds of projects require a different division of time? Could there be a project that is dominated by just one of these three kinds of work?

G. Many projects have significant dependencies on work outside your control. What techniques can you use when building a schedule to reduce the risk of those dependencies? How should you engage with the people responsible to build a schedule that makes both teams successful?

H. Your manager is pushing for a specific date and yet your experience tells you the date is ridiculous. How can you use a schedule to explain your concerns to a manager?

I. If the common oversights in this chapter affect most projects, what can a smart project manager do to: a) make a team aware of them; or, b) reward people for mitigating them?

CHAPTER THREE

How to figure out what to do

Few agree on how to plan projects. Often, much time during planning is wasted getting people to agree on how planning should be done. I think people obsess about planning because it's the point of contact for many different roles in any organization. When major decisions are at stake that will affect people for months, everyone has the motivation to get involved. There is excitement and new energy but also the fear that if action isn't taken, opportunities will be lost. This combination makes it all too easy for people to assume that their own view of the world is the most useful. Or worse, that it is the only view of the world worth considering.

> **"The hardest single part of building a software system is deciding what to build. No other part of the conceptual work is as difficult in establishing the detailed technical requirements, including the interfaces to people, to machines, and to other software systems. No other part of the work so cripples the results if done wrong. No other part is more difficult to rectify later. Therefore, the most important function that the software builder performs for the client is the iterative extraction and refinement of the product requirements."**
>
> *—Fred Brooks*

It's not surprising then that the planning-related books in the corner of my office disagree heavily with each other. Some focus on business strategy, others on engineering, and a few on understanding customers. But more distressing than their disagreements is that these books fail to acknowledge that other approaches even exist. This is odd because none of these perspectives—business, technology, customer—can ever exist without the others. More so, I'm convinced that success in project planning occurs at the intersections in these different points of view. Any manager who can see those intersections has a large advantage over those who can't.

So, this chapter is about approaching the planning process and obtaining a view of planning that has the highest odds of success. First, I need to clarify some vocabulary and concepts that different planning strategies use (it's dry stuff, but we'll need it for the fun chapters that follow). When that is out of the way, I'll define and integrate these three different views, explore the questions good planning processes answer, and discuss how to approach the daily work to make planning happen. The following chapters will go into more detail on specific deliverables, such as vision documents (Chapter 4) and specifications (Chapter 7).

Software planning demystified

A small, one-man project for an internal web site doesn't require the same planning process as a 300-person, $10 million project for a fault-tolerant operating system. Generally, the more people and complexity you're dealing with, the more planning structure you need. However, even simple, one-man projects benefit from plans. They provide an opportunity to review decisions, expose assumptions, and clarify agreements between people and organizations. Plans act as a forcing function against all kinds of stupidity because they demand that important issues be resolved while there is time to consider other options. As Abraham Lincoln said, "If I had six hours to cut down a tree, I'd spend four hours sharpening the axe," which I take to mean that smart preparation minimizes work.

Project planning involves answering two questions. Answering the first question, "What do we need to do?" is generally called requirements gathering. Answering the second question, "How will we do it?" is called designing or specifying (see Figure 3-1). A requirement is a carefully written description of a criterion that the work is expected to satisfy. (For example, a requirement for cooking a meal might be to make inexpensive food that is tasty and nutritious.) Good requirements are easy to understand and hard to misinterpret. There may be different ways to design something to fulfill a requirement, but it should be easy to recognize whether the requirement has been met when looking at a finished piece of work. A specification is simply a plan for building something that will satisfy the requirements.

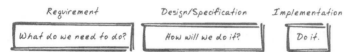

FIGURE 3-1. *An insanely simple but handy view of planning. If you don't know what you need to do, it's too early to figure out how to do it.*

These three activities—requirements gathering, designing/specifying, and implementing—are deep subjects and worthy of their own books (see the Appendix and the Annotated Bibliography). I'll cover the first two from a project-level perspective in the next few chapters, and implementation will be the focus later on in this book (Chapters 14 and 15).

Different types of projects

Several criteria change the nature of how requirements and design work are done. I'll use three simple and diverse project examples to illustrate these criteria:[1]

- **Solo-superman.** In the simplest project, only one person is involved. From writing code to marketing to business planning to making his own lunch, he does everything himself and is his own source of funding.

---

1 For another comparison of different types of software projects, see *http://www.joelonsoftware.com/articles/FiveWorlds.html*.

- **Small contract team.** A firm of 5 or 10 programmers and 1 manager is hired by a client to build a web site or software application. They draft a contract that defines their commitments to each other. When the contract ends, the relationship ends, unless a new contract/project is started.

- **Big staff team.** A 100-person team employed by a corporation begins work on a new version of something. It might be a product sold to the public (aka shrink-wrap) or something used internally (internalware).

These three project types differ in team size, organizational structure, and authority relationships, and the differences among them establish important distinctions for how they should be managed. So, while your project might not exactly match these examples, they will be useful reference points in the following sections.

How organizations impact planning

With the three project types in mind, we can examine the basic criteria for project planning. At any time in a project, there are basic questions that everyone should know the answers to. You might not always like the answers, but you and your team should know what they are. Most planning frustrations occur when there's disagreement or ignorance about these issues.

- **Who has requirements authority?** Someone has to define the requirements and get them approved by the necessary parties (client or VP). In the solo-superman case, this is easy: superman will have all of the authority he wants. On a contract team, there will be a client who wants strong control over the requirements and possibly the design. Lastly, a big staff team may have committees or other divisions in the corporation who will need to be served by the work (and whose approval in some way is required). There may be different people with high-level requirements authority ("It will be a sports truck") and low-level requirements authority ("It will get 20 mpg and have 4-wheel drive").

- **Who has design authority?** Similar to requirements, someone has to define the design of the work itself. The design is different from the requirements because there are always many different possible designs to fulfill a set of requirements. Designs, also like requirements, are often negotiated between two or more parties. One person or team might be responsible for driving the design process and developing ideas (designer), and another team provides guidance and feedback on the first party's work (VP). Note that because design skill is distributed in the universe independent of political power, people granted design authority might not be people with much design talent.

- **Who has technical authority?** Technical authority is defined by who gets to choose which engineering approaches are used, including programming languages, development tools, and technical architecture. Many of these decisions can impact requirements, design, and budget. The difference between technical decisions and design decisions is subtle: how something behaves and looks often has a lot to do with how it's constructed. In some organizations, technical authority supercedes requirements and design authority. In others, it is subservient to them. In the best organizations, there is a collaborative relationship between all the different kinds of authority.

- **Who has budget authority?** The ability to add or remove resources to a project can be independent from other kinds of authority. For example, in the contract team situation, the team might have the power to define the requirements and design, but they might need to return to the client each time they want more money or time.

- **How often will requirements and designs be reviewed, and how will adjustments be decided?** The answer depends heavily on previous questions. The more parties involved in requirements, design, and budgets, the more effort will need to be spent keeping them in sync during the project. As a rule of thumb: the less authority you have, the more diligent you need to be about reviewing and confirming decisions, as well as leading the way for adjustments.

Although I've identified different kinds of authority, it's possible for one person to possess several or all of them. However, most of the time, authority is distributed across team leaders. The more complex the distribution of authority is, the more planning effort you'll need to be effective. In Chapter 16, I'll cover how to deal with situations where you need more authority than you have. For now, it's enough to recognize that planning involves these different kinds of power.

Common planning deliverables

To communicate requirements, someone has to write them down. There are many ways to do this, and I'm not advocating any particular method. What matters most is that the right information has been captured, the right people can easily discuss it, and good commitments are made for what work should be done. If the way you document requirements does all this for you, great. If it doesn't, then look for a new method with these criteria in mind.

For reference purposes, I'll mention some of the common ways to document requirements and planning information. If nothing else, knowing the common lingo helps translate between the various methods used by different organizations. You'll find some teams document the requirements informally: "Oh, requirements…just go talk to Fred." Others have elaborate templates and review procedures that break these documents into insanely small (and possibly overlapping) pieces owned by different people.

- **Marketing requirements document (MRD).** This is the business or marketing team's analysis of the world. The goal is to explain what business opportunities exist and how a project can exploit those opportunities. In some organizations, this is a reference document to help decision makers in their thinking. In other organizations, it is the core of project definition and everything that follows derives strongly from it. MRDs help to define the "what" of a project.

- **Vision/scope document.** A vision document encapsulates all available thinking about what a project might be into a single composition. If an MRD exists, a vision document should inherit and refer heavily to it. A vision document defines the goals of a project, why they make sense, and what the high-level features, requirements, or dates for a project will be (see Chapter 4). Vision documents directly define the "what" of a project.

- **Specifications.** These capture what the end result of the work should be for one part of the project. Good specifications are born from a set of requirements. They are then developed through iterative design work (see Chapters 5 and 6), which may involve modifying/improving the requirements. Specs are complete when they provide a workable plan that engineering can use to fulfill requirements (how much detail they must have is entirely negotiable with engineering). Specifications should inherit heavily in spirit from vision documents. Specifications define the "how" of a project from a design and engineering perspective. (In most agile methods, use cases and story cards roughly translate into requirements and specifications).

- **Work breakdown structure (WBS).** While a specification details the work to be done, a WBS defines how a team of engineers will go about doing it. What work will be done first? Who will do it? What are all of the individual pieces of work and how can we track them? A WBS can be very simple (a spreadsheet) or very complex (charts and tools), depending on the needs of the project. Chapters 7 and 13 will touch on WBS-type activities. WBS defines the "how" of a project from a team perspective. (Some agile methods use task boards, showing all active story cards, which roughly translate into a WBS.)

Approaching plans: the three perspectives

You may have noticed how each deliverable mentioned represents one of two perspectives on the project: business or engineering. On many projects, these two views compete with each other. This is a fundamental mistake. Planning should not be a binary or either/or experience. Instead, it should be a synthesis of what everyone can contribute.

To make this happen, a project manager must recognize that each perspective contributes something unique that cannot be replaced by more of something else (i.e., no amount of marketing strategy will improve engineering proficiency, and vice versa). For good results, everyone involved in project planning must have a basic understanding of each perspective.

The business perspective

The business view focuses on things that impact the profit and loss (P&L) accounting of an organization. This includes sales, profit, expenses, competition, and costs. Everyone should understand their P&L: it's what pays their salaries or their contracts. When engineering teams are unaware of how their business works, many decisions made by management will appear illogical or stupid. Thus, it's in the interest of whoever is responsible for business planning to help others understand why the project exists from a business standpoint. In the tech sector, people with job titles like business analyst, marketing, business development, product planner, or senior manager represent the business perspective.

Some projects have multiple business perspectives. If you work for a firm contracted to build a database server, you have your firm's business interests to consider, as well as the business interests of the client you are serving (hopefully they are in line with each other). The intersection of these perspectives can get complicated; I'm going to keep it simple here and assume projects are of the big-staff variety. However, it should be easy to extrapolate the following questions to more complex situations.

A good business perspective means that the team has answers for the following questions:

- Why is this project needed for our business?
- What unmet needs or desires do our customers have?
- What features or services might we provide that will meet those desires and needs?
- On what basis will customers purchase this product or service? What will motivate them to do so?
- What will it cost (people/resources)? Over what time period?
- What potential for revenue (or reduced organizational operating costs) does it have? Over what time period?
- What won't we build so that we can build this?

- Will it contribute to our long-term business strategy or protect other revenue-generating assets? (Even nonprofits or IT organizations have a business strategy: there are always bills to pay, revenue to obtain, or revenue-generating groups to support.)

- How will this help us match, outflank, or beat competitors?

- What are the market time windows that we should target for this project?

Those responsible for the business perspective take bold views of the importance of these questions. They believe that the answers represent the bottom line for the organization and should strongly influence project decisions. However, the business view doesn't mean that all projects must be slaves to revenue. Instead, it evaluates projects based on their contributions to the business strategy. For example, a strategic project might be essential to the organization but never generate any revenue.

Marketing is not a dirty word

The most unfair criticism of business folks is that they are just "marketers," which is somewhat of a negative label in the tech sector. I think marketing gets a bad rap. In MBA terms, there are four *P*s that define marketing: product, price, placement, and promotion. Defining the product and price is a creative process. The goal is to develop a product idea—sold for a profit—that matches the needs of the targeted customer. Research, analysis, and creative work are necessary in order to succeed. Placement, the third *P*, regards how customers will obtain the product (through a web site? the supermarket? the trunk of Fred's car?).

Finally, promotion—what marketing is often stereotyped to mean—is how to spread the positive word about the product to influential people and potential customers. Surprisingly, promotion is a small part of a business analyst or product manager's time (maybe 10–20%). So, marketing plans define much more than what the ads will look like or what promotional deals will be made. Also, note that the four *P*s of marketing apply to almost anything. There is always a product (HR web site), a price (free), a placement (intranet), and a promotion (email) for it.

But when the business perspective is dealt with alone, it shows only one-third of what's needed. The quality of a product influences sales, but quality does not come from marketing.[2] Quality comes from successfully designing and engineering something that satisfies real customer needs. A proposed business plan that centers itself on technological possibilities (rather than conjectures) will make for good business.

---

2   Andrew Stellman, a tech reviewer of this book, threatened me with physical violence if I didn't offer references on software quality, so here are a couple: W. Edwards Deming's *Out of the Crisis* (MIT Press, 2000) and Philip Crosby's *Quality Is Free* (Signet Books, 1992).

A project manager, who uses only one perspective and fails, might never understand what really went wrong. His tendency will be to work harder within the same perspective instead of widening the view.

The technology perspective

While I was studying computer science at Carnegie Mellon University, it was common to talk to professors and students about new products. We'd focus on what components these new software products used and how they compared against what could have been. Value was quality of engineering: how much of the latest technologies they used. Generally, we thought everything sucked. Very few products survived our critiques. We wondered why the marketplace was packed with mediocrity and disappointment. We'd even invent geek conspiracy theories to explain the evil decisions, which we thought were made against engineering purity and thus made little or no sense to us. Often, we'd focus blame on the marketing departments of these companies[3] (not that many of us understood what marketers did). Even in my first few years in the industry, the same kinds of conversations took place again and again. Only then there was greater scrutiny because we were competing with many of the products or web sites that we talked about.

When we looked at the world, we saw technologies and their engineering merits only. We never understood why poorly engineered products sometimes sold very well or why well-engineered products sometimes failed to sell at all. We also noticed that engineering quality didn't always correlate with customer happiness. For these mysteries, we had two answers. First, it had something to do with the magic powers of evil marketing people. Second, we needed smarter customers. But we didn't think much about our flawed conclusions. Instead, we went back to writing code or finding other products to tear to shreds. I was able to see my view for what it was only after I'd listened to some smart marketers and some talented product designers.

The technology view places the greatest value on how things should be built. It's a construction and materials mindset. There is an aesthetic, but it's from the technology perspective, not from the customer's perspective. There is a bias toward the building of things, instead of understanding how, once created, those things will help the business or the customer. In the stereotypical engineering view, a database that satisfies the engineer's aesthetic is sufficient, even if it's so ugly it makes men cry, no customer can figure out how to do anything with it, or it fails to meet its sales projections.

As critical as that last paragraph was of technologists, many important questions come from the technology view only:

---

3   Faisal Jawdat, a tech reviewer of this book, threatened me with death by sarcasm if I didn't point out how ironic it is that I then went on to work for Microsoft.

- What does it (the project) need to do?

- How will it work? How will each of the components in it work?

- How will we build it? How will we verify that it works as it's supposed to?

- How reliable, efficient, extensible, and performant are the current systems or ones we are capable of building? Is there a gap between this and what the project requires?

- What technologies or architectures are readily available to us? Will we bet on any new technologies that will be available soon but are not available yet?

- What engineering processes and approaches are appropriate for this team and this project?

- What applicable knowledge and expertise do our people have? What won't they be working on to work on this project?

- How will we fill gaps in expertise? (Train/hire/learn/ignore and hope the gaps magically go away.)

- How much time will it take to build, at what level of quality?

The customer perspective

This is the most important of all three perspectives. Because the project is made to serve the customer (and perhaps serve the business, but only through serving the customer), it follows that the greatest energy should be spent on understanding who those customers are. This includes studying what the customers do all day, how they currently do it, and what changes or improvements would be valuable in helping them do what they do. Without this information, engineering and business are shooting in the dark.

But, sadly, the customer perspective is the weakest in many organizations. It generally receives the least staffing and budget support. There are fewer people in most organizations that have been trained in understanding and designing for customers than their business and technology counterparts. And even when customer experts are hired (such as user interface designers or usability engineers), they are often restricted to limited roles in the project decision-making process and are granted few requirements or little design authority.

In any case, the customer point of view is built from two different sources: requests and research. Requests are anything the customer explicitly asks for or complains about. This kind of information is valuable because the customer has the greatest motivation to identify these problems ("Yes, my computer explodes whenever I hit the Space bar"), but it is also problematic because, in most cases, customers are not designers. They often blur the distinction between problems that need to be solved and specific ways of solving them. They may explicitly ask for a feature, such as print preview, without describing the real problem (people throw away too much paper). If the project team can start by understanding the problem, there may be many ways to solve it that are cheaper or better than the feature requests. Even skilled designers often struggle at designing for themselves.[4]

There are two kinds of experts who understand customers and design for them: usability engineers and product designers. Usability engineers are experts in understanding how people work, and they provide metrics and research to help project teams make good decisions from day one of project planning. Product designers, or interaction designers, are people trained in how to take that data and convert it into good designs for web sites or products. If your organization is fortunate enough to employ these fine folks, involve them early on. Ask them to be advocates for this point of view. If you're working without them, you are at a distinct disadvantage to your competitors. Consider hiring someone to consult and advise on where these efforts would be of the most value.

Without expert help, the project manager must make do on her own. This is possible, but because it's often the least interesting perspective for folks with engineering backgrounds and is least understood by senior management, it typically gets less support than the other points of view. Enough resources and seniority need to be invested in the customer perspective to balance out the technology and business ones. Otherwise, surprise: the customer perspective won't be credible and won't be heard.

The important questions from the customer view include:

- What do people actually do? (Not what we think they do or what they say they do.)
- What problems do they have trying to do these things? Where do they get stuck, confused, or frustrated?
- What do they need or want to do but aren't able to do at all?
- Where are the specific opportunities to make things easier, safer, faster, or more reliable for them?
- What design ideas for how to improve how the thing should work—in terms of what people actually do—have the most potential for improving the customer experience?
- How can those ideas be explored? What prototypes, sketches, or alternatives need to be investigated to help us understand the potential for the project?
- What core ideas and concepts should the project use to express information to users?

---

4 This is a deliberately inflammatory remark designed to promote these footnotes. But seriously: when designers design for themselves, they tend to over-design, perhaps indulging in the freedom of not having a client to work for.

The magical interdisciplinary view

These three points of view always overlap. Every business consideration has technical and customer implications (which is the same for all of the other permutations). So, getting the best planning perspective requires laying out each view on equal footing and seeing where the similarities and differences are. Some decisions will need to be made that favor one perspective over another, but that shouldn't be done by accident. It should support an intelligent strategy derived from getting as much value from each perspective as possible.

By investing time in exploring all three perspectives, it's possible to see opportunities for smart strategic decisions. It might be possible to satisfy some of the top issues or goals from each of the three perspectives by defining a project targeted at where the three perspectives overlap. Those are areas that have the greatest potential value to the organization because one effort can simultaneously address business, technology, and customer goals.

Almost as important as its strategic planning value, using a Venn diagram (like the one in Figure 3-2) can defuse perspective bias of engineers or marketers. It helps teams see overlapping points of view, rather than competing ones only. Early and often during project-planning discussions, this diagram or something like it (e.g., a diagram that includes a list of potential goals from each perspective) can be used to frame suggestions made by people who have bias toward one view of the project. When ideas are suggested, they can be mapped against this diagram to see how they contribute to all three perspectives. The PM plays a key role in making this happen, by proactively using his generalist nature to unify all three views into one.

FIGURE 3-2. *The three perspectives.*

One way to accomplish this is to establish early on that there will always be great technological ideas that do not benefit the business or the customer, as well as great ideas to help customers that are not viable for the business or possible with current technology.

This gives everyone the power to identify one-dimensional ideas and call each other on them. It also generates respect across perspectives because everyone is forced to realize that they need to collaborate with people who have knowledge they don't possess in order to be successful.

But if no effort is made to bring divergent points of view together, the conflicts are rarely addressed head on. Instead, project-planning meetings become battlefields for attacking and defending opinions based on these perspective lines (and not on the true merits of the ideas themselves). Often when I've consulted with project teams, the problem I was asked to help with had nothing to do with their ability to plan a project. Instead, there was an unresolved, or even unspoken, conflict of opinion about why one department— engineering or marketing, for example—is more important than the other. Their singular perspectives not only caused the problem, but also made it impossible to see the cause of the problem.

Years ago, I was involved in one of these silly wars myself. I was the program manager for web-search features on Internet Explorer 4.0. Two business development people were assigned to us, and they were negotiating deals with the major search engines of the time (Excite, Yahoo!, Lycos, AltaVista, etc.). We argued with these business experts over design decisions, continually debating over what was best for the customer versus what was best for the business. We each believed that we held the authority (I spoke for the design/engineering staff, and they provided the business arguments). We argued on the same points for weeks, always debating the specific decisions and never stepping back to evaluate our hidden philosophies on what made for good products. Things got so bad that we brought in our group manager to help us reach a compromise.

I'm convinced a broader view would have helped everyone. We were so invested in our egos that we were willing to waste time fighting over details, instead of working to understand all of the perspectives on what we were building. A better vision document could have helped, but that was impossible because the business challenges of the Internet were so new to the industry (circa 1997). However, had we been sharing each other's knowledge, instead of resisting it, we might have had a shot at finding a mutually beneficial compromise.

Bringing an interdisciplinary view to a project enables you to make choices that cut across the very boundaries that limit your competitors. It also gives you stronger arguments for any decision you choose to make. Instead of only claiming that a specific design will be easier to build, you can also say why marketing will find more opportunities to sell that design (provided, of course, that you're not just making up these claims). Sometimes, this will require you to make sacrifices. When you're looking for the best solutions, they won't always correspond to what you're good at doing, or which ideas you personally prefer. But if you're able to make those sacrifices, you gain the conviction and sincerity required to get others to do the same. You can then call others on favoring pet ideas over what's best for the project. People will get behind decisions they don't completely agree with if they see that an open mind, working in the interests of the project, is at work making those decisions.

The balance of power

If you work in a large organization, consider the power distribution across all perspectives. For example, if engineers outnumber business analysts by 3:1, the engineering view will tend to dominate decisions. The power ratio is simply the ratio of the number of people prone to a given view. To have a balanced perspective, the ratio should be 1:1:1 (engineering to business to customer). The more out of balance the ratio is, the more leaders need to do to compensate.

Of course, the raw number of people doesn't define how much power they have. Napoleon's army had thousands of soldiers, but there was only one Napoleon. There may be 10 programmers and 1 marketer (10:1:0), but the marketer may have as much power over the project, given his role or seniority, as the others combined. This means a manager can compensate for any natural ratio by granting power to those who should have more influence on the project. And because the nature of a project changes over time, different perspectives should have more power at different times. Consider how you can delegate decisions (see Chapter 12) to find the right balance for the project at the right time.

Asking the right questions

The simplest way to frame planning work is to focus on questions that the planning work should answer. They should be pulled from the three perspectives and rolled together into a single plan.

The questions (often called project-planning questions) should be pulled from the three lists discussed earlier. If it's a new project (not a v2), you'll need basic questions to define the fundamentals. If it's a small upgrade to an existing system, there may be fewer business and customer issues to consider. But no matter what the project is, do the exercise of running through the questions. It will force out assumptions that haven't been recognized and give everyone the same starting point for discussion.

This project-planning question list should be free of perspective boundaries. Instead, you'll have a holistic point of view of the project, which can be divided, as needed, into engineering, business, or customer considerations. Here's an example list, which uses more complex versions of questions listed earlier:

- Why does this project exist? Why are we the right people to do it? Why does it need to be done now?

- What are the three or four useful groupings we can use to discuss the different kinds of customers we have? (For example, for a word processor, it might be students, professionals, and home users. For an IT database, it might be sales, receptionists, and executives.) How do their needs and behaviors differ?

- What demographic information can help us understand who these customers are? (Age, income, type of company, profession, education, other products owned or web sites used, etc.)

- Which activities is each user group using our product for? How does this correspond to what they purchased the product for? How does this correspond to how we marketed the product? What problems do they have in using the product to satisfy their needs?

- Who are our potential new customers, and what features, scenarios, or types of products would we need to provide to make them customers? (What are the demographic profiles of these new customers?)

- Do we have the technology and expertise to create something that satisfies these needs and problems? (For each identified need, answers of yes, maybe, and no can often be sufficient, at least as a first pass.)

- Can we build the technology and obtain the expertise to create something that satisfies these needs and problems? (Yes, maybe, no.)

- Are there significant opportunities in a new product or line of products? Or are the needs tied directly to the current product or line of products?

- Are there viable business models for using our expertise and technology to solve these identified problems or needs? (Will profits outweigh costs on a predictable timeline?)

- What are the market timelines for the next release or product launch? Which windows of opportunity make the most sense to target?

- What are competitors in this marketplace doing? What do we think their strategies are, and how might we compete with them?

Answering the right questions

It can take hours or weeks to answer these questions, depending on the depth and quality of the answers needed, which is defined by the project manager or group leader. As a rule of thumb, the more strategic the project is expected to be, the more important the quality is of this kind of definition and planning research. For tactical projects that are directed at minor issues or short-term needs, less depth is needed. You might need to consider only a handful of questions, and you can base your answers largely on how you answered them for the last project. But for important projects, this information will be invaluable in any midproject adjustments or changes, not only in the planning phase.

Some of these questions are best answered by business analyst types, others are best answered by lead programmers or usability engineers. Often, the best answers come from discussions among these experts and the sharing of notes, sources, and opinions. It can be expensive and time-consuming to do this work, but that's the nature of planning. Buying a house or car, moving to a new country, or writing a book requires significant planning efforts to make the process work out well. If you do it right, it enables sharper and quicker decision making throughout the rest of the project. (I'll talk more about this in Chapter 14.)

What if there's no time?

In the worst case, even if no research exists and there's no time for proper investigation, ask these questions anyway. Raising good questions always invites two positive possibilities. First, intelligent guesses at the right question are better than nothing. Even if you only have time for guessing, speculation on the right issues is more valuable than speculation on the wrong issues. Second, the absence of research into core questions can raise a red flag for leaders and management. The long-term health of an organization is dependent on its ability to make good plans, and even though investments (hiring someone or providing funding) might come too late to help this project, it might help the next one.

Catalog of common bad ways to decide what to do

There are always more bad ways to do something than good ways, and project planning is no exception. As an additional tool toward sorting out the good from the bad, Table 3-1 shows some of the lousy approaches I've seen used. I offer these in the hopes that it will help you recognize when this is going on, and why these approaches are problematic.

Bad way	Example	Why it happens	The problem
We will do what we did last time.	"Version 3.0 will be like 2.0, only better!"	Often there isn't the desire or resources to go back and do new research into the business, technology, and customer issues.	The world may have changed since v2.0. Without examining how well 2.0 did against its goals, the plan may be a disaster.
We'll do what we forgot to finish last time.	"The feature cuts for Version 2.0 will be the heart of 3.0!"	Items that were cut are arguably well understood and partially complete, making for easy places to start.	Remaindered features are nonessential. Focusing a release on them may not be the best use of resources.

TABLE 3-1. *Common bad ways to decide what to do*

Bad way	Example	Why it happens	The problem
We'll do what our competitor is doing.	"Our goal is to match Product X feature for feature."	It's the simplest marketing strategy. It satisfies the paranoid, insecure, and lazy. No analysis is required.	There may be stupid reasons a competitor is doing something.
We will build whatever is hot and trendy.	"Version 5.0 will be Java-based, mobile-device ready, and RSS 4.0 compliant."	Trends are trends because they are easy and fun to follow. People get excited about the trend, and it can lend easy excitement for boring or ill-defined projects.	Revolutions are rare. Technological progress is overestimated in the short term, underestimated in the long term. Customer problems should trump trendy fads.
If we build it they will come.	"Project X will be the best search engine/web editor/widget/mousetrap ever."	By distracting everyone to the building, rather than the reason for building, people can sometimes avoid real planning.	Does the world need a better mousetrap? People come if what is built is useful to them, not because a team decided to build something.

TABLE 3-1. *Common bad ways to decide what to do (continued)*

The process of planning

In the time left for defining the project, answer the planning questions. If possible, each perspective (business, technology, and customer) should have one person with expertise in that area driving the research of information, generating ideas and proposals, and reviewing her thoughts with peers from other perspectives. The trick is to keep this small enough to be productive, but large enough in perspective to be broad and comprehensive. A group of 10 people will be much less effective at discussing issues and developing team chemistry than a group of 5 (see Chapter 9).

From experience, I'd rather deal with the bruised egos of those who are not main contributors to planning than include too many people and suffer on a poorly planned and heavily compromised project. The mature people who you do not include will understand your reasons if you take the time to explain them, and the immature will have an opportunity for growth, or motivation to find employment better suited to their egos.

If you're using planning deliverables like the ones I briefly described earlier in this chapter, the goal of the planning group should be to create and publish those documents for the team. The planning phase (see Figure 3-3) ends only when those documents (or more importantly, the decisions they contain) are completed.

A draft version of each planning document should be prepared early enough to incorporate feedback from the team before a final version is due. As shown in Figure 3-3, there may even be a simple feedback loop between deliverables. When the draft of an MRD is created, someone may be able to start working on the vision document, raising new questions for the MRD that improve it before it's finalized. This pattern repeats

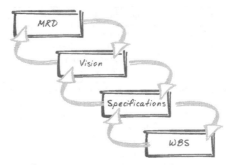

FIGURE 3-3. *The feedback between levels of planning.*

through all of the planning work. So, even if there are hard deadlines for finishing planning docs, some overlap in time is healthy and improves the quality of the process. As shown in Figure 3-4, when a project is in mid-game (implementation), it becomes harder, though not impossible, for this kind of feedback to propagate back up the planning structure. (Alternatively, Figure 3-4 can be thought to represent a contracted team that has influence over specs and work assignments only.)

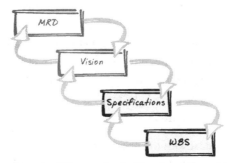

FIGURE 3-4. *As time goes by, it should become harder (though not impossible) for changes to propagate back up the planning structure.*

The daily work

As far as the daily work of planning is concerned, there's no magic way to do these collaborative tasks. People are people, and it's impossible to skip the time required to get individuals of different minds to come together, learn from each other, and make the compromises necessary to move things forward. There will be meetings and discussions, and probably the creation of email distribution lists or web sites, but no secret recipe of these things makes much difference. Be as simple and direct as possible. The leader sets the tone by starting the conversations, asking the important questions, and making sure the right people are in the room at the right time. However, there are three things to keep in mind:

- **The most important part of the process is the roles that people are expected to play.** Who has requirements authority? Design? If many people are involved, how will decisions be made? How will ties be broken? With these sorts of relationship issues defined early on, many problems can be avoided or, more probably, handled with composure and timeliness. (See Chapter 10 for more on relationships and defining roles.)

- **Everyone should know what the intermediary points are.** What are the milestones between day one of the planning effort and the day when the project definition should be complete? The timeline for deliverables—such as reports, presentations, review meetings, or vision documents—should be listed early, and ownership should be defined for each of them. When exactly does "planning" end and design or implementation begin? There should be good, published answers.

- **There should be frequent meetings where each perspective is discussed.** Reports of new information or thoughts should be presented, and new questions or conclusions should be raised. Experts from elsewhere in the organization or the team should be pulled into these meetings when they have expertise that can help, or if their opinions would be of value to the group.

The project manager is often responsible for consolidating each meeting and discussion down into key points and making sure conclusions reached are written in stone in a place the group can easily reference. Questions or issues raised should be assigned appropriately and then discussed at the next meeting.

Customer research and its abuses

There are many different ways to abuse information about customers. Simply claiming that customers are important doesn't signify much. It takes no work to say "We care about customers" or "Customer satisfaction is important" because rarely does anyone ask how those beliefs map to organizational behavior. Even though in the last decade much progress has been made in refining methods for researching and understanding customers, most of it has not penetrated through to management- or engineering-centric organizations. It's still uncommon for project teams to have an expert in customer research, interface design, or usability available to decision makers.

By far, the most prevalent mistake is over-reliance on a single research method. The fundamental problem with all research, scientific or otherwise, is that a given study assesses only one point of view on an issue (we'll discuss this again in Chapter 8). Each method for examining something is good at measuring certain attributes and horrible at measuring others (see Table 3-2). Just as you would never use a speedometer to measure your weight, or your bank account to measure your blood pressure (though they may be related), there are some things that surveys and focus groups are good for and others that they are not.

Method	What is it?	Pros	Cons
Focus group	A group of potential customers are brought together to view prototypes and give opinions in a facilitated discussion.	Can get many opinions at once. Allows for extended suggestions and open dialog.	Discussions are difficult to analyze and easy to misinterpret. Poorly trained facilitators create deceptive data.[a]
Survey	A series of questions are given to potential customers.	Low-cost way to get information from large numbers of people. Good for very broad trends.	Information reliability is low.[b] Authoring surveys without biasing answers is difficult. Easy to misinterpret data.
Site visits	Experts or team members go to the customers' work sites and observe them doing their work.	Observe the true customer experience. Often this is the most memorable and powerful experience for the team.	The data is most valuable to those who did the visit—it's hard to transfer to others or to use quantitatively.
Usability study	Selected customers use a design in a controlled environment. Measurements are taken for how many scenarios they can complete, in how much time, and with how many errors.	Quantifies how easy it is to use anything. Provides evidence for specific problems. Most valuable when done early, before project begins.	Little direct value for business or technological questions. Can be wasted effort if done late or if engineering team doesn't watch often.
Market research	The market of the product is examined to see how many customers there are, what the competing products cost, and what the revenue projections are.	Only way to capture the business view of a market or industry.	Doesn't explain why products are successful, and it focuses on trends and spending, rather than people and their behaviors.

TABLE 3-2. *Common customer research methods*

a   Focus groups tend to bias people toward being helpful. They don't want to insult their hosts, and they will often be more positive and generous in considering ideas than they would otherwise.

b   Consider how diligent you were in answering questions in the last survey you took. If you never take surveys, ask yourself about the kinds of people likely to spend lots of time taking surveys.

Experts at customer research do two things: they choose the method based on the questions the project team needs to answer, and they make use of multiple methods to counteract the limitations and biases of individual approaches. Table 3-2 outlines some of the major research methods and their high-level tradeoffs.

As a program manager at Microsoft, on the best project teams I worked on, I had many of these sources of information. I'd have to request answers to questions that went beyond the basics, but there were experts in the organization who would do this for me. On other teams with less support, I'd have to make do on my own (typically with less success because I had other things to do, and I wasn't as proficient as a full-time expert would be).

Even with no resources or budget, an afternoon of work answering those questions can provide useful results. Over time, the skills in doing research will grow and will take less time in the future. More importantly, having done some of this kind of work on your own will put you in a more informed position to hire someone to do it for you, should the budget or headcount finally exist.

With any data, skepticism and healthy scrutiny improve its value. Assumptions should be questioned, and biases of different kinds of research should be called out when the research is presented. No form of data is perfect: there are always biases, caveats, margins of error, and hidden details. The project manager has to be able to see past the biases and make intelligent use of what's available to make better decisions.

Bringing it all together: requirements

Planning creates large volumes of information, and the challenge becomes how to simplify it into a plan of action. At a high level, a vision document is where all of the perspectives, research, and strategy are synthesized. We'll talk more about that special document in the next chapter. But at a lower level, the simplest tool is requirements.

Many projects use requirements as the way to define the direction of a project. A requirement by definition is anything the team (and client) agrees will be satisfied when the project is completed. In the simplest sense, ordering a pepperoni pizza is an act of requirements definition. You are telling the pizza chef specifically what you want. He may ask you questions to clarify the requirement ("Do you want a soda with that?"), or he may negotiate the details of the requirement ("We're out of pepperoni, will you accept salami instead?"). In the more complex case of software development, good requirements are difficult to obtain. There are many different ways to interpret abstract ideas ("make it run fast" or "make it crash less often"), and the process of eliciting requirements can be difficult.

There are established methods for developing and documenting requirements, and I recommend familiarizing yourself with them.[5] Depending on what authority you have over the requirements process, there are different ways to go about doing it so that you'll obtain good results. The details of these methods are beyond the scope of this book. However, I can offer you one simple method that I think is easy to use and generally very effective: the problem statements method.

Problem statements are one- or two-sentence descriptions of specific end user or customer issues. They're derived from research or specific customer requests. They're written in a format that identifies a need from the customer perspective (as opposed to the engineering or business perspective). This ensures that the customer viewpoint is maintained and not distorted by other perspectives.

---

5   See the excellent *Exploring Requirements: Quality Before Design*, by Donald Gause and Gerald Weinberg (Dorset House, 1989).

As an example, here's what a list of problem statements for an intranet web site might look like:

- It is hard to find commonly needed items on the home page.
- Pages with department information are very slow to load and users have to wait.
- The database query page crashes when working with large tables, and users have to start over with their work.
- The site does not provide automated access to HR services, which are time consuming to do manually.
- Search results are difficult to scan with the current layout.
- The registration page doesn't warn about required fields, and it's too easy to make mistakes.
- The status page doesn't include information about email, and users cannot find out why their email isn't working.
- There is no way to save preferences or options for how the home page is displayed.

Note that these are not bug reports. These issues may have never been identified as things the web site needed to do. Problem statements should be broader in perspective from bugs because we're capturing what's missing from the customer's perspective, instead of what's broken from a technical perspective.

Each of these statements can be followed by supporting evidence or examples (say, screenshots that provide context for the issue, or references to the usability study or other research that surfaced the problem) to help tell the story and explain why and how the issue occurs (or why the omission of a kind of functionality is significant). But this supporting evidence should not mix with the problem statement itself, or with engineering plans or business objectives. For sanity, these customer problem statements should remain purely about customers and their needs.

Problems become scenarios

Because problem statements represent the current state of the world, a project needs something else to express how the world will be when the work is completed. For this purpose, problem statements need to be converted into what are called feature statements or scenarios. There are many different ways to do this; use-cases are one popular method,[6] but there are many others.

Each scenario is a short description of something a customer will be able to do as a result of the project, or the tasks they will no longer have to do because the project automates

---

6 See Alistair Cockburn's *Writing Effective Use Cases* (Addison-Wesley, 2000).

those tasks for them. The idea is to describe these things from the customer's perspective and to avoid description of how these benefits will be achieved (that comes later). For now, what's important is that the team is able to discuss which scenarios have the most value. Considerations for business potential or technological feasibility should be reflected in how the scenarios are prioritized.

The feature statements themselves should become the way to most easily represent what's been learned about customers and what the project will be focused on providing for them. Based on the previous list of customer issues, here is what some feature statements might look like.

Possible features of Project X:
- —Commonly used items will be easy to locate on the home page.
- —Search results will be easy for most users to read quickly.
- —The site will provide easy, automated access to HR services.
- —The registration page will make it easy to enter information without mistakes.
- —Department information pages will be at least as fast as the home page itself.
- —The database query interface will be as reliable as other parts of the system.
- —Users will be able to learn about email server status issues in a simple and convenient way.
- —Users will have a convenient way for the system to remember their preferences.

Feature statements should never describe a specific design, but should instead explain the solution's impact on the customer. This is easier said than done. Most creative people love to solve problems and will do it automatically. The trap is that fast solutions are often shallow. Let the problems marinate before solving them. Simply ask people to write down their solution ideas during planning meetings and discuss them later. Make exceptions for ideas that either completely eliminate problems from the lists or identify them as trivial.

These feature statements can be ordered roughly by importance, helping to define the shape of what the project will be. When the time comes to design, it will go much faster because everyone will be working toward the same results (instead of being distracted by their favorite ideas for solutions). Because so much is riding on these short descriptions, they need to be written carefully and with consideration for how long they'll be used by the project team. It often takes several passes and reviews to get them right, but once complete, they'll rarely need to be redefined over the course of a project.

Integrating business and technology requirements

With a list of features derived from user research, additional features to satisfy business or technology considerations can be added. But a primary question must be answered: what is the purpose of these additional requests if they do not help customers? Before adding features, the list should be reviewed to see which ones already represent these business and technology considerations. This forces all discussion to be centered on customer benefit, without prohibiting specific technology or business considerations. Any noncustomer-centric features should be revised to make sure they do not negatively impact the customer's experience.

Sometimes, it's necessary to add a feature to help sell a product, despite its dubious end-user value, or to satisfy a demanding client or executive. But by planning first around customer research, problem statements, and resulting features, everyone will have to make arguments within that context. This gives the project manager a level playing field of features that has the best interests of both the customer and the organization in mind.

Summary

- Different projects demand different approaches to planning.
- How planning is done is often determined by who has what authority. Requirements, design, and budget are the three kinds of project authority that impact planning.
- There are some common deliverables for planning projects: marketing requirements documents (MRDs), vision/scope documents, specifications, and work breakdown structures (WBSs).
- The most powerful way to plan a project involves use of three equal perspectives: business, technology, and customer. The customer perspective is often the most misunderstood and misused.
- Asking questions forces good thinking and directs planning energy effectively.
- The process of defining requirements is difficult, but there are good references for how to do it well.
- Problem statements and scenarios are a simple way to define and communicate requirements. They are easily converted into design ideas without losing clarity about what's important and what isn't.

Exercises

A. Make a list of who had design, technology, and business authority on your last project. Was knowledge of this made clear to the team at the beginning? Were the right people chosen to make these kinds of decisions? How did that impact the project?

B. Of the three views—business, technology, and customer—which was the least represented in the last project you worked on? What impact did that have on the quality of what was made?

C. What are some of the problems with defining requirements that aren't discussed above? If you have a customer who demands a feature that you believe is a mistake, or who changes his mind after work has started, how should the disagreement be resolved?

D. Imagine you were the manager of a project where the engineers and the businessmen did not like each other, and they fought over basic decisions. What actions could you take to improve their relationship? (Hint: What questions aren't being asked? What views aren't represented?)

E. Let's assume you decided to sabotage a project during its planning phase. Make a list of the most potent things you could do to foul things up. (If you get stuck, assume you don't care about getting fired.)

F. Make a list of how, if you were the manager instead of the saboteur, you'd prevent or respond to items in the list from question E.

G. What are the warning signs of a project around which there was too much planning? What can be done if you, as the project manager, see all the warning signs?

H. Have you ever seen a person use something you designed? Run your own super-informal usability study. Give a potential new customer your marketing literature, sit her down in front of your software, and ask her to try and do whatever the marketing literature says the software will let her. Offer absolutely no help, no matter how desperately you want to give it. You will learn more about the importance for user research than any book could possibly tell you.

I. Should the person who writes a requirement be the same person who works on designing something to fulfill it? What are the problems with having one person do both? What are the problems with having a separate person for each?

CHAPTER FOUR

Writing the good vision

One challenge in leading teams is keeping people focused on the same goals for long periods of time. All leaders fear that decisions they make won't be remembered. It's possible that the reasons people had for listening to them today will be forgotten or ignored tomorrow. Perhaps worse, managers themselves may forget in which direction they are supposed to be leading the project. So, the challenge of project management is not only to get things started in the right direction, but also to keep it headed that way.

Chapter 2 included a brief overview of planning documents, such as MRD, vision, and specifications. This chapter focuses on the vision document, the most important of all planning materials. I'll explain why vision documents are worth the effort to write, what qualities good ones have, and how to continually get value from them over the course of a project. When they are used properly, they conclude the initial planning phase of a project (see Figure 4-1).

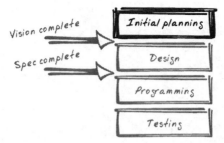

FIGURE 4-1. *A finalized vision document signifies the end of the planning phase, just as final specifications signify the end of the design phase.*

But one note before I start: there are many different ways to divide the ground these documents cover. Some organizations don't use MRDs or business justification documents at all, and instead roll that information into the vision document itself. A few times I've been on very small projects where vision-type information was collapsed down into the specification itself, or simply kept on a wiki or in email. So, don't worry about how many documents you should have or what they're called—that's not important. My advice applies well to any process you use.

The value of writing things down

Daniel Boorstin, author of the great works *The Creators* (Vintage, 1993) and *The Discoverers* (Vintage, 1985), once said that the written word was the greatest technology man ever invented. Without it, we'd be dependent on our notoriously unreliable memories[1] to do

---

1 Read Daniel Schacter's *The Seven Sins of Memory* (Mariner Books, 2002); or, watch the excellent film, *Memento*. They both should help you recognize how limited and unreliable human memory is.

complex things like make dynamite (hmmm, how much nitroglycerin goes with how much charcoal?) or nuclear reactors (the uranium goes where?). Specific to the pursuit of project work, writing things down makes it possible to define engineering work or capture the overall objectives for entire teams only once, and reuse that knowledge many times. Documenting the details of decisions offloads the burden of precision and recollection from our minds down to paper; all we need to do to recover them is look at what we wrote. That freedom of mind allows us to go at full speed at the task at hand, confident that we can return to what we wrote if needed (say, when we lose focus, have disagreements, or get confused). It follows that the more complex and involved any effort is, the more likely it is that writing down some of the details about it will improve the chances of success.

The larger a project, the more complex and involved the work will be. A team of three might be able to talk enough in the hallway to coordinate, but a team of 20, 100, or 1,000, working in different time zones, doesn't have that luxury. Instead, someone has to define the higher-level plan for all of the work before much of it begins, and she needs to document it in a way that everyone can easily use as a reference.

Writing things down also serves to communicate the intentions of a team across a large organization. If group A can represent their core ideas and high-level decisions in a short document, then groups B and C can understand group A's intentions and raise questions or provide feedback quickly. The more complex and involved a project is, the more important that short document becomes, because complex projects have higher odds for miscommunications and costly mistakes. And, as a bonus, new people to the team (senior and junior alike) can read a distilled version of the core ideas of the project and get up to speed much faster than if they had to learn those core ideas on an ad hoc basis.

How much vision do you need?

I've seen vision documents that were 50 pages long, carefully formatted with research, diagrams, and strategic thinking. I've also seen visions that were a couple of pages of bulleted items, with a few sentences describing each one. Depending on the project, different amounts of structure and planning are needed. Don't make the mistake of thinking that planning documents are fixed, rigid things: they're just documents. How deep or fancy they need to be depends on the nature of the project and the culture of the team. However, good vision documents tend to cover the same kinds of questions, but the material varies in depth and rigor.

To help you figure out how much structure and investment your vision document needs, consider the following questions:

- How many valid questions does the team itself have about the future? How much do people expect to know about what they'll be doing and why they'll be doing it?

- How many different people will be impacted by the project? How many different organizations are they in? How will you properly set expectations up, down, and across each organization?

- How much explaining of decisions do you want to have to do in person? (A good vision should stand on its own in representing the project to many people.)

- What depth of feedback on project direction do you want from others?

- How much depth of knowledge and thought should a project leader provide to the organization as part of making project-level decisions? (A vision provides the evidence of this.)

- During the course of the project, how much depth of strategic thinking should the team have access to?

- What research do executives or senior managers expect you to do as part of project planning? How will you deliver this to them?

- Will there be a need to remind the team later on of what the goals are? Are people likely to argue later about specific issues that have been agreed on recently?

The more detailed and stronger your answers are to these questions, the more value a vision document will have. If few of these questions apply, go with something lightweight and informal. If many of them apply, and reading them made your stomach churn, you'll need heavier stuff.

These questions are more accurately questions of leadership than purely about visions. However, a vision document is the only way to simultaneously address many of them. Even if working alone (solo-superman), writing down an informal vision document (e.g., a list of goals) for the week, month, and year goes a long way toward concluding those periods of time with something to be proud of. Once things are written down, it's easier to hold people accountable for them, even if you're only being accountable to yourself.

Team goals and individual goals

To talk in detail about visions, I need to define some terms. Visions, team goals, and goals are often used in overlapping ways. Here is a clarification of how I'm going to use them:

- **Vision.** Defines the high-level goals for the entire project. This may also include a vision statement or uber-goal. (High-level goals defined by a vision are sometimes called objectives to help distinguish them from lower-level goals.)

- **Team goals.** The subset of the vision a particular team is responsible for, which is defined in greater depth than the vision. (For example, team A might be responsible for the database system and its goals, and team B might be responsible for the search engine system and its goals, but both share the same project vision.)

- **Individual goals.** The subset of team goals that an individual is responsible for.

On small projects, there's little distinction between team and individual goals (see Figure 4-2). A project might even be small enough that there's no need for these distinctions. But on larger projects with 50 or more people, this layer is necessary. Working on large teams for much of my career, I'm used to seeing these three layers: one set for the entire project (vision), one set for each feature or area of the project (team), and one for the personal goals for each employee working on the project (individual). The first two are of public record for the entire team; the last one is between the employee and his manager.

FIGURE 4-2. *Three levels of goals.*

As an example, let's take project Hydra, an intranet web site:

- Hydra vision. The Hydra web site will make the most frequently used intranet sources (search, accounting, inventory, HR, travel) easily accessible from one web site, with one easy-to-use interface.

- Team A will be responsible for making search and accounting easily accessible and simple to use. Team B will be responsible for inventory, HR, and travel.

- Fred (team A) will design and implement all features required for searching. Mike (team B) will drive the overall design effort and write all user interface specifications for Hydra. Bob (team B) will design and implement all the features required for HR and travel.

There is strong inheritance from the top down: team goals inherit from project goals, and individual goals derive mostly from area team goals (the primary exception being individual needs for training or growth that can't be satisfied within the project). Provided these three levels are well crafted, everyone should show up every day, motivated to do work that makes local sense to them and contributes directly to the entire project. The time it takes to set up this structure is worth it. It creates natural synergy and makes managing a project easier (see Figure 4-2).

Different documents should correspond with these three levels of definition (or minimally, different discussions). For the entire project vision, the group manager or uber-project leader should be leading the creation of the high-level vision document. She should then expect area or component leaders to interpret those high-level directives into goals for their own areas, possibly lifting specific themes or goals from it. Finally, line-level contributors should be discussing with their team leaders what their individual goals and responsibilities are, derived from those team goals.

The five qualities of good visions

Because everything derives from the high-level vision, the team's overall leader should invest more energy in it than any other early planning material. The five most important characteristics are: simplifying, intentional (goal-driven), consolidated, inspirational, and memorable.

Simplifying

The most important quality is a simplifying effect on the project. A good vision will provide answers to core questions and give everyone a tool for making decisions in their own work. While a vision will raise new questions, these should be fewer in number than ones that no longer need to be asked. In the early phases of a project, people should be referring to the vision all the time—in discussions, emails, and meetings—actively using it as a tool to help make decisions. The project manager should be on the lookout for this and be willing to modify and revise the vision to include unforeseen questions that will make it more useful to the team. The vision should never be like a religious relic, protected inside a glass cabinet. It should be more like a rulebook to a good board game, providing clarity for everyone involved, making boundaries clear, and quickly settling disputes or miscommunications. It should be worn out from use and have notes scribbled in the margins. Its effect should be to put an end to the preliminaries quickly and get people into the heart of the action with the confidence that the project can succeed.

Intentional (goal-driven)

The vision document is a project's first source of goals. It sets the tone for what good goals look like, how many goals there should be in a plan, and how much refinement the goals may need before they are complete. A well-written goal defines a clear intention for the people on the team. Enough information is provided in the goal itself that people will know when it's been completed. They should also be able to easily separate out activities that are likely to contribute toward the goal from ones that won't. Writing good goals is difficult and highly subjective; it takes many revisions to obtain a strong, well-written goal. The fewer high-level goals, the more powerful the vision document becomes. As a rough rule of thumb, a project vision document should have somewhere between three and five high-level goals (see the upcoming catalog of good vision statements for examples).

One popular business acronym for writing good goals is SMART: Specific, Measurable, Action-oriented, Realistic, and Timely. The idea is that if a goal has all five of these attributes, it's likely to be well defined enough to be useful (however, subjective judgment remains as to how specific or realistic a goal should be). Another technique that can help with goals is playing devil's advocate: ask how a project can still fail if its goal can be satisfied as written. Then consider if there is a way to more carefully phrase the goal, or if another bit of supplemental information should be provided to support the goal.

Consolidated

For the vision document to have any power, it must consolidate ideas from many other places. It should absorb the key thinking from research, analysis, strategic planning, or other efforts, and be the best representation of those ideas. Any vision for a team is a failure if understanding it requires the reader to do even half the work of the author.

For this reason, it's best to separate out the goals and directives from all of the supporting arguments and research behind the plan. There should be one place to easily find all of those supplemental thoughts and materials (a simple web site), and it should encourage the diligent (or the skeptical) to go deeper than the vision document itself. Consolidation does not mean jamming together a random assortment of references—it means that there should be coherence among them. They should use the same template and formatting, or at least be easily printable as one volume: not for the sake of process, but because this makes it easier to read, which forces someone (preferably the head honcho himself) to consider exactly how many references or sources are important for people to be familiar with. That number shouldn't be zero, but it also shouldn't be 15 or 20 papers, essays, or reports.

Inspirational

Inspiration never comes from superficial things (and as an aside, even superficial people require genuine inspiration). To connect with people, there must be a clear problem in the world that needs to be solved, which the team has some interest or capacity to solve. While a charismatic team leader can help, it doesn't change the quality of the ideas written down in the vision. By giving the reader a clear understanding of the opportunities that exist, and providing a solid plan for exploiting it, people who have any capacity of being inspired, will be. Although with programmers and engineers there is a tendency to draw inspiration from technological challenges, it's easy to derive those challenges from the real-world problem that the project needs to solve. Make sure everyone understands that the project is being funded to solve the real-world problem and not just the technological one.

Memorable

Being memorable implies two things: first, that the ideas made sense; and second, that they resonated with readers and will stay with them over the duration of a project. They might not remember more than a few points, but that is enough for them to feel confident about what they're doing every day. (Note that if the vision is too complex for anyone to understand, it's impossible to achieve this effect. People rarely remember things they don't understand.)

Being memorable is best served by being direct and honest. If you can strike at the core of decisions and communicate them well—even if people don't completely agree with those decisions—they will stay with people longer than those from a vision full of ideas they fully believe in but were buried in weak and muddy writing. So, strive to make the vision clear and confident. Give the team strong concepts and ways of thinking about the work. Avoid flashy ideas that might inspire people in the short term, or capture a fad or flighty trend, but run out of steam after a few weeks, when the value of the idea has been spent.

The key points to cover

At the heart of a vision should be answers to many of the following questions. It's common for these topics to be major headings in a vision document or listed at the end as part of a Q&A section. (Although, when these questions are not addressed in the core document and are made into an appendix, expect to see engineers flip to the last pages, which implies something negative about the strength of the writing that preceded it.)

Answering many of these questions demands involvement from marketing, customer research, product design, or other experts who are available to you—and this should not be an afterthought. Some of the following questions are intentionally similar to questions asked in the previous chapter on planning. The difference is that these questions are angled heavily toward priorities and decisions, rather than context and understanding. During planning, there was room for exploration, but the vision is obligated to take a stand and be decisive.

- What is the one sentence that defines this specific release of this specific project? (This is often called the vision statement, or for the cynics on the team, the visionless statement. Examples for this are offered shortly.)

- How does this project contribute to the goals of the organization? Why is this project more relevant than others that also might contribute to the goals of the organization?

- What scenarios/features for customers are essential to this project? (Priority 1.)

- What scenarios/features for customers are desired but not essential? (Priority 2.)

- Who are the customers? What problems does this project solve for them? What evidence or research (as opposed to opinions and speculations) supports these claims? How will customers get their jobs done without this project?

- Who are the stakeholders for this project in the organization (the people with power over the project but who are not necessarily customers)? What role will they have in the project? (We'll cover stakeholders in Chapter 16.)

- Why will these customers buy or subscribe to this service? (Obfuscated versions of "because it's cool" or "because they have no choice" are not acceptable answers. However, summaries of what target users are currently paying for, and how the new project fits into their lifestyles, budgets, or daily habits, would be. Of course, in an IT situation, the answer may be "because they have no choice.")

- Who are the competitors, and how will this project compare to them? (Prior releases of similar projects should be included as competition, or possibly nontechnological alternatives such as pencil and paper. The Palm Pilot's simple design is attributed to seeing paper as the primary competitor, not other electronic devices.)

- What solutions for customers have been requested or suggested but will definitely not be part of this project?

- How is this not a technology in search of a problem?

- What is the project not going to accomplish? (Don't be pedantic: list the things people might guess or assume would be part of the project, but won't be. Include political, business, and customer perspectives if they're not already covered.)

- What are some likely ways for this particular project to fail, and how will they be avoided or minimized? (In early drafts, there might only be risk evaluations, but without plans for managing/avoiding them.)

- What other companies or groups is this project depending on in order to succeed? What other companies or groups are depending on this project in order to succeed?

- At a high level, how will the work be divided across the team? Who are the leaders for each major sub-area of the project, and what authority do they have?

- What assumptions are being made that the project depends on? What dependencies does this project have on other projects, companies, or organizations?

For any question or point that is considered critical, there should be rock-solid thinking behind it. The project manager should seek out the smartest and most skeptical members of the team, and enlist them to poke holes in the logic and supporting arguments behind key statements. Because these points will be the cornerstone of everything that follows, they should be irrefutable. This feedback process is often best done informally, one-on-one or in very small groups, with the project manager incorporating feedback and considering new perspectives after each discussion.

On writing well

Even for those among us who naturally communicate well, visions and leadership documents bring with them the potential for great pretension. Suddenly there's an opportunity to show to the entire organization how grand your thinking is—the ego temptation is hard to resist. But pretentious writing defeats its own purpose: instead of communicating ideas, it obscures them.

It's hard to be simple

The most common mistake in writing visions is equating complexity of thought with complexity of presentation. Contrary to what many people think, it takes significantly more work to express sophisticated ideas in a simple manner than otherwise (writing code and writing essays share this relationship). Ten pages of summaries, disclaimers, charts, and diagrams can easily obfuscate the central ideas of a vision. Their inclusion might only prove the insecurities and lack of concision on the part of the author (read any academic or philosophical journal for bountiful examples of this). Sadly, this behavior is easy to copy. It tends to start at the top of organizations and bleed down, causing near-fatal levels of poor communication. In some companies, it's hard to be sure the documents are in English.

For this reason, the vision document establishes more than just the direction of the project. It establishes the tone and communication quality people should expect from each other while working on the project. It's a chance for team leaders to demonstrate for everyone else how to cut to the chase and communicate well. On the contrary, if the vision is bloated, jargon-laden, pompous, highly speculative, inconsistent, or even delusional, it shouldn't be a surprise that the resulting project will have the same characteristics.

Good vision documents never shy away from their core ideas. They avoid prefaces, disclaimers, and introductions, and they make no attempt to hide from the key (and perhaps controversial) decisions that will define the project. Because of this, they are often short and easy to read. Many poor vision documents I've read were large volumes that were intimidating not because of the sheer brilliance of thought they expressed, but because of their physical size. The intimidation worked: no one read the document.

Writing well requires one primary writer

Many of the worst vision documents I've seen were generated by committees. Small committees can sometimes act as good sounding boards, but they should never play the role of primary authorship or decision-making authority. Unless there is exceptional chemistry and shared vision (generally anathema, given the politics of committees), the prospects of clear, concise, passionate writing are dismal. Therefore, the project manager or leader needs the authority to author the vision and drive one voice into it, with the full understanding that it's her job not to write a reflection of her own personality, but instead to encapsulate the best ideas and thinking available in the organization. The one author should be a strong collaborator who is able to incorporate the best ideas and opinions of others into a single document.

A canonical reference for primary authorship is the Declaration of Independence. In 1776, the Continental Congress formed a committee to write this document. The committee met several times, but in recognizing the importance of clarity in the document, asked Thomas Jefferson to write the draft. Much like I'm suggesting for a project team, Jefferson wrote many drafts and engaged in discussions with Congress over the course of several revisions. The group delivered a final document to Congress several weeks later. This role doesn't need to be highly visible; Jefferson did not do a book-signing tour or product endorsements for his work on the Declaration. He was simply granted the authority to make use of his skills in the best service for his team.

Volume is not quality

It should be understood that clear thought does not require many pages. The most effective leadership documents in the world were not very long. The U.S. Constitution, including the Bill of Rights, is a mere 7,000 words (about 6 pages). The 10 Commandments are 300 words. The Magna Carta is 5,000. Good, clear thinkers are able to distill ideas down to their core and central elements, and they express them in a way that is more powerful than twice as many pages. Volume should never be confused with quality. Unfortunately, because volume is easier to produce than quality, we sometimes give in to the temptation of "If we can't be good, we might as well be long and perhaps no one will notice" (another habit of committee lead authorship). Although with this in mind, it is fair to ask why I wasn't able to make this book shorter. *Mea culpa.*

All of these points imply that the ownership of drafting and revising a vision should be assigned carefully. Odds are good that the best communicator in the organization is not the person with the most senior job title. The highest probability for authoring a good vision requires the project leader to know his own strengths and weakness, as well as those of the people on his staff.

Drafting, reviewing, and revising

Every organization has different considerations to make in how they plan projects. I can't offer a simple, five-step plan for how to get from day 1, with no vision, to day 20 (or 5 or 50) with a completed and fully sponsored vision. Depending on how much authority you do or do not have, it may take considerable time to get all of the necessary approvals and have all of the needed conversations to pave the way for the project.

But what's important is that the process for defining the vision starts before the currently active project for your team is complete, and it needs to be finished before the team is expected to move at full speed on the next one. Sometimes, one individual can be pulled off a project in its last phases and can dedicate half her time to scouting out the key questions listed earlier. The project leader can then pick up the momentum from this work and drive toward a draft more quickly than he could if he were working alone.

Often, the most demanding part of this process in large organizations is working with senior management to coordinate what needs to be done (see Chapter 16). Are there plans from the CEO or executives for the entire company that impact this next project? Are there engineers or other thought leaders who need to be consulted? Who are leaders in the organization (both the local team and the entire company) that have expertise, or political influence, that you need to be aware of and build relationships with? Are there core ideas that you are expected to deliver on, or at least consider delivering on? Do other projects in the company need you to deliver something to them so that they can succeed in their efforts?

In good situations, the senior managers provide clear answers to these questions and acknowledge the uncertainty they are creating for the project when they leave good questions unanswered. In bad situations, a heavy burden is placed on the project manager to create her own answers and learn only by trial and error what the real boundaries are. (Alternatively, if you are in a small shop and have only your peers to answer to, all of these senior management questions and burdens are, for better or worse, yours.)

In any case, the nature of the work is the same. Given a projected timeline between completion of the current project and the point in time when the new project needs to be at full steam, intermediary points need to be set for rough drafts, reviews with leaders that represent the entire team, and complete first drafts of a vision for the project. Expect that at every point of review, time will be spent revising and improving the draft (as opposed to assuming that every meeting will end with the room nodding in agreement). Start small, and gradually increase support for the core ideas over time, making them better after each opportunity for feedback. The timeline for this process should be made public (see Figure 4-3), and the people in the small group shouldn't be hidden away in special offices or in other buildings. They should be visible and accessible to the team (although care should be taken not to distract them from the current project). Encouraging questions and visibility always helps smooth transitions into new work.

Part of this process must include a presentation of the key ideas, and the draft vision, to the entire team (aka all-hands meeting) early enough that it is not complete pretense, but scheduled late enough that there is something substantive to say. While this is scary for new leaders, if a meeting is held at the point in time when core ideas are strong but some

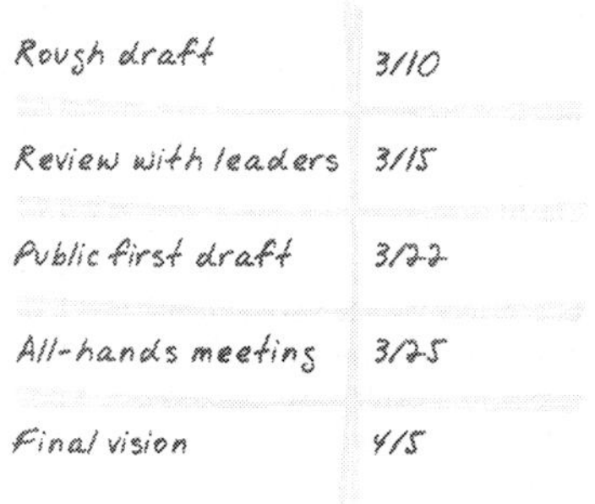

Rough draft	3/10
Review with leaders	3/15
Public first draft	3/22
All-hands meeting	3/25
Final vision	4/5

FIGURE 4-3. *A basic schedule for reviewing and revising a vision document.*

questions remain, the opportunity is created for everyone on the project to see the vision as something alive and accessible. They won't reject it if it's something they can still influence and question. If the vision has grown up through many conversations and opportunities for feedback, the rollout to the team will feel natural to everyone involved.

When the vision is completed, the planning phase is over (see Figure 4-3). The team should have the information needed to do good design work that satisfies the goals. If a review process like the one shown in Figure 4-2 has been used, the team should have a head start on design because they've been made aware of the general direction early on.

A catalog of lame vision statements (which should be avoided)

I've read dozens of vision documents in my career, and there are certain patterns the bad ones share. Lame visions have no integrity: they don't offer a plan, and they don't express an opinion. Instead, they speculate, and avoid the possibility of being wrong. If the vision doesn't take a clear stance on what should happen, the team leaders will never fully invest emotionally behind the effort, setting up the project for failure. In the film *Fight Club*, Tyler Durden says, "Sticking feathers up your butt does not make you a chicken." Writing a document with the word *vision* in the title doesn't mean you have a vision. You can have all the right meetings and use the right document templates and still miss the entire point of what vision documents should do. In the same sense that having the job title *project leader* doesn't magically make everything you do an act of leadership, calling something a vision document doesn't mean it will have the effects I've described previously.

Table 4-1 shows some of the common things I've seen in impressive-looking vision documents that disqualify them from having project leadership value.

Lame vision statement	Example	Why it happens/fails
The kitchen sink	Maximize our customer's ability to get their work done.	Too broad to be useful. This is a mission statement for an organization, not a vision for a project.
The mumbo jumbo	Develop, deploy, and manage a diverse set of scalable, performant, and strategic knowledge-management tools to best serve our constituents, partners, and collaborative organizations, improving the possibility of overall satisfaction among our diverse customer profiles.	This is jargon-based committee-speak. It uses complex language to hide the absence of strong ideas. No one can know what this means; therefore, it can't be useful.
The wimp-o-matic	We may eventually consider trying to do something that's kind of better than what we've done before. At least that's what we think our vision should be now. But don't go too far because we think it might change again pretty soon.	Everyone will see how spineless this is, and there is nothing for the team to rally around.
What the VP wants	Mr. VP's vision for our corporation is to be the best producer of widgets in mid-size markets, and we will work very hard to work up to Mr. VP's standards, using every resource at our disposal to make this happen.	"I said so" is not a supportable argument. VPs are obligated to provide reasons for important decisions, and that's what the vision is for.

TABLE 4-1. *Common lame vision statements*

Examples of visions and goals

In this section, I provide some examples of good vision statements and project goals pulled from my own experience. Although I've changed the details, it's easy to imagine what working on these projects would be like, as well as what the goals underneath the visions might contain.

Here are examples of good vision statements:

- SuperEdit 3.0, the editing tool for experienced copy editors, will make the top five most frequent customer scenarios easier to use, more reliable, and faster to operate than SuperEdit 2.0.

- *Superwidgets.com* will be the premier widget-purchasing site on the Internet for purchasing agents at medium-size corporations. It will make the entire process of widget purchasing for medium-size businesses fast, easy, and safe.

- The Helpdesk Automated Services Site (HASS) Version 5.5 will address the top 10 customer complaints across the university, without any negative impact on average performance, reliability, or response time across the system.

As an example of good project goals, here's what the team of people that developed the Palm Pilot handheld organizer used to define their project:[2]

2   From *Piloting Palm: The Inside Story of Palm, Handspring, and the Birth of the Billion-Dollar Handheld Industry*, by Andrea Butter and David Pogue (Wiley, 2002), p. 72.

1. **Size.** Fit into a shirt pocket. Be light enough not to seem unwieldy.

2. **Cost.** Less than a luxury paper organizer ($300 USD).

3. **Simplicity.** Should be as simple as paper. Turns on instantly and uses simple conventions.

4. **Sync with PC.** Use the PC as a common point of interaction for the customer.

Good project goals like these are clear and simple, and describe the world as it will be when the work is complete. Remember that simplicity is different from difficulty. It was a significant technological and design challenge to create a product that satisfied these goals. The preceding examples of good vision statements might represent huge challenges for those projects. Depending on how "premier," "easier to use," and "top complaints" are defined, those projects could have big challenges ahead of them.

Supporting vision statements and goals

The claims made in a vision statement, or in project goals, should be supported or clarified somewhere in the document. So, what these statements mean by *customer needs*, *easier to perform*, *reliability*, and *top customer complaints* should be defined well enough that informed decisions can be made. If those things are important enough to be in the vision, they are important enough to enlist expert help in fleshing them out to the same precision and detail as technological goals. If claims such as "easy to use" are made, but no one has any expertise about ease of use, the team isn't set up to meet that goal. In producing the vision, leaders should be assessing what resources are needed to be successful and how resource and skill gaps will be filled (the choices are train, hire, change vision, or cross fingers).

Visions should be visual

"A finger points to the moon. Do not confuse the finger for the moon."

—Zen parable

Visions earned their name for a reason: they are supposed to appeal to our capacity to imagine and visualize a specific kind of outcome. By looking at a picture, we absorb many levels of information all at once. For many complex concepts and ideas, pictures provide faster access and greater clarity to more people in less time than words. I've had dozens of conversations in my office with programmers or architects who are struggling to clarify points of an argument, only to end when one of us finally goes to the whiteboard, quickly sketches out the idea, and asks, "Do you mean like this?" Then usually we all laugh at how much time we wasted trying to explain object models or designs with our words or our hands, when a marker and whiteboard would have been much faster. I think American culture emphasizes verbal and mathematical skills over drawing and artistic skills, and most professional people's reflexes have been trained to go in that direction. I'm convinced that, to our detriment, we forget the power of images in expressing ideas.

The best vision documents include visual images. They provide rough drawings, mock-ups, or prototypes of what the final result might look like if the vision is followed. These were offered as suggestions and rough cuts, giving people just enough of an idea to help the goals in the vision crystallize in the readers' minds. It's made clear these mock-ups are far away from a final version of what will be built. Very far. Instead, they are presented as just one early attempt to fulfill the ideas in the vision. This kind of speculation enables people to talk about the work itself, rather than only the abstractions of the work provided by the vision.

Mock-ups and prototypes often resonate more with the most hardcore engineers and programmers than any object model diagram or code sample. Unlike those familiar and abstract forms of expression, the visual prototype shows something that doesn't exist yet, but can. Skyscraper architects and automobile designers make many physical mock-ups and prototypes to help them understand the ideas they are working with and get feedback on those ideas from others. Filmmakers use storyboards for the same purpose. Good vision documents shouldn't shy away from using similar techniques. Showing a sketch of the final thing allows every individual to put his own work in a larger context. The team members aren't just building a component anymore. They now have an idea of what their component will make possible when it's finished.

Visualizing nonvisual things

Just because a project doesn't have a user interface or interact with customers doesn't mean it can't be visualized. How will the world change when the project is finished? Perhaps the vision is about the elimination of some problem or frustration for people (slow servers, crashing databases, etc.). This can be visualized by showing before-and-after views (or simulations) of the same web site—or a prototype that compared the sequence of steps customers will have to do before and after—expressing how much simpler things will be when the new architecture or database is implemented.

There are often many ways to visually express ideas, regardless of how abstract or technical they might seem. If the project will allow customers to spend less time at their desks, show an empty chair by a desk. If the project will make the database faster, show two demos, one before and one after. If the failure rate of an embedded system API will decline by 10%, show the graph of a test case that's being used to measure this, before and after the project. Give the team a visual image no matter how dull or boring it is, to frame around their individual work.

If this end result cannot be visualized—even as just a sketch, a mock-up, or a chart—then I'd argue that the vision is not clear. If you can't find any visual representation of the impact of the project on the universe, be afraid that it's directed toward something the world doesn't need, or that it isn't well defined enough for you to be successful.

This skill of imagining the future and visualizing ideas, particularly when customers are involved, is the domain of designers. Sometimes they're called interaction, product, or even industrial designers. They are professionals who have been trained in how to convert ideas into images and abstract thoughts into the details of what customers will see. While some engineers or project managers might have these talents, few have cultivated them into skills. If ease of use and customer satisfaction are goals, then the services of designers should be acquired early on in a project, and contributing this aspect to the vision would be only one of the natural contributions they would make to the project. If brought in early enough and granted authority to be truly involved, they not only make products look good, but also will contribute significantly to making the product itself good.

The vision sanity check: daily worship

One of the original copies of the U.S. Constitution sits in a vault, behind thick panes of Plexiglas, in a museum in Washington, D.C. Although it's safe and secure, I'm certain few people read it in this format. When ideas aren't accessible or kept in the light, they fade away (unless they're important enough to get their own exhibits at museums). Even on short-term projects, it's easy to lose track of how daily decisions fit back into the larger whole, and the lack of visibility of the core ideas promotes this kind of entropy. People might be very busy and feel good about the modules and pieces they are constructing, but without frequent and common points of reference, it's hard to know whether it's all still going in the right direction. The vision, or the core ideas and goals that are part of it, must be kept alive in the hallways and offices of the people doing the work.

To keep the vision visible, a few core goals should be up on posters in highly trafficked parts of the hallway. They should be discussed openly in weekly or monthly meetings, read aloud to the entire room before the meeting starts. Slide decks or other materials used within the team should have those few core points on the first slide or the first page. Most people on the team, most of the time, should be able to name most of the goals of the project, certainly at least the ones that they are contributing to directly or are responsible for.

But this visibility doesn't necessarily keep the vision alive. The fact that people have memorized it doesn't mean they are continuing to use it in their work. Keeping the vision alive requires action on the part of team leaders. They have to continually reapply the same reasoning that led to its creation.

Ask the following questions at every status or leadership meeting through the course of a project:

1. Does the vision accurately reflect our goals for this project?

2. Is the vision helping leads and individual contributors make decisions and reject requests that are out of scope?

3. Are there changes to the vision we should consider that would make #1 and #2 true?

If the leaders of an organization can make the vision document a living thing, they empower everyone else to do the same. The vision and goals stay healthy and can be a continual source of motivation and clarity for the entire team.

This isn't to say the vision should be modified frequently. On the contrary, major changes should be rare after the project is moving at full speed. But as with a constitutional amendment, the possibility should exist that certain situations may justify change. And that potential helps to keep everyone sharp and the vision's central ideas in everyone's mind.

Summary

- Vision documents distill other planning materials into a single, high-level plan.

- Writing things down serves the author and the team. It provides the basis for discussion and a point of reference that doesn't rely on our fallible memories.

- The amount of detail in your vision document varies with the nature of the team and the project.

- Team goals should derive from goals defined in the vision. Individual goals should derive from the team goals.

- Good visions are simple, goal-driven, consolidated, inspirational, and memorable.

- Volume does not equal quality. It takes more effort to be concise than not.

- Keep the vision alive by asking questions about the utility of the vision to daily decisions on the project.

Exercises

A. Pick a movie (or book) you find inspiring. What attributes of the movie made this effect possible? Imagine you are the film director. Write a short vision statement for the film, listing the attributes you want the finished film to have. If you pick a film, watch the DVD commentary to hear how the film's creator constructed the film to have those effects on viewers.

B. Close your eyes and imagine what the project you are working on will be like when it is finished. If the finished project were made into a film, what would its soundtrack be like? Would it be muzak (the bland music you hear in elevators and waiting rooms)? Dance music? Punk rock? Compile a soundtrack for the project, with the help of your teammates, and distribute a CD or playlist to them.

C. Research visionaries. Select any two: Gandhi, Malcolm X, Thoreau, Buddha, Socrates, Jesus Christ, or Confucius. What were their visions? How did they develop their ideas? What work did they do to express their ideas? To promote and popularize them?

D. Choose a day, and record/calculate what percentage of your time is spent reading what others have written. Be sure to include text messages, email, instant messages, web sites, billboards, and letters from home, as well as project-related documents. Also, remember to count the time you spend writing down how you spent your time. This exercise will help you understand why attention to writing a vision document is important due to all of the demands on your readers' attention.

E. What can happen if someone's individual goals are in conflict with the team or project goals? Whose responsibility is it to correct this? What actions can they take?

F. When it comes time for your team to write a vision or specification, print out copies of the U.S. Constitution and leave it on any spec author's chair, with a note that says, "They wrote a spec for an entire government in six pages. How many do you need to spec a feature?" How does the team respond?

G. At the beginning of every project, make a communal list of jargon words to be avoided. Pick words you know people will want to use, but which have better, clearer alternatives (that you can offer). Put the list on a public wiki and allow people to add words over the course of the project.

H. For fun, write the anti-vision. What is the worst vision document you can imagine? What would it include? How would it be written and how long would it be? See if you can come up with vision statements worse than the lame vision statements listed in this chapter.

I. Identify every one on your team who you would trust to collaborate with you to author a vision document. Write down the reasons why. If you had to pick one person in your organization to be the vision document's primary author, who would it be?

CHAPTER FIVE

Where ideas come from

The less-than-surprising truth about the origins of ideas is that they come from people. No idea in the history of mankind has ever come from a pile of large rocks, a warm mound of dirt, or a bundle of sharp, pointy sticks. Nor have ideas come from self-help books, creativity seminars, or brainstorming sessions. While ideas might be presented or consumed through these things, it's the people who create them that are the source. It follows then that on projects, it's individuals—and not processes, methodologies, or committees—who come up with ideas and find ways to use them.

This means there is nothing magical about ideas. We are all capable of coming up with them (although some of us are better than others). Never forget that it's the fundamental nature of humans and other creatures to use their creative powers to solve problems they encounter in the world. Despite how little education we might get in our modern lives for how to apply these skills, they are there. Our species is still around primarily because we find ways to deal with challenges, and invent tools and strategies to help us overcome them. (Although it is fair to ask whether our ability to invent things, as currently applied in the 21st century, causes more problems than our inventions solve.)

Regarding projects, the ability to find good ideas is important from the first day to the last. Good ideas are needed to make early planning decisions, develop designs, write quality code, and deliver work that meets the client's needs. The scope of these ideas may be different (i.e., some impact the entire project and others impact one line of code), but the process for discovering and choosing between them is very similar. In this chapter and the next, I will explain that process. In this chapter, the focus will be on how to come up with ideas and do creative thinking. Chapter 6 will define how to manage the creative process and work with ideas once you have them.

For the most part, I'll be using the design phase of work (see Chapter 2) to illustrate the process of working with ideas. This is roughly the period of time after a high-level plan has been created (e.g., vision) but before implementation has begun. If you don't organize your project this way, that's fine: this chapter will still be of use to you. The advice here is easily applied to any kind of problem-solving or idea-generating situation.

The gap from requirements to solutions

For reasons I can't fully explain, many people have difficulty planning creative work. In most of the books I've read about software development and project management, there's a shortage of coverage on how to get from a list of requirements for what should be implemented to a good design. Schedules often have a date for when requirements are supposed to be finished, and another date for when specifications are supposed to be finished, but little instruction is provided for what goes on between those dates (see Figure 5-1).

FIGURE 5-1. *Design is often seen as a mysterious process between early planning and completed specifications.*

Now this might be fine if the work involved is incremental, straightforward, and simple. The ambiguity of that time is mitigated by the simplicity of the creative work that needs to be done. Otherwise, a lack of definition for how to go about designing something sets up the team to fail.[1] If the problems are complex, the team will need time to evaluate different approaches and learn about the best ones before they fully commit to building them.

Like a traveler at a fork in the road, knowing where you want to go ("home, please") doesn't tell you anything about the best way to get there ("all three of the roads, at least from where I stand, look the same"). Smart travelers look for ways to minimize the chances of going down a dead-end path. Perhaps they walk a short distance down each road, or find another point of view (a hill, a mountain, a remote-controlled geocentric orbiting spy satellite) that gives them more information. The further they need to go on their journey, the greater the time investment for exploration probably needs to be.

There are two simple ways to fill in the gap. High-quality requirements are one option, and design exploration is the other. Because they are highly related to each other, it's common for these activities to overlap in time.

Quality requirements and avoiding mistakes

In Chapter 3, I provided a basic explanation of requirements and their roles in the planning process. Roughly defined, quality requirements effectively communicate the needs of the customer and/or the goals of the project, with sufficient clarity to be actionable for whoever will do the work. A good requirement might not define how to solve a problem; rather, it might identify a problem clearly enough that someone with the right expertise can confidently work toward solving it. Most software and project teams I've encountered have at least an informal requirements process, possibly as simple as email exchanges with bulleted lists of one-sentence requirements.

Requirements are critical. They act as the starting point for generating ideas and potential solutions. If the requirements state "There will be a barn and it must be green," then anyone doing design for the project will be thinking about different kinds of green barns. This is helpful in two ways. First, it eliminates many ideas from possible consideration

---

1   Be afraid when a project is tasked with breakthrough work but has planned for straightforward work. It's like expecting to do brain surgery with a first-aid kit. The goals and planning don't match, so be prepared to fail in messy ways.

(anyone showing sketches of blue spaceships can be corrected easily). Second, it allows designers to ask questions to further explore the requirements. A designer can ask low-level questions, such as "Is lime green acceptable, or only dark greens?" or "How many square feet does the barn need to be?", or high-level questions, such as "What will the barn be used for? Have you considered a loft? It's probably cheaper and may be better for your needs." Depending on who has requirements and design authority (see Chapter 2), different people will have the power to decide how the questions are answered or to suggest changes to the question. But everyone should be encouraged to ask questions and probe the requirements, which improves their quality.

So, the more attention paid to carefully written requirements, the better the odds that designers will find solutions to meet them. If no requirements are written, then whoever does the design is working at her own risk (i.e., if you're designing without requirements, it's in your interest to draft some). As a rough guide to better requirements, here is a short list of common mistakes to avoid in writing requirements.[2]

- **Provide a plan for requirements negotiation and iteration.** Because requirements enable designers to ask questions, the odds are good that some of the questions will be good enough to force a rethinking of the requirements. Whoever has requirements authority should be planning for this and either begin discussions with designers early enough to incorporate them, or make provisions for modifications to the requirements later on, after some ideas have been proposed. The more focused the requirements are on specific problems to be solved, rather than specific ways to solve them, the less need there will be to modify them.

- **Hunt down erroneous assumptions.** Often, requirements assume that the client or user needs or wants something that he doesn't really need or want. Lists of possible requirements may start in email or as informal lists, and everyone may assume someone else has scrutinized and intensely reviewed them. If you're the PM, don't make this assumption. Religiously ask clarifying questions, such as "Why do we need this?", "What problem will this solve?", or "Whose requirement is this?", to push the assumptions out into the light. Remember that it's always possible someone innocently misunderstood something or passed on erroneous information by accident.

- **Hunt down missing information.** The most glaring errors in requirements involve errors of omission. This can be partial or complete. Partial means that an aspect of a requirement is missing (e.g., the date field format isn't specified, although a date field is), or that an entire requirement has been overlooked (the web site needs to be in Greek and support Firefox 1.0). Missing information can mean two entirely different things: first, the client doesn't care about this aspect of the problem; or second, the client does care but either didn't think about this aspect or forgot to put it down. Like

2   For more information, see *Exploring Requirements: Quality Before Design*, by Donald Gause and Gerald Weinberg (Dorset House, 1989).

erroneous assumptions, it's the PM's job to flag bits of missing information and confirm whether it's the result of the first or second issue.

- **Define relative priorities to each requirement.** As much as we'd like to get everything on our shopping lists, it's critical that requirements at least imply how important each one is, relative to the others. By doing it in relative fashion, it's much easier for negotiations to take place between those with requirements authority and those with engineering authority (for more on prioritizing, see Chapter 12).

- **Refine or eliminate unintentionally ambiguous language.** Words such as *fast*, *big*, *small*, *nice*, *pretty*, and *usable* require relative measures to be understood. It's fine for them to be left ambiguous, provided that everyone involved in the requirement (client, boss, programmer, etc.) is comfortable with negotiating the answers later on. Otherwise, it's in the interest of everyone involved to write requirements to be ambiguous only where intended. Boundary cases ("Our home page must be at least as fast to load in Firefox as *www.cnn.com*; preferably, it should be as fast as *www.oreilly.com*") are often the simplest way to resolve ambiguities. As in this example, absolute requirements (must have) and desired requirements (nice, but can live without) can be indicated easily.

Using one of the problem statements from Chapters 3 and 4, here's one way to write a quality requirement:

> **Search results will be easy for most users to read quickly.** Priority 1. Our goal will be to incrementally improve the usability of our search experience. We will redesign the current search result page to solve the top five customer complaints and the top five issues found in the upcoming usability study of the existing design. The newly designed page will be the results page displayed from searches entered into all primary search entry boxes (navigation bar, home page, shopping cart) and, if at negligible cost, from all search boxes.

There is certainly room for more detail, but many pitfalls of requirements have been avoided in just a few sentences. Notice that the requirement is specific about intention, but it is not specific about redesign for the page itself. The more detailed the requirement, the more risks there are for the requirement to (unnecessarily) constrain the design. This may or may not be desirable, depending on who has what authority and skill set.

Design exploration

Now that we agree (not that you have a choice) on the importance of requirements, we can discuss how to explore ideas based on them.

Once requirements are in place, designers can explore the territory framed by the requirements. There is a large space, called the problem space, of potential ways to solve any given problem. Depending on the requirements, this space can be very large; for example, there are an infinite number of ways to design a home, a meal, an accounting system, a web site, or whatever it is that you're being paid to do. So, until you have some sense of what the possibilities are (because you've explored this particular territory before), it's unwise to commit to anything discovered early on. The first ideas you find are unlikely to be very good: you're still learning your way around the problem space and developing a sense for the possibilities.

Figure 5-2 illustrates the problem space as originating from requirements. As a designer starts exploring ideas for satisfying the requirements, the problem space begins to grow. The problem space grows because each early question or sketch exposes more decisions and opportunities than could be seen before. For example, the requirements might state "The web site must provide full-text searching of all pages," but it probably won't say which search engine should be used, how it will be configured, or how its user interface will be integrated into the rest of the web site. Instead, someone has to explore what the different possibilities are—and there will be many. (However, the problem space eventually narrows; we'll talk about that in the next chapter.)

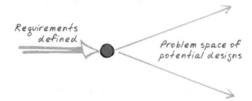

FIGURE 5-2. *Design ideas grow out from problem definitions.*

Depending on the nature of the requirements, there may be different kinds of boundaries on the problem space. If there is only a week of time to search out alternatives, and the final design must cost only $10 to build, the problem space is very limited. A designer will be constrained to a narrow set of alternatives. In fact, it's entirely possible to create requirements that are impossible to satisfy (e.g., make a perpetual-motion machine or solve NP complete problems in polynomial time). Time, budget, expertise, and specific design criteria all impact the shape or size of the problem space. This is in part why requirements definition has such a large impact on the design process.

It also explains why there must be a feedback loop between design and requirements. If some requirements turn out to be impossible to satisfy, given the constraints of a problem space, there must be some way to adjust them. Alternatively, if a designer finds a fantastic idea that satisfies the project goals, but requires adjusting a requirement, it's in the interest of the client/customer/business to consider making that change.

It's not surprising that innovative work often occurs when one person has both requirements and design authority (i.e., someone in a start-up company, an R&D lab, or a group that has given him lots of power). He can settle design and requirements changes all on his own.

Fear of the gap and the idea of progress

Perhaps many people skip over the design process because they're afraid of exploration, especially when others are watching them do it. When we explore our own work (say, trying to optimize an algorithm or revise a document), no one is there to witness the process. We're free to try embarrassing or strange ideas because the only judgment we face is our own. But with design as a scheduled activity for a team, anyone doing design will have her explorations visible to many other people. Any sketches or prototypes she makes will need to be shown to others and discussed openly. If people don't trust others to give them constructive criticism, it's not surprising that this process intimidates them.[3]

And unlike fixing bugs or producing documents, in design work most people don't know how to measure progress. Instead of watching a number get bigger or smaller, during design a manager must rely on his knowledge of the design process (which may be limited) or his subjective judgment of the creative progress (which he may not have or trust). This is compounded by the fear that too much structure will restrict creative people from doing their creative work, but not enough structure might send the project straight for a cliff. (As a final plug for Chapter 6, I promise I'll explain how to deal with this challenge in the next chapter.)

On the whole, I think that creative work—whether related to building bridges, designing spacecraft, or engineering web sites—suffers from many stereotypes. Managers and leaders need to be the first people to get past those labels. Specific to finding ideas, two of the worst stereotypes and misperceptions are represented by the following evil phrases: "there are no bad ideas" and "think out of the box." By examining these phrases and the erroneous ideas behind them, I'll provide some simple ways to think about creativity and give advice on how to find good ideas.

There are bad ideas

I do not know where the phrase "There are no bad ideas" came from, but I'm certain it's wrong. I've seen the phrase used in both television commercials and in brainstorming meetings (and quite possibly in television commercials about brainstorming meetings). This cute little phrase is typically used in an attempt to help prevent people from filtering out ideas too early in the creative process—a noble goal indeed. But when applied to almost any other situation involving problem solving or creative thinking, "There are no bad ideas" could not be more frustratingly false. I have incontrovertible evidence that there are an infinite number of awful, horrible, useless, comically stupid, and embarrassingly bad ideas. If you pay attention to the world around you, it's pretty clear that people are coming up with new ones all the time.

---

3   See "How to give and receive criticism" at *http://www.scottberkun.com/essays/35-how-to-give-and-receive-criticism/*.

Even with a top-notch set of requirements, most of the possible designs that exist or could be created will not solve the problems or satisfy the goals (see Figure 5-3). In fact, the space of good solutions for a problem is much smaller than the space of nonsolutions. Basic logic bears this out: if I ask you to climb Mount Everest, there are probably a handful of different routes that safely lead to the top. But if I ask you not to climb Mount Everest, you have an infinite number of ways to succeed (e.g., picking your nose, reading Dickens, climbing other mountains, climbing other mountains while picking your nose and reading Dickens, etc.). There are always more ways not to do something than there are to do it (a fact sure to generate much rejoicing among cynics and slackers everywhere).

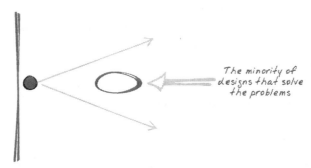

The minority of designs that solve the problems

FIGURE 5-3. *Most of the possible designs will not lead to success (and the ones that will are not all bunched together, as this diagram might imply).*

However, the problem is that it's difficult to know early on which ideas will lead to true solutions. Unlike climbing Mount Everest, most projects cover territory that isn't well mapped out. You might be using cutting-edge (i.e., unreliable) technologies, trying to solve a new or complex set of problems, or working with people who don't have the needed expertise. There are 1,000 reasons why your current project may be different from projects done in the past, and that difference means that new thinking (designing) is required to be successful.

Good or bad compared to what?

Of course this gets even more difficult because it's not always easy to know whether the idea in front of you is good or bad. Ideas are impossible to evaluate in the abstract. They are good or bad only in how they solve some particular problem or achieve a desired effect (e.g., make someone laugh, make things explode, etc.). As I stated previously, if the problem is complex, it's rare that you'll find a complete solution, which means that a good solution is good only relative to its alternatives. If you have only one idea on the table, there's no basis for comparison and no way to properly evaluate it. So, if you ever find yourself without alternatives to evaluate against each other, or a clear problem to solve, it's very difficult to judge the value of an idea.[4]

Another way to think about this is that while the discovery of $E=mc^2$ was certainly a nice piece of work by Mr. Einstein, it's not of much use to a friend struggling to balance her checkbook, or to someone who is currently lost in the Sahara Desert (not to mention someone lost in the desert *and* trying to balance her checkbook).[5] Is $E=mc^2$ a good idea? Perhaps it is if you widen your requirements and problem space to include the general idea of improving your knowledge of the universe. Perhaps it isn't if the only thing you care about is your friend in the Sahara. Ideas look good or bad only against some kind of background. No matter how smart or clever an idea seems in the abstract, when it comes to projects that must actually build something to solve some kind of problem, the failure to distinguish the abstract from the pragmatic always leads to trouble.

It's common for smart people to be led astray from the real problems at hand because of the abstract qualities of their ideas. Ideas can be elegant, clever, or creative in how they relate to other ideas we are familiar with—even when they don't solve real-world problems. Sometimes an idea may make someone feel good because it validates a claim he made or works to his political advantage. For example, a programmer might argue for idea A instead of idea B because A is more elegant—given the object model he's designed—even though idea A is less satisfactory given the customer's requirements. It's possible his personal requirements are at odds with the project requirements, but he hasn't noticed the difference. So, always make sure to sort out what your real motivations are for pursuing, or defending, an idea.

Thinking in and out of boxes is OK

The second most notorious and misleading phrase regarding ideas, "Think outside the box," has its origins in a classic brainteaser-type puzzle. The puzzle, shown in Figure 5-4, asks the puzzle victim, I mean participant, to connect all nine dots using only four straight lines—without lifting the pen off the paper. It turns out that this is impossible, unless the victim uses the space beyond the boundaries of the dots and thinks (drum roll please) outside of the box. The point is supposed to be that by erroneously assuming that constraints and boundaries are part of a problem, we limit our thinking and prevent

---

4   However, a simple formula for how to make water and a compass from sand would win best idea in a "Mr. I'm-lost-in-the-desert" competition. This is an example of a well-defined problem that is impossibly hard (simple but difficult). When people complain that requirements take the challenge out of problem solving, know that they're full of crap. Problem definitions point at which mountain to climb, but say nothing about how to get to the top.

5   One example is minoxidil, a medication intended to treat high blood pressure. It turned out to be effective against an entirely different problem: hair loss. Judged against one criterion, the formula for minoxidil was a failure; against another, it was a success. Was the formula a good idea or not? It depends which context you consider.

ourselves from finding solutions. It's a charming, almost sweet, point, and I'll give you a moment to savor it before I tear it to shreds.

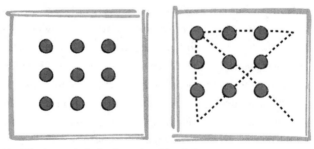

FIGURE 5-4. *The "Think outside the box" puzzle, with solution.*

Puzzles and brainteasers aside, it's not eliminating boxes that is most difficult—it's knowing which boxes to use and when to use them. Constraints are ever present: we require air to breathe and food to live. The laws of physics bind objects together. Sometimes constraints are helpful in solving problems; for example, say what you will about gravity, but I'm grateful that I can assume when I put a pointy rock down on the ground, it's not going to fly up and hit me in the face.

Thus, the real craft of problem solving and creative thinking is knowing which constraints to use or ignore and when to do so. I've seen super-creative people arrive at my door with fantastic ideas three weeks past the last possible date I could have used them. I've also been in brainstorming meetings for tiny, under-funded projects—already behind schedule—where people offered their "biggest, most radical, out-of-the-box ideas," which only infuriated the entire team because not a single one of the good ideas came anywhere near the final project plan.

Someone has to lead a team in deciding which constraints/requirements can be ignored, bent, twisted, or manipulated, and which must be followed to the line and the letter. Being creative often involves working within a constraint, with limited resources or time, and finding cunning or clever ways to do better than was thought possible (see the film *Apollo 13*). Big, radical ideas are rarely needed to succeed. More often, it's a handful of basic, solid, good ideas—applied correctly—that are needed.

My fundamental point is this: do whatever you want with the box. Think in the box, out of the box, on the box, under the box, tear apart and make a fire out of the box, whatever, as long as you manage to solve the problems identified as the goals for the project. Make the boxes irrelevant in favor of understanding the problems, cultivating people's best creative energy, and aiming all the team's power in the same direction. As Thomas Edison said, "Hell, there are no rules here. We're trying to accomplish something." Make sure any rules you create serve the process and the people in it, not the other way around.

It's also critical to consider the following questions: how do you get people thinking about the same problems? How do you bring good ideas toward you? Want to guess at where you might start? Is this paragraph annoying you yet? Well, surprise. Things often start with asking the right questions. (Really? Yes. Are you sure? Positive. Can we get on with it then? Indeed.)

Good questions attract good ideas

"Computers are useless. They can only give you answers."
—*Pablo Picasso*

To dodge a bunch of unwanted college requirements, I studied logic theory and philosophy as part of my undergraduate degree. Apart from the many things I learned and forgot, one thing I learned and remembered was how to ask good questions. I had good instincts for logic, but as the only undergraduate in graduate-level logic theory classes, I was always behind the rest of the group. I quickly learned that if I didn't ask carefully worded questions to peers or professors, I'd receive volumes of complex information that didn't help me at all. In fact, I've found that many engineers, doctors, and other intelligent experts tend to be very happy to share what they know, regardless of whether it's what I'm asking about. People just get lost in their own knowledge.

Carefully asked questions are one way to lead difficult conversations in useful directions. As an example, I had this recurring experience with logic professors that forced me to pay attention to how I asked questions. It would start with me asking something like, "Can you explain this one part of Gödel's incompleteness theorem?" The professor would answer, "Certainly. You see, all proof systems can be reduced to an essential set of characteristics defined by the core recursive primitive functions." I'd say, "Uh, OK. That's nice. But can you explain this one line here?" and I'd point to this tiny line in the proof, circled in thick red ink and with a giant question mark next to it. The professor would nod his head and say, "Oh, that, of course. <Pause>. Well, the history of logic proof systems stems from the noble attempt to express aspects of existence through a verifiable system…." I'd say, "Oh, god. No, this here <pointing again>. What does it mean? How does it relate to the line above it?" He'd answer with, "Certainly, certainly. You see, proof theory relates to logic theory because of the intangibility lemma between sets of nonordinal but infinite value…." Finally, I'd give up and head for the nearest pub.

I learned that without good questions, I'd never get good answers. Sometimes it was difficult to get good answers even when asking good questions. But I did manage to pass those classes, and I later found that at Microsoft, and in the tech sector, those question-asking skills were of great value. The communication problems I faced in the classroom were similar to problems I'd face with engineers, lawyers, executives, marketers, designers, and customers. People often insist on telling you things that have nothing to do with what you need to know. But my logic class experience aside, good questions, asked firmly, help move conversations in useful directions.

There are three kinds of questions to consider specific to creative problem solving: focusing questions (good), creative questions (also good), and rhetorical questions (evil).

Focusing questions

A good focusing question draws the attention of a person or a group to the absence of something important, useful, or even central to the work being done. These kinds of questions narrow the scope of discussion in some way and amplify the attention given to certain aspects of a situation. It's the equivalent of "Don't bother with that for the moment, look here." Assuming the recipient of the question pays attention to it, a well-considered and directed question can be more useful than any number of answers to lesser questions. "Is there any way to use the existing code base to build a system that meets this performance requirement?", or "How will users know when to go to this screen?", or "Is it possible to mix peanut butter with chocolate?" In just a few words, good questions identify an essential element of the problem (or solution)—by-passing all of the secondary and nonessential information—and create a space for an answer to be born. Smart people know instinctively when they hear a good question, or a good problem, and will enjoy attacking it at full speed once it's been recognized. Good questions act like magnets, attracting clever and creative people toward them, and bringing all of their potentially good ideas along for the ride.

Great project managers and creative thinkers are masters of questions. They sense when things are getting off track, recognize the essential elements missing from a discussion or a plan, and inject them back in with a carefully timed and phrased question. On strong teams, even if the project manager asks the wrong question, the fact that he's interrupting the discussion at the right time will cause someone else to respond with the right one. "Well, Scott, actually we rejected that requirement. So, a better question is 'are we sure this new design meets the updated list of requirements?'" And after a short discussion, the entire team is now re-energized and refocused around an improved view of the work to be done. Good questions are catalysts: they recombine the knowledge and energy of a discussion—enhancing, refining, and crystallizing it all at once—and cast that energy out again toward more fruitful terrain.

I've found that after building trust with a team, the most powerful question in all of project management, creative thinking, and problem-solving is:

What problem are you trying to solve?

Provided you have enough credibility that this question isn't seen as annoying manager-speak, it can be used in almost any discussion, at any time early or late in a project, to help ascertain two things. First, that the team can identify what it is they are really trying to figure out; and second, that everyone in the room at the time has the same answer (there's nothing worse than five smart people working together but unknowingly trying to solve different problems). This works magically well for anything from high-level strategy discussions to low-level detail decisions of code syntax, test-case minutiae, or design production issues. It's such a powerful and useful phrase that I made it into a poster and hung it up above my desk. I've found that whenever I feel like the design thinking and idea generation are confused, or people are saying conflicting things, I'm not alone—others are just as confused. So, by throwing the master question down, I make sure everyone gets reset and recharged around whatever it is we're supposed to be doing.

Creative questions

A completely different kind of question, a creative question, works in the opposite direction from focusing questions. Creative questions point to directions that haven't been considered but should be explored. "How many different ways can we present this information to customers on the home page?" or "What else can the search engine database be used for?" Design discussions usually thrive on exchanges of these kinds of questions between teammates, with lots of thinking, sketching, and exploring of answers in between. Good creative questions usually increase the number of alternatives and broaden the scope of the discussion (although not necessarily the scope of the problem). As we'll see later in this chapter, creating a wide pool of ideas is often the only way to arrive at good ideas. Asking good questions sets up a creative person to go in the right direction, or, as is often the case, in a wrong direction that eventually helps people figure out what the right one is.

Rhetorical questions

But be careful with the creative question's evil twin: the rhetorical question. Rhetorical questions are the insincere kind, asked without any intent for a literal answer. Like a parent scolding a child ("What were you thinking when you ate an entire box of Fruit Loops?" or "How could you let Sally cover the television screen with peanut butter?"), rhetorical questions tend to end discussions. They imply guilt and negative judgment. They assume that the asker of the question knows more than the recipient, and they unfairly place the recipient in a compromised position of power. People who have authority, but don't know how to use it well, often ask rhetorical questions (e.g., a frustrated boss or teacher). By asking questions in this manner, they rarely get the response they were after. If used carefully, rhetorical questions can be funny or can shake people up who need to be shaken ("Come on guys, is this really the best you can do?"). But they should be used sparingly, even for this purpose.

Both focusing and creative questions help draw out the raw materials needed for good thinking. It takes a careful hand to know when to use which kind of question and when to simply contribute to discussions and volunteer ideas. Of course, if the team is producing good work and naturally stays focused while being creative, there might not be a need to consciously seek out questions. After all, it's the quality of the ideas that's important in the end, not the questions or specific processes that led to them.

Bad ideas lead to good ideas

I first saw a designer design something when I was a junior in college. I didn't really know what designers did, and I thought that—for the most part—they made things look pretty: designer jeans, designer handbags, etc. Anyway, this young man was designing a new kind of portable stereo. He sat at his desk in the design department undergraduate studio, which was a big, open space with lots of tables, sketches, prototypes, and blueprints all over the place.[6] He was sketching out different ideas, each one an alternative design for the stereo. I asked him what he was doing, or more precisely, how what he was doing fit into "designing"—whatever that meant to him.

He thought it over for a moment, smiled, and told me, "I don't really know what the good ideas look like until I've seen the bad ones." I nodded politely, but dismissed him entirely. I chalked up my inability to understand what he was saying to my perception of him as an odd, creative-type person, and not to my own ignorance.

It was only after I'd spent a couple of years designing software that I understood what he was saying. I'd learned through experience that good ideas often require the remains of many bad ideas. Without making mistakes and oversights in many different attempts, it's often impossible to find the path of ideas that leads to success (see Chapter 1). Perhaps it's only when an idea doesn't work and we're confronted with failure that we're forced to review our assumptions. And only then, when we step back with more information, can we see the path that wasn't visible to us before.

So, the best ideas and designs require momentum. They don't arrive as the result of a magic spell or force of will ("Be brilliant, now! I mean now! How about…now!"). Every drawing, sketch, or prototype, no matter how ridiculous or pathetic, teaches the designer (or engineer or scientist) a little something more about the problem, and increases the odds that the next attempt will be better than the last. Every great mind that has pursued

---

6   It was much like the workplaces described in *Peopleware*, by Tom DeMarco and Timothy Lister (Dorset House, 1999), or *Planning Extreme Programming*, by Kent Beck and Martin Fowler (Addison-Wesley Professional, 2000).

the solving of complex problems in the world has done so surrounded by large piles of crumpled paper. Some have lied about this, others have embraced it. If nothing else, this notion that bad ideas lead to good ones frees us to start designing however we choose. We should fully expect to get our hands dirty and make lots of early mistakes because the sooner we make them, the sooner we'll move on to better ideas.

Good designs come from many good ideas

Solving a single problem isn't the goal of a project—things are much harder than that. Most software projects involve the solving of dozens of problems, preferably in a way that customers can use easily and that can be built by the engineering team in a limited amount of time. The sheer number of points of integration between parts and components involved in designing and engineering an automobile, a web site, or a software program demands that designers proceed through many revisions with the full expectation that it may take dozens of attempts and adjustments to get it all right. Revision and refinement are the name of the game, and part of the process.

All creative pursuits from engineering to the arts share this fundamental truth, as some well-known thinkers and creators have stated:

"The two most important tools an architect has are the eraser in the drawing room and the sledgehammer on the construction site."

—*Frank Lloyd Wright*

"The physicist's greatest tool is his wastebasket."

—*Albert Einstein*

"There are days when I make five of them, but one has to reckon that of 20 drawings, only one will be successful."

—*Vincent Van Gogh*

"There is no such thing as failure. Only giving up too soon."

—*Jonas Salk*

"There's a way to do it better—find it."

—*Thomas Edison*

"Fail. Fail Again. Fail Better."

—*Samuel Beckett*

"If you want to succeed, double your failure rate."

—*Tom Watson, IBM*

"I write 99 pages of shit for every one page of masterpiece."

—*Ernest Hemingway*

While the goal might not be to make every software project into a masterpiece, any project requiring design and problem solving must be given enough time to explore a range of alternative ideas. They also need time to integrate concepts and components. The cynical and the cheap might choose to provide fewer resources for these activities, but the cost will always be paid in the lower probability of actually solving customer problems.

But even if you buy all this, and you work in an organization that provides time for design, things are still difficult. Finding and creating useful ideas require different skills than most of us learn in school or are generally taught in the workplace. In fact, I myself, despite years of study and work in design, had to go back to school to get a new lesson on where ideas come from.

Perspective and improvisation

On a dare from Ayca Yuksel and Vanessa Longacre, two former co-workers at Microsoft, the three of us enrolled in an improvisational comedy class at a community college. After only the first day, I learned that my terror at the proposition of being funny on command was entirely unfounded. I discovered that most people, if they learn how to pay attention (which the class taught us to do), can find humor in many ordinary situations. It's all about learning to see the things that often go unnoticed, and making connections between them.

When I returned back to work and the world of projects and designs, I realized that the same was true about problem solving. Good problem solvers notice things other people don't. They see more detail, make more associations, and have more depth of perception to draw on to find connections between things. In an interview in *Wired* magazine,[7] Steve Jobs had this great piece of creative commentary:

> To design something really well you have to get it. You have to really grok what it's all about. It takes a passionate commitment to thoroughly understand something— chew it up, not just quickly swallow it. Most people don't take the time to do that. Creativity is just connecting things. When you ask a creative person how they did something, they may feel a little guilty because they didn't really do it, they just saw something. It seemed obvious to them after awhile. That's because they were able to connect experiences they've had and synthesize new things. And the reason they were able to do that was that they've had more experiences or have thought more about their experiences than other people have. Unfortunately, that's too rare a commodity. A lot of people in our industry haven't had very diverse experiences. They don't have enough dots to connect, and they end up

7   Issue 4.02, February 1996.

with very linear solutions, without a broad perspective on the problem. The broader one's understanding of the human experience, the better designs we will have.

The only criticism I have of this quote is that it implies something special about creative people that can't be obtained by "noncreative" people. I don't believe people are born into one of two exclusive piles of creative geniuses and unimaginative morons. If the improv class I took was any indication, most people can learn to become more observant and develop their sense of awareness about the world, themselves, and the connections between things, satisfying Jobs' criteria.

Everyone in the class (see *www.jetcityimprov.com*) invented ways to be interesting and funny, despite how almost none of the students—all adults, all from different backgrounds and professions (and a few from other countries)—had any comedy or improvisation experience before. I think improv and other good creative exercises draw on our universal ability to make use of what others show us, and help us to see more clearly and deeply by paying more attention. I fully believe that a competent, but not exceptional, software developer might improve most by studying the construction of skyscrapers, bridges, or even musical composition, than exclusively reading within her domain.

Stepping outside of a specific field (even for just the few hours required to read a book or watch a film) and then looking back is often the only way to really understand it for what it is. Mastery of something should be like standing on a peak in a mountain range: it lets you take pride in what you've accomplished, but it also makes you realize how many other mountains there are with equally good views.

I found that improv class helped me to step out of my job and my relationships and grow in ways I couldn't while inside those things. Helping this along were the four rules we used during in-class games to help us stay aware and keep ideas flowing. I found later on that they transferred easily into design discussions and small-group brainstorming meetings—situations where the goal was to seek out new ideas and create a big list of concepts and thoughts to be reviewed later.

I admit that, to the skeptical and the sarcastic (such as the author), lists of rules to follow can seem like happy fascism (tyranny with a smile). However, most times I've tried them—even with tough, quiet, cynical, pedantically sarcastic, overly intellectual, and low-social-energy teams—they've helped. They consistently led to better discussions, even if those discussions started with the team rejecting these rules and coming up with their own.

Improvisational rules for idea generation

To do the improvisational game for brainstorming (warning: it's not good for deep design thinking), you need a few things: a small group of people (2–8), a comfortable room, a nice chunk of dedicated time, at least one problem definition relevant to the project, and someone at a whiteboard to write down short descriptions of each suggested idea. If people need the whiteboard to explain ideas, that's OK. But since the goal is volume, detail shouldn't be the focus.

To start, someone acts as facilitator and stays by the whiteboard. There should be a problem statement that defines what the group is generating ideas for. This can come from the problem statements or requirements, or it can be something you come up with on your own. Once the problem is agreed upon, people start offering ideas, which the facilitator writes down.

The game begins when someone suggests an idea and a discussion ensues. There are four rules to follow for that discussion:

1. **Yes, and....** When someone else offers a thought, the only allowed response is "Yes, and <insert something here>." Your first attempt must be to continue his line of thinking. Generally, you take his idea or point and move it forward or redirect it, such as "We could use a search box here...", "*Yes, and* it would be smart enough to bring the user to the right place when they type something in." Or, "*Yes, and* it could make use of the new search engine we're building and return faster results." The intention is to keep things moving positively and to develop a habit of listening to others in order to help them with their ideas, instead of just waiting to say your own.

2. **No half-assing.** It's not acceptable to offer an idea of your own, followed by "Sorry, I know it's lame" or "I'm not good at being creative." Half-assing means not being committed to what you're saying. What you say doesn't have to be brilliant for you to stand behind it. It's OK for your idea to be bad: it just might trigger someone else to say something better. If you trust the person next to you to say "Yes, and...", she might be able to do something interesting with your "lousy" idea that neither she nor you would have thought of otherwise.

3. **No blocking questions.** Questions put ideas, and the people asking them, on the defensive. If you say, "Why the hell would you do that?", you're framing a new context around what the other person said that is not improvisational—it's judgmental. It assumes that there is no good reason for it until proven otherwise, which isn't the right atmosphere for open and free thinking (although it is the right atmosphere later on in deeper design discussions). Instead, test your own intellect: how can you direct their initial idea into something useful? Make whatever assumptions or leaps of faith you need in order to make sense of someone else's statement. Roll with it and keep going. Short, clarifying questions might be OK on occasion, but don't make them the focus. It's better to move on to the next idea than

narrow in on individual ones. If raw idea generation is the goal, the volume of ideas per hour is more important than the quality of each idea. Saying nothing can often be better for the overall goal of idea generation than making a point of how stupid one idea is.

4. **Make the other guy look good.** No one should keep score or keep track of who said what. Rewards should go to people who help amplify, express, or draw out the best ideas from others in the group. Because the odds are that whatever gets designed will be built by everyone in the room, there's no sense giving out gold stars or categorizing ideas based on their originator. If the design process starts as a healthy communal process, where the best ideas rise regardless of their origins, the rest of the project will likely have the same spirit.

The result of this kind of exercise should be a list of rough and sketchy ideas that someone will sort through later. When he does, he'll pick out the ones interesting enough to pursue or to discuss in more detail. Because these follow-up discussions are less about raw idea generation, the improv rules don't matter as much—although the spirit of them should carry on.

More approaches for generating ideas

If you're not ready for improvisational games, or if you want a more straightforward way to generate ideas, here are some traditional suggestions:

- **Pick up a book on creative thinking.** There are many good ones to choose from. Two of my favorites are *Thinkertoys*, by Michael Michalko (Ten Speed Press, 1991), and *Six Thinking Hats*, by Edward De Bono (Back Bay Press, 1999). Many other popular books are very good as well, but I've gotten the most mileage out of these two.

- **Pay attention to when you feel most creative.** Figure out what environments make it easiest for you to be creative. Are you alone? Are you with people (which people)? Is music on or off? What music? Everyone is different, and you won't connect with your own creativity until you spend some time figuring out what environments inspire you. It might involve being in a funky coffee shop, meditating on a park bench, or watching the sun set slowly over the skyline behind the Brooklyn Bridge.

- **Recognize that persistence contributes to creativity.** People who appear creative don't necessarily come up with ideas any easier than you do. But they may spend more time exercising those parts of their brains and keeping them flexible. Creativity is a skill just like any other, and while we don't all start out with the same gifts, anyone can get better at anything if they invest enough energy in it.

- **Purchase the brainstorming card deck, ThinkPak, created by Michael Michalko.** It's a set of playing cards that are designed to help individuals or groups come up with new ideas for any kind of challenge.[8] There are other sets like this that you can find, but I've had more success with this one than others.

---

8 ThinkPak is available at *www.amazon.com*.

The customer experience starts the design

"Technological visionaries can never recognize the distinction between the feasible and the desirable."

—Edward Mendelson

If the best architecture in the world is written with the best object models, finest algorithms, and fastest yet most reliable code base ever, it can still be entirely useless if the customers for whom that work was done can't figure out how to do what they need to do with it. It would be a waste of those algorithms and those man-hours of engineering effort because no one will ever experience the quality of the completed work.

The only insurance against this is to start the design and engineering effort from the top down—from what the customer will see on the screen, down to the high-level components, then down to the work items. As soon as rough concepts have been drafted for what the user will experience, the engineers and technologists should respond with how well what they've been thinking about fits against those concepts. Can the designs be built? What compromises might be needed? What constraints need to be considered? The work continues, with discussions going back and forth between layers of the design, and different experts on the team, making sure that as things progress, the integrity of the user experience is maintained, without violating what's possible (and probable) from the engineers. The design thinking will be moving in two directions: from the desired customer experience down to the technology, and from the practical technology up to the customer experience (see Figure 5-5).

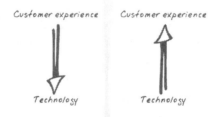

FIGURE 5-5. *The best design process integrates customer-centric design with practical considerations for the available technology. If one is designed in isolation, the other will always be compromised.*

The brainstorming sessions should clarify how and where to start design work. Many of the early ideas generated in brainstorming probably describe some way to design the system to solve a problem. Each one of those ideas has at least one visual representation—in terms of how the software or web site would actually look to someone trying to use it—that can be sketched out and discussed without writing a single line of code. (If the project is an embedded system or an OS kernel—systems that have no tangible user interface—attention should be paid to which conditions are never acceptable.)

Coming up with those representations, sketches, early drawings, or in some cases prototypes, is the first step to understanding the idea. If it can't be drawn and can't be sketched, it certainly can't be built. UML and Visio diagrams are not the same thing as a design sketch. Diagrams are abstractions. They don't show what the user will see, and therefore, they can hide all kinds of problems and details that need to be thought through.

Here is one of the sample problems I listed in Chapter 3: "It is hard to find commonly used items on the home page." Let's assume that after a brainstorming session, three decent ideas were found:

1. Dynamically prioritize the page based on what people use.

2. Get rid of stuff people never click on.

3. Organize the home page into groupings that make sense to customers.

Before any engineer thinks about how to build these things, someone has to consider the ideas' merits from the customer experience perspective. It might turn out that as wonderful as these ideas seemed in the abstract, no one in the building can come up with a good design[9] that incorporates them in a way that makes it easier for customers to do the work they need to do. For this reason, it's in the team's interest to start with the customer experience: it's the easiest way to eliminate unneeded work, clarify what design will be built and why, and reduce the odds of having to make big changes later. Managing this process isn't easy, but doing it poorly is better than not doing it at all.

A design is a series of conversations

With a few sketches of potential user interfaces, real design work can begin. An informal walkthrough of the sketches with engineers, testers, and marketers can begin the real conversations that lead to progress. An engineer can give an off-the-cuff recommendation to a designer about the work implied or suggest changes to the design that might make it easier to build. Many good questions will be asked in both directions. The engineer may also be able to make the designer aware of options that are technically possible but of which she wasn't aware ("Oh, with the new flux capacitor we're building,

---

9   Recommendations: Steve Krug's *Don't Make Me Think* (New Riders Press, 2005) for general principles of web design; *GUI Bloopers*, by Jeff Johnson (Morgan Kaufmann, 2000), which outlines common UI design mistakes. Check out *http://www.upassoc.org/people_pages/consultants_directory/index.html* to hire a usability or design consultant, or contact the author at *www.scottberkun.com/services*.

you can eliminate that screen"). The earlier this discussion can start, the faster the conversation becomes strong, and the more ideas that can be raised, considered, and reviewed.

It's important that everyone sees the process for what it is: a series of attempts, discussions, questions, and introspections that repeat until satisfactory proposals are made (eventually documented in specifications). If someone doesn't want to participate in this fluid kind of work, they should release some of their authority in the decision-making process to those who do. Designing is not the same as engineering, and although having engineers involved in design tends to improve the designs, it's better to remove individuals from the heart of the process than to try and change the process to satisfy an individual.

If the goals for the project are clear, and the problems to solve are identified, the design conversations that ensue will be good-natured. Disagreements will happen, but if everyone is trying to solve the same problem, the conflicts will go only so far. And given the points I've made earlier in this chapter about the value of perspective, these problems may lead to people expanding their perspectives. Like the rules of improvisation suggest, one person's idea can be a launching point for someone with a different background or opinion to suggest something entirely unexpected and significantly better than what was originally proposed.

> **"I like working with good people because if I come up with an idea, they come up with a better idea, then I come up with an even better one, and so on: it's a leapfrog process, and the work becomes much better than it would be if I only did exactly what I want."**
> —Terry Gilliam, film director

The kind of collaboration Gilliam describes is possible only when a team trusts each other. It's often managers and leaders who have the responsibility of creating trusting environments and who need to be open to good ideas, regardless of their origin. We'll talk more about this in Chapter 12.

Summary

- Many teams don't properly manage the time between requirements and specifications.
- Quality requirements and design explorations are the best use of that time.
- Ideas are good or bad only in relation to goals or other ideas.
- Constraints are useful in finding ideas, but thinking outside the box isn't necessarily the answer. Sometimes the best solution is finding a clever way to work within the constraints.
- Questions, perspectives, and improvisational games are tools for finding new ideas.

- The best place to start with design ideas is the customer experience.
- Ideas develop into designs through conversations between different people with different kinds of expertise.

Exercises

A. Find someone you think is more creative than you are. Ask her where she gets her ideas, and what habits she has to cultivate creativity. Pick one habit she uses and practice it for a week. (If you can't think of anyone, pick Picasso, Einstein, or someone famous for creative thinking in your field.)

B. Do you think requirements help or prevent your creativity? How can you create requirements so that they help you find creative ideas?

C. What is the craziest idea you've ever suggested to someone else? Can you think of a way to make the idea even crazier now?

D. What is the wildest idea you've ever had that you have never told anyone else? Why not? What were you afraid of? How is this fear related to your ability to be creative at work?

E. Design exploration means outcomes are uncertain, and following what seem to be the best ideas may not provide expected results. How can a project leader ensure the team's confidence isn't shaken when a favorite idea is killed, or star prototype is abandoned?

F. What problem are you trying to solve by reading this book? By doing these exercises? Is there any situation where the question, "What problem are you trying to solve?" isn't useful?

G. Pretend you are working on a redesign of your house or apartment. Make a list of 10 focusing questions you can ask to stimulate creative thinking. Then make a list of 10 creative questions.

H. In your next brainstorming meeting or creativity session, write the list of rules up on the whiteboard. Ask everyone to do an experiment, just for 10 minutes, where everyone has to follow the rules. What effect did it have? Are there rules you'd like to change or add?

I. If design is a series of conversations, what does this mean for the importance of communication skills? Can a person be a great designer if he is also hard to talk to? Can a great designer simultaneously be a horrible collaborator?

J. Is there any way to predict how many ideas you need to find a good one? Is there a relationship between the complexity of the problem you're trying to solve? Are there other factors? Or is it too hard to predict?

CHAPTER SIX

What to do with ideas
once you have them

As hard as it is to find good ideas, it's more difficult to manage them. While the project is humming along, vision document in place and a strong creative momentum moving forward, there is another level of thinking that has to occur: how will the designs and ideas translate into decisions? Even if good design ideas are being investigated, and people are excited about what they're working on, the challenge of convergence toward specifications remains. If a shift of momentum toward definitive design decisions doesn't happen at the right time and isn't managed in the right way, disaster waits. For many reasons, project failure begins here.

If the team is still struggling to make big decisions on the day programmers need specifications (or the decisions they contain), the tone has been set for the rest of the project: things will be late, they will be half-assed, and people will not be able to do their best work. More troubling is that even if things are completed on time, if the quality of ideas reflected in the designs is poor, timeliness may not matter. Depending on the goals of the project, the quality of the ideas may count as much as, or more than, being on time.

For these reasons, the time between the completion of early planning and the writing of specifications, in any milestone, is always tough. Teams naturally tense up when the first major deadline (i.e., specifications) is visible on the horizon. Even if people aren't talking about it, many recognize that not all the ideas still being discussed can survive. There won't be enough time, money, or people to build all of the different things that are being considered. People start thinking of ways to hedge on their commitments or cut corners. Worse, some of the ideas and designs may be in conflict with each other. A car can have only one engine, a house only one roof, and if three different alternatives for these things are still proposed, it's clear that most of them won't come to be.

Ideas get out of control

One frustrating observation in these times is that there are plenty of good ideas bouncing around, they just don't seem to land anywhere. Perhaps the worst experience of my career—at this stage in a project—was during the making of Internet Explorer 4.0. (If you're not interested in another war story, feel free to skip ahead to the next section.)

I remember sitting in my office staring at my whiteboard. Another PM and I had made a diagram of the larger project team and all of the features we were working on. Each time we thought it was complete, we'd remember a new requirement that had been added or changed. When we finished, it took up the whole whiteboard. Suddenly, he was off to a meeting, and I was alone in my office with the evil diagram.

I had tons of work to do, but I sat and stared at it anyway. I couldn't imagine how it happened. The size of each problem we were trying to solve was so large and overlapped so much with the other problems that I couldn't keep it in my head at the same time. I loved my team and my work, but that didn't protect me from my growing sense of despair. I couldn't see how we could finish what we had started. Although it was a promising mess, with lots of smart things in it, it was a mess nonetheless. A friend on the team poked his head in my office, saw the expression on my face and the diagram I was looking at, and understood immediately. He said, "Hey, feel the love!", which became our sarcastic rallying cry for the rest of the project.

In the early months of the IE 4.0 project, we had a perfect storm of software development. We were simultaneously trying to shift from small releases and teams (à la 2.0 and 3.0) to a major product release. We had the industry pressure of Microsoft's competition with Netscape, which the press made out to be a winner-take-all battle. And then there were the internal politics of a transformative yet strategic product. It would have been difficult for anyone to keep the ship steady. And like most projects, it's when the momentum shifts from planning to engineering that egos and opinions clash. People face their first tough decisions and feel the pressures of their commitments. As uncertainties and pressures become increasingly obvious, one thing doesn't change: deadlines. The next date sits impatiently on the horizon, getting closer every day.[1]

The solution, which is the focus of this chapter, is to carefully manage the field of possible designs. Someone has to plan and guide each milestone from exploration to specification. Unless there is an experienced design or engineering champion around to lead this effort (which, as mentioned in the previous chapter, is the best way), the burden falls on the nearest project manager. In picking up where Chapter 5 left off, we'll focus on turning the corner on idea generation and head toward the writing of specifications (a topic conveniently covered in the following chapter).

Managing ideas demands a steady hand

The most common mistake is to treat the design process as if it were a big light switch— you can just turn it on and off whenever you like. This fantasy, as it goes, runs like this: you show up one day, realize it's getting late and that there are too many ideas and designs (and not enough decisions), and you say to the team, "OK, we're done with ideas. Pick a design and let's start coding! Woohoo!" Even at the off chance that there is a design that is ready for primetime (which there won't be), this kind of unpredictable behavior will disorient and confuse the entire team. Up until that moment, everyone was

---

1   A feeling captured best by the They Might Be Giants song, "Older": "This day will soon be at an end, and now it's even sooner, and now it's even sooner. And now it's sooner still."

working on designs that required time to bake. Without a date given to them, they may have thought they had right up until 11:59 p.m. on the night before specs were due to make their big decisions.

Instead, good idea management is decisive but predictable. It should never be a surprise that the nature of the work is changing (unless there is a crisis) or that the focus of energy is shifting because the project is entering a different phase. There should be easy and natural reminders to the team as the scope and emphasis change. Like a dimmer switch for lights—the kind with a knob that gives measured control over changes—there should be a gradual shift of focus. It's the project manager's job to manage that dimmer switch and make sure it's controlled with a steady hand. There may be a moment when someone has to say, "Look. Time is up. Is it A or B?", but that moment should be expected days or weeks before it comes about. The pace might need to accelerate or decelerate, but it should be done gracefully.

To illustrate this, Figure 6-1 conveniently shows an idealized view of the creative phase of a project, with a singular point in time when problems and goals have been defined (vision document and/or requirements), and a single point in time when specifications will be completed. Between these two points are much brainstorming, sketching, designing, prototyping, and all sorts of other fun activities described in Chapter 5. For the first half or so of the available time, everyone is focused on coming up with ideas and growing the space of alternative designs. For the second half, the emphasis shifts to narrowing the field by refining and improving the best designs. Eventually, a point is reached where enough design decisions have been made to document them all in a specification.

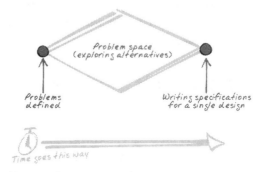

FIGURE 6-1. *The problem space has to narrow at the turning point.*

This is a good story, and a fine diagram, and I'm proud that they appear in this book. However, as is the fate of many fine diagrams, the one pictured here represents something that never quite happens. Those straight lines and perfect angles don't exist. Managing ideas, like much of project management, is always a fuzzy and subjective process (see the eight paradoxes of project management in Chapter 1), and there are several important reasons why this diagram is inaccurate.

First, the problem space tends to shift back and forth. It's never a bright yellow line that's fixed in place. Because understanding the problems to solve—and the ways to solve them—is not static, the space of possible alternatives is always growing and shrinking. Requirements will be adjusted. The trends might be for the space to grow more than shrink, or shrink more than grow, but it's never all of one or the other. It's more of a fuzzy curving line than a straight one.

Common reasons for this include:

- **New information becomes available.** The world doesn't stop because you have a project underway. Companies might go out of business. A technology may fail. Budgets may change. A usability study or customer interview might reveal a new insight into the problem ("people print documents more often than we thought" or "users can't even do their basic tasks with the home page design we prototyped").

- **An engineer's plan becomes clear, changing the rough estimates of how much work might be possible.** Early thinking always gives way to better, later thinking. This sometimes works in the project's favor, and sometimes it works against the project. For example, a programmer might find a new implementation strategy: "if we build it this new way, I don't have to do five of these other work items, and there is more time for other work, or we can finish early (yay)" or "because we can't build it how I initially thought, we have to do five additional work items, meaning less time for other work, or we can finish late (boo)."

- **Conflicts are found between two solutions for two different problems that, when integrated, work against each other.** This can happen for usability, business, or engineering reasons. Joe might have a fantastic design for the car engine, and Sally might have a great design for a transmission, but when brought together, they realize that aspects of each of their designs conflict—for example, the transmission doesn't fit with the engine.

Changes cause chain reactions

Another reason the problem space shifts is that design decisions are interrelated: one change can impact many different decisions. Given this interdependence, it's impossible to fully predict what the impacts will be. I've seen this happen many times.

On the IE 5.0 project, one of our goals was to improve people's ability to organize their list of favorite web sites. We considered four different designs and made simple user interface (UI) prototypes for each one. With these prototypes, we did rough engineering estimates and got basic usability information to use in comparing them. With specs due soon, we chose to focus on design B. But then, days later, we learned that because of a schedule change on a different project, a component that design B depended on wouldn't be available to us. So, we had to go back and reassess our choice.

When we did, we discovered that *all* of the other designs also required the same component (d'oh!). Then, when we cut the functionality (i.e., eliminated the requirement) that this troublesome component would have provided, we learned that other programmers were depending on us to provide that functionality to them through our code. This component was more important to the project than we'd initially realized. We had to sit down as a team and figure out if we could afford to design and build that functionality ourselves, or if we could live with the consequences of not having the functionality at all.

It's important to note that this story doesn't represent a failure. Without making the decision to go with design B, we never would have flushed out all of the dependencies and design considerations involved. I do believe that smart teams flush out requirements and dependencies early, but if the project is complex, you may never get them all. I don't believe that the time spent modeling complex systems to catch every dependency and interrelationship is usually worth the costs (if the pace is fast, and the project is complex, these models will be expensive to maintain), but it might be. It depends on the needs of the project. We chose to bet on the teamwork of the design process to flush them out for us, and it did.

Anyway, the back-and-forth process I went through, where paths opened and closed, assumptions were proved wrong, and new questions were raised, is precisely what designing things is all about. This is often called iteration, which means that the details need to evolve over time (because the problem is complex enough that decisions won't be right without several evolutions).

Specific to design, iteration implies a two-steps-forward, one-step-back experience. The more difficult and complex the work, the tighter that ratio tends to be (e.g., 1.5 steps forward for every 1 step back). But until you take that step forward and make a decision ("Let's run with design B!"), you won't see all of the problems and issues. Making decisions during design, even if they turn out to be wrong, is the only way to force issues and problems to the surface. If you plan correctly, you will be wrong many times during the design process, but through doing so, you will dramatically improve your chances of success. Most engineering, design, and scientific efforts have similar patterns, as the following quote expresses:

> **"There are still enormous amounts of trial and error.... You go back and forth from observation to theory. You don't know what to look for without a theory, and you can't check the theory without looking at the fact.... I believe that the movement back and forth occurs thousands, even millions of times in the course of a single investigation."**
>
> —*Joshua Lederberg, winner of the Nobel Prize, 1958*

Creative work has momentum

The second problem with Figure 6-1 is that the creative momentum of a project is always stronger than inexperienced leaders and managers expect. The effort required to narrow down a pool of ideas into a single (good) design becomes much harder, and demands different skills, than they anticipated. Figure 6-1 implies correctly that the time to close down a problem space should be as long as the time it took to grow it out. But the more innovative or creative the project is, the harder it is to estimate the time the problem space will need. This is because of the creative work's momentum.

The cause of this momentum is that the rate of new questions and issues being discovered is faster than the rate that old issues are being closed. Anyone involved in the work can sense this trend. Even when the target date for specifications is weeks away, many will believe that the schedule is going to slip (and worse, that there is nothing they can do about it because the managers don't see it happening). This is often the first major slipping point on projects. It happens gradually and is continually underestimated until it's too large to correct easily. (I'll cover general corrective actions for schedules in Chapters 14 and 15.)

So, in the diagram shown in Figure 6-2 (noticeably uglier than that shown in Figure 6-1, but, alas, more realistic), the team is working hard, but it's still very clear that the date for writing specifications is improbable. The rate of closure is good and is trending in the right direction, but its trajectory doesn't match the specification deadline.

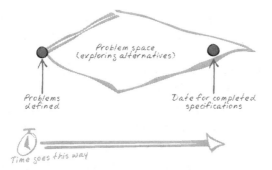

FIGURE 6-2. *The problem space grows and shrinks during design, relative to the unexpected momentum of creative work.*

This is often the first time that a project manager has reason to panic. Until this point, everything was abstract: words, goals, lists, and slide decks. But when the designs aren't together yet, and the date for specifications looms, people get scared. Some look for ways to avoid the real situation by blaming others, forcing bad decisions, or denying that the problem exists. Chapter 7 will explain one technique for dealing with late specifications; Chapter 11 will discuss what to do when things go wrong. But in this chapter, I'll focus on a better way to manage ideas and avoid these problems in the first place.

Checkpoints for design phases

The best way to manage ideas is to start any major design work with clear checkpoints for how the time should be used. Instead of having only two checkpoints, requirements (or problem definition), and spec writing, some intermediary points need to be defined before creative work is going at full speed. It's the project manager's job to make sure these points in time are created (and that everyone understands their usefulness), although it might be best if the designers or engineers define the specifics for when those points in time occur and what the criteria should be for reaching them.[2] There are many different ways to do this, and the best way will vary from project to project and team to team. But, as a basic rule of thumb, Figure 6-3 illustrates the key points in time.

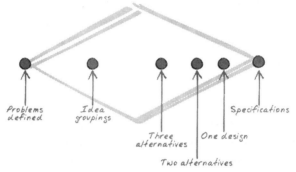

FIGURE 6-3. *Checkpoints for design.*

- **Vision and proof-of-concept.** If the vision document is delivered with a proof-of-concept prototype, the design and creative effort has a head start. There will already be design ideas and engineering concepts to investigate and build off of (or reject, but with improved understanding of the problem). It's not a good vision if it doesn't have at least a rough proof-of-concept design prototype.

- **Idea groupings/lists.** After the initial wave of new ideas and possible approaches are raised, someone has to organize and consolidate them. There should be a point in time when this happens so that the team can expect it and plan for it.

- **Three alternatives.** After the halfway mark, the goal is to narrow the possible design directions into three to five alternatives. The more complex the project, the more alternatives there should be. How much each alternative differs from the others depends on the aggressive/conservative posture of the project, the confidence of the designers, and the problems the project is trying to solve.

- **Two alternatives.** Investigate, research, prototype, and question until it's possible to confidently eliminate down to two alternatives. There should be two clear directions that define the largest remaining decision point(s).

---

2   The checkpoints themselves are not as important as the effect they have. It's often better to let the team propose checkpoints because it improves the odds they'll respect them.

- **One design.** Investigate, research, prototype, and question until it's possible to make a final direction choice.
- **Specification.** Document the single chosen design. Use the remaining time to investigate, understand, and decide on lower-level design issues.

These checkpoints should be defined by the team around the same time the vision document is completed. If schedules are short, reduce the number of checkpoints or skip some intermediary points. And if there aren't enough resources to invest in checkpoints for all the work, prioritize around the most important design challenges.

It's important to realize that these checkpoints are not used exclusively to control the process. They also serve to guide the team, break the work into manageable chunks, and give the project manager a way to understand the state of the project. When changes happen, the checkpoints give everyone a frame of reference for discussing what's happening and why. For example, after reaching three alternatives, new information or ideas might develop that temporarily expands the field of alternative designs to four or five. This might mean the design is still alive, and new thinking is being used to improve the design. But it could also mean that unnecessary directions are being explored. The checkpoints force the team to figure out which one it is, and acknowledge when the design space is growing larger than it should be. The checkpoints create natural opportunities for project managers and their teams to discuss how aggressive or conservative they need to be in their next decisions to keep the project on track.

> **NOTE**
> These checkpoints can be used at the project level or for any individual design problem from a feature to an algorithm. It's a tactic for shepherding work: it applies at any scale of the project.

From my experience, it's the earliest checkpoints that are hardest to get right and the easiest for engineers to ignore. If the first steps can be managed well, a foundation is formed for the rest of the creative process. People will see the value and buy into the process. So, take care to manage those first few checkpoints. With particularly resistant teams, simplifying the process into just three checkpoints—problems defined, the three alternatives, and writing specifications—might be a workable compromise the first time around (see Chapter 10 for more on team process creation and adoption).

How to consolidate ideas

In any creative process, once you have enough ideas, someone has to look at the possibilities and divide them into useful piles. This makes it possible to understand the different viable design directions and to begin to see their differences. (As a rule, 4 or 5 piles of things are easier to work with than 30, 50, or 150 individual things. This is true for ideas, specifications, hyperactive children, small animals, pieces of candy, annoying writers that make silly lists for no reason, etc.) It's fine if some ideas are represented in prototypes and others in scribbles, notes, or unexplored thoughts. The goal isn't to eliminate or refine individual ideas, it's to put some shape and structure around them all.

There are many techniques[3] for doing this, but the simplest one I know is an affinity diagram (aka KJ diagrams, after the anthropologist Kawakita Jiro). This approach requires four things: ideas, a wall, Post-it notes, and the team (although good beer and tasty food help). In an affinity diagram, each idea is represented as a note, described in just a few words and placed on the wall. These ideas can be the output of brainstorming sessions or a list refined by one or more people on the team. There can be anywhere from 20 to 100 or more ideas. The scope of the problem you're trying to solve, and how creative people have been, can make for wild swings in the size of ideas from project to project.

With an affinity diagram, you'll see a broader view of the ideas. It should look something like Figure 6-4. Some ideas are similar, and you want to position them together so that they are easier to identify. Working visually allows people to focus on relationships and not on how much information they can keep in their head. Affinity diagrams also have the benefit of making discussions with others about ideas natural. A small group of people can stand together at the wall and make comments about the relationships they see, changing the positions of the Post-it notes as they come to new conclusions. Affinity diagrams use Post-it notes because they can be moved around on a wall and organized easily into different arrangements.

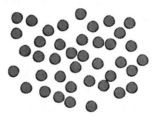

FIGURE 6-4. *Lots of ideas (yay), but they are hard to manage (boo).*

The goal of the affinity diagram is to reach something like what is shown in Figure 6-5. The same raw list of ideas is now grouped into five buckets that represent most of the available ideas. The way to do this is easy. Someone goes to the wall and starts moving ideas around. The lead designer, the project manager, or a small team should be the first to take a stab at organizing the ideas. After someone has taken a first cut, it becomes easier for others to move ideas around between groups, change the names of the groupings, or recognize that some ideas are duplicates of each other and can be removed.

---

3   See *http://www.ms.lt/ms/projects/toolkinds/organize.html* for a good list of alternatives.

As people on the team stop by and make changes, the diagram will change in shape in many interesting ways. (One tip: consider taking digital photos periodically if you want to preserve the different groupings people come up with.) Eventually, the affinity diagram settles down and groupings emerge that can be used in the next steps.

FIGURE 6-5. *Grouping ideas is a good idea.*

In case I'm being too abstract in describing how affinity diagrams work, here's an example that explains Figure 6-5 in another way. Let's say that one of the project goals was to make search results on the intranet web site easier to use. We met, brainstormed, had some beers, and came up with a long list of ideas. The next morning, people had a few more to add, so we included them. We reviewed that list, eliminated duplicates, laughed as we crossed off ideas no one could explain, and had this basic list of ideas to work with:

- Remove advanced options that no one ever uses.
- Improve the layout of the search results page.
- Use the superior HyperX search engine.
- Reduce the number of results shown.
- Allow users to set preferences for how the page should look.
- Open the results in a new window.
- Fix the performance bugs in our search engine.
- Make the query engine work properly (support Boolean searches).

After reviewing the list and using Post-it notes or some other method to group the ideas, we spent a half-hour organizing them. We moved them around, tried different arrangements, and finally arrived at a list we thought was most useful:

- Simplify
    —Remove advanced options that no one uses
    —Improve the layout of the search results page
    —Reduce the number of figures shown

- Customize

    —Allow users to set preferences for how the page should look

    —Open the results in a new window

- Remodel architecture

    —Make the query engine work properly (support Boolean searches)

    —Fix the performance bugs in our search engine

    —Use the superior HyperX search engine

The groupings here are very simple, and because there are only a total of eight ideas, it works fine. However, if there were 40 or 50 ideas, a list wouldn't work as well. Lists promote linear and hierarchical thinking, and they become hard to manage when they get too large. Later on in development, lists are a great way to push the process forward, but while still in the early stages, affinity diagrams are more powerful. They help people see ideas as fluid and tangible things that can be moved around and easily reorganized. This fluidity helps people to question their assumptions, see new perspectives, and follow other people's thoughts. For teams new to creative thinking (especially as a group), an affinity diagram is a great way to go. Use lists for your own purposes as a project manager afterward, but give the team an affinity. I'm convinced that it helps find more good ideas and brings people into the process.

Refine and prioritize

Don't worry about finding "the best" grouping—pretty good is good enough. There are many ways to group even a small number of ideas, and many of them will be good. Aim for four or five groups that cover different ground or imply different directions. Some ideas might not quite fit into any one group, but work them in as best you can anyway.

Remember that you can come back to your ideas and regroup later on if you need to. When you find something that feels good, move on. You don't ship affinity diagrams or lists of ideas to the customer, so don't overthink it.

One last exercise to consider is to take an informal pass at prioritizing the ideas (I'll cover formal prioritization in Chapter 12). Which ideas are the most promising? Refer back to the project vision and problems to be solved to make sure everyone understands the real criteria, because it's easy to fall in love with ideas for reasons that have nothing to do with the goals of the project. One person should drive this process, whether it's the project manager or lead designer. The more informal you keep this discussion, the less time it will take. It's not necessary to draw up a complex criteria checklist and evaluation procedure. All you need is a rough idea of which concepts seem stronger before you move on to prototyping. Should schedule time become shorter, this rough guide will make it easier to sort out where to use your remaining time.

Prototypes are your friends

In Chapter 5, I explained why design is an exploration. You have to explore the problem space to understand what the alternatives are. Good design depends on knowledge of alternatives because the more information you have about problems and solutions, the easier it is to make good decisions. Prototypes are the natural next step in the design process. They take everything that's been learned and apply it to the problem without taking on the risks of full implementation. Prototypes fulfill the carpenter's maxim, "Measure twice, cut once," by improving the design thinking before the team commits to a plan. And as I'll explain next, prototypes do not need to be elaborate, expensive, or require much time. If you're skeptical about the value of prototyping, jump to the section "Prototypes support programmers."

Where do prototypes start?

With four or five groupings in hand, you've paved the way for good prototyping. While people with stronger creative skills might have seen the directions for alternatives days before, groupings of ideas make it easier for the team to see how many alternatives there are. With 20 or 30 ideas, there are hundreds of different ways they could be combined, not counting how many different ways there are to interpret each individual idea.

An experienced designer will have good instincts for how to begin. She'll be comfortable sorting through the available ideas and deciding what to prototype first (not to mention how to go about doing it). But should you be designing without one, there are several simple ways to choose what to prototype:

- Pick the most promising idea from each group and try to combine them in one design.
- Do small prototypes for each group to see where they go. Could all the needed problems be solved just by remodeling the architecture or by adding customization? See how far each direction takes the design.
- Designer's judgment: allow the designer to use her experience and intuition to decide what to use in a first stab.
- Make a list of the hardest or most important design questions, and make a prototype(s) that will help answer them.

As a general rule, the more sophisticated the prototype is, the more sophisticated the questions it can answer. A sketch on the back of a napkin is fine for very early and very rough kinds of questions, but if you want to know something specific and be confident in the answer, you'll need something more involved.

With the first prototypes underway, it should become clear which additional ideas might be added without causing problems, and which ones no longer fit. Like a jigsaw puzzle, some things will slide together and make more sense than others, but it requires trial and error to find out. Because there are so many perspectives (customer, business, technology), it's impossible to predict which paths will work and which ones won't. And that's precisely what prototypes are for: making mistakes, learning, revising, and moving forward.

Prototyping for projects with user interfaces

Prototypes should be done from the top down. Start with what the users will see and the sequence in which they will see it. Involve your usability and design experts as early as possible to get to some reasonable designs and assumptions. There's not much sense in spending days planning databases and XML schemas until a few screens have been made: that's like building the frame of a house before you've seen the floor plan. If you do, you're guaranteed to throw away production-quality work, something the prototyping effort is meant to avoid.[4]

Instead, wait until there are sketches or mock-ups of the user interface that are promising (best determined through usability studies or by walking through decisions users will have to make on each screen to do their work). Engineers should then explore how it might actually get built. If similar discussions started earlier on in the project, this should be a natural and easy continuation of them.

As far as how to build prototypes, there's no magic secret. It takes some experience to learn which things can be faked or glossed over and which ones require more thought and investment.[5] The general rule of thumb is to do as little work as necessary to get the information you need. Any tool—Flash, HTML, VB, or even paper—can be used to prototype designs. It's much more about the skill of the designer and/or prototyper than the technique or tool.

Prototyping for projects without user interfaces

Even on projects with no user interfaces or web frontends, it's still sensible to prototype.[6] Instead of user interface design issues, pick the most difficult or complex technical challenges and prototype them. Confirm that the core algorithms are sound, satisfy basic test cases, or meet a subset of the performance criteria. The goal of prototyping is the same no matter what kind of project it is: work to understand whether the rough approach(es) you're considering can be built in the time allotted and actually solve the problems posed. It's a chance to deal with risk before implementation begins and to learn about what needs to be done before committing to it.

---

4 For arguments on the issues of programming before designing, see Alan Cooper's *The Inmates Are Running the Asylum* (Sams, 2004).

5 See "The Art of UI Prototyping" at *http://www.scottberkun.com/essays/12-the-art-of-ui-prototyping/*.

6 While your team might not be responsible for the users, somewhere along the way your algorithm or database does meet with living people, and decisions you make will impact their experiences.

Prototypes support programmers

In the situation where there is a designer or project manager who can lead the prototyping effort, programmers and engineers often complain that they have nothing to do.[7] They might also say that the process is a waste of time (a claim often made of anything that doesn't involve writing code). On the contrary, I think programmers benefit more from prototyping than anyone else on the team. Prototyping, when done properly, dramatically improves the probability that the designs they are asked to build have been well considered and are of high quality. Perhaps what is more important to the project manager, while prototyping is taking place, is for the programmers to have lead time to investigate the engineering approaches they'll need to use. The quality of their production code should rise if they invest their design time wisely. Worst case, I'm sure customers would appreciate additional bugs being fixed in the software.

Here's a short list of questions programmers should be responsible for answering at this time:

- At a high level, how will we build what is shown in the design prototype(s)? Is there existing code or technology that can/should be used?

- Are there reasonable design changes the designer should be aware of that will reduce engineering costs?

- What are the five or six main components needed, and how will they relate to each other? At the highest level, how expensive will these components be to build? (High/medium/low/unknown is sufficient. For the answer *unknown*, it's the programmer's job to start investigating.)

- Where are the greatest technical risks? Which components are hardest or most complex to build?

- Which interfaces, between which components, are the most complex or most likely to fail? (A dedicated tester or QA person, if available, might answer this best.)

Just like there is no way for a designer to confidently answer complex design questions without a design prototype, there is no way for an engineer to confidently answer complex engineering questions without an engineering prototype (despite what he might say). If ever multiple prototyping efforts are necessary, they should be done in sync with each other. It's best for the lead designer and the lead engineer to spend time talking to each other, asking questions, and helping each other to make good decisions. The two prototyping efforts should be on a path that could eventually join up conceptually: the engineering and design ideas should match.

---

7   I've argued with other managers on this point. They couldn't imagine their amazing engineers not coding at full speed all the time. There is hypocrisy here: if the programmer's time is so valuable, the use of it should be planned. "What will the programmers do?", they'd ask me. And I'd say, "They'll wait for a plan worthy of their time or help us find it."

Alternatives increase the probability of success

Specific to user interfaces and web designs, most prototypes I've contributed to, or made myself, had lots of brothers and sisters. With the big pool of ideas that surfaced early on in the creative process, there were many alternatives that seemed just as reasonable as the others. The only way to understand which ones were better was to try out some of them. Designers or engineers who are experienced at making prototypes have the ability to change the user interface, layout, or other details to one of any number of configurations (CSS and HTML are great examples of this, where there are layers that can be changed independently of each other). A flexible prototype can make discussions and decisions happen much faster because people don't need to imagine and visualize as much in their minds.

I've learned from experience that no matter how much it seems like people agree, if they're not all looking at the same image, they may not be agreeing at all. Each person might have something very different in her mind's eye, and when she says yes to the others, she's actually agreeing to very different things. Later on, odds are good it's the designer or the project manager who will be blamed for this kind of confusion. Prototypes are a reliable way to prevent it because they are actual things that can be shown and referred to later. "See this? You agreed to this, and everyone in the room saw you agree to this exact design." You should specifically call out aspects of prototypes or design screenshots that you're using in this way.

Questions for iterations

With the first cut at a prototype, tons of new ideas and questions will come up. This will include suggestions for changes, enhancements, and new ideas to try. If it's an early prototype, its next iteration might focus on exploring big ideas or wide changes. If it's a late prototype, iterations should be used to narrow the design space and help make decisions. As each iteration comes together, there's an opportunity for a new discussion about the progress of the design. The best framework for these discussions is a set of questions that help evaluate the design and that focus the discussion in a productive way.

Here are some questions for early prototype iterations:

- What requirements does this satisfy? Can we verify this? (Usability, use-cases, etc.)
- What's good and bad about this design relative to the problem it's supposed to solve? (Pros and cons for each of usability, business, and technology considerations.)
- What data do we need to evaluate this design? (Perhaps a usability study, an informal review by a programmer for engineering sanity, marketing, an expert's opinion, etc.)
- What did we learn from this design that we should keep in the next attempt? Eliminate?

- What might we try in the next iteration to make this better?

- Are there other ideas from the idea groupings or from other prototypes that we should include?

Here are some questions for late prototype iterations:

- What decision does this help us make?

- Which open issue will this help us close?

- Has this design confirmed the existence of a problem we need to investigate? Has it resolved a problem we needed to solve?

- What might we try in the next iteration to get us closer to writing specifications?

And with that, the designer has enough information to make another version of the prototype, perhaps integrating two different alternatives together or forking the design into two new alternatives. There shouldn't be any restrictions on what's allowed or not allowed, as long as whatever is done eventually brings the design work one step closer to completion.

The open-issues list

As the field of alternatives narrows, there is one new responsibility for the project manager: the open-issues list. An open issue is anything that needs to be decided or figured out but hasn't happened yet. It's essentially a list of questions that should encompass anything that needs to be done, prioritized by its potential impact on engineering. The form of this list isn't as important as the quality of issues listed and the diligence of the person driving to resolve them. I've used a designated spot on a whiteboard or Excel spreadsheets for this, and I can't say that the tool I chose made much of a difference either way. I don't think these lists need to be controlled or managed like source code (that is, unless the politics of your organization make it worthwhile): the simpler the tool, the better.

This list can start with a rough list of unanswered questions ("Will we use data schema A or B?" or "When do we need final UI design from Sally?"), but it should grow in detail as specifications are written. Each item should have a name next to it of the person who is driving the issue to resolution. It should be the PM's job to make sure everyone is aware of issues they've been assigned, nag them appropriately, and track them to resolution.

Programmers should have the full burden of engineering questions and research, but if there are any issues that the PM can take on, he should. Typically, items that might block engineering but are not engineering specific—such as marketing approval, usability considerations, branding, and visual design—should be tracked by the project manager, as they will impact the specification more so than the implementation (we'll cover the difference between the two in Chapter 7).

The wise project manager divides the open-issues list into two priorities: things that need to be resolved before specifications, and things that could wait until later. It's the most natural way to prioritize issues that have the potential to block engineering—and possibly the entire project. Anything on the post-specification list should be clarified with engineers because they're the only ones who can verify that the decision or information can wait. (How and why things should wait until after specifications will be covered in the next chapter.)

Every uncertainty that needs to be addressed should be listed. No one but the project manager may need to see this list, certainly not early on. But as days go by, it can serve as a tool to unify the team in meetings or hallway discussions. The goal isn't to make people feel bad, it's to remind them of what remains and to help them see what problems other team members need to resolve. Because the project manager's work affects everyone, making the list visible allows people to collaborate on resolving the issues: "Oh, that's on my list, too. Should you take it, or should I?" This is one reason I've kept my issues list up on a whiteboard in my office or in the hallway. (A wiki might work fine, but no one ever looks at that list but the person who created it. Non-virtual and informal places work much better.)

I found that whenever people came by my office and asked how things were going, I'd point to that list and say, "That's exactly how things are going. When that list is empty, I'll be able to finish those specifications." While this isn't a performance metric or something rigorously measurable over time, the state of a project manager's issues list, and the scope of the questions it includes, reveal a great deal about how well things are going. If the list is long but contains very specific issues, things are in good shape. If the list is short but asks scary fundamentals like, "What problem are we trying to solve?" or "What programming language are we using?", you know the project has a long way to go.

Summary

- Ideas have their own momentum. It will take longer to rein in creative work than you expect. Changes will cascade through a project.

- Create checkpoints for creative work to track and manage it. Common checkpoints include proof-of-concept, idea groupings, three alternatives, two alternatives, and one design.

- Use affinity diagrams to consolidate ideas.

- Prototypes enable the project to confront issues early and learn from mistakes without significant risk.

- Use iterations, or the periodic refinement of a prototype, to ask questions, evaluate progress, and decide on the next steps.

- Create an open-issues list to track questions that need to be resolved before specifications can be completed.

Exercises

A. How do you organize your to-do list, for either personal tasks or work tasks? Can you apply a similar system to how you organize, track, and manage your ideas? Why or why not?

B. Should ideas be managed openly or in private? Who on your project team should have access to: a) see; b) modify; or, c) add/delete ideas?

C. Imagine you are toward the end of a project and realize a big idea that could radically improve what you're building. What are some ways to keep that idea around so that when planning starts for the next batch of work, your idea can be used? Can you think of a way to capture ideas like this for the entire team?

D. Spend 24 hours where whenever you hear someone suggest an idea, or have an idea yourself, you write it down. How many ideas did you collect? More or less than you expected?

E. Take the list from exercise D. How many different ways to categorize them can you think of? (If you were too lazy to do the previous exercise, use any list: a shopping list, a list of people you want to see naked, anything).

F. What are the warning signs of working on a project with too many ideas? Is there a healthy ratio of ideas to time, to people, or to a project?

G. Managing creative work requires skills that might not be used in other parts of project management. What are the benefits and risks of having an engineer or designer lead the creative stages in a project?

H. Pretend you are working on a project midway through planning. No one has made a prototype; there are only written documents. You recognize there are some questions that can't be answered with documents alone. What do you do? Do you create a prototype on your own? Involve another person on the team? Who do you show the prototype to? What do you expect his reaction to be?

I. Let's assume in the previous exercise, you decided to make a prototype. You show it to the team and they love it. In fact they love it so much that they agree to abandon all other design work and implement, to the pixel, the prototype you made. You know the prototype makes many assumptions that need to be examined, but they don't care. How can you convince them other prototypes are necessary? What could you do before you show the prototype to minimize the chances this scenario happens?

J. What does it mean if a PM claims to have zero open issues? Who would you trust more, a PM with 5 items in her open-issues list or 50? Are there any dangers of spending too much time tracking open issues?

PART TWO SKILLS

CHAPTER SEVEN

Writing good specifications

I **once had an argument with a programmer** who believed that we didn't need to write specs. I walked into his office with this big template I'd been told to use by our boss, and he just laughed at it (and unfortunately, at me as well). His opinion was that if what I wanted to do was so complicated that I needed 50 pages to explain it to the programmers, it wasn't worth building anyway. He saw the need for all of this process and paperwork as a signal that communication and coordination on the team were failing, and that we weren't trusted to decide things for ourselves. We shouldn't need so much overhead and bureaucracy, he said, implying that elaborate planning was never necessary.

Having had this argument before, I smiled. I asked him if he'd make the same claim about the engineering plans for the hi-rise apartment building he lived in or the three-story highway overpass he drove on to get to work. But apparently he had heard this question before, and he smiled right back. He said that while he was glad those things were planned in great detail, he didn't think working with software was quite the same as working with the laws of physics and construction materials (and he argued in favor of methods with minimal spec writing, such as extreme programming). We quickly agreed on two points. First, that compared to traditional engineering, software is more flexible, easier to change, and rarely has people's lives at stake. But, we acknowledged that because we faced complex engineering challenges, had a team of people depending on our decisions, and had budgets and deadlines to meet, we needed more than our memories of hallway conversations to make sure the right things happened.

We also agreed that what we needed for our project was something suited to the kind of work we were doing and the kind of people we were. Some sort of written documentation would be useful if it solved real problems for our team, accelerated the process of getting things done, and improved the probability of a quality outcome (and it needed to be updatable over time without upsetting anyone). If we could make something that achieved those things, he said he would gladly use it, regardless of what we called it or what form it came in. And with that, we revised the spec process down into something we agreed would work for our small team. I went back to my boss, rehashed our conversation, and worked out a compromise. The big, tax law-size spec template went away.

The key lesson from this story is that like anything else people make, there is no one right way to write specifications or to document work. Specifications, like most things teams are asked to do, should match the needs of the current project and the people who will have to create and read them. And in the same way that web sites or software products need to go through a design process to find the best approaches, specifications need some thought and iteration to be done correctly.

But many experienced people I know have fallen into the trap of believing there is only one way to do specifications (or whatever they call them), which tends to be whatever way they did it last time. Sometimes this chain of repetition goes all the way back to the first projects they worked on. They assume that because those projects weren't complete disasters, the way they wrote (or didn't write) specs contributed positively toward that outcome—a claim that without any investigation may or may not be true (i.e., the project might have succeeded in spite of a dysfunctional spec process). Worse, if good questions about how and why specs are written have never been asked, no one on the team really understands how good or bad the spec writing process really is, or how much it does or does not contribute to the team's performance. (This is entirely similar to how the absence of good questions about writing quality code prevents the possibility of understanding how good or bad the code really is.)

My aim in this chapter is to explain the following ideas. First, that specifications should do three things for a project: ensure that the right thing gets built, provide a schedule milestone that concludes a planning phase of a project, and enable deep review and feedback from different individuals on the course the project will take. These three things are very important, and it's unlikely that a process other than written specifications provides them all at the same time. For that reason alone, I'm a fan of specs. Second, most of the complaints people have about specs are easily remedied, provided their authors understand the common pitfalls of spec writing and recognize the specific benefits specs should be used to provide.

What specifications can and cannot do

Specifications, like vision documents, are a form of communication. When used effectively, they convey important information in a simple and easy-to-consume way. When used poorly, they are hard to read, tedious to create, and frustrating for everyone who comes in contact with them. Often, teams that write lousy specs seem to need more of them (as in, "If wolves come in packs, specs come in plagues"). Most of the time, weak or failed specifications come from a misunderstanding about what specifications are capable of and what they can't possibly achieve.

Here's a list of the important things specs can do for a project:

- Describe effectively the functionality of what will be built
- Help designers clarify decisions by forcing them to be specific
- Allow the review, questioning, and discussion of detailed plans before full implementation begins
- Communicate information from one to many

- Create a team-wide point of reference for plans (and if drafted during design, use it as a living documentation of design progress)[1]

- Provide a natural schedule milestone to focus the team

- Create insurance against the author(s) getting hit by a bus[2]

- Accelerate, improve, and increase the frequency of healthy discussions

- Give leaders an opportunity to give feedback and set the quality bar

- Add sanity and confidence to the team (and author)

Things specs cannot or should not do:

- Eliminate all discussions between team members

- Prove to the team how smart the author is

- Prove how important a feature is (or why it shouldn't be cut)

- Convert people to a philosophical point of view

- Be a playground for the author's Visio or UML skills

The team's leaders should put together a list like this for the team. Everyone who will have to read or write specs should be asked to review the list and give feedback on it before specs are written. Maybe there's something listed that the team doesn't need specs for, or something isn't listed that should be added. This can be a quick discussion—a half-hour max. Even a short chat about it sets expectations for what the specs will contribute, and gives the team a chance to provide suggestions for better ways to go about doing it. If there is a team-wide template for specs, it should be written with these criteria in mind.

Deciding what to specify

Every methodology for software development or project management defines specifications differently, which is fine. There are four basic kinds of information that end up in specifications, and the easiest way to discuss them is to assume they end up in four different documents. But how these things get divided up isn't important (although some people get religious about it). What matters is that the right information is specified by the right people, and it's produced in a useful way for the people who read it. So, on smaller teams, these different kinds of specifications are often combined. On larger teams, they may need to be separate (but linked together) and even authored by different people.

---

1   Some teams put specs into source control, with check-in/check-out locks enabling multiple people to edit without stomping on each other (the Google Docs web application mimics this behavior). In similar news, it's frustrating to wander through a document trying to figure out what's changed. With any tool authors should log changes; e.g., "7/20/2008—added detail to section 6".

2   As sardonic as this might seem, it's true. In fact, the field of knowledge management is based on capturing information that otherwise would disappear if an individual were to, shall we say, not make it to the next release.

- **Requirements.** To document the many things expected of a project, a requirements specification outlines all of the requests and obligations that the work must live up to. It consolidates all other requirements work and provides a point of reference for the project. At best, this is a list of victory conditions, describing the end result, without explaining how it will be achieved. In all cases, requirements should be defined before the design process begins (although they can be improved and updated later), and they should be derived from the vision document. They should be included with feature specifications for clarity and to aid in review (will this plan satisfy the requirements?).

- **Feature.** A feature specification describes the behavior for a scenario from the customer perspective. A feature specification is the primary output of the design process. It describes the software functionality through the user interface (if there is one), and it details how things should work from the most nontechnical perspective. It should describe how the customer's experience will have changed when the work is complete, and it should contain a simple listing of the engineer-defined work items needed to fulfill it. This is different from a requirements list in that it defines a specific design that satisfies the requirements, including the user interface or other nontrivial design elements. If done well, a good feature specification can be as simple as a series of well-explained screenshots.

- **Technical specs.** A technical specification details the engineering approach needed to fulfill the feature specification. It only needs to be detailed enough to describe the most complex or reused components that other programmers might reuse, and to provide supporting evidence for the work items needed for a feature specification. Sometimes, the depth or technical nature of a feature specification eliminates the need for a separate technical spec.

- **Work-item lists.** These are roughly equivalent to work breakdown structure, WBS. A work-item list is the description of each programming assignment needed to fulfill the feature specification. It should be broken down to a level of detail that separates items of different levels of importance, with estimates that are measured in days (some boundary on work-item size should be defined, perhaps a day or half-day, but it's up to the programmers to define it). The creation of the work-item list is entirely the domain of the programmer, and it's up to the lead programmer, and possibly the project manager, to review and sanitize these lists. (Technically, work-item lists are not specifications: they are the plan for how engineering will fulfill specifications. However, they are so important and related to specs that I couldn't find a better place to introduce them.)

- **Test criteria and milestone exit criteria.** As the feature specification comes together, test criteria should be created. This must include prioritized test cases for the new functionality, along with goals for how well the code needs to perform on those cases to meet the quality goals for the milestone (aka exit criteria; see Chapter 15).

Let me provide an example of how these different kinds of specification information can be combined. Whenever I worked on a large team, it was common to write both feature and technical specifications. We'd derive requirements lists from the vision, review them with the team and customer, and then place them at the beginning of the feature specification. Work-item lists were generated by the programmer (often in a simple team-wide spreadsheet), and copied or linked into the feature spec. We'd end up with one primary specification that included many of the kinds of specification information just described.

The easiest way to think about these four types of specifications is in rough chronological order: requirements, feature, technical, and work items. Like many tasks, each kind of information provides the groundwork for the next. The larger the team and more complex the project, the more formalized the division between these kinds of specifications probably needs to be.

Who is responsible for specifications?

On a large team, PMs or designers should be responsible for the feature spec; programmers would be responsible for the technical spec. They should be writing these things so that someone reading both documents will believe that the authors actually know each other and chatted frequently. Often, technical specs are much shorter (and less generous to the reader) because their audience is smaller, and programmers tend not to be interested in writing things that don't compile. Even so, the technical spec supporting the designs in the feature spec should match up.

Business analysts, clients, or project managers often write requirements documents. It depends on who has requirements authority and what the nature of the project team is (small contract team, big staff team). Work-item lists are the responsibility of whoever is managing the programming team. In large organizations, this is typically the lead programmer.

On small teams, as usual, it's a less-structured affair. There may not be strict policies for who does what, or even what documents need to be written. The project manager or lead programmer may end up writing a single document that's an uneven stew of these four kinds of information, jumping between them to suit the immediate needs of his team. This can be fine, provided people get what they need when they need it.

Specifying is not designing

The two previous chapters defined a design process for how to work with ideas and develop them into plans. The importance of a defined design process is to separate the act of designing and planning work from the act of writing a specification for it. The creation of a specification should, as much as possible, be focused on expressing an existing plan or set of decisions in the best possible way, rather than simultaneously designing that plan. The less separation there is between these two things, the harder it is to achieve either of them. Performing one of these processes on its own is difficult enough, and the more one tries to do both at the same time, the lower the odds are of doing either task properly.

Spec authors must be aware of the different mindsets of designing and specifying. When they sit down to write the specification, they must, for the moment, stop exploring and creating and focus on expressing and explaining. Or, at least they must plan to come back and heavily revise the document to reflect the voice of an explainer rather than a creator. Whenever writing specifications (or anything else), it's important to remember that the way that we figured something out is not always the best way to explain it to someone else.

Describing the final design versus how to build it

While it's possible to combine feature and technical specifications into one document, most of the time they need to be clearly separated sections. One of the worst specifications I've read fell into the trap of doing these two things at once. The author, as smart and capable as he was, tried to describe the design while simultaneously explaining how it would be built. As soon as I opened the document, it was obvious how much time he must have spent on it.[3] He had made large and meticulously crafted diagrams showing relationships between objects and components, while simultaneously diagramming them in terms of how they would be used by customers. The result was a beautiful and highly refined disaster. The spec looked impressive, but after five minutes of reading the thing and struggling in frustration to make sense of it, I had the urge to throttle him (and apparently his team had a similar reaction). He'd tried several times to walk people through it, which, sadly, only served to increase their negative (and latently violent) responses.

In an attempt to help, I spoke to the spec writer and tried to offer some advice. He admitted that he'd lost focus and that the spec itself wasn't that important, but he still believed his approach was good. He claimed that because he knew the programmers would need a reference for both the expected behavior and the higher-level details of the object relationships, it made sense to combine them all together. My opinion was that even if a person needs both kinds of information, there's no reason to assume she needs them at the same time or on the same page. Often, it's easier to write and read at a single

---

3 It's always a warning sign to see beautiful or extensive specs. It implies the PM is worried more about the spec than what goes out the door, or he doesn't trust his team. Worse, very long specs are an indicator that no one actually read the thing (exceptions include building nuclear reactors or high-tech surgical equipment).

level of thought, and deal with the story one level at a time, than it is to combine them together. Good specifications often describe the design in layers: first, what the customer experiences described in customer language; second, a high-level overview of basic objects and architecture; and third, coverage of complex and detailed engineering design issues.

Good specs simplify

The toughest thing for technically minded people to do is to effectively choose which details to leave out and at what time to do so. Having survived many terrifyingly complex logic and math classes, I learned that the best teachers knew when to skip over nonessential, although still important, things and how to return back to them when the student (or reader) was ready for them. When specs are well written, they use the same kind of skill. The essentials come through. People gain understanding of the work and can proceed with clarity. The mental models they had for how things will be constructed are more refined after reading the spec, and the quality of the questions they can ask the PM or others on the team is improved. Look for this effect. You never get everyone, but strive to reach the important contributors to the project.

Of course, complexity is unavoidable for a complicated object model or highly detailed interface. Some things might take some explanation and time to understand, but be sure that this is truly the case. More often, complexity is a cop-out that hides poor writing or mediocre thinking. The entire point to writing the specification is to describe things in a way that minimizes the amount of work other people will have to do to understand it. In the worst possible case, it would take someone more time to comprehend the specification than it would for her to design the thing herself. But as with most matters of writing, these criteria are highly subjective. Sorting out the right level of clarity and appropriate complexity is a matter of judgment, and the decision is best left to team leaders.

But in the name of trying to describe things well, here are some writing tips and things to avoid in specs:

- **Borrow good explanations for things from other specs (even if they are authored by other people).** Use hypertext appropriately and grab useful overviews from the Web if needed—which should be encouraged by team leaders. You don't have to invent or describe everything.

- **Avoid jargon and obscure language.** Don't use it unless you're certain it helps the reader, which it rarely does. Or, put less usefully, reduce the probable obfuscation of intentional conceptual matter through attenuated concision of macro-concepts into disambiguated knowledge transformations and the general abrogation of redundant lingual assemblages.

- **Hold on to old specifications.** They make good references when you're stuck on how best to present a concept or to diagram something. When you see a good specification someone else wrote, hold on to that, too.

- **Have specific readers in mind when you write.** Even on a team of 10 people, there will likely be 4 or 5 who will depend most heavily on the spec. Add to the mix a smart person you know, who isn't on the team and isn't familiar with the particular technology you're using. How would you describe a tough concept to him?

- **Don't fall in love with Visio or flowcharts.** Maintain platonic relationships with all tools. Usually, diagrams are interesting only to the person who made them, and they are often not as effective in helping the project as their creator thinks. Sometimes, a good paragraph or a sloppy, hand-drawn sketch is better than a 500-element UML diagram. (Just because a diagram is the only way for the author to understand something doesn't guarantee it's the best way to explain it to someone else.) Tools and diagrams can be great things, just maintain objectivity about them.

- **Is it a reference or a specification?** Specifications do not generally need to be complete API references or describe every single instance or possible behavior. It's entirely reasonable to focus on explaining the 10 or 15 common or most important cases and have a separate document that exhaustively lists the rest (with less detail).

- **Before digging in, use pseudocode or even English to describe complex algorithms at a high level.** As mentioned earlier, consider how a layered approach to explanation might be the fastest way to learn—even for smart people. At a minimum, good summaries and overviews go a long way.

And here's one additional trick that I've always found helpful: whenever someone is confused by something in a draft of your spec (something you will discover only if you manage to bribe her to read it in the first place), take five minutes to explain it to her. Once she gets it, ask her if there's a better way you could have explained it in the spec. Sometimes you'll get good advice and sometimes you won't, but your understanding will always improve simply because you're forcing yourself to widen your perspective. Each time you ask another person, you'll be thinking about the particular concept in a slightly different way, improving the odds of finding a better approach. As the spec author, remember that good feedback comes more easily if you ask for it than if you wait for it.

Ensure the right thing will happen

Specifications define a set of intentions. They make this claim: "If things go as we expect, when we finish this work we will have what is described in this document," meaning that all (or a reasonably large percentage) of the behavior and functionality communicated in a feature specification should be manifested in the final working code when all is done. While it's entirely possible that the day after the spec is finished the world may change, on the day it's written the intention remains. When the world changes, the specification should be updated to reflect this new world and new intentions—whatever they are.

At an engineering level, the goal of a specification then is to communicate these intentions to everyone who needs to make use of them. For testers and quality assurance, this means having enough precision for the expected behavior of a project to write draft test cases and estimates. Marketing, documentation, and any other specialists on the project will have other questions they need answered about what the end result will be like before they can do their jobs. Technical support or account managers will need to understand how things work so they can support, or plan to support, the work.

One of the best questions to ask people after they've read a specification is: "Do you have what you need to do your best work?" By putting the focus on the readers, their interest in it will change. They will ask better questions and put the spec to use, in their minds, toward the real work that will follow.

Who, when, and how

Much like vision documents, it's very important that specifications have one author. Everyone who is going to be doing the work should be contributing by making comments and adding content, but one person needs to filter it, shape it, and make it all fit together. The reason for this is simple: if you want the specification to read like it was written by a clear-thinking individual, you can't have different people owning different parts of the document. As long as that one author understands that it's his job to incorporate good contributions and suggestions from anyone who offers them, things should work out fine.

Assuming there is one primary author, the likely candidates for the job are the project manager, designer, or lead programmer. Because specs represent cross-functional decision making, they should be written by whomever is most accountable for decisions at that level. The feature specification and the technical specification are obligated to match and reconnect with the work-item lists the programming team compiled. If engineering and design have been working together throughout the design process, making these things match up is straightforward. As a bonus, working together early on changes the perspective on the spec process: it will be seen as a happy collaboration to plan work, rather than the beginning of a process of debate and frustration.

For this and other reasons, the specification work should begin during the design phase. As prototypes are being made and ideas explored, small decisions start to fall out of the work, and rough-draft specification documents can begin (and should be marked as early drafts). They can be kept private for a while until there is enough description to be of value to more than one person. In conversations between project management, design, marketing, and programming, a slow but steady understanding grows about what the right design is, and the spec should trail those discussions. As the design process hits the point in time where there are only two major alternatives, the specification should have strong momentum behind it. With only two alternatives on the table, specifications can minimally include all of the common elements and engineering work required in both alternatives (e.g., a search engine that is needed for both designs), as well as a high-level listing of the remaining major decisions and their potential implications.

Writing for one versus writing for many

For project managers, specifications are a convenient place to put information of use only to them. There are often so many questions from different people that the single spec document becomes, on the surface, the easiest place to track them. Unfortunately, for anyone but the project manager, this becomes noise. Reading a specification shouldn't feel like reading the author's work diary (although like many scientists and engineers, keeping a separate work diary can help you discover good ideas). The larger the team, and the more specialized roles there are, the worse this problem can be.

However, one of the important functions of the spec is to help the PM directly. Because she has to organize and lead the effort, the document will likely be modified and read more often by her than by anyone else. The diary-like dialog that surfaces in the specification has an important function; there can be value in tracking specific and detailed bits of information about a project. The trick is to do it in a way that doesn't obscure the basic narrative and decisions the spec is trying to describe.

So, when authoring a spec, care should be taken to separate out which details service only the PM and which ones are of value to the rest of the team. The simplest way to do this is to separate explanations of behavior or functionality in the spec from issues or questions about the current descriptions. There could be one single list of open issues at the end of the specification, which is the simplest solution.

When are specs complete?

For any development schedule that has a planning phase, the writing and reviewing of specifications is its natural conclusion. In theory, the team should know most of the details for what will be built and how it will be done when the specs are complete. The project is ready to go at full speed, and the balance of the work shifts from planners and designers to programmers and testers.

How much is enough?

Deciding when a specification is complete is a judgment call. There are always lingering issues and questions or dependencies on other companies and projects that haven't completely sorted themselves out yet. The "spec complete" stamp of approval can mean very different levels of completeness and quality depending on the project and the team.

There's no right or wrong here: sometimes the risk of weaker specifications is outweighed by schedule pressure or other considerations. Just like any other high-level aspect of a project (code quality, stability, performance), only the judgment of team leaders can decide the right level of investment. And, of course, the more iterative the general engineering strategy is, the more flexibility there will probably be in how specifications are written.

But as a universal rule, the stronger the specification is, the greater the probability will be of a timely outcome. The question then is how much probability do you need? Is it worth the time it takes to make a specification 5% better? Or would the programmers or PM have figured out those details in the natural course of doing the work? There's no easy answer. Looking at any given specification, I'd have to use my own judgment. I think it takes project experience, more so than programming or writing skills, to make that call.

However, the important point is that no matter what level of completeness is expected before the specs are considered complete, the only way to achieve it is through the process of review. Because it is very subjective and comparative, the only way to get specs of a certain quality is to have team leaders (and spec consumers) review and give feedback on them. (I'll describe this process in the next section.)

How to manage open issues

No matter how well a team manages the design process, there will always be unresolved issues during spec writing. If these issues aren't managed properly, disaster waits. Many mid-project disasters are the offspring of mishandled or overlooked spec issues. It's critical that the PM take initiative in collecting and reviewing these issues, pushing the team to acknowledge them early on. This is a tough challenge for less-experienced PMs, as they will be so consumed by other spec-writing tasks that they won't give proper time to open-issue management. Often, it takes being bitten by an issue late in a project to recognize the value of early issue tracking.

Effective management of open issues is purely about diligence. Someone has to both investigate potential problems and take the time to write them down. There's no magic here. Once they're written down, they can be prioritized, assigned, and resolved; but if no one takes the time, preventing major problems will be a matter of chance, not skill.

Assuming you do track issues in some way, even if it's just a list on your office whiteboard, here are some basic questions to help prioritize and refine them:

- When does this issue need to be resolved? Who is the best person to make the decisions needed to resolve it?
- Can the issue be isolated in some way, perhaps to a specific component or scenario? Or does it impact the entire feature or project?

- What are the possible resolutions for the problem that are still under consideration? (For example, we'll use ASP or PHP, but not JSP.) How will each alternative impact the specification?

- Can we cut this issue? How does it really impact the customer in our priority 1 user scenario?

- Can the issue be divided into smaller issues that can (should) be delegated to other people?

- Who or what is blocking resolution of this issue, and are efforts being made to resolve the block? (This resolution may be technical or political.)

If there are many big issues and it's difficult to divide them, something has gone wrong, and the design process and/or team leadership has failed. The way out of the problem is beyond the scope of open-issue management (see Chapter 11).

Closing the spec gap

If you manage open issues well, it's possible to close schedule gaps by making estimates about how those issues will be resolved. The basic idea, often cynically referred to as "shot-gunning," is illustrated in Figure 7-1. If this is done properly, a specification can be reviewed and considered spec-complete on time, even though there are still unresolved design issues. Shot-gunning does introduce risk: you are estimating how well the team will resolve remaining issues, instead of waiting for the team to actually resolve them all. However, it's not necessarily a high-risk move. It all depends on how well-understood the issues are and how good the assumptions are that have been made about them. Consider, if you will, two teams. The A-team has a long but well-understood issues list. The B-team has a small but poorly understood issues list. Which team do you think will most likely meet its dates? I'd bet on the A-team (play A-Team theme music). If nothing else, skepticism dictates that the B-team's small issues list implies that they haven't found all of their spec issues yet. The A-team has spent more time understanding their open issues and is better prepared for whatever challenges the project holds for them.

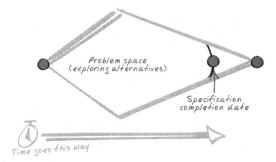

FIGURE 7-1. *Closing the design/spec gap.*

It's important to note that closing the gap doesn't mean abandoning the design work required to finalize those decisions. It means that the PM tries to step back for a moment and carefully make judgment calls for the sake of maintaining the schedule.

To help in closing the gap, consider the following questions for each open issue:

- Are there work items that will need to be done regardless of which alternative is chosen? If so, they should be estimated and added to the spec. If necessary, these work items can be started before the specification is finalized.

- Can the PM or designer resolve this issue? Will the closure of this issue result in new work items? (For example, it may be possible to work in parallel with the programmer starting on understood work items, while the PM drives the open issue to resolution.)

- What are the possible alternatives for resolving this issue that are still in consideration?

- Of the probable alternatives, which is the most expensive? Consider estimating work items based on this approach, and make the specification and work-item list into a worst-case design plan.

- Is this a central or core component? When will the programmer need to implement this? Can this be designed later on during the implementation phase? Is it something we know few other components are dependent on?

- Can this issue be contained, narrowed, divided, or cut? If not, bump it to the top of the priority list.

Closing the gap can't always be done successfully. It's possible you'll make a solid push and progress things forward but still find you're too far away. Even so, the push to close never hurts. Inexperienced teams often need this kind of pressure to force them to confront all of their issues (technical and otherwise), and managers might not fully understand the complexity of what remains until this happens. A good argument can be made for closing the gap proactively, instead of waiting until the schedule is at risk.

The significance of hitting spec complete

There should be a date on the project schedule for hitting spec complete, and it's perhaps the most important date for PMs as individual contributors to the project. Often, the writing of the specification is their primary, or perhaps only, significant literal deliverable to the project. Once specs have been completed, the PM's focus will shift toward guiding and leading the project, including helping the team transition into full development.

After spec complete, there should be a change in attitude on the project team. The feeling should be that for the current milestone, the preliminaries are over: many tough decisions have already been made. The team has gone through some big challenges in figuring out the right designs to find one coherent plan. It's up to the PM to make sure that everyone involved in the effort thus far has some of this perspective and has his work acknowledged.

Face to face is the best way to tell people you appreciate their work. Don't depend on an email to the entire team to mean much to anyone. Go door-to-door or call them on the phone. A short conversation carries more emotional weight than any email.

Although morale events and pep talks are hard to do well, there should be some kind of team-wide acknowledgment for the work done to date. Simple things work best: an afternoon off, a long lunch in the sun, or a week of free beers or snacks in the coffee room. Some kind of positive break in the routine (e.g., get out of the workplace) is the best way to help teams transition and recharge in preparation for the different pressures they will face in the coming weeks or months.

Reviews and feedback

The biggest mistake people make with specifications is waiting until a formal review process takes place to get feedback. Reviews should be used to refine, not to make a first pass and a final decision at the same time. This is another reason why a design process is so important: it means that design decisions have had many iterations, and the authors have had lots of chances to incorporate good suggestions. Team leaders should make this happen by being available for informal earlier reviews and by making the draft specs available on the intranet. But this isn't to say that spec review meetings should be a cakewalk; everyone should walk into the review process with a very clear idea of what is expected of her.

There are different ways to review specifications, but most involve a meeting where the document is discussed to someone's satisfaction. How formal this meeting is depends on the attitude of team leaders. However it's done, the goal is to answer the same two questions: "Is this specification sufficiently detailed to guide us through development?" and "Will the result satisfy the requirements and goals for this part of the project?" There are certainly many more specific questions to ask, but they all derive from these two key ones. The process of review should be directed at answering them confidently.

How to review a specification

The review of a specification should be a team process. While the center of attention is the document and the people who wrote it, the goal should be to confirm that everyone who has to do the work agrees with what's in the document. The easiest and fastest way to do this is by getting them all together in a room so that they will all know the answers to any questions that are asked. I've seen spec reviews done via email or conference call, and I can't say I was happy with the results. As soon as a contentious issue came up, I wished I were in the same room with the team so that I could use whiteboards or hand gestures to explain things in real time. The more complex the spec, the more you want people in the room. (If you're forced to work virtually, and believe everyone needs to be in on the review, do it in small groups of three to five. For complex tasks like reviewing specs, conference calls and video conferences with large groups quickly become tragicomedies.)

A one- or two-hour block of time should be reserved in a mid-size conference room several days in advance. If the spec is ready for review (as determined by the author, with guidance from criteria defined by team leaders), it should go out as part of the meeting invite. As far as I can remember, I've been able to do this only a handful of times. More often, I booked the meeting a week or so in advance and informed everyone they'd get the document via email 24 hours before the spec review meeting. Some people hated this, but I've learned it's the most successful way to provide an updated document and get people to read it. With the early warning, people can plan to read the thing in that 24-hour period.

By the same token, I think it's fair to require that those attending the spec review must read it before they show up. By natural selection, people who really need to read it will find the time to do so because it will be one of the most important things they're doing. No matter what they say, if they honestly can't find the time to at least skim the document for glaring problems, the work is not a top priority for them and they don't belong in the room.

Whenever I had the authority to do so, I made reading specs before the meeting a rule for the entire team. This ensures two things. First, it reduces the number of people who show up to only those who really need to attend. Odds of a packed room filled with unimportant nitpickers go way down. Second, the review meeting will go much faster because everyone is starting from a similar depth of understanding. People who did not read the specification will tend to stand out based on the questions they ask. If their questions are valid, they should be considered; if they are well covered in the spec, it's fair to ask them to read that section and follow up with the spec author after the meeting.

Who should be there and how does it work?

There should be at least one person from each major role in the room (programming, testing, etc.), plus any other major contributing roles (business, design, documentation). Reviews should be open to the entire team: if testers or programmers were interested in the spec, and took the time to read it, they should be welcome to attend, even if they don't work on the specific feature. Team leads should be optional invites, and it's up to them to decide whether they need to participate in the meeting. If they're doing their jobs well, they may know enough of the details to attend only the most contentious spec reviews. On the other hand, if it's an inexperienced team, they may need to attend every meeting.

The actual meeting should be run by the PM (or spec author). The process is simple: answer questions. If there are no questions (i.e., fantasyland), and the right people are in the room and are happy with the spec, the review ends. Some PMs like to do walkthroughs of the final prototype, which is fine. Others prefer to walk through the document section by section. Personally, I think this is a waste of time (if I wrote a good spec, and everyone has read it, why go through the whole thing?), but some teams like it, so use whatever works. The only important thing is that people are engaged in a healthy discussion, asking good questions, and working together to sort things out.

For any question raised, it's up to the people in the room to discuss the answer to the question asker's satisfaction or to add a new item to the open-issues list in the spec. When the questions end, the PM reviews the open-issues list (a whiteboard in the conference room works well for listing new items) and decides if there is anything worthy of holding another review discussion. If nothing reaches that bar, the spec is deemed reviewed, pending investigation and resolution of those new open issues.

After the spec review is complete, the PM should have a timeline for responding to new questions or issues raised in the meeting. Immediately after the meeting, everyone who was invited to attend should receive an email with a short summary of the open issues, a date of the next review (if one was scheduled), and a timeline for when open issues need to be resolved. This is particularly important if an open issue blocks another person on the team from doing her work. In fact, blocking issues should be called out during the spec review and given special attention.

The list of questions

There are some questions that need to be asked in every spec review based on the common things people have seen go wrong over the years. Even if asking tough questions doesn't find specific issues, they do force the team to think more critically about what they are doing. Remember, this isn't a final exam—it's OK for everyone to know what the questions will be before they show up. It's in your interest to make sure everyone walks into the review prepared.

Because designing and spec writing are optimistic processes, it's up to the people in the review to be skeptical and probe for things that might have been overlooked. (Be careful not to be mean. Being critical does not require going out of your way to be cruel or to make people feel bad. If a team is woefully under prepared for spec reviews, the responsibility is often as much on the team leaders as the individuals.) Even if the team knows the right questions, someone has to push and dig to make sure real answers come out.

Here's my list, although I encourage you to revise these questions and add your own:

- Does the programmer's list of work items match the spec? How does each major component in the spec relate to each work item? Where in the design is it most likely that we'll find overlooked work items?

- How is this design most likely to break? What are the weakest components or interfaces? Why can't they be improved?

- What is the strongest aspect of this design? What is the weakest? What are we most and least confident about? Are our strength and confidence centered around the most important components?

- Do we have the right level of quality? Will this be as reliable, performant, and usable as our project vision demands? Are the test estimates realistic?

- Why isn't a simpler design better? Do we really need this much complexity or functionality? What evidence do we have or what sound argument can be made not to make this simpler?

- What dependencies does this design have? Are there technologies, corporations, projects, or other specifications that might fail in a way that damages or prohibits this work? Do we have any contingency plans?

- Which elements of the design are most likely to change? Why?

- Do test, documentation, marketing, and all other specialized roles assigned to this project have all the information they need to do their best work? What are their top concerns, and how will they be addressed? Or, are there sound reasons we can ignore them?

- What are the PM's, programmer's, and tester's major concerns with this specification? With this feature?

- Are there opportunities to share or borrow code with other features being built for this project?

- Have we met our accessibility and localization requirements for the UI?

- What are the security risks of this design? Why doesn't it make sense to eliminate them? Are they documented in the specification, including potential remedies (i.e., threat models)?

- Do we have credible evidence indicating that specified users can use this UI design to successfully do what they need to do?

Summary

- Specs should do three things: ensure that the right product gets built, provide a schedule milestone that concludes a planning phase of a project, and enable deep review and feedback from different individuals over the course of the project.

- Specs solve only certain problems. Team leaders should be clear on what problems they are trying to solve with specs, and what problems need to be solved through other means.

- Good specs simplify. They are primarily a form of communication.

- Specifying is very different from designing.

- There should be clear authority for who writes and has control over the spec.

- Closing the gap is one approach to managing open issues and to accelerate the end of the specification process.

- A review process is the simplest way to define and control spec quality.

Exercises

A. Get a big bunch of LEGO pieces and find another project manager. Divide the LEGOs into two piles, putting the same number and type into each pile. Sit back to back with the other PM, while one of you creates something with the LEGOs (doesn't matter what it is). After it's made, the person who made it must instruct the other, using only words, how to make the same object. Compare the results. Then repeat, switching roles.

B. Why do PMs try to use specifications for things they cannot do? What problem are they trying (and failing) to solve?

C. What does the quality of a specification tell you about a project manager? Can you guess, based on a specification alone, what the quality of the software will be?

D. Visualize something you do often and almost effortlessly, like tying your shoes, setting an alarm clock, or starting a DVD. Write down how you do it so that another person could follow your directions. Draw a sketch to illustrate how to do it. Try to follow what you wrote, exactly as written, or ask someone else to. Pay attention to the results, revise, and do it again.

E. Find the worst specification you've ever seen (ask your friends, teammates, anyone you know who works in a field that has specifications). Now ask them for the best specifications. Make your own list of the common attributes found, both positive and negative.

F. How can you be sure a specification has the right level of detail? Can you think of ways to detect when you've gone too far, or haven't gone far enough?

G. Do you know someone who is addicted to Visio, UML, or another tool? Do you have evidence this addiction is leading to bad specifications? Do something good for your team: stage a Visio intervention. Get all the people together who consume his specs, have them all sign a petition for less Visio documents, and give it to the PM. Include the list of what specifications can and cannot do.

H. If you know spec complete is only a few days away, how can you make sure your remaining time is used effectively? Can you prep the rest of your team to help you? What can you do to maximize the odds that your spec review will go well?

I. Imagine this scenario: you write a brilliant spec, with amazing pictures, clear writing, and thorough documentation. But your best engineer hates it. She hates not only how it is written, but also the ideas it represents. Spec complete is only two days away. What can you do? What might you do next time to prevent this situation?

CHAPTER EIGHT

How to make good decisions

In the process of writing this book, I interviewed more than a dozen project managers. One question I asked was how to make good decisions. Their answers included weighing options, defining criteria, and seeking out different ways to resolve the situation at hand. But when I asked how many decisions they made a day, and how often they used the techniques they named, they often realized something was wrong. Many admitted (after looking over their shoulders to make sure no one else would hear) that it was impossible to always follow any formalized process for making decisions, given the limited time they had and the number of things they needed to get done.

Instead, they conceded that they often work on intuition, reasonable assumption, and a quick projection of the immediate issue against the larger goals of the project. If they can, they will reapply logic used for previous decisions or make use of experience from previous projects. But as reasonable as this answer sounded every time I heard it, the project manager and I found something disappointing about it. I think we all want to believe that all decisions are made with care and consideration, even though we know it can't possibly be so. There is limited time and limited brain power, and not all decisions can be made equally well.

Failures in decision making occur most often not because the decision maker was weak-minded or inexperienced, but simply because he invested his energy poorly across all of the different decisions he had to make. There is a meta-process of deciding which decisions to invest time and energy in. It takes experience and the willingness to review mistakes and learn from them to get better at this higher-level decision making. (Different types of training can be done to develop these skills,[1] but I've never seen or heard of them as core components of any computer science or project management curriculum.)

It's the ability to make effective decisions that explains how some people can manage five times as much work (or people) as others: they instinctively divide work into meaningful pieces, find the decisions and actions that have the most leverage, and invest their energy in making those decisions as good as possible. For the decisions they must invest less time in, any errors or problems caused by them should be easier to recover from than the mistakes they might have made in important decisions.

It's curious then that when "decision-making skills" are taught in universities, students typically learn the methods of utility theory or decision tree analysis: processes where choices are assigned numerical values and computations are made against them (cost-benefit analysis is another commonly taught method). Many MBA degree programs

---

1   Training through simulation is the best way to develop decision-making skills. Simulations put students at the center of the experience, instead of the teacher. See *Serious Games*, by Clark Abt (Viking, 1970).

include this kind of training.[2] But little coverage is offered for higher-level decisions or other practical considerations of decision making outside of the classroom. Methods like decision tree analysis demand the quantifying of all elements, which works well for exclusively financially based decisions, but is a stretch for design, strategy, or organizational decisions.

It's not surprising then that of the project managers I interviewed, few had formal training in decision making, and of those who did, few used it often. This anecdotal observation fits with what Gary Klein wrote in his book, *Sources of Power: How People Make Decisions* (MIT Press, 1999): "…be skeptical of courses in formal methods of decision making. They are teaching methods people seldom use." Klein goes on to explain the many different ways that skilled airline pilots, firefighters, and trauma nurses make decisions, and how rare it is that formalized methods found in textbooks are used to get things done. This doesn't mean these methods are bad, just that the textbooks rarely provide any evidence about who uses the methods or how successful they are, compared to other techniques.

Much like project managers, Klein observed that these skilled professionals rarely have enough information or time to make those decision methods work. Instead, they have four things: experience, intuition, training, and each other. They make good decisions by maximizing those resources. In some cases, such as with fighter pilots or medical students, training is designed with this in mind. Instead of memorizing idealized procedures or theories during training, an emphasis is placed on developing experience through simulations of common problems and challenges.

In this chapter, my coverage of decision making focuses on three aspects: understanding what's at stake, finding and weighing options (if necessary), and using information properly.

Sizing up a decision (what's at stake)

Everything you do every day is a kind of decision—what time to wake up, what to eat for breakfast, and who to talk to first at work. We don't often think of these as decisions because the consequences are so small, but we are always making choices. We all have our own natural judgments for which decisions in our lives demand more consideration, and the same kind of logic applies to project management decisions. Some choices, like hiring/firing employees or defining goals, will have ramifications that last for months or years. Because these decisions will have a longer and deeper impact, it makes sense to

---

2   *The Ten-Day MBA*, by Steven Silbiger (Quill, 1999) includes a compact chapter on basic decision tree theory. The book does a good job of summarizing the core of many MBA programs.

spend more time considering the choices and thinking through their different tradeoffs. Logically, smaller or less-important decisions deserve less energy.

So, the first part of decision making is to determine the significance of the decision at hand. Much of the time, we do this instinctively—we respond to the issue and use our personal judgment. Am I confident that I can make a good decision on the spot, or do I need more time for this? It often takes only a few moments to sort this out. However, this is precisely where many of us run into trouble. Those instincts might be guided by the right or wrong factors. Without occasionally breaking down a decision to evaluate the pieces that lead to that judgment, we don't really know what biases and assumptions are driving our thinking (e.g., desiring a promotion, protecting a pet feature, or ignoring decisions that scare us).

With that in mind, here are questions to use in sizing up a decision.

- **What problem is at the core of the decision?** Decisions often arise in response to new information, and the initial way the issue is raised focuses on the acute and narrow aspects of the problem. So, the first thing is to ask probing questions. For example, the problem might be defined initially as, "We don't have time to fix all 50 known bugs we've found," but the real issue is probably "We have no criteria for how to triage bugs." Redefining the decision, into a more useful form improves decision quality. Being calm in response to a seemingly urgent issue helps make this happen. Ask questions like: What is the cause of this problem? Is it isolated or will it impact other areas? Whose problem is it? Which goals in the vision doesn't it put at risk? Did we already make this decision in the spec and, if so, do we have good reasons to reconsider now?

- **How long will this decision impact the project? How deep will the impact be?** A big decision, such as the direction of the vision or the technology to use, will impact the entire project. A small decision, such as what time to have a meeting or what the agenda should be, will impact a small number of people in a limited way. If it's a long-term decision, and the impact is deep, patience and rigor are required. If it's a short-term decision with shallow impact, go for speed and clarity, based on a clear sense of the strategic decisions made in the vision. Generally, it's best to make big decisions early on or in a given phase of a project so they can be made with patient thought and consideration, instead of when time is running out. (This is similar to some of the considerations discussed in Chapter 2.)

- **If you're wrong, what's the impact/cost? What other decisions will be impacted as a result?** If the impact is small or negligible, then there isn't much to lose. However, this doesn't mean you should start flipping coins. For aspects of projects such as usability or reliability, quality comes from many small decisions being aligned with each other. The phrase "Death by a thousand cuts"[3] comes from this situation, where it's not one big mistake that gets you: it's the many tiny ones. So, you

---

3   The complete phrase is "Death by 1,000 cuts"—as in paper cuts. Yuck.

must at least consider whether the choice is truly isolated. If it isn't, it's best to try and make several choices at once. For example, either follow the same UI design guidelines on all pages, refactor all the code that uses the same API, or cut those features completely. Get as much mileage as possible out of each decision you make.

- **What is the window of opportunity?** If you wait too long to make the decision, it can be made for you—routes will close and options will go away. In this universe, big decisions don't necessarily come with greater amounts of time to make them. Sometimes, you have to make tough strategic decisions quickly because of the limited window of opportunity you have. And sometimes, the speed of making a decision is more important than the quality of the decision itself.[4]

- **Have we made this kind of decision before?** This is the arrogance test. If I put you in an emergency room with a patient squirming on the operating table and asked you to perform heart bypass surgery, how confident would you be? There is no shame in admitting ignorance: it generally takes courage to do so. If you're working on anything difficult, there will be times when you have no idea how to do something. Don't hide this (unless you're choosing speed over quality for the decision in question), or let anyone else hide it. Instead, identify that you think the team, or yourself, is inexperienced with this kind of choice and needs outside help, or more time. If a leader admits to ignorance, she makes it OK for everyone else to do the same. Suddenly, decision making for the entire team will improve because people are finally being honest.

- **Who has the expert perspective? Is this really my decision?** Just because someone asks you to decide something doesn't mean you're the best person to make the call. You are better at some decisions than others, so don't rely on your own decision-making limitations. Never be afraid to pick up the phone and call the people who know more than you do about an issue. At least ask for their consultation and bring them into the discussion. Consider delegating the choice entirely to them: ask whether they think it's their call to make or yours. If the relationship is good, it might be best to collaborate, although this requires the most time for both parties.

- **Whose approval do we need? Whose feedback do we want/need before we decide?** The larger the organization, the more overhead costs there are around decisions. A trivial decision can become complex when the politics of stakeholders come into play (see Chapter 16). A good test of your authority is how often trivial decisions require approvals or the formation of committees. The more processes there are around decisions, the more you must work through influence rather than decree. There are political costs to decisions that have nothing to do with technology, business, or customer considerations, and the impact of a decision includes them.

---

4 This is often true in competitive situations. Quick action can shift what in military terminology is called the burden of uncertainty. By taking early action, you force the competitor (or partner) to respond. Often, whoever feels they have an advantage (resources, skills, terrain, brains) takes this initiative.

Finding and weighing options

In *Sources of Power: How People Make Decisions*, Klein identifies two basic ways people make decisions: singular evaluation and comparative evaluation (see Table 8-1). In singular evaluation, the first option is considered and checked against some kind of criteria (do I want to wear this green shirt today?). If it meets the criteria, it's chosen and the decision maker moves on to more important things. If it doesn't meet the criteria, another idea or choice is considered, and the process repeats (how about this yellow shirt?). Examples include finding a bathroom after drinking a liter of soda, or finding something to eat after fasting for three days. The first available restroom or restaurant you find is sufficient, and there's no need to explore for alternatives.

At the other end of the decision-making spectrum, comparative evaluation requires seeking alternatives before deciding. Considering what city to move your family to is a good example of a common comparative evaluation decision.

Decision approach	How it works	Example
Singular evaluation	The first reasonable alternative found is accepted.	You've been wounded by zombies and need to find a hospital.
Comparative evaluation	Several alternatives are evaluated against each other before deciding.	You have only one extra anti-zombie inoculation and must decide who on the planet to save.

TABLE 8-1. *The two basic ways people make decisions*

Singular evaluation makes sense for situations where the difference between a great solution and a decent solution isn't important. Klein describes these situations as being in the zone of indifference because the decision maker is indifferent to major aspects of the outcome as long as a basic criterion is met. Being able to recognize when all of the alternatives are in the zone of indifference (see Figure 8-1) can save a project significant time, enabling you to end debates and discussions early on and to focus energy on the complex decisions worthy of more thought. Good decision makers don't waste time optimizing things that don't need to be optimized. As Tyler Durden says, "That which doesn't matter truly should not matter."

Comparative evaluation is best for complex situations that involve many variables, have consequences that are difficult to grasp quickly, or require a high quality outcome. New situations or problems that are strategic in nature are prime candidates for comparative evaluation. The more that is at stake in a decision, and the less familiar everyone is with the nature of the options, the more appropriate a comparative evaluation is. With teams, comparative evaluation is the best framework to use if you have to convince others or want their participation in the decision-making process. Comparative evaluation forces you to make relative arguments and develop deeper rationales for action, which is useful for group discussion and communication.

FIGURE 8-1. *The zone of indifference contains the aspects of a problem you do not care about; single evaluation implies that you have a larger zone of indifference than comparative evaluation.*

Most of the time, there's every reason to do quick comparisons. There are many different ways to do comparative evaluation, and some are less elaborate than others. For example, it doesn't take more than a few minutes to list out a few alternatives for a decision on a whiteboard and to make some quick judgments about their relative value. And even when working alone, I've found that making a short list of comparisons is a great way to check my own sanity. If I can't come up with more than one choice, I clearly don't understand the problem well enough: there are always alternatives.

Emotions and clarity

Few people talk about them, but there are always emotional and psychological issues involved in decision making. Richard Restak, author of *The Secret Life of the Brain* (Joseph Henry Press, 2001), wrote, "There is no such thing as a non-emotional moment." We always have fears, desires, and personal motivations for things, whether we acknowledge them or are even aware of them. Even altruistic motivations, such as wanting the best outcome for the project or for the people involved, have emotional components.

This means that even the most logical business-like person in the room has feelings about what he's doing, whether he is aware of them or not. Sometimes emotions are useful in making decisions, but other times they slow us down or bias us against things we need to consider. And beyond personal feelings, the act of decision making itself involves pressure and stress, and it can create emotions and feelings that have nothing to do with the matter at hand. By externalizing the decision-making process through writing or talking, you can share emotional burden and increase the odds of finding clarity.

The easy way to comparison

Comparative evaluation can happen only if you've clarified the problem or issue to be decided. You also need a sense for desirable outcomes (ship sooner, improve quality, make the VP happy, etc.). Borrow words and phrasing from the vision document, specifications, or requirements lists. Those documents reflect big decisions that have already been made, so use them as leverage. Sometimes a quick conversation with the client, customer, or author of those documents is better than the documents themselves.

If you're familiar with the specifics of the issue, or can get in a room with someone who is, it takes only a few minutes to come up with a decent list of possible choices. With a quick list, you'll start to feel better about your alternatives and will have a basis for bringing other people into the discussion. Sometimes, it will be obvious that one choice is dramatically better than the others, and no further analysis is necessary. But often you'll find the opposite: what appeared to be a no-brainer is more complicated than first thought. By writing down the choices, you get a chance to recognize that other issues were hiding from you.

The simplest way to do this is with a good old pros and cons list (see Figure 8-2). I'm not sure when in life we learn it, but most everyone I've ever taught or managed was somehow familiar with making this type of list. What's strange is that it's uncommon to see people use these lists in meetings or discussions, perhaps because they're afraid that by writing down their thought processes, others will think they're not smart enough to keep it in their heads.

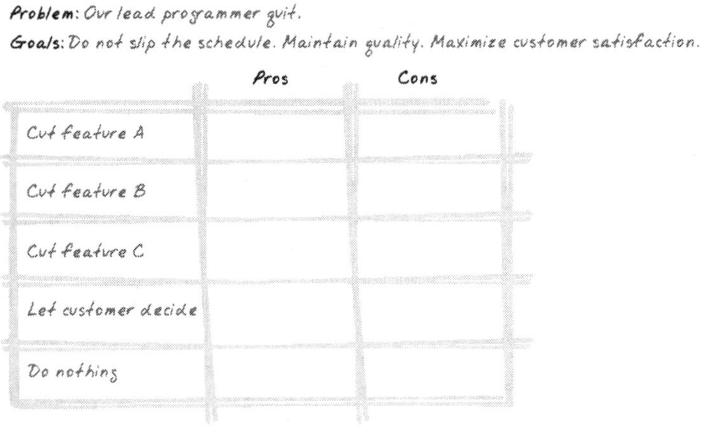

Problem: Our lead programmer quit.
Goals: Do not slip the schedule. Maintain quality. Maximize customer satisfaction.

	Pros	Cons
Cut feature A		
Cut feature B		
Cut feature C		
Let customer decide		
Do nothing		

FIGURE 8-2. *The pros and cons list.*

Apparently, the pros/cons list dates back to at least the 15th century, when it was used as a tool to help settle public debates. Then, centuries later, Benjamin Franklin applied the technique to his own decision making, so he is credited with popularizing it in the U.S.[5]

As simple as this kind of list is, there are important considerations for using it effectively:

---

[5] A short history of the pros/cons list can be found in the pamphlet, "How to Make a Decision" (Who's There, Inc., 2003), which can be purchased from *http://www.knockknock.biz*. In 32 entertaining pages, this title covers techniques like flipping coins, rock-paper-scissors, eenie-meenie-minie-moe, etc.

- **Always include a "do nothing" option.** Not every decision or problem demands action. Sometimes, the best way to go is to do nothing, let whatever happens happen, and invest energy elsewhere. Sunk costs are rarely worth trying to recover. Always give yourself this option, even if only to force the team to understand exactly what's at stake in the decision. Depending on your local politics, having "do nothing" on the list can give more relative value to any other decision that you make because it reminds people that there is no universal law that says you must do something about a problem.

- **How do you know what you think you know?** This should be a question everyone is comfortable asking. It allows people to check assumptions and to question claims that, while convenient, are not based on any kind of data, firsthand knowledge, or research. It's OK to make big unsupported claims—"I'm 100% positive this function will be reliable"—as long as everyone knows the only thing behind it is the opinion of the person making it (and can then judge it on that merit). As appropriate, seek out data and research to help answer important questions or claims.

- **Ask tough questions.** Cut to the chase about the impact of decisions. Be direct and honest. Push hard to get to the core of what the options look like. (See the section "Keeping it real" in Chapter 13.) The quicker you get to the heart of the issue and a true understanding of the choices, the sooner you can move on to the next decision. Be critical and skeptical. Ask everyone to put feelings and personal preferences aside: don't allow good ideas to hide behind the fear of hurting someone's feelings. Show the list to others on the team, and add in their questions or meaningful comments. Put any questions or possible assumptions in the pros or cons column for a given idea; an unanswered question can still help clarify what a given choice really means.

- **Have a dissenting opinion.** For important decisions, it's critical to include unpopular but reasonable choices. Make sure to include opinions or choices you personally don't like, but for which good arguments can be made. This keeps you honest and gives anyone who sees the pros/cons list a chance to convince you into making a better decision than the one you might have arrived at on your own. Don't be afraid to ask yourself, "What choice would make me look the worst but might still help the project?" or "Are there any good choices that might require that I admit that I'm wrong about something?"

- **Consider hybrid choices.** Sometimes it's possible to take an attribute of one choice and add it to another. Like exploratory design, there are always interesting combinations in decision making. However, be warned that this does explode the number of choices, which can slow things down and create more complexity than you need. Watch for the zone of indifference and don't waste time in it.

- **Include any relevant perspectives.** Consider if this decision impacts more than just the technology of the project. Are there business concerns that will be impacted? Usability? Localization? If these things are project goals and are impacted by the decision, add them into the mix. Even if it's a purely technological decision, there are different perspectives involved: performance, reliability, extensibility, and cost.

- **Start on paper or a whiteboard.** When you're first coming up with ideas/options, you want the process to be lightweight and fast. It should be easy to cross things out, make hybrids, or write things down rapid-fire (much like early on in the design process). Don't start by making a fancy Excel spreadsheet, with 15 multicolored columns enabled for pivot tables; you'll miss the point. For some decisions that are resolved quickly, the whiteboard list is all you'll ever need. If it turns out you need to show the pros/cons list at an important meeting, worry about making an elaborate spreadsheet or slide deck later.

- **Refine until stable.** If you keep working at the list, it will eventually settle down into a stable set. The same core questions or opinions will keep coming up, and you won't hear any major new commentary from the smart people you work with. When all of the logical and reasonable ideas have been vetted out, and showing the list to people only comes up with the same set of choices you've already heard, it's probably time to move on and decide.

> **NOTE**
> A simple exercise for the reader is to add to the list shown in Figure 8-2. Given how little detail of the situation is provided, there are at least a dozen other reasonable options that could be added. A nice prize will be given to anyone who names them all.

Discuss and evaluate

Effective decisions can be made only when there is a list of choices and some understanding of how the choices compare to each other. With a list in place, a person can walk through the choices and develop an opinion about which options have the greatest potential. It's often only through discussion that strong opinions can be developed, and the list of choices acts as a natural discussion facilitator (we'll discuss facilitation in Chapter 9). I always try to put these decision matrixes up on a whiteboard, so when people walk into my office and ask about the status of an issue, I can point them to exactly where I am and show them why I'm leaning in a particular direction. Even if I don't have a conclusion yet, it's easy for them to understand why (perhaps buying me more time to make the decision). More so, I can ask them to review it with me, hear out my logic, and offer me their opinions. Instead of trying to explain it all on the fly, the pros/cons list documents all of the considerations and adds credibility to whatever opinion I've developed.

On teams that communicate well, it's natural to discuss critical decisions as a group. Each person in the discussion tries to string together assumptions pulled from the pros/cons list and makes an argument for one particular decision. You'll hear each person voice her opinion in terms of a story—"If we do this, then X will happen first, but we'll be able to do Y"—and then someone else will chime in, refining the story or questioning one of the assumptions. The story gets refined, and the pros and cons for choices get adjusted to capture the clearer thinking that the group has arrived at. Over time (which might be minutes or days), everyone involved, especially the decision maker, has a full understanding of what the decision means and what tradeoffs are involved. When the pros and cons list stabilizes, and little new information is being added, it's time to try and eliminate choices.

Sherlock Holmes, Occam's Razor, and reflection

The character Sherlock Holmes once said, "If you eliminate the impossible, whatever remains, however improbable, must be the truth." And so it goes with decision making: if you eliminate the worst choices, whatever remains, however bad, must be your best choice. This is admittedly a cynical way to decide things, but sometimes eliminative logic is the only way to gain momentum toward a decision.

If you've created a list of possible choices and need to narrow the field, look for choices that do not meet the minimum bar for the project. You might have included them earlier on because they added to the discussion and provided an opportunity to find hybrid choices, or because the requirements were being reconsidered, but now it's time to cut them loose. Review your documents and requirements lists, check with your customer, and cross off choices that just won't be good enough.

Another tool to narrow the possibilities is a principle known as Occam's Razor. William of Occam was a medieval philosopher in the 12th century who's credited with using the notion of simplicity to drive decisions. He believed that people add complexity to situations unnecessarily. He suggested that the best way to figure things out was to find the simplest explanation and use that first because, most of the time, it was the right explanation (i.e., in modern parlance, "Keep it simple, stupid").[6]

Occam's Razor refers to the process of trying to cut away all of the unneeded details that get in the way and return to the heart of the problem. It also implies that the solution with the simplest logic has the greatest odds of being the best. There might be a promising choice that requires risky engineering or new dependencies on unreliable people. Applying Occam's Razor, that choice's lack of simplicity would be a reason for taking it off the list of possibilities.

But to apply Occam's Razor effectively, you need time to reflect. After long hours pounding away at the same issues, you lose perspective. When all the choices start looking the same, it's time to get away. Go for a walk, get some coffee with a friend, or do anything to clear your mind and think about something else. You need to be able to

---

6 The weakness of Occam's Razor is its vulnerability to local maximums. For example, if you stand on a hill, and can't see anything on the horizon taller than you, you'd assume you were on the tallest point on Earth. There can be information you don't have, that if you had it, would invalidate your assumption.

look at the choices with a clear and fresh mind in order to make an effective decision, and you can't do that if you continue to stare at it all day.

Reflection is highly underrated as a decision-making tool. To reflect means to step back and allow all of the information you've been working with to sink in. Often, real understanding happens only when we relax and allow our brains to process the information we've consumed. I find doing something physical like going for a run or walk is the best way to allow my mind to relax. Other times, doing something purely for fun does the trick, like participating in a Nerf fight or playing with my dog. It's also hard to beat a good night's sleep (perhaps preceded by a collaborative romp between the sheets) for clearing the mind. But everyone is different, and you have to figure out for yourself the best way to give your mind time to digest everything you've been thinking about.

When you do come back to your comparison list, briefly remind yourself what the core issues are. Then, thinking of Occam, look at the alternatives and ask yourself which choice provides the simplest way to solve the problem at hand. The simplest choice might not promise the best possible outcome, but because of its simplicity, it might have the greatest odds of successfully resolving the problem to a satisfactory level.

Information is a flashlight

Most people educated in the Western world are taught to trust numbers. We find it easier to work with numbers and make comparisons with them than with abstract feelings or ideas. Decision and utility theory, mentioned briefly earlier, depends on this notion by claiming that we make better decisions if we can convert our desires and the probabilities of choices into numbers and make calculations based on them. Despite my earlier criticism of these theories, sometimes forcing ourselves to put numerical values on things can help us define our true opinions and make decisions on them.

But decisions aside, we commonly like to see evidence for claims in numeric form. There is a difference in usefulness and believability in someone saying "Our search engine is 12% slower on 3-word queries" than "The system is slow." Numerical data gives a kind of precision that human language cannot. More so, numerical data is often demanded by people to support claims that they make. The statement "The system is slow" begs the question "How do you know this?" The lack of some kind of study or research into the answer makes the claim difficult to trust, or dependent solely on the opinion and judgment of the person saying it. Sometimes a specific piece of information answers an important question and resolves a decision much faster than possible otherwise.

Data does not make decisions

The first misconception about information is that it rarely makes a decision for you. A good piece of information works like a flashlight. It helps illuminate a space and allows someone who is looking carefully to see details and boundaries that were invisible before. If there is currently no data into a claim, taking the time to get data can accelerate the decision-making process. The fog lifts and things become clear. But returns diminish over time. After the first light has been lit and the basic details have been revealed, no amount of information can change the nature of what's been seen. If you're stranded in the middle of the Pacific Ocean, knowing the current water temperature or the subspecies of fish nearby won't factor much in your survival decisions (but knowing the water currents, trade routes, and constellations might). For most tough decisions, the problem isn't a lack of data. Tough decisions exist no matter how much information you have. The phenomenon of analysis paralysis, where people analyze obsessively, is symptomatic of the desperate belief that if only there was enough data, the decision would resolve itself. Sadly, this isn't so. Information helps, but only so much.

It's easy to misinterpret data

The second misnomer about data is that it's all created equally. It turns out that when working with numbers, it's very easy to misinterpret information. As Darrell Huff wrote in *How to Lie with Statistics* (W.W. Norton, 1993), "The secret language of statistics, so appealing in a fact-minded culture, is employed to sensationalize, inflate, confuse, and oversimplify." Huff categorizes the many simple ways the same data can be manipulated to make opposing arguments, and he offers advice that should be standard training for decision makers everywhere. Most of the tricks involve the omission of important details or the exclusive selection of information that supports a desired claim.

For example, let's say a popular sports drink has an advertisement that claims "Used by 5 out of 6 superstars." It sounds impressive, but which superstars are using the product? What exactly separates a star from a superstar? Whoever they are, how were they chosen for the survey? How do they use the drink—to wash their cars? Were they paid first, or were they rejected from the survey if they didn't already use the drink? Who knows. The advertisement certainly wouldn't say. If you look carefully at all kinds of data, from medical research to business analysis to technological trends, you'll find all kinds of startling assumptions and caveats tucked away in the fine print, or not mentioned at all. Many surveys and research reports are funded primarily by people who have much to gain by particular results. Worse, in many cases, it's magazines and newspaper articles written by people other than those doing the research that are our point of contact to the information, and their objectives and sense of academic scrutiny are often not as high as we'd like them to be.

Research as ammunition

The last thing to watch out for is ammunition pretending to be research. There is a world of difference between trying to understand something and trying to support a specific pet theory. What happens all too often is that someone (let's call him Skip) has an idea but no data, and he seeks out data that fits his theory. As soon as Skip finds it, he returns to whomever he's trying to convince and says, "See! This proves I'm right." Not having any reason to doubt the data, the person yields and Skip gets his way. But sadly, Skip's supporting evidence proves almost nothing. One pile of research saying Pepsi is better than Coke doesn't mean there isn't another pile of research somewhere that proves the opposite. Research, to be of honest use, has to seek out evidence for the claim in question and evidence to dispute the claim (this is a very simple and partial explanation of what is often referred to as the scientific method). Good researchers and scientists do this. Good advertisers, marketers, and people trying to sell things (including ideas) typically don't.

The best defense against data manipulation and misinterpretation is direct communication between people. Talk to the person who wrote the report instead of just reading it. Avoid second-, third-, and fourth-hand information whenever possible. Talking to the expert directly often reveals details and nuances that are useful but were inappropriate for inclusion in a report or presentation. Instead of depending exclusively on that forwarded bit of email, call the programmer or marketer on the phone and get his opinion on the decision you're facing. There's always greater value in people than in information. The person writing the report learned 1,000 things she couldn't include in it but would now love to share with someone curious enough to ask.

Aside from using people as sources, a culture of questioning is the best way to understand and minimize the risks of information. As we covered earlier in matters of design and decision making, questions lead to alternatives, and they help everyone to consider what might be missing or assumed in the information presented. Questioning also leads to the desire for data from different sources, possibly from people or organizations with different agendas or biases, allowing for the decision maker and the group to obtain a clear picture of the world they're trying to make decisions in.

Precision is not accuracy

As a last note about information and data, many of us forget the distinction between precision and accuracy. Precision is how specific a measurement is; accuracy is how close to reality a measurement is. Simply because we are offered a precise number (say, a work estimate of 5.273 days) doesn't mean it has any greater likelihood of being accurate than a fuzzier number (4 or 5 days). We tend to confuse precision and accuracy because we assume if someone has taken the time to figure out such a specific number, the analysis should improve the odds that his estimation is good. The trap is that bogus precision is free. If I take a wild-assed guess (aka WAG) at next year's revenue ($5.5 million), and another one for next year's expenses ($2.35 million), I can combine them to produce a convincing-sounding profit projection: $3.15 million. Precise? Yes. Accurate? Who knows. Without asking "How do you know this?" or "How was this data produced?", it's impossible to be sure if those decimal places represent accuracy or just precision. Make a habit of breaking other people's bad habits of misleading uses of precision.

The courage to decide

"All know the way; few actually walk it."

—*Bodhidharma*

There is a big difference between knowing the right choice and making the right choice. Often many people can figure out the right decision, but very few will be willing to stand up and put themselves and their reputations behind it. You will always find more people willing to criticize and ridicule you for your decisions than people willing to take on the responsibility and pressure to make the decision themselves. Always keep this in mind. Decision making is a courageous act. The best decisions for projects are often unpopular, will upset or disappoint some important people on the team, and will make you an easy target for blame if things go wrong.

These burdens are common for anyone trying to engage in leadership activity. Decision making is one of the most central things leaders and managers do, and the better the leader, the more courage that's required in the kinds of decisions that she makes (see the section "Trust in yourself (self-reliance)" in Chapter 12).

Some decisions have no winning choices

One of the ugliest decisions I've made as a project manager involved the explorer bar component of Internet Explorer 4.0. The explorer bar was a new part of the user interface that added a vertical strip to the left part of the browser to aid users in navigating through search results, their favorites list, and a history of sites they'd visited. With a few weeks left before our first beta (aka test) release, we developed concerns about a design issue. We'd known about the problem for some time, but with the increasing public pressure of what were called the "browser wars," we began to fear that this problem could hurt us in the press if we shipped with it.

The issue was this: it was possible, in special cases, to view the explorer bar in the same window as the filesystem explorer, allowing for a user to create a web browser that divided the screen into three ugly vertical strips, leaving a small area for actually viewing web pages. After seeing the press and the industry scrutinize IE 3.0, we feared beta users or journalists might discover this condition, make a screenshot of it, and release it as part of their reviews. Product reviews were critically important, especially for beta releases.

There was consensus on the team and pressure from senior management that we had to take action and do something.

I made a pros and cons list quickly, discussed it with my programmers and other project managers, and identified three viable choices. They were all bad. Fixing the problem properly required five days of work, which we didn't have. We'd have to cut another major feature to do that work in time, and it would be devastating to the quality of the release to do so. There was a hacky solution, requiring two days of work, that eliminated some of the cases that caused this condition, but it was work that would have to be thrown away later (the work was good enough for a beta release, but not good enough for a final release). The last choice was to do nothing and bet that no one would discover this issue. I desperately looked for other alternatives but didn't find any. Every idea people came to me with led back down to these three choices. I remember sitting in my office one night until very late, just staring at my whiteboard and going around in circles on what I should do.

Every project manager can tell stories of tough choices they had to make. If you have responsibility, they come with the territory. They can involve decisions of budget, hiring, firing, business deals, technology, litigation, negotiation, design, business strategy, you name it. When faced with a tough decision, there is no single right answer. In fact, it's entirely possible that things may happen to make none of the available choices (or all of them) lead to success. Decision making, no matter how well researched or scrutinized, is another act of prediction. At some level, any tough decision comes down in the end to the project manager's judgment and courage—and the team's courage—to follow it.

In this particular situation on IE4, I chose to do nothing. After a sleepless night, I decided I'd rather manage the press issues if and when they occurred (which would consume my time, not the programmers') instead of investing in insurance against something that hadn't happened yet. I wasn't happy about it, but I felt it was the best choice for the project. The team had agreed early on that it was my decision to make, so we moved on.[7]

Good decisions can have bad results

Our hindsight into past events has been unfair to many good decision makers. Simply because things didn't work out in a particular way doesn't mean they didn't make a good choice with the information available. It's impossible to cover every possibility when dealing with complex, difficult decisions (although some people will try). The more time you spend trying to cover every contingency, a common habit of micromanagers, the less

---

7   Was I right? The day after my decision, our lead developer, Chee Chew, did the work on his own. Without telling anyone he got the balance of work done, *on his own time*. The original five-day estimate was by someone with less experience. By chance, I showed up at his office the next day and found a surprise. He smiled at me as he showed me the version of the browser with his changes. I was speechless.

time you'll have to spend on the probable outcomes. There's little sense in worrying about getting struck by lightning if you have a heart condition, eat poorly, and consider typing really fast as a form of exercise.

Simply because part of a project fails doesn't necessarily mean a bad decision was made. It's common for things to happen beyond the control of the project manager, the team, or the organization. Many things are impossible to predict, or even if predicted, impossible to be accounted for. It's unfair to hold decision makers accountable for things they couldn't possibly have known or done anything about. Yet, in many organizations, this is exactly what happens. If a team loses a close game, public opinion tends not to credit the hard work and heroic effort of the players who got the losing team even that far. Blame should be wielded carefully around decision making. Courageous decision makers will tend to fail visibly more often than those who always make safe and cautious choices. If you want courageous decision makers, there needs to be some kind of support for them to make big bets and to help them recover when they fail.

Project managers are definitely responsible for the fate of the project. I'm not suggesting they should be patted on the back for imploding a team. It's just that care should be taken not to blame a PM for making a good decision that turned out to have a bad outcome. If his logic and thought process were sound *before* the decision was made, then even in hindsight, his logic and thought process are still just as sound *after* the decision was made. The state of the world at the moment a decision occurs doesn't change later on simply because we know more now than we did then. If there was something the PM and the team didn't know, or couldn't see, despite their diligence in trying to know and see those things, they shouldn't be roasted for it. Instead, the team should be thinking about how collectively they might have been able to capture the data and knowledge that they missed and apply that to the next decisions they have to make.

Paying attention and looking back

To improve decision-making skills, two things need to happen. First, you have to make decisions that challenge you and force you to work hard. If you never make decisions that you find difficult, and if you are rarely wrong, it's time to ask your boss for more responsibility. Second, you have to pay attention to the outcomes of your decisions and evaluate, with the help of others involved, if you could have done anything differently to improve the quality of the outcome. Experience benefits only those who take the time to learn from it.

In training and in real missions, fighter pilots meet in debriefing sessions to review what took place. These sessions are led by senior and experienced staff. The central theme is that the only way to develop and learn about something as complex as being a fighter pilot is to review missions, correlate with everyone involved regarding what happened and why, and see if there were any ways to improve the outcome. These discussions often include analysis of strategy and tactics and an exchange of ideas and opinions for alternative ways to deal with the same situation.

The medical community does something similar in what are called M&M or morbidity and mortality sessions (jokingly referred to as D&D, death and doughnuts), though these are typically done only for fatal cases or where something particularly novel or complex was done.

In both cases, it's up to the leaders of the session to avoid making the session a trial or to embarrass people for their mistakes. The goal should be to make them feel comfortable enough with what happened that they are willing to spend time reviewing and re-evaluating what occurred, so they learn something from it, and give others in the organization a chance to benefit from the costs of whatever took place.

Here's my rough list of questions for reviewing decisions. When I'm called in to help teams evaluate previous work, this is the decision-making framework I start with. This works best as a group activity (because you'll benefit from different perspectives), but it also functions for reviewing your own thinking.

- **Did the decision resolve the core issue?** This should be part of the decision-making process itself. Even if you make the right call, the difference is how well the team executes the decision. Two hours, one day, two days after a decision, the decision maker needs to check in and ensure the decision is being carried out. Those first few hours or days are when unforeseen problems arise.

- **Was there better logic or information that could have accelerated the decision?** Where was time spent in making the decision? Was there any knowledge or advice you could have had that would have accelerated the process of finding or exploring alternatives? What research tools were used? Did anyone go to the library? The bookstore? Search the Web? Call a consultant or expert? Why weren't these sourced used?

- **Did the vision, specification, or requirements help?** Good project-level decisions should contribute to lower-level decisions. Did this decision reveal a weakness or oversight in the vision? Was the vision/spec/requirement updated after the decision was made to eliminate the oversight?

- **Did the decision help the project progress?** Sometimes making a bad decision moves the project forward. Decisions catalyze people. By making a quick decision to go east, and changing the perspective, it might become crystal clear that the right direction is actually north. But until the team started moving east, they might never have figured that out. In looking back, clarify why the initial decision was successful: was it because you made the right call or because you made the decision at the right time?

- **Were the key people brought into the process and behind the decision?** Was there anyone whose support or expertise was needed that wasn't involved? Did you attempt to contact them and fail, or did you not even try? Was there some way to bring them in more effectively than you did? (You need to get their opinions on this if you want an honest perspective.)

- **Did the decision prevent or cause other problems?** The immediate issue might have been solved, but were other problems caused? Did morale drop? Was a partner company or team burned by the decision? What negative side effects did the decision have, and could they have been avoided? Were they anticipated, or were they a surprise?

- **In hindsight, were the things you were worried about while making the decision the right things?** Pressure and paranoia can distort one's sense for which issues are worthy of attention. In hindsight, you should be able to see the things that were distorted in importance, by you or others, and ask yourself how it happened. Whose opinion or influence contributed to the distortion? Who tried to minimize it but was ignored?

- **Did you have sufficient authority to make the right call?** Perhaps you had an idea you wanted to run with, but you ditched it for political reasons. Or maybe you spent more time fighting for control over issues, which you felt should have been under your authority from the beginning. Consider how power played a role in the decision and how changes in the distribution of power might have changed how things went.

- **How can what was learned in making this decision be applied elsewhere in the project?** Don't limit lessons learned to the specifics of the decision. Look at the next wave of decisions coming to the project (next important date or task), and apply the lessons to them. Use the new perspective and look out into the future, rather than only the past. Remember the Burmese saying: "A man fears the tiger that bit him last, instead of the tiger that will bite him next."

Summary

- There is an important skill in meta-decision making, or decisions about which decisions to invest time in.

- Size up decisions before spending too much time on them.

- Look for the zone of indifference and opportunities for effective use of singular evaluation.

- Use comparative evaluation for the decisions worthy of more investment.

- All decisions have emotional components to them whether we admit it or not.

- Pros and cons lists are the most flexible method for comparative evaluation. They make it easy to involve others and get additional perspectives on decisions.

- Information and data do not make decisions for you.

- You improve at decision making by reviewing past decisions and exploring them for lessons and opportunities for better tactics.

Exercises

A. How did you decide to pick up this book? Did you consider alternatives? How do you decide how to decide in everyday life?

B. Think about what you are going to do this weekend. Make a pro/con list for each of your options. Include a do-nothing choice and at least one hybrid choice.

C. What is a good decision you have made in the past that had a bad outcome? Were you blamed for the result anyway? What does this tell you about how people perceive decisions? Should this influence how you make decisions?

D. If data is so easy to manipulate, why are so many meetings in the world focused on the exchange of unquestioned surveys and reports? How come it can be easier to point to someone else's logic to defend a decision, rather than simply explain your own?

E. There is more to a decision than deciding which option to choose. A decision also has to be communicated to others, explained sufficiently well to persuade people to agree, and carried through to successful completion. Which one of these is most difficult for you? Does it vary from decision to decision? How can evaluating the challenges of a particular decision increase the odds of its success?

F. How did you decide which of the above exercises to read? To complete? How will you decide if it's worth reading the next one?

G. Who in your life do you debrief your major life decisions with? Why do you pick them for this important role? Make a list of people you work with, and create a pro/con list of their value to you in reviewing past decisions.

H. When is it more important to do the right thing than to do what everyone wants you to do? Is logic or emotion more important in finding courage?

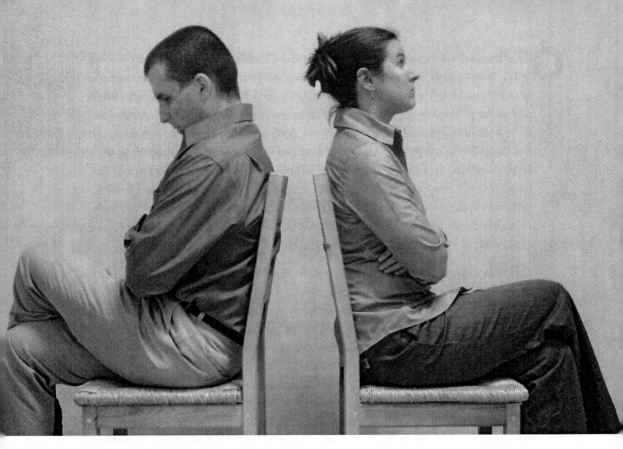

CHAPTER NINE

Communication and relationships

One of the earliest engineering stories in Western history is the story of the Tower of Babel, from Genesis, and at its core is a lesson about communication. As the story goes, humanity was happily united in the desert. They soon figured out how to make bricks and mortar. Things were going so well that, for no particular reason, they decided to build a tower high into the sky. Things went along brilliantly until the workers suddenly lost the ability to use the same language (can you say "divine intervention"?), at which point everything literally fell apart. The once-united people were scattered across the world (more divine intervention), and different languages and societies were formed. It's suggested in the story that had they been able to continue to communicate well with each other, nothing would have been impossible (which is perhaps, as the story also suggests, what motivated the divine intervention).

This biblical story is quite short: barely a page. However, through the centuries, it has captured the attention of many artists and writers who used the story to explore contemporary issues. The vivid images of the tower painted by Brueghel[1] and others gave the story increasing relevance to engineering and project management tasks of their times. The interpretations of the story have shifted from age to age, as have the depictions of what the Tower actually looked like, but the general themes are the same. Some believe the story is a warning about humanity's hubris and a reminder that some things should be unattainable to us. Others see it as a story of people striving to achieve all they can by pushing the boundaries of what's possible. But for me, and for the sake of this chapter, the central lesson of the story of Babel is simple: if you can't communicate, you can't succeed.

For much of the history of civilization, the slowness of communication caused problems. Even as late as the American Civil War (1861–1865) there were no radios, telegraphs, or semaphore (flag) systems in common use. Generals sent messages by horse to coordinate battle information with commanders at different camps (which, depending on distance, took hours or days, assuming the messenger didn't get lost). As a result, decisions were made days in advance with no way to change attack assignments. Many disasters and frontline miscommunications resulted from these limitations. (Imagine a battlefield commander who has just sounded the charge, sending all his troops to attack, when an exhausted messenger stumbles into his tent. The messenger, struggling to catch his breath, says, "Dispatch from command.... 'Dear commander: The reinforcements you were depending on were sent elsewhere. Sorry. Good luck.'" No wonder messengers were often shot.)

---

1   Brueghel was a Flemish painter in the 16th century, famous for his paintings of landscapes and peasant scenes. You can see his *Tower of Babel* painting, and his full biography, at *http://en. wikipedia.org/wiki/Pieter_Brueghel_the_Elder*.

Today, communication is still important, but two things have changed. First, speed is no longer the primary problem (how can you get faster than instant messaging?). Instead, the problem has become the quality and effectiveness of communication. Second, communication isn't enough for complex work: there need to be effective relationships between the people who are working together. Unlike the military command structure of an army, most software teams rely on peer-to-peer interaction and other, less hierarchically driven relationships. Although there are often clearly defined leaders, who sometimes give orders, projects are heavily dependent on the team's ability to make use of each other's knowledge, to share ideas, and to work in synchronicity (as opposed to relying on strict lines of authority, rigorous discipline, and the compulsion to follow orders without question).

Because project managers spend much time communicating with individuals and groups, they carry more responsibility for effective communication than others on the team. If it's the health of the social network of a team that prevents it from becoming another Tower of Babel, it's the project manager who has the most natural role in building up and maintaining that network.

Doing this doesn't require an extroverted, game-show-host personality; nor does it demand a brilliant sense of humor or magical powers (although these may help). Instead, it starts by admitting communication and relationships are critical to success, and there's room for improvement for yourself and your team. If you admit it's important, you'll want to understand where most communication problems occur and learn how to deal with them.

Management through conversation

This sounds strange, but it took me years to understand the value of talking to people in the workplace. I'd chat and joke around, but rarely confused socializing with the actual doing of work. My experiences led me to believe I had to solve problems on my own. In my first year at Microsoft, I'd rarely seek out the opinion of others or find someone who had more knowledge than I did and reuse it. Instead, I'd grind it out and work hard instead of smart. At the same time, I watched two of my earliest managers, Ken Dye and Joe Belfiore, exhibit the curious behavior of spending a great deal of time talking to other people. I'd see them, sitting in various other people's offices, chatting away. As busy as I was, I couldn't help but wonder how they could afford to spend so much time "socializing." Being new, I didn't ask them about it. Instead, I just labeled them "extroverts," which, at the time, I considered a minor insult. Their behavior annoyed me (shouldn't they be working at least as hard as I am?), and I didn't see value in what they were doing. How wrong I was.

As my responsibilities grew, I understood what Ken and Joe had been doing. Through trial and error I learned manhandling, bullying, dictating, or demanding things wasn't an effective tactic when I needed things from people who weren't obligated to listen. I noticed similar results in noncommunicative programmers or testers, and they were ineffective when getting work done that involved other technical people. (This is significant if you look at Figure 9-1. The implication is everyone can benefit from better relationships, no matter how isolated their work supposedly is.)

How developers spend their time	
Kind of work	Percentage
Working alone	30%
Working with one other person	50%
Working with two or more people	20%

Quoted from *Peopleware*, DeMarco and Lister (Dorset House, 1999) summary of the Gerald McCue study (IBM, 1978).

FIGURE 9-1. *There's evidence programmers are not as solitary as we think.*

I found that the more I demanded things from people ("You need to code it this way, OK?"), the lower the probability was that I'd get their best work. Even if they did what I asked, something about my approach killed their motivation or minimized the probability they'd add value beyond what I'd asked for. However, I found that when I conversed with them ("Hey, I think we need to do X, and I think you're the right person to do it. What do you think?"), instead of barking orders, I received what I needed sooner than when I used those other tactics. And, as a bonus, the odds increased of them suggesting good improvements on my ideas. I learned dialogs are better than monologs.

Relationships enhance communication

Despite how obvious it is that you need to have a positive relationship with someone in order to have a good conversation with him, people are rarely rewarded for their skills in doing so. Those informal chats and conversations Ken and Joe invested time in were not a way to kill time. Those conversations were investments in people and information, giving Ken and Joe knowledge and insight into what was going on that few others had. But specific to my point: when they needed to request advice, an opinion, or a task, they could talk to almost anyone on the team, at any time, and start from a healthy and positive place, rather than from scratch. Their relationship with the team accelerated their ability to communicate with everyone.

This made it easier to cut to the chase without being rude, or even to make exceptional requests of people that ordinarily would be rejected. In matters of opinion, they had built enough trust to get honest opinions from the right people in a casual manner, and, if so inclined, they could incorporate those suggestions and ideas into their own thinking well in advance of larger discussions. Ken and Joe were ahead of the rest of the team. They knew more about what was going well and what wasn't, and they had more influence on it through their investment in relationships. They'd paved the way for all kinds of additional support and benefits, simply by talking and listening to people.

In Tom Peters' and Nancy Austin's classic, *A Passion for Excellence* (Warner Business Books, 1985), this sort of behavior is called management by walking around (MBWA). It's described as a central quality in the successful managers they observed (an entire chapter in their book is dedicated to it). But it's not easy to do well. They recommend explicitly picking a small number of people, at different levels and roles in the team, and investing time in building this kind of informal relationship with them.[2] More importantly, it requires an understanding of how healthy communication and relationships work and a commitment to growing those skills. Even if you don't choose an MBWA approach to build relationships, core communication and interpersonal skills will still be essential to everything you do.

A basic model of communication

Few people in the workplace have any proficiency in diagnosing communication or relationship problems, or have the necessary authority to sort them out. However, it is easy to learn a simple framework for what the goals of communication are—from a project management perspective—and apply it to daily situations. With this knowledge, you can break down where things are failing and become more capable of resolving problems because you'll have a better understanding of what's not working.

> **"Good communication centers around highly developed individual awareness and differentiation. A good communicator is aware of both internal processes in themselves, and external processes in others."**
>
> —*John Bradshaw*

In the simplest framework, there are five basic states that any act of communication can be in.[3] Each is progressively more important and harder to achieve than the previous

---

2 As Peters says, " If you are not a regular wanderer [into people's offices], the onset of wandering will be, in a word, terrifying...." It takes time to build that kind of rapport with people, especially those who have reason to fear you.

3 I was unable to find references for this framework. I'd heard the first three, but could not find a source. Another good framework is the Satir model, which Weinberg uses in his books. See *The Satir Model: Family Therapy and Beyond*, by Virginia Satir et al. (Science and Behavior Books, 1991). Yes, this is a book on therapy. And yes, if that bothers you, it's exactly the book you need to read.

state. Communication is successful only if it reaches the third state (understanding), if not the fourth (agreement) or fifth (action). To help illustrate each state, I'll use an example from the film *2001: A Space Odyssey*. Dave, an astronaut, is in a small spacecraft and wants to get back inside the mother ship. Hal, inside the mother ship, is the only entity capable of opening the doors to let him in.

1. **Transmitted.** When you send an email or leave a voice mail, you are transmitting a piece of information to someone. This doesn't mean she has read or heard it, it just means the message has left your hands with the intent to arrive in hers. With email and the Web, it's very easy to transmit information, but there is no guarantee anyone is ever going to read it. Example: Dave says, "Do you read me Hal?" (Dave hears only silence in response.)

2. **Received.** When someone checks his email or signs for a FedEx envelope, the message has been received. However, reception doesn't mean the message was opened or that the recipient has any intention of reading it or spending any time trying to figure it out. While read receipts for email do tell you it was opened, nothing else is confirmed. Example: Hal responds, "Dave, I read you." (The transmission is received and acknowledged.)

3. **Understood.** Digesting and interpreting a message's information correctly is a big jump in effort from simply receiving a message. Actual cognitive activity has to take place in order to understand something ("What does this mean?"), whereas receiving it does not require that same activity ("Hey, I got some email!"). Understanding a message may require time. Often, the recipient needs to ask questions to clarify the original message. (This complicates the simple five-stage framework, creating a tree of simultaneous nested communications as each question, and each response, starts its own sequence of transmission, reception, understanding, etc.) Dave asks "Hal, open the pod bay door." And Hal responds, "I'm sorry Dave, I'm afraid I can't do that." Hal understands, but doesn't agree.

4. **Agreed.** Understanding something doesn't mean a person agrees with it. I might fully comprehend every aspect of a request from an executive, a day before final release, to do a Linux port of our Mac-only video-editing program, but that has no bearing on how insane I think the idea is. Achieving agreement between two intelligent, opinionated people can be a complex and time-consuming activity, especially if the objections aren't stated clearly. Despite how difficult it is, agreement is the basis for making decisions that impact a team.[4] Dave says, "What are you talking about Hal?" and Hal responds, "This mission is too important for me to allow you to jeopardize it." Dave is unable to get agreement from Hal, and the door stays closed.

---

4 Sometimes agreement can be as simple as deciding which person gets to make a certain decision. Instead of debating the issue, debate who should decide the issue. See Chapter 8.

5. **Converted to useful action.** Despite how much energy it can take to understand something properly and perhaps reach a level of agreement on it, significantly more energy is required to get someone to do something about it. Even if the message explicitly called for the receiver to take action, there's often no strict obligation on her part to do so. Perhaps she assumes it's OK to meet the request next week or next month (when you need it done in the next 10 minutes). And perhaps, worst of all, it's entirely possible an action is taken but it's the wrong action, or it is an action the sender of the message doesn't agree with. Even if Dave had convinced Hal he should open the door, until he does it or agrees to when it will happen, Dave is still helpless in space.

Good communicators think about how deep into this five-step model they need to go to be effective, and they craft communication to make that possible. They use language and examples that will make sense to the recipient, instead of just using what is convenient for them. More so, in the message they clarify what the likely points of argument are and identify what action they want the recipient to take in response.

So, every time you receive or send an email, or stop in at someone's office to ask him something, there is a natural progression of communication taking place. Use this framework to help you diagnose why what you want to have happen isn't happening.

Common communication problems

There are a handful of reasons why communication breaks down. In many teams, these behaviors exist because the group manager either exhibits them herself or tolerates them in others. Until someone with some authority steps in, identifies the problem as a communication issue, and takes at least partial responsibility for helping to sort it out, those bad communication habits will continue.

This short list covers many of the common communication problems, briefly describes why they occur, and offers some simple advice for avoiding or recovering from them.

- **Assumption.** When you walk into someone's office and ask him why he hasn't sent out that important email yet, you're assuming: a) he knew he was supposed to send it; b) he knew *when* he was supposed to send it; c) he understood what was supposed to be in it; and d) he was supposed to notify you somehow when he did it. Before yelling at this person (let's call him Sam) or blaming him, good communication involves clarifying these assumptions. "Sam, did you send that email yet?" Sam replies, "What email?" "Sam, remember yesterday we spoke in the hall and you confirmed you could do this?" "Oh yes, I sent it a few minutes ago." Good communicators habitually clarify assumptions during discussions at key points, such as when commitments are made, and confirm them again before the deadline.

- **Lack of clarity.** There is no law in the universe claiming others will understand what you're saying simply because you understand it yourself. No matter how eloquent you may be, if the other person doesn't understand you, you're not eloquent enough for the situation at hand (as Red Auerbach said, "It's not what you say, it's what they hear"). The natural remedy is to step back, slow down, and break down ideas into smaller and smaller pieces until a point of clarity is reached, and then slowly build up from it. Find a story or analogy to give a rough framework that people can follow, and add detail to it until you don't need the analogy anymore.

- **Not listening.** In the movie *Fight Club*, the main character, Jack, says in reference to one of the many support groups he's recently joined, "They actually listen to me, instead of just waiting for their next chance to talk." We are compulsively bad listeners, and we tend to prefer the sound of our voices to others. Worse, even while people are speaking to us, we are often calculating our next response—continuing our original argument—instead of listening to their point. (The extreme form of this problem is simply not paying attention, as in reading your email while someone is talking to you. Despite doubtful claims of multitasking proficiency, it still sends a negative message to the person who's talking to you: "You are not worthy of eye contact.") The remedy is to accept the possibility that they know something you don't. Your goal is not to force them into a position, but instead to achieve the best possible outcome for the project.

- **Dictation.** The evil twin of not listening is dictating. Instead of giving even the pretense of listening, people who dictate simply give orders. Any objections to the order are rejected or responded to with derision, as if it should be obvious why the order is being given without explanation ("What are you, stupid?"). This is not an act of communication because it's a violation of the framework covered previously: no attempt is made to reach understanding. Giving orders should be the exception. Instead, strive to make decisions in an environment where people have the right to ask good questions and propose challenges to your logic.

- **Problem mismatch.** Communication can mask many other problems. It's only when we communicate with someone that they have a chance to surface their feelings about other issues. What comes back in response to a request may be an expression of feelings that have nothing to do with the specific request ("Hey, can you read this spec?" "No! Never! Death first!"). There might be an unresolved issue about another decision that he hasn't expressed yet. If neither party recognizes there are different issues being discussed under the guise of a single issue, the discussion will be difficult to resolve. Someone has to separate them: "Wait, what are we really talking about here? How to code this feature, or why you didn't get that promotion you wanted?"

- **Personal/ad hominem attacks.** Situations become personal when one party shifts the discussion away from the issue and toward an individual. This is called *ad hominem* (against the person). For example, Fred might say he doesn't have time, to which Sam replies, "That's the problem with you. How come you never have time for reviewing test plans?" This is unfair to Fred because he has to defend not only his opinion, but also his personal behavior. Personal attacks are cheap shots.[5] Often, the person taking the cheap shot feels vulnerable and sees the attack as the only way to win the argument. It's up to a more mature person (or perhaps Fred himself) to intervene and separate the issues.

- **Derision, ridicule, and blame.** When a person has a new idea, she is making herself vulnerable to whomever she chooses to share it with. It requires a feeling of trust to be forthcoming and honest. If she is consistently ridiculed or demeaned in the process of communicating important but unpleasant information, she will stop doing it. The first response to a problem shouldn't be "How could you let this happen?", or "You know this is entirely your fault, don't you?"

There are other problems that arise in communication, but this basic list covers many of the possible situations. The more people involved, the harder it is to isolate what the problem is and fix it. Sometimes group discussions are the wrong place to solve communication issues because there are too many people and conflicts involved to resolve any problem effectively. Group communication is an issue I'll touch on briefly in Chapter 10, but for most of this chapter, I'll focus on simpler situations.

A simple tactic for making the previous list actionable is to share it with people on your team, and ask them to identify when someone is behaving in a problematic way. The team will now have a language for the problems they see, making it easier to resolve them. Specific to team leaders, a commitment should be made to re-examine their own behavior and pay more attention to what they're doing and saying. Odds are high they'll identify habits that need to be worked on. (Change of any kind is tough. Organizational change requires those in power to take action. See Chapter 16.)

However, no matter how much you read or study about human psychology and communication, it's always subjective. There's no mathematical formula you can use, or detection device you can buy, to help you recognize when you're about to cause a communication problem. The same applies to making others aware of communication problems they are causing. It's sensitive and complicated, and some people have years of experience with bad communication habits that they're unwilling to give up simply because you suggest they should. This is one of the many reasons why project management is a tough role: you have to invest in relationships with people, regardless of how much they're investing in you.

---

5   A comprehensive list of conversational cheap shots, conveniently categorized and listed with examples, can be found at *http://www.vandruff.com/art_converse.html*. Please, please, please do not use this as a playbook to follow.

Projects depend on relationships

Project managers are only as good as their relationships with the people on the team. No matter how brilliant the PM is, his value is determined by how well he can apply his brilliance to the project through other people. This doesn't mean micromanaging them or doing everything, instead it's about seeing the PM role as amplifying the value of others in any way possible.

The challenge is how. Every time I've given a lecture on project management and convinced a group of this point, someone invariably raises her hand and asks: "I understand it's something I should do, but how do I go about amplifying their value without annoying the crap out of them?" This is a fair question. Few people come to work wanting to be amplified or to have some person they might not like involved in their daily business. The answer is relationships: depending on the person you're dealing with and what expectations have been set, your approach must be different.

Defining roles

"The cause of almost all relationship difficulties is rooted in conflicting or ambiguous expectations around roles and goals."

—*Stephen Covey, author of* The 7 Habits of Highly Effective People

In the previous list of communication problems, one important issue is assumptions and how to clarify them. Leadership roles are the most ambiguous and prone to assumptions by others. Any programmer or tester will always carry the first experience he had with a PM (bad or good) as his model when working with all future PMs. The first time you walk in the door, the new team sees you as a projection of all of their previous experiences with PMs. They will assume different things than you will about what you can do and what value you might add to the team. No matter how well defined you think the job descriptions are where you work, there's always plenty of room for bad assumptions.

The easiest remedy is to clarify roles with any important person you know you will be working with: programmers, testers, marketers, clients, or even executives. Sit down with one person you work with and make three lists on the whiteboard. The first list is things you are primarily responsible for. The second list is things both of you share responsibility for. And the third list is things the other person is primarily responsible for. As you work together to make the lists and discuss which items belong where, you will quickly recognize what expectations you have of each other (see Figure 9-2). Role definition flushes out all of the assumptions and baggage people have about what project managers, general managers, developers, testers, or anyone else is supposed to do.

What the PM does	What we both do	What the programmer does
- write specs - manage clients - manage executives - track progress - lead team communication	- triage incoming bugs - discuss tradeoffs that impact dev cost & design - warn each other of risks or problems - help each other problem solve or brainstorm	- write code - drive build process - work w/test on builds - review checkins - review specs

FIGURE 9-2. *Role-definition discussions help every relationship (this is just an example—your lists may look different).*

At a minimum, you'll identify the places where you disagree, and, even if you don't resolve them all, you'll be aware of potential problems and can work more sensitively on those tasks. Often the role discussion will reveal how dependent both parties are on each other to be successful. But perhaps most important is that this discussion provides a framework both parties can use for relationship problems in the future. The ice has been broken, and it's now easier to talk about roles, collaboration, and responsibility. Should there be a problem later, all someone has to do is pull out the list and point to where something isn't working out as it should have.

The fear in having these discussions is about control. When you write down something important and offer it for discussion, you're vulnerable to having it taken away from you (or so the fear goes). But as far as the PM is concerned, typically the things of greatest interest (high-level decision making, cross-discipline work, strategy) are the last things more specialized people want responsibility for. In fact, often there is ignorance among the team about what the PM does all day, and without discussing roles, they have no way of ever discovering what the PM is doing.

In the worst case, where there are huge gaps in perceived roles ("I don't care what your last PM did, I will not do your laundry"), it's time to talk to your boss and possibly the manager of the person you spoke with. There's no cause for alarm: the framework you used is the easiest way to bring the discussion to others and work toward a resolution. On larger teams, I've sometimes started this discussion with the manager of the programming team first, got his buy-in, and then worked my way down to line-level programmers. This makes sense if you think the PM's support is necessary up front, or if you have a better shared understanding of roles with him than you do with some of the line-level programmers.

The best work attitude

An unspoken assumption is that people are working hard and trying to do their best work. But because there's no way to measure how hard people work,[6] or what their best work looks like, managers rarely spend time talking about it. This is a mistake.

It should be entirely natural and acceptable for a PM to ask anyone the following question: "What can I do to help you do your best work?" No preface is needed, nor any caveats about what you might not be willing to do. Just by asking this simple question, three positive things happen:

1. You establish the possibility that the person you are talking to is capable of doing her best work on the current project, and that perhaps there is something preventing her from doing so.

2. You put her in a framework of evaluating her own performance and identifying things she can do that might make a difference.

3. You make it possible to have a discussion about what both of you can do to improve the quality of the work being done. By framing the discussion around "best," you dodge the possibility that she feels criticized or that her current work isn't good enough.

This approach has nothing to do with trying to make people like you. Getting the best performance possible out of the team is a direct responsibility of the PM. Figuring out how to make people more effective is not simply doing them a favor, it's improving the quality and speed of the work done on the project. Of course, for a project to succeed, it might not require everyone's best work, but so what. If their pursuit of a higher standard doesn't hurt the project—and it clearly improves their own morale and personal investment in the team—then it's worth the cost of asking a few simple questions.

Sometimes when you ask people how to get their best work, the answer might be "Leave me alone," or "Stop asking me silly questions," or other less-than-useful responses. Even if they don't seem receptive, they will be thinking about your question, whether they admit it or not. I've had programmers shrug off my initial question ("No, Scott, there's nothing you can do"), and then come back to me a week later and make a great suggestion that ended up helping the whole development team. Plus, they thanked me for respecting them enough to ask their opinion.

The underlying attitude implied is that when a programmer is falling behind, the PM's job is not to assign blame and yell at him to work faster. Instead, it's to help him to understand the problem and contribute time to help resolve it. Asking about his best

---

6 Every measure of work has its problems. Lines of code imply quantity, not quality. Hours imply length of work, not intensity.

work is an easy way to establish a supporting relationship with him. Even if there are other demands on the PM's time, it's often best to prioritize assisting direct contributors to the project ahead of secondary political or bureaucratic matters. The former will always have a direct impact on the project schedule, but the latter may not.

How to get people's best work

Great leaders rarely force people to do anything. Instead, they use every other means in their power to convince people to do things. Everybody has different strengths and weaknesses when it comes to motivating others, and it follows that better leaders tend to have a wider range of tools to use and more command over them.

Something I've seen in weaker managers and leaders is the over-reliance on one approach or method to try to get the best work out of people. If that one method doesn't work, they give up, claiming that there's nothing that can be done. Sadly, not much happens when the team leader claims there are no alternatives. Instead, when stuck, there's probably another angle to take that might work. It's possible that you're capable of trying another tactic, but also consider that someone else on the team might be able to help by lending a talent to the situation that you don't have.

- **Follow advice.** Listening to suggestions is one thing, but doing something about it is another. When they ask for more time for certain tasks, make it happen. If they suggest that there are too many meetings, let them suggest ways to shorten them. Invest real energy in following through on what they need. Even if it doesn't pan out, if you take the challenge of fulfilling requests seriously, they'll notice. People can spot real managerial effort from miles away (they have lifetimes of experience observing token, lip-service effort).

- **Challenging/making demands.** The most obvious way for a person in authority to get work out of people is to demand it: "40 push-ups, now!" The more intelligent the people you work with are, the less likely this approach will work. If the vision is good, the work is interesting, and people get along, there's little need to demand anything. Motivation should come naturally. When you need to light fires, find clever ways. Place friendly wagers: "If we make this date, I'll dye my hair blue" or "Whichever team of programmers fixes all the bugs first will get an afternoon BBQ on my boat."[7] Demands have their place, but don't get mean, get honest. "Look, this needs to be done. It's too late to debate this, and I'm sorry if I wasn't clear before. Please, just deliver on this for me. OK?"

- **Inspiring.** It's difficult to fake inspiration. Either you believe in what you're doing, or you don't. If you do believe, you have to find some way to express it in a positive manner so that other people can feed off of it. "Look. I love this project. We are paid

---

7   The clever, but sneaky, thing to do is to plan on inviting both teams, regardless of who wins. But don't tell them that until the competition is over.

to learn new technologies and figure out how to apply them. That's rare, and it gets me to come here every day." It doesn't have to be elaborate or eloquent. If it's honest, it works. Human nature reciprocates positive emotion, and when you bring something real out, you invite others to follow. More direct methods include asking people what they like about writing code and helping them to make connections between those feelings and the work they have in front of them.

- **Clearing roadblocks.** Every great running back in American football had an unsung hero who paved the way for him. That unsung hero is called the blocker (aka fullback). He runs out in front of the running back and knocks over the first guy who tries to tackle the running back (usually someone much larger than he is). If you look carefully at any highlight reel where someone runs for 70 yards, you'll see another guy lying flat on the ground, buried under various large people, who made the play possible. Good PMs make plays possible. They eliminate issues that are slowing down the team. Ask people: "Are you blocked by anything?" If they say they are waiting for a decision, or trying to track down information, it's your job to figure out if there's any way you can accelerate that process. They should know you are available to help if they ever feel blocked.

- **Remind them of your respective roles.** The most frequent way to enable best work is to remind people of their roles. When a programmer complains that she is getting too many new-feature requests, the response should be that it's probably not her job to field requests: she should direct people to you (the PM). She's free to involve herself if she feels it's appropriate, but if it's late in the schedule, she should be using the PM to run interference. Sometimes people, especially programmers, are so focused on the work itself that they lose sight of the testers, designers, and managers around them who are often better suited to drive certain kinds of tasks than they are.

- **Remind them of the project goals.** As the PM or leader, you have more perspective on the project than any individual. It's easy for people to get lost in the complexity of their narrower areas of responsibility and lose track of what issues are truly important. A short conversation with you, where you refresh their understanding of what they're really accomplishing and why, can restore their focus, motivation, and effectiveness. Like the landing lights that identify an airport runway at night, making it easy for pilots to spot their way to safety, good PMs light the way.

- **Teaching.** If you have a skill or trick that people you work with can make use of, why not offer to teach it to them? Giving them a new skill or a tip for using an old one doubles the value of that knowledge. By teaching, you make it possible for people to get more work done faster and improve the chances of them doing good work, as well as possibly improving the quality of what their best work is. If instead of waiting for you to do a basic task, you can teach your team to do it themselves, everyone wins.

- **Asking.** It seems obvious, but it's rarely done. Simply ask them for their best work. You don't need to explain why, or even necessarily offer anything in return. Just say, "Hey, I'd love to see your best work here. This work is important and if you have more to give, I'd like you to give it now."

The motivation to help others do their best

Early on in my time with the Windows team, I remember feeling like I spent all my time helping other people do their jobs. I was a relatively new manager (as in having direct reports), and after running around helping people put out fires and giving advice, I just wanted to be alone. I tried going to my office and closing the door, but people kept coming by. My voice mail light wouldn't stop blinking, and I didn't even want to look at the email that had accumulated while I was running around the building. I remember questioning why I spent so much time in other people's offices, and it took me awhile to come up with an answer I believed. But I found one, and here it is.

Those conversations were not ethereal or anecdotal things. In each of those conversations, I was doing something directly related to the goals of the project. This goes beyond the abstract importance of good relationships. Every time I answered a question at my door, negotiated with another organization, or argued for resources for my team, I was doing as much as any developer or tester to move the project forward. I was enabling them to write code, find bugs, and do 1,000 other things faster or easier than they would have otherwise.

My point is that if you carefully examine the conversations you have with people, and consider their impact on the project, you'll generally find every conversation contributes to one of the following things:

- Improves the quality of what's being made
- Increases the chances it will be finished on time
- Helps make the product/web site/software more useful for people
- Increases the chances the product/web site/software will generate profit or traffic
- Protects people from needless work, stupid politics, or bureaucracy
- Makes what's built easier to maintain
- Increases the morale or happiness of the people on the team
- Helps the team to work smarter and faster, and to apply (and learn) new skills
- Eliminates or clarifies behavior that is detrimental to the project or the team

So, even when you tire of clearing roadblocks, answering questions, or checking in with various people for different reasons, remember that the effort you put into those things is not wasted. As long as you can connect those discussions, pep talks, fire drills, arguments, and discussions back to positive trends in the project (or the prevention of negative ones), they're essential to moving the project forward. You're doing work, however unglamorous or unrewarded, that no one else can do as effectively as you can. However, if you find that you can't tie those actions back to important things, stop doing them. Prioritize your time and relationships so that your energy has the greatest positive impact.

Summary

- Projects happen only through communication. In modern times, speed isn't the communication bottleneck, quality is.

- Relationships enhance and accelerate communication.

- There are several frameworks for how people communicate with each other. PMs should be familiar with them so that they can diagnose and resolve communication breakdowns.

- There are several common communication problems, including assumptions, lack of clarity, not listening, dictation, personal attacks, and blame.

- Role definition is the easiest way to improve relationships.

- Ask people what they need in order to do their best work. Ways to do this include: listening, clearing roadblocks, teaching, and reminding them of goals.

- Relationships and communication are not low-priority work. They are essential to all of the individual activities that take place during a project.

Exercises

A. Block off a half-hour on your schedule every Wednesday afternoon. Use it exclusively to walk your team's hallway and talk to the individuals working on your project. Ask what they're working on, how things are going, and if there's anything you can do to help them. If your team is virtual, use that half-hour to catch up on any communication you're behind on with them. After a month, ask yourself if it improved your relationships with anyone? If yes, continue; if not, find a better use for that half-hour.

B. You learn your project is dependent on the successful completion of Project X. Project X is being postponed so that the team can be redirected to work on Project Y, a project you do not care about. Write a plea to Project X's sponsor to convince him to keep Project X on track.

C. You are the project manager on a high-risk project. For the last several report periods, you've included a graph that illustrates the dwindling budget. You've even drawn attention to it in your periodic conference calls, but you've heard only indifference from the project's sponsor. A week from being bankrupt, you confront the sponsor directly and ask when you can expect additional funds. The sponsor is incredulous and asks why he wasn't notified before. How could you have communicated the situation and call to action more effectively?

D. Your manager interrupts a status meeting to announce your team will discard the current design and pursue a different one. She describes a solution she saw on a television show. Given your understanding of the project sponsor's requirements, you feel the current design is superior and also cost-effective. How can you convince your manager to rescind her announcement?

E. Next time you are in an argument with a friend, significant other, or coworker, think about the five-step model of communication every time you open your mouth. Are you acknowledging what they are saying? Are you taking time to make sure they understand what you are saying? Write the five steps down on a piece of paper and keep it with you.

F. You're halfway through a project and learn the team is behind schedule. You learn the lead programmer is a friend of the project client and has been entertaining change orders after work at a local bistro. The programmer has clout with the development team, and the client has clout with your supervisor. What action do you take?

G. Make two ordered lists, one of the most important people on your team, the other of the best relationships you have with people on your team. Look at the two lists for opportunities for improving relationships: if you could improve a relationship by 25%, which one would have the greatest impact on the project?

H. Turn the list of common communication problems into a poster, and place it prominently on the wall in the main conference room for your team. Invite your team to use it to point out when you're communicating poorly.

I. When do you decide to do your best work? Can someone else motivate you to do it, or do you have to motivate yourself? What does this tell you about how to motivate others to do their best work?

CHAPTER TEN

**How not to annoy people:
process, email, and meetings**

Bureaucracy (n): An administrative system in which the need to follow rigid or complex procedures impedes effective action.

The larger your team, the greater the odds are that your project management activities will annoy someone. Anytime you track someone else's work, or make decisions that impact others, you will potentially annoy them; it comes with the territory. If you're smart, you'll look for ways to minimize annoyances. They'll be happier, the project will run better, and you'll get fewer dirty looks from people in the hallway.

The three activities with the greatest odds of annoying people are email, meetings, and team processes (i.e., build or spec procedures). This chapter will run through the common mistakes and basic approaches for performing these tasks with a minimal annoyance risk factor (aka MARF).

A summary of why people get annoyed

Because I couldn't find a published history of annoyance, I'm relying on my own observations in summarizing why people get annoyed. I have a fair amount of experience in this area: I've been annoyed many times, have witnessed other people in a state of annoyance, and have been known to, on occasion, annoy others.

For the full effect in understanding these examples, they are described in the first person (it may help to think of a specific person you have experience working with, who you respect, when reading through these).

- **Assume I'm an idiot.** If I have been hired to do X, which I am capable of doing, anytime someone treats me as if I cannot do X—or need a 20-step procedure, rulebook form, template, daily evaluation, committee, or other process to enable me to do X—I will be justifiably annoyed. Part of my job should be to help define my work in a way that satisfies whatever objectives management decrees. But until I fail and prove incompetence, I should be treated as competent. I should be free to define, within reason, the best way to get my work done.

- **Don't trust me.** If, on a daily basis, I am expected to check in, double-check, triple-check, and report on decisions that are well within the range of my responsibilities, I will be annoyed. If I must confirm everything, what authority do I really have? Why does everything need to be documented and recorded if I'm doing a good job? Even if I'm not initially trustworthy for some reason, it should be management's job to provide a fair path for me to earn trust and to progress along that path.

- **Waste my time.** If the way the team functions forces me to repeat (tedious) tasks many times, or go far out of my way to protect against contingencies and management paranoias that are comically unlikely and insignificant, I will be annoyed. This includes flip-flopping on important decisions or being grossly inconsistent in messaging or behavior without making any attempt to explain it (or at least apologize for it), even when asked.

- **Manage me without respect.** If I am ever sent on a wild goose chase, given assignments that have no basis in reality, or set up to fail and take the blame for things beyond my scope of responsibility, I will be annoyed. Someone should be looking out for me and making sure my efforts align with the project's, guiding me toward success. Therefore, my requests for assistance should be taken seriously and not be excessively delayed or ignored.

- **Make me listen to or read stupid things.** Anytime I am required to listen to someone else or read something another person has written that has no meaningful bearing on the work we are doing, I will be annoyed. We have a triage bar for bug quality—why not one for stupidity? Just because someone calls a meeting, writes a paper, or sends an email doesn't mean it's worth my time. The more secondary or tertiary things are that I'm asked (or forced) to do, the less productive and happy I am.

Most of these reasons for annoyance explain why many people loathe the idea of work processes. They fear that any attempt to systematize their work can result only in bureaucracy or other forms of suffering. I think the fear is unfounded. People design processes, just like everything else, and if the designer is smart and has the right goals in mind, the processes can benefit everyone. Process can help people instead of restricting and annoying them.

The effects of good process

I define a process as any repeatable set of actions a team decides to perform on a regular basis to make sure something is done in a certain way. Processes go by many names: rules, guidelines, forms, procedures, or restrictions. (For example, how code gets checked in, tested, and built is a common example of an engineering process. Others include spec writing and managing calendars and schedules, etc.) A good process improves the odds of the project being completed and has benefits that outweigh its costs. However, because time is rarely spent considering why certain processes exist, or what problems they (should) solve, many teams live with lots of processes, without the benefits they can provide.

Sometimes the problem is who's in power. Any idiot with power can come up with the most mind-numbingly idiotic system for doing something and force the team to follow it. Then, when the team manages not only to survive that process but actually ship something, the person in power may even point to the process as a contributor to the success (blind to the fact that the team was successful in spite of the stupid process). If he has enough power, he can quell any mutinies and continue torturing the team by adding even more procedures.

Other times, the problem is the philosophy: "X worked before, so let's do X." In this situation, a team leader who has done something a certain way in the past insists on inflicting that method or process on every new team he leads (this bad management habit is mentioned in Chapter 8). This is bad because prior success with X is relevant only if the current situation is similar to past situations. The real acceptance test for a process should emphasize the needs of the present over observations about the past.

But often the problem is the complexities of creating processes. A process tries to organize how people work and how they interact, two critically important but very organic things. People work differently—they have different preferences and tolerances for formal controls. If the person creating the process isn't careful, the process can easily become a bottleneck, slowing people down and constricting their (sense of) freedom and empowerment.

The trick in creating good processes is to understand two things: what makes projects and teams successful in general, and what makes the current project and team different from others (see Figure 10-1). It's not enough to know how, say, good team decisions are made in general: you have to account for the culture, personality, and habits of the current team you're working with. Sometimes, the culture or the project demands a different approach (e.g., decisions for car antilock-brake-embedded systems versus decisions for Steve's punk rock band's web site). Instead of regulating from above, it's often best to let the team self-regulate. Instead of reusing the standard template, let them modify and create their own. Much like any kind of negotiation (see Chapter 11), when it comes to process, you have to be clear on the interests you care about and not the specific positions.

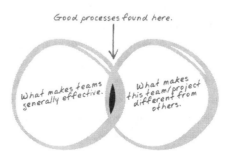

FIGURE 10-1. *Good process requires having a sense for projects in general, as well as the unique attributes of the current project.*

To help you both find and recognize good processes, here is a list of attributes and the effects they'll have on the project. This can be used as a checklist when sitting down to create or refine a process.

- **They accelerate progress.** As counterintuitive as this seems, good procedures make people more efficient. For example, the white lane separators on American highways restrict where you can drive. But because they provide the same restriction for everyone, individual drivers can go very fast. Good process provides a system that people can depend and base decisions on. In some cases, the process defines roles that people will play, which makes it easy for Steve to get what he needs from Molly (e.g., finding someone to do a code review). A canonical example is automated build tools that allow people to build projects with a few keystrokes, provided they follow the programming conventions defined by the build system.

- **They prevent problems.** The most common motivation for putting a process in place is to prevent stupidity from happening (again). The challenge is to do this without simultaneously making progress more difficult, or encouraging new stupidity. This requires understanding the causes of the problem and what factors are most important to progress. Ask the question, "What is the least intrusive, least annoying, and least expensive way to make sure that X, Y, and Z never happen again?" Or, going the other way, "What problem does this prevent from happening? How serious or likely is that problem?" If a process doesn't prevent problems or accelerate progress, get rid of it.

- **They make important actions visible and measurable.** Processes for opening bugs or publishing specs make it easy to track how often those things are done. You can track their status, the results, and the team-wide trends. For bugs, specs, and tests, a good process will make it easy to find out the state of the project. This is important for mid-game and end-game strategies (see Chapters 14 and 15).

- **They include a process for changing or eliminating the process.** Because projects are changing all the time, a process that is useful one month may not be useful the next. The process must have a built-in mechanism for deciding when it needs to be updated or discontinued. Never assume that a process will go on forever, and avoid defining jobs around processes for this reason. Someone who identifies his job as "The guy who runs test pass 5" will defend test pass 5 with his life. Instead, make people responsible for the effects and results that the process has on the project, not the process itself.

- **People impacted by them are in favor of them.** People like helpful processes. A good process will be seen as desirable to those who need it. If you are proposing a new process that impacts programmers, and your process is valuable to the project, it should be easy to get them to try it. People should be directly involved in coming up with new processes they will use. Alternatively, if the people who the proposed process will impact can enumerate dozens of reasons why the process is a bad idea, they're probably right.

A formula for good processes

One way to think about process is the value of its positive effects versus the costs of putting it into place and running it. There's a formula for this that can help. You don't need to come up with actual numbers for this formula to be useful. I offer it mostly as an exercise to help you think about the tradeoffs involved in adding engineering processes. If you don't like exercises or formulas, skip to the next section: you won't miss a beat.

First, consider the costs of the process: the time to design the process (DT), the time for the team to learn it (LT), the actual time to do work with the process, multiplied by how often it's done (AT * N). Total costs for any process are:

$$DT + LT + (AT * N)$$

Then, consider the benefits of the process: the costs of failures the process avoids (FC), multiplied by the probability that those failures will occur (FP) without the process within a given unit of time, multiplied by how many of those units of time are in the project (T).

$$\text{Total benefits} = (FC * FP) * T$$

The result is roughly this:

$$\text{Process value} = ((FC * FP) * T) - (DT + LT + (AT * N))$$

I fully admit there are gross oversimplifications in this formula, but the spirit of it is close enough to make it interesting. If the result is a high number, there is more value than if it is a low number. A negative number means that the benefits of the process were outweighed by the costs.

This formula implies, at first, that it's very easy to create a process that effectively eliminates a problem. However, the price of doing it may cost more than a lifetime of living with the threats of that particular problem (i.e., buying a $5,000 security system for the cookie jar). If you include design and learning time, and recognize that there's only a probability of failure, cost-benefit works against changing the process.

However, you must consider the lifetime of the benefits: they will often span more than a single project. More importantly, the probability of the failure occurring over the next several projects may increase to 100%. The T value in the formula is significant—even if the probability of a failure (FP) is low, if T is big enough, it will eventually happen. In other words, the longer the time interval, the greater the odds of failure, which also means the greater the value of having something in place to prevent that failure. (This exposes one of the major challenges of being a leader: deciding when to pay the tangible short-term costs for less tangible long-term returns. This challenge comes up all over the place: hiring, equipment, facilities, training, etc. You reap what you sow; long-term investments are the only way to get long-term improvements.)

A last note about this formula: the value AT (actual time to use the procedure) is more important than it might seem. A good process should make things take less time; AT should have a negative value compared to how work was done without the procedure, if it's really saving time. This changes the relationship of costs/benefits as it's structured in the equation. For example, if AT=5 hours, but previously the task took 7, the net value is 2 hours. That means that the task now takes two hours less to do, and the overall value of the process is much higher.

How to create and roll out processes

When you identify a problem you think can be solved with a process, follow the same rough procedure I will outline in Chapter 11. (Even though you're not in a crisis, the basic procedure of executing a short-term plan is similar.) Clearly define the problem you're trying to solve and the small group of people best able to help solve it. Work as a small group generating alternative proposals and then pick the most promising one.

Next, identify an isolated low-risk part of the project to pilot this new process on. If possible, pick individuals who are interested in and receptive to the process change and involve them in the creation of the process. Agree on what desired effects the process change should have, and if possible, set up measurements for them. Then, have the people involved make the change. Set a date in the future to evaluate how effective the process change has been.

When this evaluation day arrives, meet again with the small group and the people involved in the pilot. Discuss what happened. If the pilot was a disaster, repeat the process and do a second small pilot. Otherwise, revise the process based on what you've learned, and roll it out to a larger group (possibly the entire team). It should be clear to everyone you ask to use the process what problems you're trying to solve and why you're convinced the proposed solution will actually help (the evidence and testimonials you have from the people involved in the pilot should help a ton).

Managing process from below

"Never underestimate the power of stupid people in large groups."

—Todd Blanchard

Sometimes, people with more power than you inflict processes on your team that you don't agree with. You might simply be outnumbered or without the authority to revise the process. It happens to the best of us. I know of three ways to deal with this situation. They don't always work, but they're worth a shot.

- **Shield your team from the process.** Sometimes, you can absorb the process for your team. If some paperwork needs to be done, do it yourself. This might make you feel like the team secretary, but if it's only a matter of you burning an afternoon, so your team doesn't have to, the trade might be worthwhile. In some cases, you will score many trust points with your team for protecting them against stupid things. Time cards, expense reports, mandatory (but ridiculous) HR-type meetings, equipment requisitions, and other annoying trivia are common examples of easily shielded processes.

- **Bet against the process.** Rally your team around a counterproposal. Find out what things the process is trying to prevent or ensure, and guarantee to the powers that be that your team will meet those goals without the process. Set a certain amount of time to make an evaluation. If your team fails after that time, you'll agree to adopt the process. But if they succeed, you'll take the proposal off the table. If nothing else, this focuses the process discussion on the right issues (what problem are we trying to solve?), so even if you fail, it will be an improved process. (In rare cases, research into other similar and successful organizations that don't do whatever the process is, or do it in a different and less stupid way, can score points and avoid the need for the bet.)

- **Ignore the process.** I have a tendency to ignore distant, ambiguous, bureaucratic, organizational things that I don't understand. My theory is that by ignoring it, I force one of two things to happen. Either the person responsible for the thing will contact me and ask me why I didn't do it, giving me a chance to have a dialog with him about why I should do it at all; or, if no one asks me why I didn't do it, then it can't possibly be that important. I'll go about my business, be successful without the thing in question, and have a good justification should someone ask me one day why I didn't do that thing ("Oh. Well, we did X just fine without it. Perhaps you can convince me how Y would have helped?"). This often works best in a new organization because you have the added excuse of organizational ignorance. Be warned, though: your political landscape may make it dangerous to ignore bureaucracy.

Non-annoying email

As remedial a subject as it seems, email is the most annoying system people on projects deal with. Simply as a result of the volume of email we receive, it's easy to feel pressure to read and respond to new messages as quickly as possible, often sacrificing good reading and writing skills. Most of us just don't read or write email very well. What's ironic is that the convenience of email is squandered when we can't understand what the hell the other person is trying to say, or we can't get her to understand what we're trying to say.

Of most importance to project managers is that email is a primary means of communication for leaders. In both creating new mail and responding to mail sent by others, a leader influences the flow of information through a project. If a leader has clear thoughts and asks solid questions, she encourages others to do the same. One response to a large discussion with dozens of people can send a wave of clarity through the organization. But the leader hurts the team's ability to communicate well if she expresses fuzzy thoughts and makes obscure or obfuscated points.

One major challenge is that few admit they send bad email. For example, take the following test: using your own subjective judgment, what percentage of email that you receive from people within your own organization is high quality? Average quality? Totally useless? Now ask yourself what percentage of the email you send fits into each of these categories. As an experiment, I once asked a small group of PMs, testers, and programmers this very question. By a factor of almost 2 to 1, everyone claimed that other people wrote crappier mail than they did. Because they all worked together, this anecdotal data implied that everyone thinks the problem is email generated by others, not themselves. I don't have harder data to support this claim, but it rings true. Somehow, when there's a communication failure, on average people tend to blame the other guy (for copious evidence, see any history of international politics in Western civilization).

The good piece of email

One habit I learned at Microsoft was the reward for the good piece of email. Many important debates took place on email, and it was common for these discussions to include people at multiple levels of hierarchy—line PMs, middle managers, and VPs might all be exchanging mail back and forth, treating each other mostly as equals. I often found myself in the middle of these debates, usually because something I was responsible for suddenly became very important to the division.

Every so often in these email discussions, I'd make a really strong point in response to something someone else said. I'd carefully word it, revising it over and over to get it just right: simple, strong, and clear. Then I'd send it out. Sometimes my arguments would get torn apart; sometimes I'd be ignored. But on occasion, I'd hit a home run. When I did, I'd often get a private email a few minutes later from a VP or "other person much more important than I" that said only two words: "Good email." The discussion might still rage on, but I'd know that I scored some points in the argument. More important was this: someone took the time to let me know that my points were good, and that I was expressing them in a praiseworthy way.[1]

Smart managers value good email. Managers read so much poorly written email every day, and if they don't take the time to reward those who communicate well, they're

---

[1] It's embarrassing, but I kept those notes of appreciation, probably because there wasn't enough outward praise from management. IM and email provide no equivalents to head nods or smiles that give secondary feedback during meetings: perhaps these side emails compensate for that in some way.

unlikely to see more people do it. Little side emails take about 15 seconds to send, and as my story indicates, may mean more to others in your organization than you think.

But praising others is easier than taking responsibility for your own bad email habits. As I mentioned previously, I'm convinced that most people think they write better email than others think they do (and the more senior you are, the harder it might be to get honest feedback about your email etiquette). Because leaders and managers send more email than others, it's critical to sort out what bad habits you have and invest energy in curbing them. Here is some project management-style advice on what good email looks like and what some of the common bad habits are.

- **Be concise, simple, and direct.** Pascal, the mathematician for whom the language is named, once wrote, "If I had more time, I'd write a shorter letter." Language, like code, can be optimized. Instead of optimizing for logical efficiency, you want to optimize for communication efficiency. Unlike code, a grammatically and logically correct three-word message is useless if the recipient can't figure out what the hell it means.[2] Consider who is reading the email and how you would explain what you need to say if you were talking face to face. What details would be needed? Omitted? What concepts can you assume he knows? What metaphors can you use? For important email, step away from it for a few minutes and then reread it, with these questions in mind, before you send it. Or for important mail, or mail going to a large number of people, have one of the people on your team skim it over and give you feedback.

- **Offer an action and a deadline.** The best email has a specific request that is clearly stated, and, if appropriate, is tied to a reasonable deadline. It should be easy for people reading the email to understand why they are receiving it, how they are impacted by the action, and what they need to do (before the deadline). Assuming you enforce the deadline ("Requests must be in to me by Friday"), you set yourself up for people to be attentive to future actions you communicate through email, which puts you in a position of power.

- **Prioritize.** Is it necessary to send that email? The more emails you send, the more work others will have to do to prioritize your requests. How many of the things you're mentioning are important? If you have 10 issues to discuss, break them into two groups and focus on the most important group. Consider if some things can be better handled on the phone, in the next team meeting, or by going door-to-door. If you don't prioritize, expect the recipients to prioritize for you—in a way that serves their interests, not yours.

---

2   A possibly apocryphal story about Victor Hugo describes a clever use of compact communication. When *Les Misérables* was published, Hugo sent a telegram to his publisher asking for results. His telegram was as concise as possible, consisting of one character: "?". The response also consisted of one character: "!". Apparently sales were spectacular. If there's a lesson here, it's that two people that know each other well can communicate more efficiently than those who don't, which is another reason for developing relationships with coworkers.

- **Don't assume people read anything (especially if it's important to you).** It's arrogant to assume that because you sent it, someone has read it. People get tons of email every day, much of it from people just as important as you are. The more important the issue is to you, the more energy you have to expend to make sure people are actively doing something about it. The more trust you've built with the people on your team, the more assumptions you can make about how people will respond to things you send.

- **Avoid giving a play-by-play.** It's rare that anyone needs to know the sequence of events that led to something happening. Avoid writing emails that focus on the contributing actions by different players: "When Sally first designed our build process, she was interested in…", or narrative-driven prose like "The meeting started off fine, with Bob and Steve talking through their slides with great passion and conviction. That is, until…." Instead, focus on impact: what happened, how this changes the world, and what we're going to do about it. If you're compelled to include background details, list them below the critical points. The same goes for references to slide decks, web sites, papers, etc. Make it possible for anyone to skim the first two lines and know immediately if it's important enough for them to read any further.

- **Sequester FYIs.** I've been on teams that persisted in forwarding tons of semi-interesting-but-not-directly-relevant-to-anything email. Some people call these FYIs, or for your information emails. Curiosity and industry awareness are fine habits, but don't let them dominate communication forums used for more tangible work. Set up an email alias or discussion group for "industry trends" or "tech watch," where your team can post the cool things they find. If your email client supports it, ask everyone to set these kinds of emails to low priority, or add "FYI:" to the front of the subject line. Make this stuff easy for people to filter out.

- **The telephone is your friend.** If ever you don't understand something in an important email you've received, don't respond with an elaborate five-part question. See if you can reach the sender of the email on the phone. Interactive communication is always better at resolving confusion and conflict than email. A 30-second phone conversation is often equivalent to a long series of time-consuming email exchanges. If you do get the sender on the phone and resolve the issue, you can then share your clarified understanding in an email sent to everyone—odds are good that if you were confused, so were others. Telephones (or a walk down the hallway) are the great expediters of group email communication.[3]

---

3 There's probably some law of communication claiming that the dominant mode of communication (email) still depends on the previously dominant mode (telephone) as its fallback: IM → Email → phone → snail mail → smoke signals → face-to-face → etc.

An example of bad email

Awful email is easy to recognize. Awful email is often very long, poorly written, has many attachments, and is hard to skim. It can be spotted from very far away, and it is usually either ignored or challenged appropriately: "Fred: I found this email very confusing. If others agree, can you either revise or call a meeting? If not, I'll call you. Thanks." For this reason, awful email is not the most dangerous kind.

The really dangerous emails are the ones that look like well-written communication but are, in fact, ripe with distractions, half-baked thoughts, and ambiguities. What follows are two examples of the same email: one bad and one good. Here's the bad one.

From: Jack Colono
To: Striker development team
Subject: Summary of recent check-in discussions

Over the last four weeks, many of us have wondered when the process for redesigning our code check-in procedures would finally be complete. I know it's taken a long time and that there has been much debate in hallways and meetings about the right way to go about deciding on, much less figuring out, the actual design for the new procedure as well. Choosing the members of the committee was not easy for me, and as many of you know, took more time than expected. Apologies for that, but these things happen.

So, first I'd like to give you some of the highlights of our new proposal, in case you missed one of the weekly discussions we've had, or didn't come by to chat with me about it over the last two weeks:

1) Check-ins are very important. They determine what we're really building.

2) Everyone has opinions. We've all heard Randy and Bob each describe in detail why they think the current system is so bad.

3) There are no easy answers. Most of the changes we've discussed all have downsides. So, when we do finally reach a conclusion, there will be some rough edges on transition and possibly on an ongoing basis.

With that out of the way, I'd now like to let you know that later this week I'll be sending out the revised proposal. Please be on the lookout for the next piece of email from me. It should be coming soon.

Thanks,
Jack

An example of good email

Unlike the bad example, this email does not tell any stories or try to justify anything: it's all action. It's short, clear, and to the point. Instead of talking about proposals, it actually offers one. While it has the flavor of an ultimatum, it serves the purposes of creating escape velocity for the proposal, helping to push it out the door.

From: Jack Colono
To: Striker development team
Subject: New check-in process

The final proposal for the new check-in process is complete and is up on the web site: *http://intman/proc/checkin/*.

Because this has been a contentious issue, I've discussed this proposal one-on-one with much of the team and incorporated everyone's feedback. If this didn't include you and you have strong opinions, please send me mail ASAP.

But be warned: this is the second public notice about these upcoming changes. The opportunity for making changes is currently small and is getting smaller by the day. Please act now or prepare to hold your peace.

Friday at 5:00 p.m. is the deadline for contacting me with feedback on the above proposal. I will consider and respond to any questions or comments raised before then (in collaboration with appropriate folks). Otherwise, this matter is closed and will become effective next week.

Thanks,
Jack

As clear as the difference between these two emails should be, don't read too much into these examples. They're not meant to be templates for things to always or never do. Each email you send might have a different purpose, and it might make sense to contradict these examples. As long as you're writing it thoughtfully and with clear reasons, do whatever is necessary to get the job done. But always be on the lookout for ways to cut to the chase and use email to make things happen.

How to run the non-annoying meeting

Here is my meeting confession: I do not like regularly scheduled meetings. Unless there is a force keeping them lean and tidy, they will eventually slide into slow, bloated, frustrating, dysfunctional wastes of time. However, if there is that force in place, meetings can be energizing, centering experiences for everyone in the room. The challenge is that whoever organizes and runs the meeting needs to know what he's doing.

For starters, understand how expensive meetings are. If a meeting lasts an hour, and 10 people are there, that meeting costs 10 person-hours. Instead of fixing bugs or closing issues—two guaranteed forms of progress—the entire team is locked up in a conference room waiting for something to happen that is worth the expense of their time. Maybe it happens, maybe it doesn't. So, I think programmers and others are justified in complaining about meetings; relative to the value of time in front of a computer, time in meetings doesn't usually score well.

However, if the meeting requires participation because important ideas or decisions are on the table, reveals information that changes everyone's post-meeting behavior, or conveys inspiration or understanding for what's going on across the project, then the value of the meeting is much higher. Instead of a chore, it becomes a way to consume or exchange information difficult to obtain through other means.

The art of facilitation

Years ago, I remember being in a big argument over how we were going to architect an important part of Windows. I had arrived early and watched everyone walk in the room and take their seats, smugly confident in their own opinions. I watched them lean back in their chairs and run through their arguments in their minds before the meeting even started. And, of course, argue is exactly what we did. For 10 minutes, the discussion shifted back and forth in big waves. Conflicting diagrams were violently sketched out across whiteboards, hands flailed in disagreement, and sarcastic statements and rhetorical questions abounded. Finally, my group manager, Hadi Partovi, stood up. He quietly walked to the whiteboard at the front of the room.

Without saying a word he wrote a list of questions. The room became silent. Everyone stopped arguing and watched what he was doing. When he finished, he asked if he had the right issues on the board. Everyone nodded. He then led us through them one at a time. There were still arguments, but when structured, they were dramatically less continuous. Hadi didn't offer his own opinion (although I knew he had one). Instead, he used his energy to help the rest of us navigate through the questions we'd agreed on. This is the art of facilitation.

Facilitate (v): The act of making things easy or easier.

Good meetings happen only when someone in the room understands how to facilitate. Some people do it instinctively, and others can't even recognize when it's being done. Like other interpersonal skills, people have different levels of awareness about the many ways interaction occurs and how to influence it.

Facilitating can be a semiformal role, held by a designated person who runs the show (often the PM), or by whoever called the meeting. Some teams have strong enough cultures of facilitation (meaning that many people have the skill) that they can switch who's playing this role naturally in the course of conversation. But most of the time, on most projects, meetings are desperately in need of facilitation talent.

Facilitation pointers

Facilitation is a skill that most teams take for granted. There are good books[4] and courses on how to facilitate, but your best bet to understanding the skills involved is to watch someone who does it well, and then apply what you've observed in the next meeting you organize. However, there are some pointers worth mentioning. It took me a long time to figure these out, and they go a long way in helping you to develop whatever natural facilitation skills you have.

- **Establish a host position.** If you're the organizer of the meeting, you're the de facto facilitator. Start the meeting by introducing people, clarifying the agenda, and beginning the discussion. If you behave like a host from the moment people walk in the door, they will behave like guests and treat you with respect. Carefully choose where you sit in the room: sitting at the head or center of a table gives you the most authority, and sitting in the corner gives you the least.

- **Listen and reflect.** The core function of the facilitator is to help other people communicate. If someone says something half-baked (but not completely worthless), help him to develop the idea. Try the reflection trick of restating what people say: "So Mike, what I think you're saying is <insert better way for Mike to express his point here>. Do you agree?" This refines his point and demonstrates for everyone how to make the discussion collaborative. However, be careful to separate your desire to champion your own opinions—it's hard to be a good facilitator if you're caught up in your personal agenda. Some organizations hire professional facilitators who help out with contentious meetings and offsites.

- **Direct the conversation.** With the agenda as your guide, jump in to push the discussion back on track when necessary. Be flexible and let people have their say, but if the conversation is heading south when the agenda demands you go west, something must be done. Politely interrupt, point to the agenda on the wall, and ask that they table the discussion at hand until the issues in the agenda have been covered (or offer to adjust the agenda if this new issue is worthy). Pay attention to who is speaking too much and who isn't speaking enough, and manage the floor accordingly ("Bob, hold on one second...Steve do you have any thoughts on this?").

- **End the conversation.** Have a threshold in mind for when an issue should be resolved elsewhere. It's often enough to identify a problem, and an owner for the problem, and ask that owner to go off on his own and come back tomorrow or the next day with a proposed solution. This is a great way to end side debates that have taken over meetings: "Whoa, hold on guys. Sam and Bob—you two go off and figure

---

4   Two good places to start are *The Facilitator's Fieldbook*, by Tom Justice (American Management Association, 1999) and *Mining Group Gold*, by Thomas A. Kayser (McGraw-Hill, 1991).

this out, OK? Then come back and let us know what you've decided." Never let two people dominate the floor, when five or six other people are bored out of their minds for the entire hour.

- **Make history.** Take time to document the discussion (if possible, as it happens). As a facilitator, this helps you track where you are in the agenda and communicate this to the group. For this reason, I am completely infatuated with whiteboards. They're the easiest way to capture what people are saying, make to-do lists, or identify points of (dis)agreement. But how you do it doesn't matter. What's important is that when the meeting is over, the next steps and important points are recorded and emailed out to those who attended the meeting. Some say that being the scribe is a position of power because you can influence how things are recorded and what aspects are emphasized. Even if that's not the case, sending out notes does provide a forcing function for others to clarify anything you've misrepresented.

Even if you don't agree with these pointers, I hope they've helped you to recognize that there is a leadership role to be played in meetings. If no one is actively playing this role, meetings will tend to be frustrating and/or boring affairs. The general refrain is "Meetings suck and should be avoided," but the real problem is how the meetings are run, not the idea of meetings themselves.

Three kinds of meetings

The greatest trap for meeting organizers is forgetting how versatile meetings are. Not all meetings should be run in the same way or should have the same structure. The reason why many meetings are boring for 90% of the people there is because the goals are in conflict with the meeting's structure and size. You can't have highly interactive discussions with more than seven or eight people, no matter who's facilitating. As a very rough rule of thumb, there are three kinds of meetings, with different constraints and applications. Always consider what kind of meeting will best serve the problem that needs to be solved.

- **Highly interactive discussion.** Everyone in the meeting is expected to participate. Goal: depth and intimacy. Focus: exploring or resolving specific issues or seeking out alternative ideas. Size: small to medium (2–8). Examples: design discussion, brainstorming, crisis management, and triage.

- **Reporting or moderate discussion.** One person has content to cover, and she needs people to respond to or understand that content. Goal: get high-level feedback or share knowledge. This can be highly interactive, but it occurs only for a subset of the group. Several different people may take the floor during the meeting, changing the roles for who's driving and who's responding. Size: medium to large (5–15). Examples: spec review, architecture review, management review, and small presentation.

- **Status and project review.** Objective is to summarize the status of a team or an entire project. Gives leaders a chance to make course corrections and present new directives from management to the entire group at once. When these meetings include the activity of collecting status, or force everyone to listen to the reporting of status, they are often the most boring experiences in the known universe. Size: medium to large (10–100). Examples: status review, project review, big presentation, and all-hands meeting.

The most evil meetings occur when there is a mismatch of the goals and how they're organized. If there are more than 10 people in the room, it's very difficult to have a highly interactive or deep discussion. There isn't enough time for everyone to participate, and what will happen is that a small group of dominant personalities will use up most of the available time (unless someone facilitates the meeting to avoid this; however, a small group of dominant personalities isn't always a bad thing). Most committees take this form and have the expected mediocre to crappy results.

The evil of recurring meetings

The second most evil meeting is the one that recurs (weekly, daily, monthly), and then lives on for weeks despite it not being needed anymore (some buildings at Microsoft were impossible to reserve meetings in because abandoned recurring meetings clogged up the conference-room scheduling system). Recurrence is great in that it sets a rhythm for work and forces people to be in the same room together at the same time. All sorts of small issues can be resolved quickly and casually when people are physically together and can depend on seeing each other in person once or more a week. "Oh. Hey, Sam, I've been meaning to ask you…is this API going to change? I saw your check-in and I thought it might impact me, but I wasn't sure." Email and telephone calls don't guarantee responses, but when the person is sitting next to you, you can usually get what you need.

The problem is that it becomes too easy for recurring meetings to live on long after the value of the meeting has disappeared. When people stop coming, or others use the time to check email on their laptops, something is wrong; the meeting doesn't warrant the time anymore. The fear managers (and other meeting organizers) often have is that by canceling the meeting, they are losing control. But on the contrary, torturing teams with unneeded meetings is how managers lose the influence they're trying to protect.

Here's a good rule: opt-in meetings. Keep the recurring meeting on schedule and ask everyone to check his email for an agenda five minutes before the meeting is supposed to start. If there is a solid agenda, the organizer sends it out, and the group meets. If there's no agenda, you send out email saying so, and the meeting is canceled (for that week). This gives the team a reserved timeslot if needed, but doesn't force people to attend bogus meetings. The recurrence should be canceled entirely if no meeting occurs for more than three or four weeks.

Meeting pointers

This last section is a list of commonly overlooked tactics for successfully running and participating in meetings. There's nothing sexy or interesting about this: there's just certain things you have to deal with when working with small groups of people. Anyone who has run many meetings will have her own pet list of tricks or tips. If nothing else, I hope this list helps you to think about what things have worked for you in the past.

- **Are the right people in the room?** Some people will come if you invite them. Some people won't come unless you knock them unconscious and drag them (and/or bribe them with candy). Much of the work PMs do is getting the right people in the room at the right time, so don't be afraid to run down the hallway or barge into other meetings if the person who's supposed to be in your meeting hasn't arrived yet. Even worse: if you're starting a meeting and can't find the right people, stop the meeting. Don't waste an hour of time doing stuff you'll just have to do again tomorrow or the next day when you finally get a quorum. Lastly, if you do have the right people, but see people in the room who don't need to be there, tell them so. Be diplomatic, offer to send them notes or summaries, but get them out of the room, especially if they are going to get in the way.

- **Sit or stand.** One trick to keeping meetings short is to have everyone stand up (e.g., meet in the hallway or outside). The theory is that this forces people to get to the point and only raise issues truly worthy of group discussion. The meeting needs to last for only 5 or 10 minutes, tops. The SCRUM[5] process advocates a daily standing meeting for status purposes, where only three questions are asked: What have you done since the last meeting? What is blocking you? What will you do by tomorrow's meeting? With this kind of hardcore commitment to lean meetings, even the crankiest engineer should be willing to attend. Traditional seated meetings are reserved for smaller groups. It's worth at least trying this as an experiment; if nothing else, it inspires people to consider that a meeting scheduled for one hour doesn't need to consume the full hour.

- **Prepare.** Meetings often fail because of lack of preparation. Always consider how much preparation time you'll need for a meeting to serve its purpose. Sometimes, this will be minimal: a list of questions or open issues, or an email you send out the day before with the agenda. Other times, it's elaborate: a slide deck, a demo, stapled handouts. Whenever you have a meeting not go as well as you'd like, ask yourself what could have been done differently. Most of the time, the answer will involve some form of negligent preparation. A trick is to consider this when you send out a meeting invite, and add time to your own calendar before the meeting for the appropriate amount of prep.

---

5 For more information about SCRUM, see *http://c2.com/cgi/wiki?ScrumMeetings* or *http://www. controlchaos.com/*.

- **Laptops and gadgets.** I have a strong bias against the use of gadgets and laptops during meetings. If the people in the room don't think what's going on is important enough to warrant their full attention, then they shouldn't be in the room (unless it's a status or project-review-type meeting, where there's a low signal-to-noise ratio). Face time is precious and should be used for things people naturally feel are important and worth their time, whereas email and voice mail are designed to wait. If you have an opinion about this, talk to others on the team and see if you can agree on a policy for appropriate laptop use in meetings.

- **Being on time.** This is a seniority-driven behavior. If the VP tends to arrive late, everyone else will. If she usually arrives on time, everyone else will. You can try to start on time to make a point, but if the important people aren't there, you'll only end up repeating yourself once they do show up—it's a lost cause. However, if it's peers or reports you're waiting on, try comedic annoyance tactics. My favorite trick is to call the office of each person who is late. If he's still there, mildly ridicule him on the phone in front of everyone else: "Hi Sam. We'd be honored by your presence in conference room 5." If he's not there, leave him a voice mail. Put him on speakerphone and have everyone in the room say, in unison, "We love you Sam!" or sing Happy Birthday. Do this at every meeting for whoever is late or is last to arrive. You'll start meetings off with something fun—and an additional motivator to get there on time.

- **End with clear steps and owners.** When a meeting ends, all that matters is what happens next. You can have the ugliest, nastiest, most brutal meeting ever in the history of mankind, but if you leave the room with the right list of five things that need to be done, and the names of five people who have agreed to get those things done, you've succeeded. Never let people leave a room without a clear plan for what the next step is. Part of your preparation should be based on how you think you can achieve this outcome and who the right people are for each task.

Summary

- Project managers are prone to annoying others. Some of it is avoidable.

- People get annoyed for many reasons. Often, it's when they feel their time is wasted, when they are treated like idiots, or when they are expected to endure prolonged tedium and mistreatment.

- Good processes have many positive effects, including accelerating progress and preventing problems. But, they are difficult to design well.

- Non-annoying email is concise and actionable, and it quickly allows readers to determine whether they are impacted enough to need to read more than the subject line or first sentence.

- Meetings run well when someone facilitates them.

- Frustrating meetings occur when the goals are mismatched to the type of meeting.

Exercises

A. Who is the most annoying person you know? What about him annoys you? Do you think anyone has ever given him feedback on these annoyances? If you want to be less annoying to your team, how can you invite their feedback?

B. What is the best work process you've experienced? What made it so good? Was it still as beneficial to the project a year after it was first used?

C. What is the worst work process you've experienced? What made it so bad? Could leaders have done something different? Did you suggest changes that were ignored, or did you keep quiet? How can a team leader get input from her team about annoying processes?

D. When was the last time you complimented someone for his simple, clear emails? Over the next week, every day, thank the person who sent you the clearest, most effective email.

E. Take control over your email. There is no law that says you must read it as it comes in, or respond to it within an hour. Some studies show that if you do your email in batches, two or three times a day, your time spent working on email drops and your general effectiveness climbs. As an experiment, keep a log of every time you check your email. Make it a goal to check it one less time tomorrow, and again the day after, until you are in control of it.

F. Here's a team experiment: pick one afternoon a week as a no email zone; for example, from 2–5 p.m. no one is expected to answer any emails. This frees everyone to take more control over their work for a few hours. After the experiment, ask the team if they felt more productive, less productive, or no difference.

G. Bring a notepad with you to the next few meetings you attend. For each meeting, identify who is facilitating the meeting and take notes on how they perform. At the end of the week, make a list of the best tricks and habits you saw and make a goal of emulating them in your own meetings.

H. If you find yourself in a meeting mismatch (the meeting is the wrong size for the goals), what should you do? a) Wait to see if anyone else complains; b) suggest to the meeting organizer that changing the meeting's size will increase the odds it goes well; or, c) start a game of musical chairs and kick people out until the meeting is the right size?

I. Every bureaucracy in history grew out of a simple, lean process. Research the history of the bureaucratic system that frustrates you the most (e.g., government tax system, HR hiring procedures, expense reporting at work, etc.). Find out what the first version of that system was like and how it grew into the system you know today. Could the bureaucracy have been prevented? What would you have done differently now that you know the history?

J. Take a look at all of your recurring meetings and rank them by importance. Cancel the least important recurring meeting, and try to replace whatever purpose it served with other meetings or email.

CHAPTER ELEVEN

What to do when things go wrong

No matter what you do, how hard you work, or who you work with, things will still go wrong. The best team in the world, with the best leaders, workers, morale, and resources, will still find themselves in difficult situations. The only way to completely avoid difficult situations is to do nothing of importance or to consistently put yourself in situations, and on projects, where you are safe from all forms of risk—two things that rarely contribute to success.

> "All successful projects are simply a long series of adversities that must be overcome. Far from it being unusual to face adversity, it is normal, and our business is to overcome it. The real test is not when we are successful when there is no adversary, but when there is and we triumph."
>
> —William A. Cohen

For these reasons, good PMs must be prepared to deal with difficult situations. It takes a certain kind of wisdom to realize that when bad things happen, they happen. Nothing can be done to change them after the fact. Instead, how the team responds to adversity may be a larger factor in project success than the team's ability to avoid adversity in the first place. Both are important, but resiliency and recovery ability are the attributes that make dealing with the unexpected possible. Without them, a perfect team and perfect plan can spiral out of control with just a nudge in the wrong direction.

This chapter will provide three things: a rough guide (or first-aid kit) for what to do when things go wrong, thoughts on how people and teams respond to difficult situations, and coverage of tactics and approaches for managing in tough times.

Apply the rough guide

> "You can blame people who knock things over in the dark, or you can begin to light candles. You're only at fault if you know about the problem and choose to do nothing."
>
> —Paul Hawken

This section is a primer on how to handle difficult situations. Later, I'll cover common situations and offer advice, but this guide should help you work through whatever it is that led you to flip to this chapter.

1. **Calm down.** Nothing makes a situation worse than basing your actions on fear, anger, or frustration. If something bad happens to you, you will have these emotions whether you're aware of them or not. They will also influence your thinking and behavior whether you're aware of it or not. (Rule of thumb: the less aware you are of your feelings, the more vulnerable you are to them influencing you.) Don't flinch or overreact—be patient, keep breathing, and pay attention.

2. **Evaluate the problem in relation to the project.** Just because someone else thinks the sky has fallen doesn't mean that it has. Is this really a problem at all? Whose problem is it? How much of the project (or its goals) is at risk or may need to change because of this situation: 5%? 20%? 90%? Put things in perspective. Will anyone die because of this mistake (you're not a brain surgeon, are you?)? Will any cities be leveled? Plagues delivered on the innocent? Help everyone frame the problem to the right emotional and intellectual scale. Ask tons of questions and get people thinking rather than reacting. Work to eliminate assumptions. Make sure you have a tangible understanding of the problem and its true impact. Then, prioritize: emergency (now!), big concern (today), minor concern (this or next week), bogus (never). Know how long your fuse is to respond and prioritize this new issue against all existing work. If it's a bogus issue, make sure whoever cried wolf learns some new questions to ask before raising the red flag again.

3. **Calm down again.** Now that you know something about the problem, you might really get upset ("How could those idiots let <insert incredibly stupid thing here> happen!?"). Find a way to express emotions safely: scream at the sky, workout at the gym, or talk to a friend. But do express them.[1] Know what works for you, and use it. Then return to the problem. Not only do you need to be calm to make good decisions, but you need your team to be calm. Pay attention to who is upset and help them calm down. Humor, candor, food, and drink are good places to start. Being calm and collected yourself goes a long way toward calming others. And taking responsibility for the situation (see the later section "Take responsibility"), regardless of whose fault it was, accelerates a team's recovery from a problem.

4. **Get the right people in the room.** Any major problem won't impact you alone. Identify who else is most responsible, knowledgeable, and useful and get them in together straight away. Pull them out of other meetings and tasks: if it's urgent, act with urgency, and interrupt anything that stands in your way. Sit them down, close the door, and run through what you learned in step 2. Keep this group small; the more complex the issue, the smaller the group should be.[2] Also, consider that (often) you might not be part of this group: get the people in the room, communicate the problem, and then delegate. Offer your support, but get out of their way (seriously— leave the room if you're not needed). Clearly identify who is in charge for driving this issue to resolution (see "Roles and clear authority," later in this chapter), whether it's you or someone else.

---

1   A common destructive habit, especially among men, is to pretend that nothing ever bothers you. This is called denial. At some emotional level, we are affected by everything. Those people with more awareness are called—get ready for this—healthy. Have feelings and explore them. They're good for you.

2   This is cultural. I've been on teams that had a culture of very good communication. Things stayed intimate even with seven or eight people in the room, even on contentious topics. However, most teams don't have this kind of intimacy. To cover ground quickly, you have to start small, build momentum, and then bring people in.

5. **Explore alternatives.** After answering any questions and clarifying the situation, figure out what your options are (see Chapter 8). Sometimes this might take some research: delegate it out. Make sure it's flagged as urgent if necessary; don't ever assume people understand how urgent something is. Be as specific as possible in your expectation for when answers are needed.

6. **Make the simplest plan.** Weigh the options, pick the best choice, and make a simple plan. The best available choice is the best available choice, no matter how much it sucks (a crisis is not the time for idealism). The more urgent the issue, the simpler your plan. The bigger the hole you're in, the more direct your path out of it should be. Break the plan into simple steps to make sure no one gets confused. Identify two lists of people: those whose approval you need for the plan, and those who need to be informed of the plan before it is executed. Go to the first group, present the plan, consider their feedback, and get their support. Then communicate that information to the second group.

7. **Execute.** Make it happen (see Chapter 13). Ensure whoever is doing the work was involved in the process and has an intimate understanding of why he's doing it. There is no room for assumption or ambiguity. Have specific checkpoints (hourly, daily, weekly) to make sure the plan has the desired effect and to force you and others in power to consider any additional effort that needs to be spent on this issue. If new problems do arise, start over at step 1.

8. **Debrief.** After the fire is out, get the right people in the room and generate a list of lessons learned. (This group may be different from the right people in step 4 because you want to include people impacted by, but not involved in, the decision process.) Ask the question: "What can we do next time to avoid this?" The bigger the issue, the more answers you'll have to this question. Prioritize the list. Consider who should be responsible for making sure each of the first few items happens.

Common situations to expect

There are certain bad situations that inevitably occur on projects. Much of this book is about minimizing the chances of these situations happening, as well as minimizing the severity of them should they occur. But the universe is a difficult place for projects, as there are more ways for things to go wrong than right. The more projects you work on, the more likely it is you'll experience all of the things listed here and have the chance to learn firsthand how to deal with them.

My first disaster was in 1996, when I was working on the parental control features of IE 3.0. We were working to support the W3C standard for parental control systems, planning to be the first web browser to try to make the Web "safe." I thought the project was going well, until we had our first review meeting. Of the 10 people there, 9 were so disappointed by my answers to their questions that they stopped listening to me and the meeting spiraled out of control. They were all experienced developers and architects, and their questions were much better than my answers. Everything seemed wrong: people were yelling and my team was demoralized. Ten minutes into the meeting, I knew it was a disaster. Twenty minutes in, I wished I could disappear. When the hour was over, I could barely get up off the floor.

Folks at Microsoft sometimes call this sort of thing "trial by fire." The idea is that work is pressure and there are no kid gloves. I have a vivid memory of that day because it was the first time I understood how much was required to do a good job. I had heard stories of similar experiences, but until it happened to me, I didn't fully understand. But afterward, things were clear: it was my job to have things working well enough that a meeting like that would never happen again. As painful as it was, it gave me an opportunity to learn things I couldn't have learned any other way.

From my experience training other managers, I've learned that it's difficult for people to relate to a problem they haven't experienced (another reason simulations should be used in training). Despite how easy it seems to relate to someone else's story about slipping schedules or changing requirements, most of us manage to believe we're immune. Or more precisely, that the problems we had (or are having) were unique in some way that made them unavoidable and unlike anything anyone else has ever experienced.

So, in an act of sheer optimism, I'll offer you, dear reader, a list of common difficult situations. If nothing else, skimming this list should help you reconsider the experiences you've had, as well as the ones you're currently in.

How to know you are in a difficult situation

As far as projects are concerned, I consider a situation difficult if it meets any of the following criteria:

1. There is an acute gap between reality and the current plan. ("We're supposed to release to web in an hour, but Fred says the entire customer database is corrupt, the power has gone out, and the programming team is drunk.")

2. Confusion exists about what the gap is, what's causing it, whose job it is to resolve it, or possibly whether it even exists. ("What iceberg? I don't see an iceberg.")

3. It's unclear how resources should be applied to resolve the gap. There may be fears that taking action or doing nothing may make things worse. ("Don't just stand there, do something! Wait, no…don't just do something, stand there!")

The snide comment about this list is that for some evil projects, these traits might apply from day one. Fair enough. Status quo in one organization is a fire drill in another. While it is management's job to minimize chaos—hopefully to the point that it's only specific problems at specific times and not a general trait of the work environment—we all know that sometimes management isn't able to do their job (insert second snide comment here). That said, the advice in this chapter applies equally well no matter how often you have to apply it. But if you find yourself reading this chapter often, it might be time to look for a new manager or a new place to work.

The list of difficult situations

The rough guide at the beginning of this chapter can be applied in all of the following situations, though the domains and skills involved may differ. For reference, I've included some of the possible responses to consider (fodder for step 5, "Explore alternatives," in the rough guide) for each of these situations:

- **Oversight or realization.** Most of what goes wrong on projects are oversights. Some decision made days ago didn't pan out and now something doesn't work. The problem is that the schedule remains—something new needs to be done. Possible responses: change the requirements, change the schedule to reimplement (cut the next-lowest-priority feature), or if necessary, explore new design alternatives. If you did design exploration (see Chapters 5 and 6), there may be a good fallback alternative design that's already well understood.

- **You or your team is forced to do something stupid.** This can be the result of a decision by management or a client who refuses to acknowledge an aspect of the problem. This is frustrating because you know better, but you don't have enough power to prevent it. Possible responses: recognize you may be in a management trap. If you do manage to succeed, you'll be put in the same situation again in the future. If you fail, you may be blamed for never believing. So, if this is a chronic problem, you need to invest more in managing up (see Chapter 16). Prioritize your objections, have specific recommendations, and use your political and negotiation skills (see "Conflict resolution and negotiation," later in this chapter) to work toward a compromise. You won't win, but until you find better management, you can protect your team. Try to isolate the stupidity to a feature or milestone where it will do the least damage (see the upcoming section "Damage control").

- **Failing schedule or resource shortage.** Whenever the likelihood of making the next date drops below 75%, the dates are no longer probable. It's possible, but not probable. Possible responses: see Chapters 2 and 14. It's all about exit criteria and its implied priorities. Either you cut features, add time to the schedule, or ignore all known logic, write up your last will and testament, and try to make the date anyway. Try to consider if schedule risk can be isolated and moved off the critical path, or if it can be traded into a future milestone for something deemed less important. Brook's Law[3] implies that adding people in the face of slipping schedules can have less value than expected.

---

3   Brook's Law, roughly, is that adding people has two negative effects: first, it takes time for them to get up to speed; second, the overhead required to get anything done increases. So, even in the best situations, adding additional people will have diminishing value. But there are exceptions.

- **Quality is low.** You won't know if quality is low if you don't know what the quality is. If you're using daily builds or have some frequently tracked metrics (bug count, etc.), you'll know early on. There are many kinds of poor quality: fragile code, failure to fulfill requirements, poor performance, or instability. There are also many causes of poor quality: engineering (core development practices), process (check-ins and tools), or schedule/planning. Possible responses: firm up the team's understanding of what good quality is and set daily goals for it (see Chapter 15). Sacrifice something (features, time) to afford more quality. Often, the best move is to slow the rate of progress until the quality bar has been met and everyone understands how to meet it, then accelerate the rate of progress again.

- **Direction change.** Management or the market itself can demand change. This isn't necessarily bad (it might even be a form of progress)—it's just unlikely to be fun. Budget cuts or new high-level goals may be involved. Possible responses: can the change be sequestered to certain components? Separate out what specs or parts of specs are still viable, and keep them in the development pipeline (see Chapter 14), then prioritize what needs to be changed. Make sure you're not being dictated to: being told, "Do X" is not the same as being told, "We have to generate 10% more revenue." The former is a directive; the latter is a problem to solve. Fight to find out what the problems are, and get involved by proposing palatable solutions (see "Conflict resolution and negotiation," later in this chapter).

- **Team or personnel issues.** One or more people are upset about something, and it's negatively impacting the team. This could be personal ("I can't stand working with Fred") or it could be systemic ("I hate how we do code reviews"). Possible responses: start by talking one-on-one to people involved. Ask them what's going on and what can be done (by you or by them) to make things better. Flush out the problem and let people vent. Seek out causes, not just symptoms (see "Conflict resolution and negotiation," later in this chapter).

- **Disagreement and conflict.** People openly disagree about what should be done (which can be healthy), but the disagreements are now preventing progress from taking place. More time is spent debating and constantly revisiting what should be done, instead of doing it. In extreme cases, different factions are secretly working in different directions. Possible responses: see the section "Conflict resolution and negotiation," later in this chapter.

- **Lack of faith.** The team just doesn't believe in the project direction. They are doing the work, getting along, and not actively disagreeing, but they think the ship is heading straight for the iceberg. Possible alternatives: see if they're right. If they're not, use influence (see Chapter 16) to help build support behind the direction. Start small: who has the most faith? How can you cultivate her belief and send it out to the rest of the team? Try setting smaller goals for the team and building momentum. Go door-to-door and ask for people's trust: "Look, I know you don't believe in this, but I do. Is there any way I can convince you to get behind this? If not, is it possible for you to trust me anyway, at least for the next week?"

- **Threats of mutiny.** This is the violent, acute form of lack of faith. A moment is reached where the team's threshold of frustration has been surpassed and they respond poorly to every new problem that surfaces, no matter how small it is. More so, people complain more about meta-problems (e.g., "Why does management/test/ marketing keep doing this?") than actual problems. If action is not taken, veterans may support the complaints, and small or symbolic acts of subversion will start taking place (e.g., certain bugs may become suddenly difficult to fix). Someone has to address this head-on and defuse it. Publicly acknowledge the matter, make a list of all the complaints, and visibly address at least some of the items from the list.

What can make these situations difficult is not the situation itself, but the context. The later in the schedule a problem happens, and the weaker the morale of the team (or the PM), the harder it is to deal with. Toward the end, there are fewer available moves to solve the problem, and the stakes in making moves are much higher. Sometimes, this fact makes it easy to end debates by pointing to the timeline. During end-game, many kinds of issues become prohibitively expensive to change, and it becomes easier to argue for living with the problem now and fixing it in the next release (or milestone). But note that defaulting out of a problem doesn't solve it; it just means you have an easy path for refusing to deal with the problem, which can be the right thing or the wrong thing for the project.

It's important to realize that difficult situations often have fuzzy beginnings and endpoints. No red warning light will go off on your desk telling you that morale is low or that an oversight has just been made. You have to look for it, and even if you do, it won't always be 100% clear what's going on. And then if there is a problem and you decide to take action, you might only be able to mitigate it and minimize its impact—it might not be entirely solvable. This means you have to manage minor issues caused by the problem for weeks or even months on end. (For example, managing two programmers or testers who just don't get along well. You can help patch things over, but you can't fix their conflict completely.) So, part of what to do when things go wrong is to dedicate time for maintaining chronic problems at a tolerable level. The more problems you're managing in this way, the more time you'll need to dedicate to maintenance and damage control.

Make practice and training difficult

Good training for project managers must include exercises that simulate putting PMs into these situations. I've learned that teaching people ideal cases might be the best way to learn basic theories, but improving project management skill and making theories understandable is achieved only by teaching failure and challenge cases. The most successful courses I teach focus on situations and challenge exercises, rather than formulas and concepts. Thinking cynically again, the challenge of managing projects isn't sailing in calm, open waters with clear skies. Instead, the challenge is in knowing how to juggle, prioritize, and respond to all the unexpected and difficult things that you're confronted with. (Although perhaps the ultimate skill for PMs is to change rough seas into calm water before the team sets sail.)

So, if you work with or manage other project managers, and you don't have opportunities for proper training, it's critical to use these difficult situations as learning opportunities when they occur. As stressful and frustrating as they are, the experience of going through them is pure gold for the next project—if you take the time afterward to review them. Stewart Brand once said, "In haste, mistakes cascade. With deliberation, mistakes instruct."[4] Even in the worst disaster, PMs still have control over how they respond. And unless the situation is literally fatal for the team, there is always the opportunity to learn from something after it's happened.

Regarding other difficult situations: there are many different ways to break down the possible problems you might encounter. If you're looking for bigger lists to learn from, the best single source I've seen is Chapter 3 of *Rapid Development*, by Steve McConnell (Microsoft Press, 1996). The second best source is the antipatterns catalog (*http://c2.com/cgi/wiki?AntiPatternsCatalog*), which is actually a more interesting and colorful read, but it's harder to apply and isn't consistently well written (which isn't surprising because it's a wiki system).

Take responsibility

Taking responsibility for something doesn't make it your fault: it means that you will be accountable for resolving the situation. Many people fear taking responsibility because they don't want to be held accountable and put at risk for reprimand. A good manager should have the opposite disposition: in matters involving his team, he should seek out responsibility and use it to help the team and the project succeed. If relieving an engineer or tester of fear of blame will get me a better solution, or the same solution faster, I'd gladly take the trade. If my own manager is any good, taking responsibility for a problem might earn me praise. By lending real responsibility to the problem, I instantly make the problem less dangerous to the project (see the later section "Roles and clear authority").

This idea of taking responsibility can extend not just to blame or failure, but to all relations with other people. As Larry Constantine wrote in *Beyond Chaos: The Expert Edge in Managing Software Development* (Addison-Wesley, 2001):

---

4 This is part of Brand's Pace Law. From *Edge* magazine's annual question, which, in 2004, was "What is your law?" See *http://www.edge.org/q2004/page6.html#brand*.

Instead of wondering why some person is so difficult, I find it more useful to ask myself why I am having difficultly with that person. It is, of course, usually far easier to spot the mote in a colleague's eye than to see the macaroni in your own, but every frustrating encounter with a difficult person is an opportunity to learn more about yourself. Over the long term, you may find yourself meeting fewer and fewer people who are difficult for you to handle.

This is especially valuable in difficult situations when other people might be more sensitive or prone to losing their tempers. If you can rely on your own maturity and wisdom to overcome other people's fears or irrationalities, you become capable of leading a project to success in spite of the frustrating or counterproductive behavior of others.

Taking responsibility, even for failures, is always a growth opportunity. By volunteering your own hide, you give yourself power because you are placing yourself in the middle of the situation. Deflecting blame or dodging responsibility might help you avoid the short-term problem of cleaning up a mess, or answering to senior managers on a difficult matter, but it also eliminates any opportunity to learn something or to grow and demonstrate your abilities. You have to be willing to get burned if you want to develop the skill of putting out fires.

At a practical level, use your willingness to take responsibility to empower others during crises. Add the following phrase to your playbook for working with others: "I'm not sure how this happened, I don't care right now. We can sort it out later, and when we do, I'll help take responsibility for what's happened. But because it did happen, we need to do X, Y, and Z, and we need to do it now. Can you help me figure out how to do X, Y, and Z?"

Alternatively, in some situations, the most powerful thing you can do is to give your responsibility away. (In Chapter 12, I'll cover the importance of trust and how delegation is one major form of it that managers can use to the project's advantage.) In tough times, reconfirming your trust in someone's abilities might have more of a positive effect than any intellectual or technical contribution you could make: "Sally, look. I trust you. I know this issue is hard, but you're the expert. However you think we should deal with it is the opinion I'll stand behind. But here's my feedback. Think it over. If you still disagree, we'll go your way."

Damage control

If enough problems occur at the same time, or if something truly devastating happens, the first move must be damage control. This means that from the first moment onward, your top priority is to return the project to an acceptable state. Imagine being the pilot of a 747 that has just lost all engine power. Until you've restored power, not much else matters. All of your energy is focused on solving the one problem that all other problems are dependent on. You're in damage-control mode.

What pilots and captains are trained to do in damage-control situations is to diagnose the problem, and try to isolate both the symptoms and the causes. Aircraft pilots and astronauts usually have a specific procedure for doing this for each major situation that might occur (often these procedures are kept in a book because there are many of them). The idea is that when the shit has really hit the fan, there won't be time to invent a procedure—and maybe not even enough time to follow one. So, when pilots do find themselves in an emergency, they begin the diagnostic sequence and systematically work at the problem until they find a resolution (or, if they fail, crash).

As a project manager, you will eventually find yourself in a damage-control situation. There won't be time to explore alternatives or consider options. There will be something very important that is very broken, and it won't be clear how it can possibly be resolved. To handle this situation, follow this list:

- **Call an all-hands meeting.** Word spreads quickly through a team when something very important is clearly very wrong. The longer you wait to address it, the more dissention and fear the team will have when you do. Take the bull by the horns and call a meeting, or send high-priority email out to the team. Briefly explain the situation and that you are working on it. If possible, explain what you're doing over the next 24 hours (see "Apply the rough guide," earlier in this chapter), and define the next point in time when you will have an update. Don't hide from big problems: your team will sense that something is wrong no matter how good you are at hiding it from them.

- **If people are in disagreement, find the point of agreement.** We'll cover this more in the next section. But if you are in a room full of people who seem to only disagree about what's going on or what should be done, take control and reset the discussion. Bring it back to the last point of agreement: "Do we all agree that our goals are A, B, and C, and in that order?" Once you have a point of agreement, however simple it is, work forward into the problems you're facing. Take issues one at a time and don't allow the discussion to move past them until they've been resolved or assigned to someone outside of the meeting who will drive them.

- **What is the most recent known good state for the project and the team?** If the damage you're controlling is technical, go back through the daily builds (which you should keep an archive of) to find the last good build. Put it on the table to reset the project back to that state. This might be faster than continuing the project from the state that it is in. Programmers can manually reapply changes that are lost, and you can apply higher controls to eliminate the cause of the problem. This is a radical move, but it assures stability and confidence at the expense of schedule time.

- **Can the problem be isolated?** Think of a boat that is currently on fire. Can the fire be contained? Can the most critical parts of the ship be protected against the fire? Think about how you can sequester the problem and prevent it from impacting the most critical parts of your project. This may require sacrificing less important commitments or trading resources from one part of the team to another. It might require the short-term assistance of other people from other areas to help isolate and contain the problem, but because it will assure a stable state for the project, it's worth the tradeoff.

- **Can resources be applied to help with the damage?** In some cases, you can spend your way (in terms of money or staff) out of a problem. Consider a real disaster such as an earthquake or tornado: you could spend money to relocate the project or to buy new equipment immediately to help keep the project alive while longer-term solutions are found. If you discover a large gap in quality assurance coverage, you can sometimes outsource for additional staff to cover currently unmanned test cases or build processes. Throwing money or other resources at things can sometimes work if your aim is good and it's the right kind of target.

Conflict resolution and negotiation

"What should worry us is not the number of people that oppose us, but how good their reasons are for doing so."

—Alain de Botton

Settling differences is something managers must do all the time. The fact that negotiation appears only in this chapter doesn't imply that having to resolve disagreements means something has gone wrong. On the contrary, a healthy team should have enough opinions that disagreements occur regularly. As long as people are respectfully debating the merits of different ideas, disagreements provide alternative points of view and lead to progress. What's important is how people treat each other when they disagree, how those disagreements are resolved, and whether debates are converted into positive action.

That said, in times of crisis, the ability to resolve disagreements is essential. By far, the best resource for learning the right attitude and skills to do this is the short book *Getting to Yes*, by Roger Fisher et al. (Penguin Books, 1991).[5] I didn't find this book until later in my career, and reading it gave me a better understanding of what happened in my previous negotiating experiences. I realized negotiation took place in many different forms. Sometimes, I was helping two people on the team resolve an issue. Other times, I was one of the two people in disagreement, but without the benefit of a third party interested in helping resolve the conflict, I was forced to act as negotiator. In all these cases, I found one basic approach that worked for me, which I've outlined here:

- **Find the point of unification.** Two people, no matter how much they disagree, agree about some things: the world is round, the sky is blue, the project needs to be on time. Find the important points of unification and agreement and use those to start any discussion you have. You want to start any negotiation with positive momentum.

---

5   Also see *Bargaining for Advantage*, by Richard Shell (Penguin Books, 2000). It provides more tactics and techniques than *Getting to Yes*, and it makes for a great second book.

Address any contentious issues inside a framework of mutual interest and shared perspective. Make a Venn diagram of things that interest party A and things that interest party B, and note the intersections. If there are no intersections, something is missing: why would they have any basis to disagree if they have no shared interests?

- **Recognize personality conflicts and then ignore them.** It's very easy to fall into the trap of allowing someone's personality traits to distract you from the goal of negotiation, especially if you are one of the two parties. Instead of trying to find situations that benefit everyone, it's easy to slide into seeing negotiation as a competition: you want to win, or worse, make the "opponent" lose. This is a complete distraction from your real goals. If you find you don't like the person you're negotiating with, or the people whose conflict you're trying to resolve, find a way to separate those feelings from the task at hand (or delegate your role to someone else). Focus on how the project is served by resolving the issue, and make that your motivation.

- **Look for mutual interest.** If you lay out the possible ways to resolve a situation, you will find choices that benefit both sides. They become visible by framing the discussion around interests and not adversarial positions. A position is a set of specific demands ("I will eat only chocolate cake"). An interest is a higher-level goal ("I want a tasty and satisfying dessert"). Interests can be satisfied in many ways, but positions have few solutions. Often, people who are in conflict are unaware of each other's interests, and their energy is spent battling different positions. Yet, interests are easier to work with than positions. Force people to talk about interests and reach agreement (or at least understanding) at that level first, before discussing positions. List interests for both sides and relate them back to the point of unification.

- **Be strong but supple.** If you have a hard position that you need to maintain, look for other, less-important positions you are flexible on. If you can't slip your dates, can you change your features? If you can't give more time, can you give more money? Know what points you are flexible on and can work with, and which ones are fixed. The better you understand the person you are negotiating with, the better you will be at offering things that are of value to them, but cost you little. It's safe to say that if you are flexible on nothing, you probably do not fully understand your interests (perhaps because management has informed you only of their position, not of their interests).

- **Know the alternatives.** Never enter negotiation without understanding what it will cost you to walk away from the table, and what it will cost them to walk away from the table. *Getting to Yes* calls this your BATNA—Best Alternative To Negotiated Agreement. The better your BATNA is relative to your counterparts', the more bargaining power you probably have. For example, let's say you're stranded in the desert with a dozen people, and you have the only gallon of fresh water. Fred offers $5 for it. You could say no and find a better offer from the others, but Fred can only negotiate with you. Fred has few reasonable alternatives, while you have many. Fred could be the best negotiator in the world, but this is irrelevant if you are aware of the superiority of your options, relative to his.[6]

- **Use persuasion and argument.** In most cases, the interests and desires of both parties are based on subjective opinions about the relative value of things. This means that if you can develop a true understanding of one party's feelings, you can possibly persuade them that one aspect of the situation is more (or less) desirable than they thought. Being persuasive is a skill: it combines charisma, communication abilities, logic, and psychology—all things that can be learned with experience and effort. Try to be tactful when persuading others, and focus your efforts on the points most important to progress.

The act of negotiating is just a special form of discussion. Get the right people in the room (see "Apply the rough guide," earlier in this chapter), set an agenda that includes discussion of issues and interests, and then work to find possible alternatives that resolve them. If the people in conflict are in the same organization, you can rely heavily on the project's goals to frame what should be the highest-level interests for everyone involved (the point of unification). Proposals and counterproposals are made until a resolution is reached.

If the people in conflict are in two different organizations, things become more complex—there may be less trust and weaker relationships between the people involved. The first goal has to be to replicate something similar to project goals: why are we in business together? What are the mutual beneficial reasons for us to exchange work or resources? As a rule of thumb, this should be done when that relationship begins (contracts are a simple form of this kind of agreement). It clarifies everyone's interests and provides a baseline to refer to should conflicts or disagreements arise later on (as well as minimizing the chances of those disagreements forming in the first place). But in lieu of a preemptive agreement, it can be done after the fact. It will be more difficult to do because trust and goodwill won't be high, but it's the only path toward finding a resolution.

Roles and clear authority

There are two lessons I learned from playing competitive sports. First, real trust is earned only when challenges surface and are overcome. It's only when there is a dispute, where someone is upset and the truth comes out, that relationships have the opportunity to grow. Second, good teams function effectively because each individual understands his own role as well as the role of every other person on the team. Things go well when each

---

6   This is where negotiations become complex. If Fred doesn't believe you're willing to use your options, he will see your BATNA differently. He may tell you so ("You won't let me sit here and die, will you?"). Negotiations become complex when people bluff, lie about their interests, or lack trust in the other party. In less ridiculous situations, things tend to normalize as BATNAs are executed. If a business really can get a better deal, eventually they will. If they can't, they'll give in.

individual can depend on the contributions of others to the point that he can comfortably focus on his own tasks. A lead guitarist in a rock band can't do a great solo if the bassist and drummer aren't providing a reliable rhythm structure for him to work in. It is the same with forwards and point guards in basketball, or quarterbacks and offensive linemen in American football. And, of course, it's definitely true for programmers, testers, and others on technical teams.

The ability to depend on each other in team activity becomes more important as pressure rises. Things are likely to break down, and people have the first opportunity to fail, feel afraid, or blame others when things go wrong. Complex work is often highly interdependent, meaning that Fred knows he will fail at completing his test pass if Sara doesn't get her code working on time. He has good reason to worry: he hasn't worked with her enough to build real trust in her ability to deliver in tough situations.

So, when the pressure is on, it's common to see immature teams struggle with their roles. Individuals will question the ability of others on the team and do what they can to protect themselves from the possibility of failures caused by others (often wasting energy in the process). Even experienced people may do this if they are working on teams made up of people who haven't built much trust in each other.

This means much of what the PM must do during tough times is reinforce the role structure of the team. Remind everyone of what others are depending on them to do and what they should be expecting others to do for them. As a leader, it's up to you to identify those who are becoming rattled, and remind them of how confident you are in the team. Be aware of who feels vulnerable, and work to change their perception. Holding a team together is not something done with big speeches or grand gestures. Instead, just go to people and make sure they feel connected to what's happening and have what they need to believe they can contribute to it successfully.

In some cases, people need support to play their roles. The PM should back up people who are trying to do their job but are receiving unfair questioning from others. Often, this happens around role divisions, such as between programming and testing or engineering and marketing. So, when you overhear an unfair comment, such as "My god, Bob must be an idiot if he still hasn't finished that test pass," you should say, if appropriate, "Steve, Bob is behind now because the dev team was behind all last week. Maybe you can help him out like the test team helped you guys out back then, hmmm?" Be the conscience of the team and keep people honest when necessary.

If there is real incompetence somewhere (i.e., Bob is actually an idiot), it's up to the PM to engage managers directly, and make sure the problem is identified to those who are in the best position to do something about it. (Base the feedback on the role the person is supposed to be playing and what parts of it aren't happening. It may not be incompetence as much as a miscommunication about roles or commitments.) But most of the time, the problems of a team under stress are communication, honest mistakes, lack of trust, and role failures, not pure acts of stupidity or inaptitude.

Everyone should know who the decision maker is

In tough times there needs to be a clear line of decision-making authority. If the team is deadlocked and a tough call has to be made in the next five minutes, with the fate of the project hinged on the outcome, who should do it? In military organizations, the chain of command exists to make sure the answer to this question is always clear. Because decisions will be made under great stress and with short timelines, they need a management structure that is indisputable and can be relied on to execute effectively, regardless of how confusing a situation might be. Much of the training soldiers receive is focused on trusting the chain of command. For projects, the rule of thumb should be as follows: the more pressure and the higher the stakes, the less doubt there should be over who has authority.

On projects, the chain of command for tough decisions should hinge on management—most specifically, project management. If the challenge at hand involves business, technical, and requirements issues, no one expert (marketing, engineering) is going to have the best overall perspective. However, the PM, given the breadth of her involvement in the project, has the strongest understanding of the different considerations and possible impacts of these tradeoff decisions. If multiple people do PM tasks, there simply needs to be a clear process for who decides what and who gets to be involved. The role discussions described in Chapter 9 should include coverage of decision-making authority, and they can be used to clarify other authority issues.

But remember that the decision maker, whoever it is, always has the right to delegate or collaborate. What's critical then is not that Bob or Michelle or Mr. VP makes all the tough decisions, but that everyone in the organization knows who to go to when certain kinds of decisions need to be made, well before a crisis occurs. This will increase the speed of decision making on a team, which can stop minor threats from becoming major disasters.

An emotional toolkit: pressure, feelings about feelings, and the hero complex

This last section of this chapter will cover emotion-related topics relevant when working on teams where something has gone very wrong. My goal here isn't to provide you with a treatise on stress management, but instead to provide a primer of issues you will face and the considerations needed to overcome them.

Pressure

The best definition I found for the word *pressure* is this:

> Pressure (n): A compelling, constraining influence or force.

The key word here is *constraint*. To be under pressure means that there are constraints that can't be moved and must be dealt with. This might be time, resources, the raw difficulty of the situation, or all of the above. The existence of these constraints means that there are fewer choices available and even less time to solve whatever the problem is.

But when people use the word *pressure*, as in "I'm under pressure," they mean there is some perceived threat of failing to overcome the constraint. A pressure situation, such as a political debate or taking a last-second game-winning shot, means that something important is at stake that can easily be lost (or at least is believed to be so). There are often other people involved who will suffer if they fail to succeed, amplifying the sense of pressure on them.

What's important to realize about pressure is the different ways people respond to it. Each individual has different sensitivities and will feel more or less pressure in different situations. They will also have different ways of dealing or coping with it. For some, the best release of pressure or stress is physical activity; for others, it's humor. But, sadly, many people haven't yet figured out how to deal with these things.

During difficult situations, one additional task for leaders is to make sure there is support for different kinds of stress relief. If the team witnesses the leaders poking fun at their own stress responses ("When I get home, I'm grabbing a six-pack and taking the longest bath in history"), it allows others to follow suit. If the lead programmer invites other programmers to the gym (or the paintball arena) after work to blow off steam, others will have the chance to see if that helps them with their stress. Even those who don't participate will have the opportunity to consider what stress they're under and where the best place might be to release it. On the contrary, if leaders are repressive and deny their stress, pretending they don't feel it or don't need a form of release (typical stupid macho behavior), they make life harder for everyone else. Never let your team think that the need to release stress is a sign of weakness.

Watch out for the disguised threat, "Oh. Well, if you feel so stressed out that you need relief, maybe you shouldn't be on this team." And avoid the dismissive ridicule, "Oh, yoga? I guess that's OK if you need that much help." These come from managers who don't know what's good for them. Stress relief is often cheap or free, and it has no downside. Even if it doesn't help relieve stress, supporting people in pursuing it (or making it available to them for free) provides morale bonus points. I've seen smart managers bring massage therapists in during tough times, and go door-to-door, offering each person a 10-minute massage. It worked wonders: even those who didn't participate talked about it for days.

Natural and artificial pressure

Pressure is a force that management controls. Management's actions change the nature of pressure in several different ways, and managing a team through stressful times requires an understanding of them. There are four types of pressure: natural, artificial, positive, and negative (see Figure 11-1).

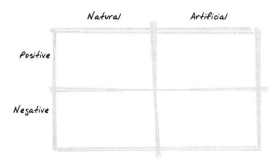

FIGURE 11-1. *The four kinds of pressure.*

I think of natural pressure as the feeling people have when a personally significant commitment they have made is at risk ("Oh, wait. I told Sam I'd have the demo working by 2 p.m."). If they believe in the commitment, and are emotionally invested in the quality of their work, they will, all on their own, increase their focus and energy level in response to pressure. I call it natural pressure because it comes directly from the work and the person's relationship to the work. In this situation, all leaders need to do is guide and protect that energy, and support the individuals on the team in their pursuit to meet their goals. This kind of pressure is generally positive because personal motivation and team needs are aligned. However, it can become negative if people feel guilt or shame about failing to meet their commitments, especially if others are causing the problems that led to those failures.

Artificial pressure is any tactic leaders perform to try and amplify the team's sense of pressure. This can be both positive and negative. The positive form is reward driven, where people are rewarded for working harder and raising their performance through tough times (e.g., raises, promotions, bonuses). Or, the additional work could be voluntary, where the leader asks (but doesn't demand) that the team work harder (perhaps with incentives like expensing dinner for those who stay late, or letting more people work from home). Sometimes, artificial pressure can take the form of a spirited team meeting, where the positive spirit behind the project is rekindled (perhaps generating some natural pressure for some of the team), and a new wave of energy is cultivated.

Negative forms of artificial pressure include scolding, guilt-tripping, or threatening as ways to get people to work harder. Sometimes, this involves leaders blaming the team for certain failures, and asking them to work harder to fix the problems that they may have caused. This is the stereotypical drill sergeant mentality: the team needs to be constantly disciplined and yelled at to perform at its best (or so the theory goes).

Most of the time, it's some combination of natural, artificial, positive, and negative forces that managers use to keep a team performing well. As much as I prefer using positive forces, sometimes it's only the careful use of negative forces that can bring a team around and get it focused again. On the whole, it's a careful balance and there's no formula for it. It's only through experience with managing teams, and observing human nature, that you get better at applying these kinds of forces. You'll find that most experienced managers have developed theories about the application of pressure. But all too often the theories aren't derived from diverse enough experiences to justify the confidence people have in them.

Formulations of pressure aside, it is clear that a team has limitations on how much pressure it can handle. Figure 11-2 shows a diagram adapted from Volume 1, *Systems Thinking*, of Gerald Weinberg's *Quality Software Management* (Dorset House, 1996). It shows a performance curve for teams working under pressure. For a time, most people and teams show improved performance as pressure increases. But over time, this relationship diminishes and then flattens out completely. When a team is at its maximum performance level (aka redlining or maxed), no amount of additional pressure will get the team to work harder, better, or faster. If the application of pressure continues, eventually the team (or individual) will snap and things will get much worse.

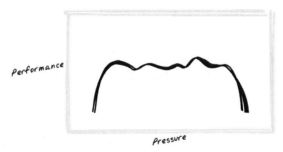

FIGURE 11-2. *There is a limit to the value of pressure in increasing performance.*

So, however you decide to use pressure to manage a team, be aware of the thresholds that you're working in. If the team is unresponsive, it might be that you need to apply a different kind of pressure, but it can also mean that the team is redlining, and no amount of management activity will get it to perform any better. It takes experience to recognize the difference. In short, people on a redlining team will have their heads down in the hallway and won't be smiling much. They'll seem nervous and tired at the same time.

They will wilt when asked to take on another task or make a minor change to something already completed. It's much more expensive to recover from burnout than slow the project down, so it's best to do the latter. Release some pressure by giving people an afternoon off, playing an impromptu game of touch football in the parking lot, or adjusting the workload or schedule to something sane.

Feelings about feelings

Before you skip past this section, assuming it's touchy-feely stuff that doesn't concern you, let me ask one question. Have you ever wondered why people behave differently under stress? If you don't care, or don't see the relevance to project management, feel free to move on. But I pity anyone who works for you. (See, guilt-tripping has its place.)

OK, that was unfair, but it worked. To reward you, let me tell you a precious nugget about human behavior. Virgina Satir, author of several books on psychology, has a simple model for helping explain why people are unpredictable. Simply put, sometimes when we feel a certain way (say, upset or hurt), we quickly have a second feeling about that first feeling, and it's that second feeling that we tend to act on. For example, let's say I tell you that you smell funny. This makes you feel sad. But perhaps you feel angry about the fact that I made you feel sad. So, instead of expressing your feelings of sadness, all you are able to do is express the secondary feeling of anger (Figure 11-3 shows a simple example of this). Later on, you might get around to realize the core feeling was sadness and then feel sad, but in the moment, it's all about your feelings in response to other feelings.

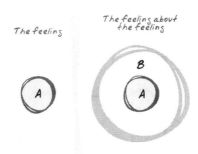

FIGURE 11-3. *The Satir model explains that the feelings we act on are not necessarily the core feelings we have.*

In Volume 1, *Systems Thinking* of *Quality Software Management*, Weinberg goes on to explain that Satir's model has other useful implications. Often, what causes that second feeling is a belief that we've been taught, which isn't consistent with healthy emotional behavior. Feeling angry about feeling sad is not a universal behavior for human beings: it's learned. In fact, according to Weinberg, our responses to many emotions are simply what we were exposed to in our own emotional development.

The funny thing about childhood development is that we all get hand-me-down belief and emotional systems. Most of the behaviors we follow are learned from our parents, who learned their behaviors from their parents, and so on. Until someone stops and examines the value of their behaviors and emotional responses, independent of where they learned them from, it's difficult to grow in emotional maturity—or even to know how emotionally mature and healthy we are. And worse, we potentially pass destructive or confused behavior on to others (e.g., our students, coworkers, friends, and children).

Some of the rules we learned might be good, and others might be bad. But simply because we historically respond in a certain way to something doesn't mean those responses are healthy for us or useful for making progress happen.

The lesson here for PMs is that sometimes the emotions you receive from people you are working with will not be related directly to the actions you have taken. You may point out a bug in someone's code and he'll get upset at you, even though you were polite and pointed out something important.

What you want to prevent from happening is a cascade of these nondirectly related feelings. Imagine if, in Figure 11-3, someone else responded to an expression of feeling B with a statement reflecting feeling C, further obscuring the real cause of the whole situation (feeling A). It's entirely possible to end up with a meeting of five people, all arguing and yelling, yet no one is in the same emotional context: they're all expressing and responding to different feelings about the actual topic of discussion (for example, think of your last family reunion).

Other notable writers on human emotion, such as Leo F. Buscaglia or John Bradshaw, go on to point out that the healthier and more emotionally mature a person is, the more aware he is of his own emotions and those of others, giving him a wider range of choices for how to respond to the emotions of others.[7] This implies that a leader in a crisis situation has better odds of success if she can see emotional patterns and make use of different ways to manage them.

The hero complex

There is one special kind of person when it comes to dealing with pressure: the person who has a hero complex. This is any individual who compulsively creates dangerous situations simply so he can resolve them. He may so depend on the thrill and challenges of extremely difficult situations that he will not do very much to prevent trouble from starting in the first place. In the minor form, it's simply someone who likes working in

---

7 For an informal introduction to basic emotional dynamics, try Leo F. Buscaglia's wonderful *Living, Loving & Learning* (Ballantine Books, 1985). For a more formal introduction, try *Bradshaw On: The Family*, by John Bradshaw (Health Communications, 1990).

risky situations. In the major form, a person with a hero complex may be putting the project at risk, or even trying to sabotage it.

When things go wrong on a project, people with hero-complex tendencies will thrive. Whereas some people wilt or shy away from stepping into the fire, these people jump right in, as if the project is finally getting interesting to them. Having people on the team with minor forms of the hero complex is great because they seek out fires and put them out, but they will rarely cause fires of their own. It's the full-blown cases of hero complex that you have to watch out for because their behavior may deliberately cause the project to become unstable. Or more commonly, they will fight to the death against actions that will make high-risk situations impossible.

The hero complex most commonly develops in people who started their careers in start-ups or very small (volatile) firms. Heroic and superhuman efforts are often required just to make ends meet because such organizations rarely have enough resources to match their ambitions.[8] If things work out well, the survivors look on their heroic efforts as a large part of why they succeeded. In that original context, they're right. However, there are bad habits hiding behind this logic: just because heroics were needed in situation A doesn't mean heroics are needed, or even beneficial, in situations B, C, and D.

The hero complex has several motivating beliefs, which are explained or refuted in the following list:

- **Planning is unnecessary: I've proved it.** Because the hero has experience succeeding without specs or schedules, he believes those things are never necessary. This belief fails because of how different projects can be. A 5-person, 1-month project has fundamentally different constraints and risks than a 200-person, 12-month effort. It may demand different approaches to management, planning, and engineering. Part of this (flawed) belief is the notion that the hero has experienced everything there is to experience about software development. This hubris blinds him from the specific problems in each project that demand a unique balance of management, process, and team structuring to resolve. *Always* and *never* are not valid answers to the question of when a process is necessary—it always depends on the details of the project.

- **I work for me alone.** The most selfish motivating force for hero behavior is simply that the hero likes being the hero. She likes it so much that she doesn't care what gets put at risk or destroyed in the process of her playing the role. Symptoms of this are destructive competition with peers or an indifference to the work of others (or even the goals of the project). She may not realize that her desire to be the hero has any possible implications (those downsides are largely for other people, not for her). In

---

8 A more favorable way to look at start-ups is that the creative force needed to innovate comes only from a small, tight group of people working hard. A "shortage" of people is desirable because it gives everyone tremendous autonomy. *Hackers and Painters* by Paul Graham (O'Reilly, 2004) makes interesting arguments about the rewards and risks of start-up work.

some cases, she may not even understand why her heroic efforts aren't always received in the way she expected. ("Didn't I rescue the cute, fuzzy animals from getting burned when I ran into the building to save them?" "Yes, but you also set the fire.")

- **The pseudo-hero.** I've seen this only a handful of times. The idea is that by making management think something is much worse than it is, and then, magically, making it much less worse than it seemed, an individual can cultivate the perception of being very good at whatever he does (our hero!). The more ignorant or uninterested management is, the easier this is to do. It tends to work only a few times before peers or others catch on. This isn't exactly the hero complex because the person in question doesn't actually want to do heroic things, he just wants to be perceived as being heroic.

- **Heroes have their foolish kings.** Most of the situations that create heroic opportunities are management failures. If the project is weeks behind, or bad strategy choices force huge design changes, only management is responsible. Sometimes, you will see codependent relationships between management and engineering, where management depends on engineering heroics to cover (and hide) their mistakes. So, instead of admitting to their own failings, they depend on rewarding the brilliant, but possibly avoidable, heroic work of the engineering team. Meanwhile, engineering loves the thrill of those problems and doesn't really want management to get better at planning or managing risk, despite how often they complain about management. An entire codependency culture is created, which depends on heroes and rewards both the creation of risks and their resolution.

- **The failure complex.** This is different from the hero complex but is related enough to make it onto this list. Some people don't feel comfortable unless there are things to complain about. When presented with a challenge, they feel more comfortable finding excuses for failing and convincing people of their validity, instead of investing that energy in rising to the challenge and trying to succeed. They prefer to blame rather than to win. These folks come in clusters from bad teams (or families) where blame and denial were more important than anything else. They need someone to demonstrate for them that there's a healthier way to go about living.

The best way to minimize the risks of hero culture is to have an active management team. If someone believes that the difference is important, it's easy to tell whether an 80-hour workweek is the result of a truly heroic crisis response or a self-inflicted chain of incompetence. As a PM, you may not have enough influence to make the team aware of its hero-driven habits, but the only way to know is to try (see Chapter 16).

It's only by someone calling attention to this behavior that there is any possibility of it changing. Minimally, push hard for a policy of review around heroic acts. Whenever a hero does her thing, there should be a public discussion of what could have been done to avoid it in the first place. Credit can be given to the hero, but rewards should also be distributed for those who find a way to prevent that kind of situation from occurring again in the future.

Summary

- No matter what you do, things will go wrong.

- If you can stay calm and break problems down into pieces, you can handle many difficult situations. (Remember the rough guide.)

- There are some common situations to expect, which include oversights, being forced to do stupid things, resource shortages, low quality, direction changes, personnel issues, and threats of mutiny.

- Difficult times are learning opportunities. Make sure you and your team take the time to examine what happened and how it could have been avoided.

- Taking responsibility for situations, regardless of who caused them, always helps to expedite resolving the problem.

- In extreme situations, go into damage-control mode. Do whatever it takes to get the project to a known and stable state.

- Negotiation is useful not only in a crisis situation, but also in management. Good negotiators work from people's interests, not their positions.

- Have clear lines of authority at all times. People should know who has decision-making power before a crisis occurs.

- People respond to pressure in different ways. Be observant and open in how you help the team deal with the different kinds of pressure.

Exercises

A. Walk around the office and find five things that could go wrong. For each, describe how you'd handle the problem if you were charged with fixing it. Who would need to be in the room to fix the problem? What would you do to fix the problem? What would you do if you were not in a position of authority?

B. Pick a project you were involved in before, in a role other than program manager, that went off the rails. Who needed to be involved to fix it? Who needed to be told about how you were going to fix it? Who needed to be told afterward? What was done well? How could it have been handled better? What could you change in your organization to reduce the chances of it happening again?

C. You are the program manager for a contractually obligated but internally disfavored software development project. One of your lead engineers, who used somewhat gnarly code that few people could understand, was laid off without warning. Your schedule has not changed. How would you manage the situation?

D. You are the CEO of a Fortune 500 company. CNN informs you that in one hour, a videotape will be broadcast in which several of your company's vice presidents will be heard making offensive comments about other employees, the company in general, and your leadership abilities. What do you do?

E. You are the project manager for an upcoming Xbox game, with a $20 million budget to support 50 staff and all the project's expenses for the 12-month schedule. To speed completion, you made a decision to buy a component for the project, rather than developing internally. Half way through the project you learn, from a reliable source, that the vendor will probably have to delay their delivery date by a year; however, the vendor has not actually told you this yet and insists that everything is fine. Tomorrow you are scheduled to present a project review to your executives. How do you handle this potential crisis?

F. You are the director of FEMA (Federal Emergency Management Agency). A major American city has just been flooded by the catastrophic failure of an upriver dam. Fifty thousand people are stranded in (and on top of) houses and offices, with no power, no way to get power, and declining food supplies. Your communication network is not working. What do you do?

G. One week into development, space aliens attack your office and your entire programming staff is hit with an alien space ray that makes them 50% less talented. You are the only witness to the event, as the ray erased the staff's memory of the event. What do you do with your schedule? Do you fire the staff? How honest would you be with your managers or clients?

H. What was the biggest crisis you've dealt with at work or in your life? What emotions did you go through and how did they impact how you handled the situation? Were you aware of how you were feeling in the moment, or only afterward? What does this suggest about how you handle crisis?

I. Here is a hypothesis: if you work on a project where nothing has ever gone wrong, it means one of two things: either you are doing work that is too easy for you, or things are going wrong, but you are ignoring them. What is your opinion?

PART THREE MANAGEMENT

CHAPTER TWELVE

Why leadership is based on trust

I **have had more than a dozen managers.** Many were forgettable and some were awful. But those I admired took time to earn my trust. They wanted my best work, and they knew this was possible only if I could rely on them on a daily basis. This didn't mean they'd do whatever I asked or yield to my opinions by default, but it did mean that their behavior was predictable. More often than not they were up front with me about their commitments, motivations, and expectations. I knew where I stood, what my and their roles were, and how much support was available from them for what I needed to do.

As a leader on a team, everything depends on what assumptions people can make of you. When you say "I will get this done by tomorrow" or "I will talk to Sally and get her to agree with this," others will make silent calculations about the probability that what you say will be true. Over time, if you serve your team well, those odds should be very high. They will take you at your word and place their trust in you.

Although movies portray leadership as a high-drama activity—with heroes running into burning buildings or bravely fighting alone against hordes of enemies—real leadership is about very simple, practical things. Do what you say and say what you mean. Admit when you're wrong. Enlist the opinions and ideas of others in decisions that impact them. If you can do these things more often than not, you will earn the trust of the people you work with. When a time comes where you must ask them to do something unpleasant or that they don't agree with, their trust in you will make your leadership possible.

This implies that to be a good leader, you do not need to be the best programmer, planner, architect, communicator, joke teller, designer, or anything else. All that is required is that you make trust an important thing to cultivate, and go out of your way to share it with the people around you. Therefore, to be a good leader, you must learn how to find, build, earn, and grant trust to others—as well as learn how to cultivate trust in yourself.

Building and losing trust

Trust (n): Firm reliance on the integrity, ability, or character of a person.

> **"Trust is at the core of all meaningful relationships. Without trust there can be no giving, no bonding, no risk-taking."**
>
> — *Terry Mizrahi, Director of ECCO (Education Center for Community Organizations)*

As an experiment, I asked a sampling of acquaintances who they trust in their current places of work, and why. The answers were roughly the same: trust is earned by people who do their jobs well, are committed to the goals of the project, treat people fairly, and behave consistently through tough times. Not a single person mentioned whether they liked these people or would want to invite them over for dinner. It seems that trust cuts beneath other personality traits. We can trust people we do not like or do not wish to spend time with.

Unlike other attributes about people, trust has little to do with personal preference. We don't choose who to trust on the basis of superficial things. Instead, there is a deeper set of calculations we make about who we can depend on. If I asked you who you would trust to save your life in a dangerous situation, you would pick people very differently than if I asked you who you'd want to go to the movies with. There is no obligation for personal chemistry and reliability to be connected to each other in any way.

But to examine trust in the context of projects, we need to break down the concept into workable pieces. One simple unit of trust is a commitment. A commitment, or promise, is the simplest kind of contract between two people about something they both agree to do.

Trust is built through commitment

When you make a new friend, and he tells you he'll meet you somewhere, you take it on faith that he'll be where he says, when he says. But if two or three times in a row he stands you up, and you end up watching a movie or standing in a club alone, your trust in him will decline. In effect, he's broken his commitments to you. If it continues, your perception will change. You will no longer see him as reliable, and you will question your trust in him in matters of importance.

According to Watts S. Humphrey's *Managing the Software Process* (Addison-Wesley Professional, 1989), one of the central elements of well-managed projects is the leader's ability to commit to her work, and to work to meet her commitments. Humphrey believes this is so important that he precisely defined the elements of effective commitments. His list, with a few modifications, follows.

The elements of effective commitment

1. The person making the commitment does so willingly.
2. The commitment is not made lightly; that is, the work involved, the resources, and the schedule are carefully considered.
3. There is agreement between the parties on what is to be done, by whom, and when.
4. The commitment is openly and publicly stated.
5. The person responsible tries to meet the commitment, even if help is needed.
6. Prior to the committed date, if something changes that impacts either party relative to the commitment, advance notice is given and a new commitment is negotiated.

There are two things of particular interest here. First, commitments work in two ways. The two people involved are mutually committed. If Cornelius commits to Rupert that he will walk Rupert's dog while he's out of town, both parties are bound to respect the other's interests. Cornelius should never have to travel the 25 city blocks to Rupert's apartment, intending to walk Rover in Central Park, only to find Rupert lying on the couch watching television ("Oh, sorry. I meant to call you yesterday—my trip was canceled."). Each party's trust is granted to the other in a trust exchange, and the expectation is that the trust will be respected—not violated or forgotten. Allowing someone to waste his time or money is a violation of trust.

Second, we make commitments all the time. In every conversation we have in which we ask or are asked to do something, and agree to a timeline for it, we're making a commitment. This includes simple statements such as, "Hey, I'll call you after lunch" or "I'll read that draft by tomorrow." Two people may have different ideas on how serious the commitment is, but there is rarely any doubt that some kind of commitment has been made. The less seriously we take our commitments to others, the greater the odds their trust in us will decline. There are different levels of commitment (e.g., if you forget to call your wife one afternoon, she won't assume this means you want a divorce), but they all connect together and contribute to our perceptions of others' trustworthiness.

Trust is lost through inconsistent behavior

Getting back to projects, people fracture trust when they behave unpredictably. When someone consistently takes action without regard to her commitments, she creates waves of concern that disturb the team. Energy is taken away from people who have to work (or contend) with her. Instead of applying their energy toward completing work, they now have to expend energy calculating whether she will actually do what she says she will. Contingency plans have to be devised, and levels of stress and doubt rise ("If Marla doesn't get that code checked in by the end of today, we're hosed."). The more careless someone is with the responsibility she has, the larger the waves will be.

One interesting (albeit painful) story about failed trust involves one of my former managers. I was a program manager working with five programmers and testers, and we got along well. Jake, the team lead, was my manager and had authority over me and several other PMs. The problem was Jake's habit of changing his mind. For example, he and I would discuss big decisions I was making that needed his support. We would come to quick agreement on the best approach. But then as soon as we entered a meeting where strong personalities or people with equal or more seniority than Jake disagreed with him, Jake, in dramatic fashion, would cave in (he did this about one-third of the time, but I never knew which third). He'd run the other way and agree with whatever decision was popular.

I remember standing at the whiteboard during meetings, halfway through explaining my plan A, when he'd agree to someone's suggestion to go with plan B. I'd stop and stare at him, amazed that he could do this without feeling a thing. Had he really forgotten? Was he this much of a brown-noser? Was he unaware of what he was doing to me? Or was this weathervane-like behavior (following the wind of the room) really beyond his control? I didn't have the skills then to sort it out, and I wasn't savvy enough to talk to others about the behavior I experienced, so I suffered. My workouts at the gym were never so good.

Eventually, I discussed this behavior with him. I also documented decisions we'd made as soon as we made them (email is good for this), and I used them later on for reference. I even went so far as to prep him right before meetings. But all this only made for minor improvements (instead of supporting plan B, he'd just stay out of the discussion, but not help with plan A). I soon found myself working around him. I'd go out of my way to have things decided in meetings without him present. By comparison, it was less work and more effective. This created other problems on our team (and with my relationship with Jake), but I was able to manage my areas and get things done.

The sad thing was that Jake was smart and fun to work with. But because I couldn't trust him, it didn't matter. He would have been more useful as a manager if he were less smart, but twice as trustworthy. We certainly would have made better products, and I would have spent less energy managing him and more energy helping the team.

Make trust clear (create green lights)

The good managers I've had made trust explicit. They told me, flat out, that I had the authority to make decisions for my areas of responsibility, provided I had the support of my team. They (my managers) would identify specific things they were concerned about and ask me to check in with them on those points. They'd ask me what I needed from them, and we'd negotiate to see if they could provide it to me. Otherwise, they directed me to focus on making things happen, instead of seeking anyone else's approval. Imparting trust, the real meaning of delegation, is a powerful thing. Some sports have specific lingo around this kind of delegation of authority—for example, getting the "green light" in basketball.

Years before I played basketball in high school, I played on Coach Rob Elkins'[1] team at the Samuel Field Y, in Douglaston, New York. He pulled me aside one day during practice, which usually meant it was time for a reprimand. I'd been goofing off during practice, pulling down other players' shorts so that they couldn't get back on defense.

---

1 Rob and Eric from the Samuel Field Y in Douglaston, New York taught me so much more about coaching and managing than the high school and college basketball coaches I had later on. If you know these guys, please tell them to get in touch with me.

When I sat down, I hung my head low, just in case. But he said nothing. We sat for long moments and watched the rest of the team scrimmage on the court. Finally, he said, "Scott, you have the green light." I looked at him. "Green light?" I asked. "Yes" he replied, smiling, but not looking at me. "OK, Coach," I said, and ran back out on the floor. Though few people ever hear these words, somehow all players know what they mean. Whereas players are normally obligated to shoot the ball only in accordance with whatever play the coach calls, the green light meant exemption. I could shoot the ball whenever I thought appropriate—I could supersede any play and exercise authority when I thought necessary.

A large amount of trust is imparted in telling a player something like this, which is precisely why most players go their entire career and never hear it. (I continued to play basketball in high school and on Division III college teams, but I never heard it again and hadn't heard it before.) Coaches are generally terrified to give up any authority. Much like managers, they feel their power is tenuous. Standing on the sidelines (or sitting alone in a corner office) is a vulnerable place to be. Many managers and coaches fear what will happen if they grant their team additional freedoms. They forget that they can always adjust levels of trust; had I misused the trust Coach Elkins put in me, nothing prevented him from taking some of it back (change the green light to yellow). More important, perhaps, is that the level of trust managers are afraid to give is often the precise amount that their team requires to actually follow their manager's leadership.

It's safe to say I played harder for Coach Elkins than for any other coach I had. I instinctively felt that I now had a higher bar to live up to (although in one game I took seven jump shots in a single quarter, and missed them all, which I'm sure was some kind of club record for both attempts and misses). I also worked with more intensity for managers who imparted similar amounts of trust in me than for those who did not. It wasn't because I liked them (although that helped). It was because I was granted the space to thrive. It's the transfer of trust that creates true empowerment because it gives people the room to work closer to their peak performance.

If maximum potential for success is your goal, you have to look for ways to give people green lights. It's the manager's job to create opportunities for her team, as well as help her team have the strength and preparation to take on those opportunities.

The different kinds of power

There are two models of power that I'll use in this book. The advanced form will come later, in Chapter 16. For now, I'll stick to the simple, but potent, form of functional power.

Functional power comes in two flavors: granted and earned. Granted power comes through hierarchy or job titles (sometimes called *ex officio* or "of office" power). For example, the coach of a basketball team has the power to decide which players will be in the game and which ones stay on the bench. Or the boss of a small sales office might have the power to hire and fire anyone he chooses. But this power doesn't have anything to do with how much respect people have for the person wielding it, or even how much skill and knowledge people feel the manager has. In contrast, earned power is something that has to be cultivated through performance and action. Earned power, or earned authority, is when people choose to listen, not because of someone's granted authority, but because they think he is smart or helpful.

Do not rely on granted power

"I distrust all systemizers and avoid them: the will to a system is a lack of integrity."

— *Nietzsche*

The use of granted power as a primary force in leadership limits relationships. It excludes the possibility of exchanging ideas, and it places the focus on the use of force, rather than smarts. While there are situations when use of autocratic power is required, good leaders keep that sword in its scabbard as much as possible. As soon as you draw it, no one is listening to you anymore—they're listening to the sword. Worse, everyone around you will draw their own swords to respond (and their swords may be better than yours). Instead of explaining to you why you are wrong, they will use their own granted power to challenge your power. This results in a competition of forces that has nothing to do with intelligence or a search for the best solution. Granted power (like the "dark side of the force") is temping because it's easier: you don't have to work as hard to get what you want.

I once faced a situation that put me at the crossroads of granted and earned power. It was during Internet Explorer 2.0, when I had my first major program management assignment. The first day I was introduced to the two programmers who I'd be working with, Bill and Jay. Jay was friendly, but Bill was quiet and intimidating. He was also very senior in the organization (a level 13 in the Microsoft jargon of the time, which meant he was about as senior as a programmer could be). I remember sitting in his office, looking at him across his desk. I'd been talking for 10 minutes and he'd said next to nothing. He just leaned back in his chair and stared at me.

I tried going to the whiteboard to see if that would help get Bill talking. No effect. He spoke up only to say sarcastic or ambiguously disconcerting things, like "Oh, is that so?" and "Wow...interesting you would think that." He was just toying with me, like a cat with a half-dead mouse. You see, I was just an arrogant 23-year-old; I had no idea what I was doing, despite how convinced I was that I could fake it. Bill, on the other hand, was a seasoned veteran who had gone through this routine dozens of times before. In fact,

I'm sure there were only two thoughts running through his mind: "How on earth did I get stuck with the new guy?" and "Is he the first or second most stupid person I've ever met?" The encounter ended with me babbling in a "straight from the HR training video" sort of way about how great it was going to be to work together. (I'm sure this confirmed for him that I was, in fact, worthy of first place.)

At the time, a friend (another PM) gave me this advice: lay down the law. I should tell Bill that because I was the PM, and he was the programmer, he should do what I said regarding high-level decisions. This fit the Microsoft mythology of PMs ("get in my way and I will kill you") that I'd heard about, and so I rallied up the courage to go try and live up to it. But before I drew my sword and charged up the hill, I chatted with my manager. Between good-natured laughs, he said not to do anything so rash. He reminded me that Bill was smart and knowledgeable about his areas, and I should find a way to make use of that. He also added that working with Bill would be, as he put it, "good for me." Trusting my manager, despite his laughter, I put my sword away and approached the problem from the standpoint of getting as much value out of Bill as possible.

Work to develop earned power

Over the weeks that followed, I slowly earned Bill's trust. It was painful at first. In the process of getting him to help me, I had to prove what I was capable of and build from the small to the large. I found that when I acknowledged he knew more than I about something, good advice came from him more easily. When I made commitments and followed through, he became more generous. I had to make good decisions, and defend my points of view with good arguments, but eventually we developed a solid working relationship. Bill granted me authority to make decisions that impacted him significantly. He just needed me to first demonstrate that I was worthy of his confidence.

Had I exercised whatever granted power I had during those early days, I would have lost any chance at earned power. Bill might have yielded to me on that first day, but because he would be responding only to my power, it would be difficult to move past that and on to more collaborative ways to work together. And if I continually relied on using power (which is what tends to happen when you start using power), it would have become less effective over time. Every time a manager or leader says, "Because I say so," they are ending discussions and shutting off the potential for better opinions. Any smart or passionate people around them will not be contributing their best work and won't be happy about their limited roles.

From an organizational standpoint, autocratic behavior pushes strong thinkers away. It simultaneously encourages those comfortable with being told what to do to stick around. Tyrants create environments that only minions could tolerate, and vice versa. Worse, tyrants create other tyrants beneath them. These patterns of behavior (granted power or nothing) get passed down through organizations, eventually poisoning them.

Persuasion is stronger than dictation

In managing others, I learned that I was more effective at making good things happen if I convinced people to do something before making them do it. Any idiot can use tyrannical power and demand specific kinds of behavior—it takes no skill. But to convince an intelligent person (or group of people) that something they initially didn't want to do is right, good, or even perhaps in their interest, is much more powerful. When they are hours into the work, and begin to question why they're doing it, they can't blame you. They'll be able to rely on their own intelligence, influenced by your arguments, for why they are spending their time doing what they're doing.

Eventually, people listened to me because of their confidence in my ability to have good reasons for my opinions. They'd ask fewer questions and take on trust that I had thought through my request of them before I'd made it. They had fewer fears about my taking advantage of them because they had so many experiences where the interests of the project and the team motivated my behavior. The more people trust you, the easier it becomes to persuade them. Like with Bill, over time, I spent less and less energy convincing people of things—even though that's where I started my relationships with them—and more and more time getting things done.

Be autocratic when necessary

Granted power does have its place. When things get out of control, granted power can be the fastest way to achieve order. If a meeting is falling apart, big commitments are being broken, or other fundamental problems are occurring, use the sword. If you're convinced that the use of direct power is the only real possibility of a successful outcome, regardless of the consequences, by all means make use of it. Be clear, be direct, and use the executive authority you have to move the project forward.

However, the more it's used, the more it covers for fundamental organizational problems. If the only way to make it through the week is to yell your way through meetings or bark orders in cubicles, it means the project vision, organization structure, or your leadership ability needs to be examined.

Trusting others

The larger an organization becomes, the more common it is to rely on granted power. There is greater fear among leaders about how to keep the masses working together (or perhaps, to prevent a revolution), and there is the belief that there isn't time to engage everyone in the organization in a kind of discussion and communication that requires using earned authority. Even on small teams, I know some leaders who don't believe they have the energy or time to engage all of their key contributors in this kind of leadership style. The solution to this problem is another kind of trust, called delegation: trusting others to make decisions.

Authority and trust often accumulate around different tasks or areas of knowledge. Joe might have the most authority when it comes to C++ objects, and Sally might be the best person for database work. Healthy, communicative teammates trust each other enough to know when someone else has more skill or a better perspective, and then solicit that person's advice without fear of embarrassment or ridicule. This is a real fear because engineering disciplines have ripe cultures of passive-aggressive behavior around asking for help (i.e., RTFM). Even in computer science departments in college, self-reliance is seen as a core competency, and students asking peers for help is often considered a sign of weakness.

From a project perspective, Sally's authority on database design is only as good as its application to the project. If she sits alone in her office, and no one enlists her authority to help solve problems, then Sally's authority is squandered, or at best, limited to the tasks Sally is doing on her own. A key responsibility of a project leader or manager is to model the delegation and sharing of knowledge for the entire team. If they do it right, the rest of the team will have a much easier time following along.

Delegation of authority

Traditionally, delegation is used to describe the act of handing off specific tasks or responsibilities. I think a more powerful form of delegation is when decisions, or the ability to influence decisions, are distributed. This can happen in meetings or group discussions. When the leader or manager is asked "So, how are we going to solve this problem?", he has the chance to hand that power over to someone else. "Well, Sally, you're our best database designer. What do you think we should do here?" As long as this isn't done unfairly (say, in the middle of a tense VP review meeting, during a failing demo, when Sally has no idea she's going to be expected to answer any questions), this sets a tone of collaboration. People can be free to acknowledge each other's expertise, and they will yield authority appropriately. Of course, for the project manager, nothing is risked. If Sally's suggestions aren't good, the discussion continues. But without that first question, the discussion may never happen at all.

Of course, delegation also extends to explicit handoffs of authority. By publicly declaring that a work area or feature is going to be managed by someone, a manager transfers her authority to that person. It's important that delegations are done with enough visibility that everyone who needs to see the transfer actually sees it. Any time I handed off responsibility to someone who worked for me, I made sure to contact every programmer or tester who would be affected so that they would know that whatever power and authority I had for that work would be transferred to someone else. Of course, sometimes people don't want to see things delegated, and it's the leader's job to use her power to enforce it.

John, a project manager on my team, was ready to take on more responsibility. So, when the time came to reorganize the distribution of work on my team, I was able to give him an area I had been responsible for in the past. After the appropriate discussions with John and Steve (the programmer on the area), I handed the responsibility off to John. A week later, Steve came into my office asking for PM help with the area. While I listened, I tried to figure out why he was talking to me and not John. I interrupted him: "Steve, why are you talking to me about this?" "Well Scott, you used to own this, didn't you?" "Yes Steve, but John owns it now. Did you talk to him?" He shrugged. "Steve, go talk to John," I said. "He's smart. He's good. Trust him." Steve came back a few days later, and we had a shorter version of the same conversation. But after that, I never heard from Steve again (at least not about this).

John probably never knew about this and never needed to. Steve preferred working with me for some reason, and he wanted to continue our relationship despite the change in ownership. But to delegate, I had to get myself out of the discussions. I could probably have answered Steve's question myself, and I might have enjoyed it, but I'd be betraying my own decision to delegate. Until I had a reason to get involved in that area of the project, I had to trust John and Steve to do their jobs, which included using Steve's trust in me to convince him to trust John.

Many managers have trouble delegating. They rose in seniority because of their ability to get work done on their own, and leading requires a different balance of skills than being an individual contributor (see the section "The balancing act of project management" in Chapter 1). These managers are usually held back by the fear that they don't have enough control. Of course, this is a trap because if that fear drives their decisions, they can never learn to trust anyone, and without trust, leadership is impossible.

Sometimes the solution is a compromise. The manager just has to discuss, with the member of her team at the moment of delegation, what considerations the delegate is expected to make. ("John, I'm worried about Steve. He's been late on every estimate. So, pay extra attention to that, OK?") By setting expectations around assignments, leaders transfer some of the experience and guidance, and probably increase the odds of success.

Trust is insurance against adversity

As we discussed in the last chapter, all projects will have things go wrong. Competitors have a habit of not doing what you expect them to (that's their job), technologies come and go, and important people change their minds. As a project manager, it's guaranteed that things will happen that were not predicted or accounted for. In tough or uncertain times, you want your team or your peers to be able to rely on you and trust in each other.

If trust has been cultivated and grown over time, and people have experience making decisions with each other (instead of in spite of each other), the project will be highly resilient to problems. When people believe in the team, they can summon forms of confidence and patience that aren't available through other means. Like soldiers in a foxhole, each person can rely on someone else to watch his back, freeing him to give more energy to the task ahead.

When a team trusts each other, it also buys the project manager time to focus on solving the problems at hand, instead of trying to calm down the hallways of panicked or frustrated employees. Sometimes the leader might need to ask for this kind of support explicitly. He has to demonstrate the respect he wants from the team by acknowledging the problem and asking, but not demanding, their support. (Yelling "Support me now!" doesn't work.) On the whole, it's connections between people that get them through tough times: not their salaries, not the technologies they work on, and certainly not how much power an individual does or does not have.

So, the wise leader, like a ship's captain, knows that unseen storms and dangers lurk across the sea, and he gets himself and his crew ready as best as he can against what he cannot prepare for. If uncertainty is guaranteed, the project manager's best investment is likely to be having a strong network of trust between him and everyone who's contributing to the effort. On larger teams, more time should be spent building trust on the relationships that are most critical to the project or most likely to fail under stress. While specs, vision documents, and other tools do help bind people together, it's the trust in the people behind those things that carries the real power.

Models, questions, and conflicts

The golden rule—do unto others as you would have them do unto you—applies to managers. No decree from leaders is ever followed as well as the ones they follow themselves. Humans are social creatures, and we learn behavior throughout our lives, predominantly on models from others. We often learn best by seeing someone we respect or admire do something, and then try, consciously or subconsciously, to emulate that behavior. As a matter of trust, it's up to leaders of projects to demonstrate the behavior they ask for in the people they work with. Michael Jordan, among his other qualities, developed a reputation for an intense work ethic. Even though he was the highest-paid and most well-known basketball player in the NBA, there were few who worked as hard as he did. This eliminated any possibility of lesser players asking to sit out of practice or to spend less time in the gym. The leader set a model that others would need to follow.

Work ethic aside, the golden rule for leaders is that they trust their own judgment enough to follow the same rules as everyone else (see "Trust in yourself (self-reliance)," later in this chapter). Doing this means allowing others, peers or subordinates, to question or challenge the leader's judgment or behavior. If someone has been granted power, there needs to be some kind of feedback loop for challenging it (i.e., who is permitted to say the emperor has no clothes?). Good leaders trust their teammates enough to—on occasion, perhaps in private—ask for feedback on their behavior and performance. Of course, there's no obligation for the leader to take action on the feedback or even to comment on it, but it's hard to imagine success occurring if there is no healthy and safe path for this kind of information to reach the project manager.

Leaders define their feedback process

People are hesitant to give feedback to authority figures. As a manager, I made a habit of asking people who reported to me, during weekly one-on-one meetings, if they had anything they wanted me to think about, regarding my work, my behavior, or my performance. It was rare that they'd say anything, although I knew this wasn't because I was a perfect manager (there are no perfect managers). I found the only solution was trust and time. I had to be persistent in creating the confidence they would need to feel comfortable critiquing my behavior—without them worrying about me becoming defensive or reprimanding them for their comments. Eventually they'd offer a small criticism, and if I handled it well, they'd offer more next time.

But once I had established a feedback loop with them, I learned that their perspective was much more useful toward me becoming a better manager than the feedback I received from my own boss. I certainly didn't have this kind of relationship with everyone, but most people, sooner or later, answered my questions with useful feedback. A suggestion for running a meeting differently, a question about a decision I'd made, or any other comment guaranteed that the ensuing discussion helped us both to feel better about whatever the thing was.

Every time I was in a discussion, I tried to expose the difference between criticizing an idea and criticizing the person who came up with the idea.[2] Just because person A disagrees with something person B says doesn't mean person A is judging person B. I wanted the team to feel that they trusted each other enough to say what they thought and openly disagree without apologizing. A sense of humor helps in making this possible, and it starts with the leader demonstrating when sarcasm or mockery are appropriate, perhaps by using himself as the target of the jokes. But my main point is that the leader has to demonstrate the behavior himself, rein in people who go too far, and reach out to those who struggle to get involved.

---

2   See "How to give and receive criticism" at *http://www.scottberkun.com/essays/35-how-to-give-and-receive-criticism/*.

This extends to conflicts and disagreements. Granted and earned authority don't help if they just sit quietly on their asses while bad things are happening. There are few better uses of power than to interrupt stupid arguments and to take the floor away from people who abuse it. When differences of opinion slide into ad hominem attacks, or the use of bogus arguments to justify decisions, someone has to interrupt and raise the bar. By not tolerating that behavior, everyone gets the same message at the same time: don't try that kind of cop-out again because we don't accept it here.

Of course, it follows through the golden rule that the true leader needs to prepare herself for the possibility (or perhaps inevitability) that others will challenge her own bogus arguments, if she should try to use them. The best leaders are the ones who take pleasure in the team being so committed to its intellectual standards that it's not afraid to question even the leader's behavior.

Trust and making mistakes

It's easy to trust people when they succeed; managing people's mistakes is much more complicated. This is where managers earn their pay.

I know from my own experience that every time someone showed up at my office door with a problem he caused, I'd try (but not always succeed) to maintain three thoughts:

1. I'm glad he's coming to me about it. I'd rather he come to me instead of hide it or try to solve it on his own and make it worse. I should let him know this right away.

2. How can I help fix this problem? Is it even fixable? What are the options? How involved should I be? I should give him as much advice as he needs, but, if possible, have him carry out what needs to be done. However, I have to make sure he's not in over his head. Sending him into battle with a 99% certainty of instant death isn't exactly good management practice.

3. I need to make sure that if there is a lesson here, he'll learn it.[3] Mistakes are where real learning happens because the mistake maker has a personal and emotional investment in what happened, and he will have tremendous motivation not to repeat it (especially if he feels that the team trusts him).

If you ask any wise masters of any discipline for their great lessons, they will tell stories about how they screwed something up, probably an important thing, and finally learned a better way to go about doing whatever it was. It follows that to become great, you not

---

3   In many military organizations, only situations described as incidents or missions require debriefings. So, if something stupid happens, and it's not really anyone's fault and the impact is minimal, there might be no lesson at all, and it's not worth the effort to make a big deal out of it. In fact, the best response might be to express that your approval isn't needed for similar minor issues in the future.

only need to make mistakes,[4] but you need someone to give you the opportunity to do so. Managers earn their pay when they manage problems because they not only have to help in the recovery, but because they also have to lead the process of converting the mistake into a lesson for the team to learn from.

Good management is about giving people as much responsibility as their abilities allow, but somehow never letting them feel that they are working alone, or that they have your support only when things are going well. It makes sense that the potential to make mistakes is the exact same potential needed to contribute and succeed. This means it's unfair to pin people to the wall for errors in judgment or for problems that arise from decisions they've made.

Instead, the ideal environment to create is one where people are comfortable being ambitious, but will admit to and take responsibility for their mistakes. They should feel trusted enough to want to learn as much as they can so that it won't happen again. If the team collectively shares this culture, it becomes self-correcting. When there is a healthy system for recognizing, responding to, and learning from mistakes, over time fewer of them tend to happen (or when they do, they are dealt with quickly), and people are more confident taking all kinds of action in the nonmistake majority of their time.

Never reprimand in real time

The worst thing in the world, especially during a crisis, is for a manager or leader to reprimand someone while the issue is still unresolved. It solves nothing, and it minimizes the probability that the problem will be solved because the person who knows the most about the issue (the blamed) is made to feel guilty and defensive. Imagine that someone who worked with you ran into your office screaming, "My office is on fire! My office is on fire!", and all you could offer was, "Gee, that was stupid. Why did you do that? I'm so very disappointed in you." Managers do this all the time, and it's hard not to wonder why. My theory is that some people believe, due to osmosis from bad managers or parents, that the way to start fixing issues is by pointing fingers and distributing blame. Of course, making people feel bad and establishing who should feel the worst does nothing to improve the situation (knowing who started the fire doesn't often help put it out). Instead, it's the time after the issue has been resolved, when heads are cool and the pressure is off, that there is every opportunity to come back and figure out what happened and why, and what are the resulting lessons for the individual, the leader, and the team.

---

4   See "How to learn from your mistakes" at *http://www.scottberkun.com/essays/44-how-to-learn-from-your-mistakes/*.

Trust in yourself (self-reliance)

**"To thine own self be true, and it must follow, as the night the day,
thou canst not then be false to any man."**

— *Shakespeare*, Hamlet

The last point about the relationship between leadership and trust is for you to learn to trust in yourself. This is a matter of philosophy and goes beyond the scope of this book. However, I have enough trust in both of us that we can cover some important ground in this short section.

If you look at high school and college curriculums in the United States, there is one class that you will not find: how to figure out who you are. This is very strange. For a nation that places primary importance on individuality and freedom, the U.S. doesn't do very much to teach its citizens about self-discovery, much less self-reliance. Self-discovery is the process of learning about who you are as an individual, independent from your friends, family, employer, or nation. Self-reliance is the ability to apply your individuality to the world, based on a framework of emotional, physical, and financial support for yourself. It doesn't mean you have to live naked in the woods, living off the land. But it does mean that you can look inside yourself and find strength to make choices you believe in, even if others do not agree with those choices.

**"Believe nothing, no matter where you read it or who has said it, not even if I
have said it, unless it agrees with your own reason and your own common sense."**

— *Buddha*

Leadership, in the traditional sense, demands that individuals have some sense of self-reliance. You can take a risk or make a tough choice only if you have an inner compass guiding you toward what you think is right. Without self-reliance, all of your decisions will be based heavily on the opinions of others, or your desire to please them, without any centering force to guide those influences. Tom Peters, John P. Kotter, and other authors call that centering force a value system. They suggest that a set of values can act as your core, or an organization's core, guiding you through difficult situations. This approach can work, but I'm suggesting something deeper and more personal.

Self-reliance starts by trusting your own opinions—it's possible for you to believe something is true, even if others do not. Differing opinion should negate yours only if you consider it and, in thinking through it on your own, change your mind. Otherwise, there is no reason to give up your opinion on a subject (you might still give in on a decision, yielding your authority to theirs, but this doesn't require you losing your own opinion). Your beliefs should be self-sufficient. If you were to change your mind only because other people think differently than you, you'd be committing an act against trusting yourself. Betraying trust in yourself can be just as dangerous as betraying trust in your team.

For the brave, self-reliance goes further. Not only do you trust your own opinions, you trust your core enough to allow your opinions to change, and even to admit to your mistakes. Without change and the occasional struggle, we can't learn or grow. But if you do trust yourself, you'll recognize that you are still you, even when you fail or grow into new ideas. Emerson wrote: "A foolish consistency is the hobgoblin of little minds." He meant that keeping the same ideas just for the sake of keeping those same ideas makes no sense. A wise person should be learning more all the time, which will require him to develop new ideas and opinions, even if they contradict ones he had in the past. If you lead an active intellectual and emotional life, your ideas will grow with you.

This means a self-reliant person can be confident in herself, while finding ways to let others influence her and help define her vision of the future, allowing all kinds of positive changes. You are free to make mistakes, admit to them, and change your mind, without violating your own identity.

So, if you can learn to trust yourself in these ways, you will, as a by-product of your leadership role, help others learn to trust themselves. No act of delegation in the worlds of projects or human psychology is more powerful than helping people believe in their own ability to become more self-reliant.

I recommend the essay "Self-Reliance" by Ralph Waldo Emerson. It's available in most editions of his collected works, or it can be found online at *http://www.emersoncentral.com/ selfreliance.htm*. The best general book on self-discovery is *Chop Wood, Carry Water,* by Rick Fields (Jeremy P. Tarcher, 1984). For the philosophically adventurous, try reading Albert Camus' *The Myth of Sisyphus* (Vintage, 1991).

> **"It is only as a man puts off all foreign support, and stands alone, that I see him to be strong and to prevail.... He who knows that power is inborn, that he is weak because he has looked [only] for good out of him and elsewhere, and so perceiving, throws himself unhesitatingly on his thought, instantly rights himself, stands in the erect position, commands his limbs, works miracles; just as a man who stands on his feet is stronger than a man who stands on his head."**
>
> — *Ralph Waldo Emerson, from "Self-Reliance"*

Summary

- Trust is built through effective commitments.
- Trust is lost through inconsistent behavior on matters of importance.
- Use the granting of authority and trust to enable people to do great work.
- Granted power comes from the organizational hierarchy. Earned power comes only from people's responses to your actions. Earned power is more useful than granted power, although both are necessary.
- Use delegation to build trust on your team and to ensure your team against adversity.

- Respond to problems in a way that will maintain people's trust. Support them during crises so that they bring issues to you instead of hiding them.

- Trust in yourself is the core of leadership. Self-discovery is the way to learn who you are and to develop healthy self-reliance.

Exercises

A. Make a list of the five people you work with most often. Who do you trust most and why?

B. Is there a risk-free way to earn someone's trust? Can you play it safe in a relationship and simultaneously make it deep and trustworthy?

C. Of the managers you've had in your life, which ones relied on granted power and which on earned power? How did this relate to their performance?

D. Think of the big commitments people have broken with you. What impact did this have on your relationship with them? Did you ever discuss what happened? What commitments have you broken with teammates? Is there any way to recover from a broken commitment?

E. How did your manager respond the last time you made a mistake? How does this differ from how you handled the last time someone who works for you made a mistake?

F. As an exploration into self-reliance, what decision have you fought for despite its unpopularity? Can you think of moments when you knew the right thing to do—and did it—even though you knew others would criticize you?

G. When was the last time you changed your mind about something important? Make it your goal to change your mind about something in your life. Invite your team or a group of friends to lunch, and tell them you'll pay the check if they can change your mind about something.

H. Research the leadership styles of any two of the following leaders: Gandhi, Abraham Lincoln, Alexander the Great, Napoleon, Genghis Kahn, Queen Elizabeth I, Nelson Mandela. Who would you rather work for? Why? What techniques did they use to earn (or manipulate) the trust of their followers? How much granted and earned authority did they have?

I. Can leadership be taught or is it instinctive? Make a list of traits that make for being a good leader (reuse anything you wish from this book or start from scratch). Score each trait from 1–9: 1 being purely instinctive, 9 being purely teachable.

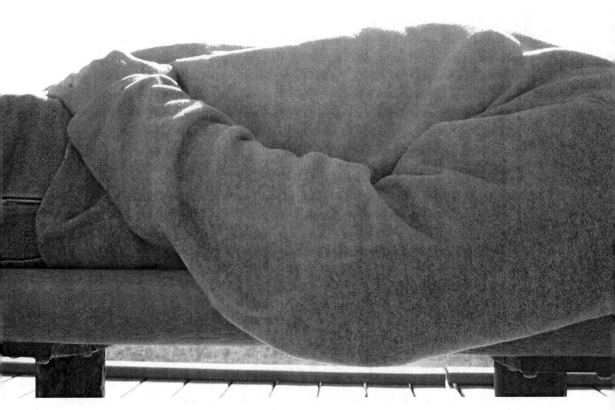

CHAPTER THIRTEEN

Making things happen

One myth of project management is that certain people have an innate ability to do it well, and others do not. Whenever this myth came up in conversation with other project managers, I always asked for an explanation of that ability—how to recognize and develop it in others. After debate, the only thing we identified—after many of the other topics covered in this book—is the ability to make things happen. Some people are able to apply their talents in whatever combination necessary to move projects forward, and others cannot, even if they have the same individual skills. The ability to make things happen is a combination of knowing how to be a catalyst in a variety of different situations and having the courage to do so.

This is so important it's used as a litmus test in hiring project managers. Even if PMs can't precisely define the ability, they do feel that they can sense it in others. For example, many hiring managers ask the question about candidates: "If things were not going well on an important project, would I feel confident sending this person into that room, into that debate, and believe he'd find a way to make it better, whatever the problem was?" If after a round of interviews the answer is no, the candidate is sent home.[1] The belief is that if he isn't agile enough to adapt his skills to the situations at hand, he won't thrive on a typical project. This chapter is about the ability to make things happen.

Priorities make things happen

Much of my time as a PM was spent making ordered lists. An ordered list is just a column of things, put in order of importance. I'm convinced that despite all the knowledge I was expected to have, in total, all I really did was make ordered lists. I collected things that had to be done—requirements, features, bugs, whatever—and put them in an order of importance to the project. I spent days refining and revising these lists, integrating new information, discussing them with others, always making sure they were rock solid. Then, once we had that list in place, I'd lead the team as hard as possible to follow things in the defined order. Sometimes, these lists involved how my own time should be spent on a given day; other times, the lists involved what entire teams of people would do over months. But the process and the effect were the same.

I invested so much time in these lists because I knew that having clear priorities was the backbone of progress. Making things happen depends on having a clear sense of which things are more important than others and applying that sense to every single interaction that takes place on the team. These priorities have to be reflected in every email you send, question you ask, and meeting you hold. Every programmer and tester should invest energy in the things that will most likely bring about success. Someone has to be dedicated to both figuring out what those things are and driving the team to deliver on them.

---

1 The bar was not "Can this person do everything?", but "Will this person know when to seek out help for situations that are beyond him?" This is just another kind of situation to deal with.

What wastes the most time on projects is confusion about which things should come before which other things. Many miscommunications and missteps happen because person A assumed one priority (make it faster), and person B assumed another (make it more reliable). This is true for programmers, testers, marketers, and entire teams of people. If these conflicts can be avoided, more time can be spent actually progressing toward the project goals.

This isn't to say those debates about priorities shouldn't happen—they should. But they should happen early as part of planning. If the same arguments keep resurfacing during development, it means people were not effectively convinced of the decision, or they have forgotten the logic and need to be reminded of why those decisions were made. Entertain debates, but start by asking if anything has changed since the plans were made to justify reconsidering the priorities. If nothing has changed (competitor behavior, new group mission, more/fewer resources, new major problems), stick to the decision.

If there is an ordered list posted on the wall clarifying for everyone which things have been agreed to be more important than which other things, these arguments end quickly or never even start. Ordered lists provide everyone with a shared framework of logic to inherit their decisions from. If the goals are clear and understood, there is less need for interpretation and fewer chances for wasted effort.

So, if ever things on the team were not going well and people were having trouble focusing on the important things, I knew it was my fault: either I hadn't ordered things properly, hadn't effectively communicated those priorities, or had failed to execute and deliver on the order that we had. In such a case, working with prioritization and ordered lists meant everything.

Common ordered lists

By always working with a set order of priorities, adjustments and changes are easy to make. If, by some miracle, more time or resources are found in the schedule, it's clear what the next most important item is to work on. By the same token, if the schedule needs to be cut, everyone knows what the next least important item is and can stop working on it. This is incredibly important because it guarantees that no matter what happens, you will have done the most important work possible and can make quick adjustments without much effort or negative morale. Also, any prioritization mistakes you make will be relative: if work item 10 turns out to have been more important than work item 9, big deal. Because the whole list was in order, you won't have made a horrible mistake. And besides, by having such clear priorities and keeping the team focused on them, you may very well have bought the time needed to get work item 10 done after all.

For most projects, the three most important and most formal ordered lists are used to prioritize project goals, features, and work items (see Figure 13-1). The project goals are typically part of the vision document (see Chapter 4) or are derived from it. The lists of features and work items are the output of the design process (see Chapters 5, 6, and 7). Because each of these lists inherits priorities from the preceding list, by stepping up a level to reach a point of clarity and then reapplying those priorities back down to the level in question, any disputes can begin to be resolved. Although this may not always resolve debates, it will make sure that every decision was made in the context of what's truly important.

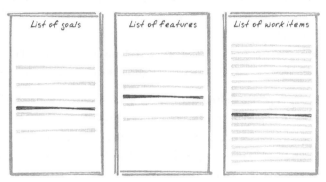

FIGURE 13-1. *The three most important ordered lists, shown in order.*

Other important things that might need ordered lists include bugs, customer suggestions, employee bonuses, and team budgets. They can all be managed in a similar way: put things in the order most likely to make the project or organization successful. No matter how complex the tools you use are (say, for bug tracking), never forget that all you're doing is ordering things. If the tools you use don't help you put things in order, find a different tool. Bug triage, for example, where people get in a room and decide when a bug should be fixed (if at all), is really just a group process for making an ordered list of bugs. The bugs might be classified by group rather than on an individual bug-by-bug basis, but the purpose and effect are the same.

If you do use the three most common ordered lists, make sure that they always map to each other. Every engineering work item should map to a feature, and every feature should map to a goal. If a new work item is added, it must be matched against features and goals. This is a forcing function to prevent random features. If a VP or programmer wants to slip something extra in, she should be forced to justify it against what the project is trying to achieve: "That's a great feature, boss, but which goal will it help us satisfy? Either we should adjust the goals and deal with the consequences, or we shouldn't be investing energy here." If you teach the team that it's a rule to keep these three levels of decision making in sync, you will focus the team and prevent them from wasting time.

Priority 1 versus everything else

These ordered lists have one important line dividing them into two pieces. The top part is priority 1: things we must do and cannot possibly succeed without. The second part is everything else. Priorities 2 and 3 exist but are understood to be entirely different kinds of things from priority 1. It is very difficult to promote priority 2 items to priority 1.

This priority 1 line must be taken very seriously. You should fight hard to make that list as small and tight as possible (this applies to any goal lists in the vision document as well). An item in the priority 1 list means "We will die without this." It does not mean things that are nice to have or that we really want to have; it gives the tightest, leanest way to meet the project goals. For example, if we were building an automobile, the only priority 1 things would be the engine, tires, transmission, brakes, steering wheel, and pedals. Priority 2 items would be the doors, windshield, air conditioning, and radio because you can get around without those things. The core functionality of the automobile exists without them; you could ship it and still call it a car.

Putting this line in place was always difficult, with long debates over which things customers could live without. This was fine. We wanted all of the debating to take place early, but then move on. As painful as it would be, when we were finished, we'd have a list that had survived the opinions and perspectives of the team. We could then go forward and execute, having refutations and supporting arguments for the list we'd made. Having sharpened it through debate and argument, we were ready for 90% of the common questions or challenges people might have later on (i.e., why we were building brakes but not air conditioning) and could quickly dispatch them: we'd heard the arguments before, and we knew why they didn't hold up.

The challenge of prioritization is always more emotional/psychological than intellectual, despite what people say. Just like dieting to lose weight or budgeting to save money, eliminating things you want (but don't need) requires being disciplined, committed, and focused on the important goals. Saying "stability is important" is one thing, but ranking it against other important things is entirely different. Many managers chicken out of this process. They hedge, delay, and deny the tough choices, and the result is that they set their projects up to fail. No tough choices means no progress. In the abstract, the word *important* means nothing. Using ordered lists and defending a high priority 1 bar forces leaders and the entire team to make tough decisions and think clearly.

Clarity is how you make things happen on projects. Everyone shows up to work each day with a strong sense of what he is doing, why he's doing it, and how it relates to what the others are doing. When the team asks questions about why one thing is more important than another, there are clear and logical reasons for it. Even when things change and priorities are adjusted, it's all within the same fundamental system of ordered lists and priority designations.

Priorities are power

Have you ever been in a tough argument that you thought would never end? Perhaps half the engineers felt strongly for A, and the other half felt strongly for B. But then the smart team leader walks in, asks some questions, divides the discussion in a new way, and quickly gets everyone to agree. It's happened to me many times. When I was younger, I chalked this up to brilliance: somehow that manager or lead programmer was just smarter than the rest of the people in the room, and saw things that we didn't. But as I paid more attention, and on occasion even asked them afterward how they did it, I realized it was about having rock-solid priorities. They had an ordered list in their heads and were able to get other people to frame the discussion around it. Good priorities are power. They eliminate secondary variables from the discussion, making it possible to focus and resolve issues.

If you have priorities in place, you can always ask questions in any discussion that reframe the argument around a more useful primary consideration. This refreshes everyone's sense of what success is, visibly dividing the universe into two piles: things that are important and things that are nice, but not important. Here are some sample questions:

- What problem are we trying to solve?
- If there are multiple problems, which one is most important?
- How does this problem relate to or impact our goals?
- What is the simplest way to fix this that will allow us to meet our goals?
- If nothing else, you will reset the conversation to focus on the project goals, which everyone can agree with. If a debate has gone on for hours, finding common ground is your best opportunity to move the discussion toward a positive conclusion.

Be a prioritization machine

Whenever I talked with programmers or testers and heard about their issues or challenges, I realized that my primary value was in helping them focus. My aim was to eliminate secondary or tertiary things from their plates and to help them see a clear order of work. There are 1,000 ways to implement a particular web page design or database system to spec, but only a handful of them will really nail the objectives. Knowing this, I encouraged programmers to seek me out if they ever faced a decision where they were not sure which investment of time to make next.

But instead of micromanaging them ("Do this. No do that. No, do it this way. Are you done yet? How about now?"), I just made them understand that I was there to help them prioritize when they needed it. Because they didn't have the project-wide perspective I had, my value was in helping them to see, even if just for a moment, how what they were doing fit into the entire project. When they'd spent all day debugging a module or running unit tests, they were often relieved to get some higher-level clarity and reassurance in what they were doing. It took only a 30-second conversation to make sure we were all still on the same page.

Whenever new information came to the project, it was my job to interpret it (alone or through discussion with others), and form it into a prioritized list. Often, I'd have to revise a previous list, adjusting it to respond to the new information. A VP might change her mind. A usability study might find new issues. A competitor might make an unexpected change. Those prioritizations were living, breathing things, and any changes to our direction or goals were reflected directly and immediately in them.

Because I maintained the priorities, I enabled the team to stay focused on the important things and actually make progress on them. Sometimes I could reuse priorities defined by my superiors (vision documents, group mission statements); other times, I had to invent my own from scratch in response to ambiguity or unforeseen situations. But more than anything else, I was a prioritization machine. If there is ever a statue made in honor of good project managers, I suspect the inscription would read, "Bring me your randomized, your righteously confused, your sarcastic and bitter masses of programmers yearning for clarity."

Things happen when you say no

One effect of having priorities is how often you have to say no. It's one of the smallest words in the English language, yet many people have trouble saying it. The problem is that if you can't say no, you can't have priorities. The universe is a large place, but your priority 1 list should be very small. Therefore, most of what people in the world (or on your team) might think are great ideas won't end up matching the goals of the project. It doesn't mean their ideas are bad; it just means their ideas won't contribute to this particular project. So, a fundamental law of the PM universe is this: if you can't say no, you can't manage.[2]

Saying no starts at the top of an organization. Senior managers determine whether people can actually say no to requests. Despite what the priorities say, if a team leader continually says yes to things that don't jive with the priorities, others will follow. Programmers will work on pet features. PMs will add (hidden) requirements. Even if these individual choices are good, because the team is no longer following the same rules or working toward the same priorities, conflicts will occur. Sometimes, it will be disagreements between programmers, but more often, the result will be disjointed final designs. Stability, performance, and usability will all suffer. Without the focus of

---

2   For additional discussion on saying yes and no, see Richard Brenners' essay, "Saying No: A Short Course" at *http://www.ayeconference.com/Articles/Sayingno.html*.

priorities, it's hard to get a team to coordinate on making the same thing. The best leaders and team managers know that they have to lead the way in saying no to things that are out of scope, setting the bar for the entire team.

When you do say no, and make it stick, the project gains momentum. Eliminating tasks from people's plates gives them more energy and motivation to focus and work hard on what they need to do. The number of meetings and random discussions will drop and efficiency will climb. Momentum will build around saying no: others will start doing it in their own spheres of influence. In fact, I've asked team members to do this. I'd say, "If you ever feel you're being asked to do something that doesn't jive with our priorities, say no. Or tell them that I said no, and they need to talk to me. And don't waste your time arguing with them if they complain—point them my way." I didn't want them wasting their time debating priorities with people because it was my expertise, not theirs. Even if they never faced these situations, I succeeded in expressing how serious the priorities were and how willing I was to work to defend them.

Master the many ways to say no

Sometimes, you will need to say no in direct response to a feature request. Other times, you'll need to interject yourself into a conversation or meeting, identify the conflict with priorities you've overheard, and effectively say no to whatever was being discussed. To prepare yourself for this, you need to know all of the different flavors that the word *no* comes in:

- **No, this doesn't fit our priorities.** If it is early in the project, you should make the argument for why the current priorities are good, but hear people out on why other priorities might make more sense. They might have good ideas or need clarity on the goals. But do force the discussion to be relative to the project priorities, and not the abstract value of a feature or bug fix request. If it is late in the project, you can tell them they missed the boat. Even if the priorities suck, they're not going to change on the basis of one feature idea. The later you are, the more severe the strategy failure needs to be to justify goal adjustments.

- **No, only if we have time.** If you keep your priorities lean, there will always be many very good ideas that didn't make the cut. Express this as a relative decision: the idea in question might be good, but not good enough relative to the other work and the project priorities. If the item is on the priority 2 list, convey that it's possible it will be done, but that no one should bet the farm assuming it will happen.

- **No, only if you make <insert impossible thing here> happen.** Sometimes, you can redirect a request back onto the person who made it. If your VP asks you to add support for a new feature, tell him you can do it only if he cuts one of his other current priority 1 requests. This shifts the point of contention away from you, and toward a tangible, though probably unattainable, situation. This can also be done for political or approval issues: "If you can convince Sally that this is a good idea, I'll consider it." However, this can backfire. (What if he does convince Sally? Or worse, realizes you're sending him on a wild goose chase?)

- **No. Next release.** Assuming you are working on a web site or software project that will have more updates, offer to reconsider the request for the next release. This should probably happen anyway for all priority 2 items. This is often called postponement or punting.

- **No. Never. Ever. Really.** Some requests are so fundamentally out of line with the long-term goals that the hammer has to come down. Cut the cord now and save yourself the time of answering the same request again later. Sometimes it's worth the effort to explain why (so that they'll be more informed next time). Example: "No, Fred. The web site search engine will never support the Esperanto language. Never. Ever."

Keeping it real

Some teams have a better sense of reality than others. You can find many stories of project teams that shipped their product months or years late, or came in millions of dollars over budget (see Robert Glass' *Software Runaways* [Prentice Hall, 1997]). Little by little, teams believe in tiny lies or misrepresentations of the truth about what's going on, and slide into dangerous places. As a rule, the further a team gets from reality, the harder it is to make good things happen. Team leaders must play the role of keeping their team honest (in the sense that the team can lose touch with reality, not that they deliberately lie), reminding people when they are making up answers, ignoring problematic situations, or focusing on the wrong priorities.

I remember a meeting I was in years ago with a small product team. They were building something that they wanted my team to use, and the presentation focused on the new features and technologies their product would have. Sitting near the back of the room, I felt increasingly uncomfortable with the presentation. None of the tough issues was being addressed or even mentioned. Then I realized the real problem: by not addressing the important issues, they were wasting everyone's time.

I looked around the room and realized part of the problem: I was the only lead from my organization in attendance. Normally, I'd have expected another leader to ask tough questions already. But with the faces in the room, I didn't know if anyone else was comfortable making waves when necessary. A thousand questions came to mind, and I quickly raised my hand, unleashing a series of simple questions, one after another. "What is your schedule? When can you get working code to us? Who are your other customers, and how will you prioritize their requests against ours? Why is it in our interest to make ourselves dependent on you and your team?" Their jaws dropped. They were entirely unprepared.

It was clear they had not considered these questions before. Worse, they did not expect to have to answer them for potential clients. I politely explained that they were not ready for this meeting. I apologized if my expectations were not made clear when the meeting was arranged (I thought they were). I told them that without those answers, this meeting was a waste of everyone's time, including theirs. I suggested we postpone the rest of the meeting until they had answers for these simple questions. They sheepishly agreed, and the meeting ended.

In PM parlance, what I did in this story was call bullshit. This is in reference to the card game Bullshit, where you win if you get rid of all the cards in your hand. In each turn of the game, a player states which cards he's playing as he places them face down into a pile. He is not obligated to tell the truth. So, if at any time another player thinks the first player is lying, she can "call bullshit" and force the first player to show his cards. If the accuser is right, the first player takes all of the cards in the pile (a major setback). However, if the accuser is wrong, she takes the pile.

Calling bullshit makes things happen.[3] If people expect you will ask them tough questions, and not hesitate to push them hard until you get answers, they will prepare for them before they meet with you. They will not waste your or your team's time. Remember that all kinds of deception, including self-deception, work against projects. The sooner the truth comes to light, the sooner you can do something about it. Because most people avoid conflict and prefer to pretend things are OK (even when there is evidence they are not), someone has to push to get the truth out. The more you can keep the truth out in the open, the more your team can stay low to the ground, moving at high speed.

The challenge with questioning others is that it can run against the culture of an individual or organization. Some cultures see questioning as an insult or a lack of trust. They may see attempts to keep things honest as personal attacks, instead of as genuine inquiries into the truth. You may need to approach these situations more formally than I did in the story. Make a list of questions you expect people to answer, and provide it to them before meetings. Or, create a list of questions that anyone in the organization is free to ask anyone at any time (including VPs and PMs), and post it on the wall in a conference room. If you make it public knowledge from day one that bullshit will be called at any time, you can make it part of the culture without insulting anyone. However, leaders still have the burden of actually calling bullshit from time to time, demonstrating for the team that cutting to the truth quickly can be done.

3   See "How to detect bullshit" at *http://www.scottberkun.com/essays/53-how-to-detect-bullshit/*.

Know the critical path

In project management terminology, the critical path is the shortest sequence of work that can complete the project. In critical path analysis, a diagram or flowchart is made of all work items, showing which items are dependent on which others. If done properly, this diagram shows where the bottlenecks will be. For example, if features B and C can't be completed until A is done, then A is on the critical path for that part of the project. This is important because if A is delayed or done poorly, it will seriously impact the completion of work items B and C. It's important then for a project manager to be able to plan and prioritize the critical path. Sometimes a relatively unimportant component on its own can be the critical dependency that prevents true priority 1 work from being completed. Without doing critical path analysis, you might never recognize this until it is too late.[4]

From a higher-level perspective, there is a critical path to all situations. They don't need to be diagrammed or measured to the same level of detail, but the thought processes in assessing many PM situations are similar: look at the problem as a series of links, and see where the bottlenecks or critical points are. Which decisions or actions are dependent on which other decisions or actions? Then consider if enough attention is being paid to them, or if the real issue isn't the one currently being discussed. You dramatically accelerate a team by putting its attention directly on the elements, factors, and decisions that are central to progress.

Always have a sense for the critical path of:

- The project's engineering work (as described briefly earlier)
- Human relationships (which relationships between people are the true high risks?)
- The project's high-level decision-making process (who is slowing down the team?)
- The team's processes for building code or triaging bugs (are there needless forms, meetings, or approvals?)
- The production process of propping content to the Web or intranet
- Any meeting, situation, or process that impacts project goals

Making things happen effectively requires a strong sense of critical paths. Anytime you walk into a room, read an email, or get involved in a decision, you must think through what the critical paths are. Is this really the core issue? Will this discussion or line of thinking resolve it? Focus your energy (or the room's energy) on addressing those

---

4 Many project management textbooks cover critical path analysis in detail. A summary can be found at *http://en.wikipedia.org/wiki/Critical_path*. For deeper coverage, see Stephen Devaux's *Total Project Control* (Wiley, 1999).

considerations first and evaluating what needs to be done to ensure those critical paths are made shorter, or resourced sufficiently, to prevent delays. If you can nail the critical path, less-critical issues will more easily fall into place.

For some organizations, the fastest way to improve the (non-engineering) critical path is to distribute authority across the team. Instead of requiring consensus, let individuals make decisions and use their own judgment as to when consensus is needed. Do the same thing for approvals, documentation, forms, or other possible bureaucratic overhead (see Chapter 10). Often the best way of improving critical paths in organizations is to remove processes and shift authority down and across a team, instead of creating new processes or hierarchies.

Be relentless

"The world responds to action, and not much else."
—Scott Adams

Many smart people can recognize when there is a problem, but few expend the energy to find a solution, and then summon the courage to do it. There are always easier ways: give up, accept a partial solution, procrastinate until it goes away (fingers crossed), or blame others. The harder way is to take the problem head-on and resist giving in to conclusions that don't allow for satisfaction of the goals. Successful project managers simply do not give up easily. If something is important to the project, they will act aggressively—using any means necessary—to find an answer or solve the problem. This might mean reorganizing a dysfunctional team, getting a room of difficult people to agree on goals, finding answers to questions, or settling disagreements between people.

Sometimes this means asking people to do things they don't like doing, or raising questions they don't want to answer. Without someone forcing those things to happen, the easier way out will tend to be chosen for you. Many projects consist of people with specialized roles who are unlikely to take responsibility for things that are beyond their limited scope (or that fall between the cracks of their role and someone else's). Perhaps more problematic is that most of us avoid conflict. It's often the PM who has to question people, challenge assumptions, and seek the truth, regardless of how uncomfortable it might make others (although the goal is to do this in a way that makes them as comfortable as possible). PMs have to be willing to do these things when necessary.

Many times, situations that initially seem untenable or intractable crumble underneath the psychological effort of a tenacious project manager. A classic story about this attitude is the *Apollo 13* mission. In his book *Failure Is Not an Option* (Berkley Publishing, 2001), Gene Kranz describes the effort that went into fixing the life-support system on the damaged spacecraft. It was one of the hardest engineering challenges the team faced, and there were grave doubts among those with the most expertise that even a partial solution was possible. Kranz took the position that not only would they find a way, they would do so in limited time. He refused to accept any easy way out, and he pushed his team to explore alternatives, resolving their disputes and focusing their energy. All three versions of the story—the film *Apollo 13*, Kranz's book, and *Lost Moon* (Pocket, 1995), by Jim Lovell (the mission captain) and Jeffrey Kluger—provide fascinating accounts of one of the greatest project management and problem-solving stories in history.

Effective PMs simply consider more alternatives before giving up than other people do. They question the assumptions that were left unchallenged by others, because they came from either a VP people were afraid of or a source of superior expertise that no one felt the need to challenge. The question, "How do you know what you know?" is the simplest way to clarify what is assumed and what is real, yet many people are afraid, or forget, to ask it. Being relentless means believing that 99% of the time there is a solution to the problem (including, in some cases, changing the definition of the problem), and that if it can't be found with the information at hand, deeper and more probing questions need to be asked, no matter who has to be challenged. The success of the project has to come first.

One of my managers in the Windows division at Microsoft was Hillel Cooperman, perhaps the most passionate and dedicated manager I've ever had. I remember once coming into his office with a dilemma. My team was stuck on a complicated problem involving both engineering and political issues. We needed another organization to do important work for us, which they were unwilling to do. I had brainstormed with everyone involved, I had solicited opinions from other senior people, but I was still stuck. There didn't seem to be a reasonable solution, yet this was something critical to the project, and I knew giving in would be unacceptable. After explaining my situation, the conversation went something like this: "What haven't you tried yet?" I made the mistake of answering, "I've tried everything." He just laughed at me. "Everything? How could you possibly have tried everything? If you've tried everything, you'd have found a choice you feel comfortable with, which apparently you haven't yet." We found this funny because we both knew exactly where the conversation was going.

He then asked if I wanted some suggestions. Of course I said yes. We riffed for a few minutes, back and forth, and came up with a new list of things to consider. "Who haven't you called on the phone? Email isn't good for this kind of thing. And of all the people on the other side—those who disagree with you—who is most receptive to you? How hard have you sold them on what you want? Should I get involved and work from above you? Would that help? What about our VP? How hard have you pushed engineering to find a workaround? A little? A lot? As hard as possible? Did you offer to buy them drinks? Dinner? Did you talk to them one-on-one, or in a group? Keep going, keep going, keep going. You will find a way. I trust you, and I know you will solve this. Keep going."

He did two things for me: he reminded me that not only did I have alternatives, but also that it was still my authority to make the decision. As tired as I was, I left his office convinced there were more paths to explore and that it was my job to do so. My ownership of the issue, which he'd reconfirmed, helped motivate me to be relentless. The solution was lurking inside one of them, and I just had to find it. Like the dozens of other issues I was managing at the same time, I eventually found a solution (there was an engineering workaround), but only because I hunted for it. It was not going to come and find me.

Among other lessons, I learned from Hillel that diligence wins battles. If you make it clear that you are dead serious and will fight to the end about a particular issue, you force more possibilities to arise. People will question their assumptions if you hold on to yours long enough. You push people to consider things they haven't considered, which is often where the answer lies. Even in disagreements or negotiations, if you know you're right and keep pushing hard, people will often give in. Sometimes they'll give in just to get you to leave them alone. Being pushy, provided you're not offensive, can be an effective technique all on its own.

Being relentless is fundamental to making things happen. There are many ways for projects to slide into failure, and unless there is at least one positive emotional force behind the project—pushing it forward, seeking out alternatives, believing there is always a way out of every problem—the project is unlikely to succeed. Good PMs are that force. They are compelled to keep moving forward, always on the lookout for something that can be improved in a faster or smarter way. They seek out chaos and convert it into clarity. As skeptical as project managers need to be, they are simultaneously optimistic that all problems can be solved if enough intensity and focus are applied. For reasons they themselves cannot fully explain, PMs continually hold a torch up against ambiguity and doubt, and refuse to quit until every possible alternative has been explored. They believe that good thinking wins, and that it takes work to find good thoughts.

Be savvy

Being relentless doesn't mean you have to knock on every door, chase people down the hallway, or stay at work until you pass out at your desk. Sheer quantity of effort can be noble and good, but always look for ways to work smart rather than just hard. Be relentless in spirit, but clever and savvy in action. Just because you refuse to give up doesn't mean you have to suffer through mindless, stupid, or frustrating activities (although sometimes they're unavoidable). Look for smart ways around a problem or faster ways to resolve them. Make effective use of the people around you instead of assuming you have to do everything yourself. But most importantly, be perceptive of what's going on around you, with individuals and with teams.

A fundamental mistake many PMs make is to forget to assess who they are working with and adjust their approach accordingly. Navy SEALs and Army Rangers are trained to carry out missions on many different kinds of terrain: deserts, swamps, jungles, tundra. Without this training, their effectiveness would be limited: they'd struggle to survive on unfamiliar terrain because their skills wouldn't work (imagine a solider in green and olive camouflage, trying to hide on a snow-covered field). The first lesson they learn is how to evaluate their environment and consider what tactics and strategies from their skill set will work for where they are. The same is true for PMs. Instead of geographic environments, PMs must pay attention to the different social, political, and organizational environments they are in, and use the right approaches for where they are.

Being savvy and environment-aware is most important in the following situations:

- Motivating and inspiring people
- Organizing teams and planning for action
- Settling arguments or breaking deadlocks
- Negotiating with other organizations or cultures
- Making arguments for resources
- Persuading anyone of anything
- Managing reports (personnel)

Here's the savvy PM's rough guide to evaluating an environment. These questions apply to an individual you might be working with or to the larger team or group:

- **What communication styles are being used?** Direct or indirect? Are people openly communicative, or are they reserved? Are there commonly accepted ways to make certain kinds of points? Are people generally effective in using email? Meetings? Are decisions made openly or behind closed doors? Match your approaches to the ones that will be effective with whomever you're talking to.

- **How broad or narrow is the group's sense of humor?** What topics are forbidden to laugh at or question? How are delicate/difficult/contentious subjects or decisions handled by others?

- **Are arguments won based on data?** Logical argument through debate? Adherence to the project goals? Who yells the loudest? Who has the brownest nose? Consider making arguments that use the style, format, or tone most palatable to your audience, whether it's a lone tester down the hall or a room full of executives.

- **Who is effective at doing <insert thing you are trying to do here>, and what can I emulate or learn from her?** Pay attention to what works. Who are the stars? Who gets the most respect? How are they thriving? Who is failing here? Why are they failing?

- **In terms of actual behavior, what values are most important to this person or group?** Intelligence? Courage? Speed? Clarity? Patience? Obedience? What behaviors are least valued or are deplored? Programmers and managers might have very different values. Know what the other guy values before you try to convince him of something.

- **What is the organizational culture?** Every university, corporation, or team has a different set of values built into the culture. If you don't think your organization has one, you've been there too long and can't see it anymore (or maybe you never saw it at all). Some organizations value loyalty and respect above intelligence and individuality. Others focus on work ethic and commitment.

Depending on the answers to these questions, a PM should make adjustments to how she does her work. Every time you enter another person's office, or another meeting, there should always be some adjustments made. Like a Marine, assess the environment and then judge the best route to get to the project goals. Avoid taking the hard road if there is a smarter way to get where you need to go.

Guerilla tactics

Being savvy means you are looking for, and willing to take, the smarter route. The following list contains tactics that I've used successfully or have been successfully used on me. While your mileage with them may vary, I'm sure this list will get you thinking of other savvy ways to accomplish what needs to be done to meet your goals. Some of these have risks, which I'll note, and must be applied carefully. Even if you choose never to use these yourself, by being aware of them, you will be savvier about what's going on around you.

- **Know who has authority.** Don't waste time arguing with people who have no influence over the issue. To be effective, you need to know who makes decisions or influences a particular situation. Find out who it is (it's not always the most senior person in the room, and the identity of the person may change from issue to issue), get time with her one-on-one, and make your case. Or, at least find out what she truly objects to. If you can't get to the most influential person (Sally, the VP), find the person who has the greatest influence on her (Sally's best employee). Go to the highest point on the chain you can reach. Warning: don't end-run people. Go to the point of authority, but invite the opposing viewpoint if necessary, or disclose to him what you're doing. "Look, we disagree, but we can agree that it's Sally's decision. I'm going to go talk to her about this tomorrow. I'd like you to be there." (See Chapter 16.)

- **Go to the source.** Don't dillydally with people's secondhand interpretations of what someone said, and don't depend on written reports or emails for complex information. Find the actual person and talk to him directly. You can't get new questions answered by reading reports or emails, and often people will tell you important things that were inappropriate for written communication. Going to the source is always more reliable and valuable than the alternatives, and it's worth the effort required. For example, if two programmers are arguing about what a third programmer said, get that third programmer in the room or on the phone. Always cut to the chase and push others to do the same.

- **Switch communication modes.** If communication isn't working, switch the mode. Instead of email, call them on the phone. Instead of a phone call, drop by their office. Everyone is more comfortable in some mediums than others. (Generally, face to face, in front of a whiteboard, trumps everything. Get people in a room with a whiteboard if the email thread on some issue gets out of control.) Don't let the limitations of a particular technology stop you. Sometimes switching modes gets you a different response, even if your request is the same, because people are more receptive to one mode over another. For anything consequential, it's worth the money and time to get on a plane, or drive to their office, if it improves the communication dynamic between you and an important coworker.

- **Get people alone.** When you talk to someone privately, her disposition toward you is different than when you talk to her in a large group. In a meeting, important people have to craft what they say to be appropriate for all of the ears in the room. Sometimes, you'll hear radically different things depending on who is in earshot. If you want a frank and honest opinion, or an in-depth intense conversation, you need to get people alone. Also, consider people of influence: if Jim trusts Beth's opinion, and you want to convince Jim, if you can convince Beth first, bring her along. Don't ambush anyone, but don't shy away from lining things up to make progress happen.

- **Hunt people down.** If something is urgent and you are not getting the response time you need, carve out time on your schedule to stake out the person's office or cubicle. I've done this many times. If he wasn't answering my phone calls or emails, he'd soon come back from a meeting and find me sitting by his door. He'd usually be caught so off guard that I'd have a negotiating advantage. Don't be afraid to go after people if you need something from them. Find them in the coffee room. Look for them in the café at lunchtime. Ask their secretary what meetings they are in and wait outside. Be polite, but hunt and get what you need. (However, please do not cross over into their personal lives. If you hunt information well, you shouldn't ever even need to cross this particular line.)

- **Hide.** If you are behind on work and need blocks of time to get caught up, become invisible. On occasion, I've staked out a conference room (in a neighboring building) and told only the people who really might need me where I was. I caught up on email, specs, employee evaluations, or anything important that wasn't getting done, without being interrupted. For smaller orgs, working from home or a coffee shop can have the same effect (wireless makes this easy these days). I always encouraged my reports to do this whenever they felt it necessary. Uninterrupted time can be hard for PMs to find, so if you can't find it, you have to make it.

- **Get advice.** Don't fly solo without a map unless you have to. In a given situation, consider who involved thinks most highly of you, or who may have useful advice for how you can get what you need. Make use of any expertise or experience you have access to through others. Pull them aside and ask them for it. This can be about a person, a decision, a plan, anything. "Hey Bob, I'd like your advice on this budget. Do you have a few minutes?" Or, "Jane, I'm trying to work with Sam on this issue. Any advice on the best way to convince him to cut this feature?" For many people, simply asking their advice will score you credibility points: it's an act of respect to ask for someone's opinion.

- **Call in favors, beg, and bribe.** Make use of the credibility or generosity you've developed a reputation for. If you need an engineer to do extra work for you, either because you missed something or a late requirement came in, ask her to do you a favor. Go outside the boundaries of the strict working relationship and ask. Offer to buy her dinner ($20 is often well worth whatever the favor is), or tell her that you owe her one (and do hold yourself to this). The worst thing that can happen is that she'll say no. The more favors you've done for others, the more chips you'll have to bank on. Also, consider working three-way trades (e.g., in the game Settlers of Cattan) if you know of something she wants that you can get from someone else. It's not unethical to offer people things that will convince them to help with work that needs to be done.

- **Play people off each other.** This doesn't have to be evil—if you're very careful. If Sam gives you a work estimate of 10 days, which you think is bogus, go and ask Bob. If Bob says it will take less than 10 days, go back to Sam and bring Bob along. A conversation will immediately ensue about what the work estimate really should be. If you do this once, no engineer will ever give you bogus estimates again (you've called bullshit). However, depending on Sam's personality, this may cost you relationship points with him, so do it as tactfully as possible, and only when necessary. Good lead programmers should be calling estimate bluffs on their own, but if they don't, it's up to you.

- **Stack the deck.** Never walk into an important meeting without knowing the opinions of the important people in the room. Always arrive with a sense for who is likely to support your opinion and who is likely to be against it, and have a strategy developed for navigating through it all (see Chapter 16). If something important is at stake, make some moves to sway those against you, or rally their support, before the meeting. Don't lie, manipulate, or mislead, but do seriously prepare and understand the arguments and counterarguments that will come up.

- **Buy people coffee and tasty things.** This sounds stupid, but I've found that people I've argued with for days on end are somehow more receptive over a nice cup of coffee at a local coffee shop. Change the dynamic of the relationship: no matter how much you like or don't like the person, make the invitation and invest the 20 seconds of effort it requires. Even if he says, "No, why can't we talk here?", you've lost nothing. Moving the conversation to a different location, perhaps one less formal, can help him open up to alternatives he wouldn't consider before. Think biologically: humans are in better moods after they've eaten a fine meal or when they are in more pleasant surroundings. I've seen PMs who keep doughnuts or cookies (as well as rum and scotch) in their office. Is that an act of goodwill? Yes…but there are psychological benefits to making sure the people you are working with are well fed and associate you with good things.

Summary

- Everything can be represented in an ordered list. Most of the work of project management is correctly prioritizing things and leading the team in carrying them out.

- The three most basic ordered lists are: project goals (vision), list of features, and list of work items. They should always be in sync with each other. Each work item contributes to a feature, and each feature contributes to a goal.

- There is a bright yellow line between priority 1 work and everything else.

- Things happen when you say no. If you can't say no, you effectively have no priorities.

- The PM has to keep the team honest and close to reality.

- Knowing the critical path in engineering and team processes enables efficiency.

- You must be both relentless and savvy to make things happen.

Exercises

A. Think of a nonwork situation where there was no predefined leader—perhaps a social event or a class project. Who emerged as the leader and why? Did she explicitly ask for permission to lead, or did she just take control?

B. Volunteer to lead something where no one has to work for you and the only way to make things happen is through persuasion and influence. Start a social group on Meetup (*www.meetup.com*), or a rec league sports team in your neighborhood. Do it purely for the experience of exploring your ability to make things happen.

C. Who in your organization has a reputation for making things happen? How did they earn it? How about people who have reputations for making things not happen? Is there any relationship between their seniority and their MTH (making things happen) ability?

D. For every goal you have, identify the single most important person for making that goal happen (often it's a single programmer or team leader). Make sure he is aware of his importance to the goal and your willingness to do whatever you can to make him successful.

E. How are you tracking priorities for your team? How do you make those priorities visible and clear to everyone? Ask people on your team for feedback on ways to make the priorities easier to remember.

F. Imagine a project where the critical path for most work items goes through one single person. What are the pros and cons of this situation? What is the range of possible things you can do to either reduce the risks of this situation or increase the chances?

G. Have you ever worked for someone who kept changing her mind? What impact did this have on your ability to get things done? What about someone who never changed her mind?

H. If being savvy is part of making things happen, what does this say about how project managers and leaders should be hired? How can someone's ability to be persuasive be evaluated during the interview process?

I. You decide to become a relentless project manager. You push hard to make things happen and never give up. Your boss and other team leaders notice and clearly feel threatened by your new attitude. How can you make things happen without rocking the boat and upsetting other leaders?

J. When is it appropriate to go to your boss, or your boss' boss to make things happen? How can you be savvy when escalating an issue up the management chain?

K. Simply saying "Failure is not an option" doesn't do much on it's own. Many people say lines from movies hoping that saying the words will bring with it all of the other things necessary to succeed. Show the *Apollo 13* movie at work and invite people from your team. Discuss as a group what assets Gene Kranz and his team possessed that made success possible. How is this different from your team?

CHAPTER FOURTEEN

Middle-game strategy

The title of this chapter, "Middle-game strategy," refers to the game of chess. Chess games are divided into three parts: opening, middle game, and end-game. The middle-game is when the player's general strategy becomes evident and is applied through moves he makes. Most moves in a game are made during middle game. End-game is the conclusion of play, where resources are slim and every single move counts. This chapter focuses on project mid-game, and the next chapter covers project end-game.

> **"Chance favors the prepared."**
>
> —*Louis Pasteur*

Mid-game on projects is the middle of the overall schedule. You'll know you're in mid-game when some things are working, but some things aren't, some issues have been discovered and resolved, but you know others haven't even been found yet. Mid-game is challenging because many things are happening at the same time, and it's difficult to maintain clarity on what's going well and what's not. The term *fog of war*—used by Clausewitz[1] in reference to how chaotic warfare can seem while you are in it—applies well to mid-game. There is an inevitable fog of development activity that surrounds the team, and it's easy for the inexperienced to get lost. It's the responsibility of team leaders to bring the team through the uncertainty of mid-game and out into end-game, where things become clear again.

In the simplest possible view, mid-game and end-game are all about high-level maintenance:[2]

1. If things are going well at the end of the first day, the goal for the next day is to keep it going well.

2. If on any day the project is not going well, it's your job to figure out what the issues are and then take action to make the project run well again. This might take hours, days, or weeks.

3. Repeat until the project is complete.

The obvious challenge is there are many things that can happen to make a project run poorly. Worse, there is limited time to figure out what's wrong and less time to resolve it. Not to mention the effort required to keep the healthy parts of the project from running into trouble.

---

1 Karl von Clausewitz was an influential 19th-century Prussian military thinker. See *http://en.wikipedia.org/wiki/Clausewitz*.

2 CMM, the Capacity Maturity Model for software development developed by the Software Engineering institute, has defined several best practices around mid-game project-level management. See *http://www2.umassd.edu/SWPI/sei/tr25f/tr25.html* or *http://www.sei.cmu.edu/cmm/*.

For these and other reasons, energy and stress levels during mid-game and end-game are very high. The team is moving at increasing speed and the margins of error get smaller every day. And then as end-game approaches, someone has to find the right way not only to apply the brakes, but also to slow the movement down progressively so that things end well.

In this chapter and the next, I'll be using the same inclusive assumptions about methodology that I made in Chapter 2 (this advice applies well, independent of the methodology you use). It might be worth a quick skim of the section "Silver bullets and methodologies" in Chapter 2 before digging in here.

While this chapter applies mostly to mid-game and the next applies mostly to end-game, there is much overlap in how and when these techniques can be applied (e.g., end-game of one phase can be considered part of the mid-game of the entire project). So, be warned that I will sometimes move back and forth between these two different topics.

> NOTE
>
> The coverage of mid-game and end-game management in this chapter and the next is industrial strength. If you see situations that don't apply because of the size of your project, feel free to skip them. I don't expect everything I cover to apply to any single project. However, I'm trying to provide value not only to your current project, but also future projects.

Flying ahead of the plane

Piloting large, dangerous objects requires more than a steady hand. The larger the thing you're steering, and the more people in it, the more inertia it has. Like project management, novices at piloting large machines (cars, planes, aircraft carriers, etc.) underestimate the time it takes for changes at the helm to be reflected in the behavior of the thing they are steering. As shown in Figure 14-1, the trajectory of large vehicles, or projects, changes significantly depending on how much momentum or other forces are involved. Most people fail to set their expectations properly for the results of their actions. Often this is because they don't understand the dynamics of the thing they're operating. Like someone learning to drive who skids out in the snow for the first time, there are too many unexplained forces interacting for her to stay in control.

When people who are supposed to be in control lose control, their common response is to panic. They might not admit this (people in panic mode rarely admit they are panicking), but it's true. The first response is usually to take a bold corrective action in direct response to the problem. But since they don't really understand all of the forces, this corrective action will typically be much too strong (see Figure 14-2). By the time they realize what they've done, another corrective action is needed, which they perform immediately. But since they're still using the same logic that got them into this fun situation in the first place, more problems ensue.

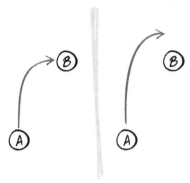

FIGURE 14-1. *The same action can have different results, depending on how much project inertia there is.*

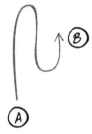

FIGURE 14-2. *To the dismay of those who are supposed to be in control, corrective actions on unknown forces have unpredictable (and often maddening) results.*

The fact is when an airplane, automobile, or project becomes unstable, it's dangerously hard to control—even for someone with expert skill and experience. (Smaller projects are certainly more agile and responsive, but they have their momentums, too.) Instability makes the result of most actions unpredictable because there are too many variables changing too quickly. Good project management, then, is largely about staying one or two steps ahead of the project, investing whatever energy is necessary to avoid getting into these situations in the first place.

Fighter pilots have a phrase for what happens when a pilot fails to stay ahead: flying behind the plane. It means that the pilot has failed to stay (at least) one step ahead of what's happening to his machine, and he is now a victim of the interaction of forces on his aircraft. Like flying high-performance airplanes, projects require the management of many different interactive forces. They are both nonlinear systems, meaning that changing one element (speed, angle, schedule, goals) may have more than one effect, or may affect the system with more force than expected, because it's amplified across many different factors or people. The warning is this: even with a stable but high-speed project, the complex nature of both the code base and the team means any management action may have unexpected consequences. Sometimes these consequences won't be visible for days or even weeks. When these delayed consequences do surface, it's all too easy to assume something more recent caused the problem, making it difficult to effectively resolve it.

Check your sanity

For project managers, the most effective way to fly in front of the plane is having a daily sanity check. Programmers use the term *sanity checking* to ensure that certain important things are true in their code (in C terminology, think assert( )). This is a very good idea because assumptions are very dangerous things. In code, when one of these sanity checks fails, everyone can skip past the hopeless search for red herrings (problems that don't exist), and ask the more fundamental question of why an insane condition has been introduced into the system.

If you want to "fly in front of the plane," you have to constantly make sure the conditions you're expecting are still true. And then if you find one that's false, you know immediately where your attention needs to be.

The challenge is there are many other possible sanity checks. Between goals, schedules, technologies, morale, competition, budget, and politics, it's impossible to verify everything all the time (although this doesn't prevent some paranoid managers from trying). It's a fatal mistake to torture a team by confirming dozens of random assumptions every day. The more pokes you make at a team to confirm things that should generally be true, the less you trust them, and the more you waste their time. You want to know the state of the project without disturbing the state of the project.

There are three ways to do this: tactical questions, strategic questions, and transparent progress measures for the team. We'll cover progress measures in the next chapter. For now, let's focus on tactical and strategic questions for sanity checking.

The process is simple: keep a short list of questions that will help put you in front of the plane and make a ritual of asking them. Ask tactical questions once a day; ask strategic questions once a week. You can do this alone, or pick specific members of the team to be involved in this process with you. You should also encourage individuals on the team, especially those who are experienced or seasoned, to do similar high-level sanity checking all on their own and to correlate their findings with yours.

My approach to this was as follows: I'd lock into my schedule a half-hour weekly meeting with myself (if I don't protect my time, who will?). I'd close my door, put on some tunes, and run through my question list. Often it only took a few minutes. I'd then be able to reprioritize my day, or my team, accordingly. On some teams, I've pushed to make this kind of questioning part of the team culture, and I did smaller versions of this type of questioning and answering during team meetings.

Tactical (daily) questions for staying ahead

- **What are our goals and commitments? Are these still accurate?** There is so much work that needs to be done on any given day that it's inevitable you and others will lose sight of the goals. Simply looking at them every day resets your focus and priorities. More important for the team, if the official goals don't match the real goals (say, due to a VP's whim) or the team goals (make stuff we think is cool), then the goals are not accurate. If the goals are not accurate, the team is in conflict. When a team is in conflict, symptoms will surface. Don't wait for symptoms if you see obvious conflicts that will eventually cause them. Stay in front, especially on issues that impact the goals directly.

- **Is what we're doing today contributing to our goals?** Look at the work items your programmers are working on today, tomorrow, and this week. Is it clear how they are contributing to the goals or fulfilling requirements? If not, the ship is starting to drift. Work with the appropriate programmer(s) to refresh everyone's understanding of the goals and the work's value toward the goals. Then adjust one of three things: the goals, the work, or both. This is sometimes called work alignment; like the wheels on your car, you have to periodically check to make sure things are moving in the same direction.

- **Are the work items not only being completed, but being completed in a way that satisfies the requirements and scenarios?** There are 1,000 ways to complete a unit of work that do not meet the full spirit and intention of the design. Any good design or specification will have defined things such that work items will satisfy the real customer scenarios. However, the subtleties of usability, business requirements, component integration, and visual design are often lost on programmers with 15 other work items to do. If a dedicated interface designer (or other expert) is around, she should be actively reviewing check-ins and the daily build to make sure the work items satisfy holistic, not just line item, requirements.

Strategic (weekly/monthly) questions for staying ahead

These questions are often the subject of leadership meetings. If there is a weekly or monthly status discussion, it's these sorts of issues that deserve leadership attention. But even for an individual PM working on a small area, these questions apply.

- **What is our current probability to hit the next date/milestone/deliverable at the appropriate level of quality?** Things have changed since work estimates were done. How do people feel about the work now that they're in it? Ask yourself, and key people on your team, what the probability is of successfully meeting the next date. 100%? 90%? 50%? High? Medium? Low? Be honest, and ask others to do so as well. Be sensitive to the team: don't make this guilt- or challenge-driven, as if you're trying to prove that their estimates are bad or that they need to work harder. Instead, make it clear that you need honest answers as of the current moment. (Why they have low confidence or who's to blame for it doesn't change the fact that they have tangible doubts. You want to be aware of and understand these doubts.)

- **What adjustments are needed to improve this probability?** It should be exceedingly rare to get 100% confidence in the next date from anyone who's honest and sane. The follow-up to the probability question should always be how you can make the probability higher. Fewer meetings and interruptions? Faster decisions? Cut features? Better decisions? Clarify goals? Better code reviews? What? Ask the people who are most involved in the daily frontline work. Make it a high-priority item for yourself and the team to actively ask this question and invest in the answers.

- **How do we make adjustments carefully and in isolation?** Always think surgically first. What is the smallest amount of action necessary to successfully resolve the problem and improve our probability? A phone call? An email? Making an important decision visible? Firing someone? Don't be afraid to take big action if that's the smallest amount that will do the job. If no surgical options are available, think holistically. Do the goals need adjusting? The check-in process? What system process or attitude can be adjusted to resolve the symptom and the cause? (See the next section, "Taking safe action.")

- **What are the biggest or most probable risks for today/next week/next month? What are our contingencies if they come true?** Simply by identifying three or more dangerous or likely risks, you take a large step toward preventing them; you will have turned your radar on, and you'll be sensitive to any warning signs that might indicate these problems are occurring. Even if you take only 5 or 10 minutes a week to list out possible risks, and your possible responses to those risks, you'll be putting yourself in front of the plane. This kind of project insurance is often cheap—a few minutes a week buys a great deal of protection.

- **How might the world have changed without me knowing it?** Is my VP or stakeholder still on board? Have his goals changed? Are key players on my team worried about something I don't know about that will impact the project if they are right? What has our competitor done that we might need to respond to? Are our partners or dependencies still on track? What is going wrong today that I won't find out about until tomorrow? A few short phone calls or hallway wanderings typically answer this question. Be careful not to micromanage, act out of paranoia, or breed fear in others. Make it a common and casual thing to make these kinds of inquiries. More so, encourage and reward people who proactively get this kind of information (about their own or others' responsibilities) to you.

However, no matter how experienced, prepared, or smart you are, there will always be days that you end up flying behind your project. Learn to see the difference between having a ton of work to do and being behind the plane—they're not the same thing. Odds are good you'll often feel there is more work to do than you have time for. However, if you've built ordered lists to prioritize work (see Chapter 13), you'll know there are always things waiting for your time. But when you're behind, you'll feel frozen, depressed, or even apathetic. You'll believe that no matter how late you stay at the office, you can never get the project back under control.

Three important last things:

1. **When you're behind, know you're behind.** Remember that schedules are probabilities. How sure are you that what needs to be completed will get done this week? 80%? 50%? If odds are 50-50 (or worse) that you'll make it, you're behind; your margin of error is small, and you will make mistakes if you haven't already.

2. **When you see others behind the plane, offer your support to them.** Don't deny the problem: tell them you see it and that you'll try to help. Avoid letting anyone in your sphere of influence flail or panic. Stay calm, help others to stay calm, and work together to get back in front of the plane.

3. **Don't hesitate to get help from peers or supervisors.** This may be the only way to recover and get back out in front. Use their help in prioritizing your time and the team's time, picking up some of your work, or just to listen to you blow off steam. Take someone's hand if it's offered to you. Ask for a hand if it isn't offered.

For more coverage of how to deal with crisis situations, refer to Chapter 11.

Taking safe action

During mid-game, most actions are smaller, tighter versions of PM activity done during planning or design. If a requirement was missed and needs to be incorporated, the process for defining and documenting it is just a double-time version of what was done during the requirements process (understand needs, consider tradeoffs, define, and prioritize). Or if something was overlooked in the spec, the process for resolving it is a double- or triple-time repeat of the specification process. Few new skills are employed during mid-game. It's usually just a leaner and faster version of a skill that was used earlier on. The problem is that working at speed breeds risk. Taking safe action during mid-game simply means that the integrity of the project is not unintentionally disrupted as a result of the action.

Safe action is difficult because the ammunition is live in mid-game. Things are already in motion and many decisions have already been made, which may conflict with any new action. For example, if halfway through the construction of your house you decide to change the plan from a standard A-frame to a geodesic dome, you will have to throw away lots of materials and effort, and possibly require new work to be done under greater pressure. It takes experience to learn how changing a requirement, cutting a feature, or modifying a design will affect both the code base and the team.

The PM's goal must be to take safe action. She needs to move and behave in ways that simultaneously keep the project on track toward goals that might change, while causing as little damage to the project as possible. Some damage is inevitable and should be expected. But the more efficient a PM's actions are, the less negative impact there will be.

As Figure 14-3 shows, the further along a project is, the harder it is to take safe action. This is because the probability that an action will have expensive consequences goes up over time: the odds are higher that work already completed will need to be modified or thrown away. Those expenses might be entirely warranted, but taking safe action means that there is some knowledge about costs before decisions are made.

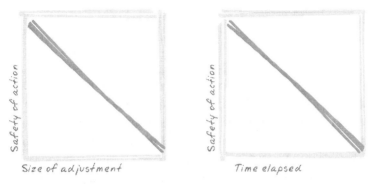

FIGURE 14-3. *Making safe adjustments is more difficult if the adjustment is large or it's made late in the project.*

When considering adjustments (feature/goal/requirement changes) during mid-game, there are five questions to consider:

1. What problem are we trying to solve? Do we need to solve this problem to be successful? Do we need to solve this problem during this milestone? Can we just live with the problem?

2. Is this problem a symptom or a cause? Is it acceptable to only resolve the symptom?

3. Do we understand the state of the code or the team well enough to predict how an action will impact them?

4. Are the costs of the adjustment (including the time to understand the state of the code/team, consider alternatives, and get political support for the decision) worth the benefit of the change? Finding and then resolving the causes might cost more than just living with the symptoms, much less fixing them.

5. Are the risks of potential new problems worth the benefit of the change?

The decision of whether to take action relies on the same decision-making strategies discussed in Chapter 8. Any design, specification, communication, or political action required makes use of the tactics discussed in Chapters 6, 7, 9, and 16, respectively. The attitude and approach are the same, but the timeline and margin for error are much smaller. The lack of time to consider options means two things. First, rely on knowledge gained during any prototyping or design effort early on; some of the adjustments you're considering now should have surfaced back then. Use the team's knowledge to aid in current analysis. Second, be conservative. The less you know, the more risks you can't see. The later you are in the schedule, the higher the bar should be for taking action.

Breaking commitments

Part of safe action is considering the commitments team leaders have made. As we discussed in Chapter 12, the trust leaders earn from their team is defined by how the leaders manage their commitments. The vision document, the requirements, and the schedule are all forms of commitment between management, team leaders, programmers, and the customer. Any action you take during mid-game may invalidate the prior commitments you've made.

To maintain trust with your team as changes happen, you must pay respect to previous commitments. As author Watts S. Humphrey stated, "If something changes that impacts either party relative to the commitment, advance notice is given and a new commitment is negotiated."[3] Changes are allowed, but they should follow a process of negotiation similar to the one that led to the first set of commitments (vision, requirements, schedule). You don't need to draft documents or have big meetings, but you do need to inform people as commitments are changing, and involve them in the process of deciding how those changes will happen.

If you are asking your team to throw away two weeks of work, make sure that you included those costs when calculating the decision. Provide them with reasoning as to why the new change is the right one, and tell them what factors contributed to this opinion. If possible, bring people on the team into the discussion before final decisions are made.

Don't be afraid to make changes. Change is good, and it's inevitable. But there are many different kinds of change, and many different ways for a leader to manage a team through it. If you were heading west, and now want the project to head north, you will need to apply the same kinds of skills (although twice as fast and half as formal) required to get the team moving north, as you did to get them moving west. Look back at Chapters 3, 4, 11, and 12 for guidance on leading through change.

---

3   From *Managing the Software Process* (Addison-Wesley Professional, 1989).

The coding pipeline

The pragmatic view of mid-game work focuses on programmers writing code. The only way the project moves forward is with each line of code written that brings the project closer to completion (pet features, unneeded optimizations, etc., do not move the project forward). All of the planning and design effort that takes place before programmers write code, whether done by them or by others, is done to create an efficient sequence of work for them to do while the clock is ticking. This is called the coding pipeline, and there are many techniques for how it's managed.[4]

It's the PM's job to make sure the coding pipeline is running smoothly. While programmers might own the management of the pipeline and decide who works on what,[5] it's still the PM's responsibility to make sure that the programming team has as much support as necessary to make it work. This may involve gopher tasks, organizing meetings, nagging various people to finalize decisions, or, in some cases, resolving the remaining design issues[6] (see Figure 14-4). The PM may have to work a few days in front of the programmer, finalizing designs and feeding the pipeline. If a PM is responsible for the work of several developers, she will have to carefully prioritize her time to ensure she can juggle the competing demands of multiple pipelines (another reason why the lead programmer should be doing some or more of this work).

In *Web Project Management: Delivering Successful Commercial Web Sites* (Morgan Kaufmann, 2001), author Ashley Friedlein calls this process briefing the team, and the details for the next piece of work they are to do is called a brief. As Friedlein writes, "To maximize efficiency and speed of development, your briefs need to be created so that they are always ahead of where the work is at the moment. As soon as a piece of work is finished, you have the brief for the next section of work ready." These briefs are derived from the specs (if still relevant), but include anything new or changed that the programmer might need to know. Without actively briefing programmers during mid-game, there can be any number of things that block a work item and slow down the pipeline: usability issues, visual design work, work items done by other programmers, marketing issues, technical

---

4   Some Agile methods use planning boards, where story cards for each unit of work are tracked. Other teams use a spreadsheet or database to track who is working on what, and what work items will come next.

5   There are formalized ways to do this. Some teams have a weekly meeting where the pipeline for each programmer is briefly discussed: everyone knows the work items for the team (for individuals, for the week). The PM is there to make sure any timing issues are integrated into the pipeline.

6   On UI intensive projects, it was management of the coding pipeline that allowed us to iterate on the design. We'd manage the pipeline to do part of work item A, get it in the usability lab, learn a ton of great stuff, refine the design, and then do the remaining parts of A. Provided we kept the pipeline full, and didn't go over budget for dev time or milestone, designers could do low/mid-level UI design work in parallel with the programming team.

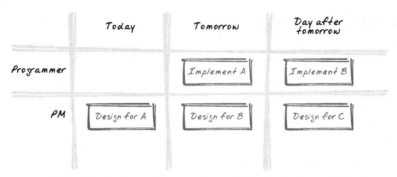

FIGURE 14-4. *The final details of a spec/design can be verified or finalized in parallel by the PM or designer. This contributes to the value of the coding pipeline.*

problems, or external dependencies. Because PMs often have the most diverse set of skills, they're the best people to run point for the coding pipeline, flagging or resolving issues, and smoothing things out before the programmer starts on them. (This includes seeking out frustrated programmers who are blocked, but either won't admit it or haven't realized it yet.)

Four questions define how to do this well:

- **What work items are actively being coded?** Are there any issues blocking programmers from completing their currently active work items? If so, eliminate them (the blocking issues, not the work items). This is a red-alert state for a project. If a programmer is blocked from actively writing code, the project is stalled. Nothing is more important than resolving an issue that blocks a programmer. Simply ask them, "How can I help you resolve this?" They'll let you know if you can help. If the blocking issue is a dependency (e.g., Fred has to finish work item 6 before Bob can start on work item 7), consider what other work a programmer can do until that block is removed.

- **Does the programmer know and understand everything needed to implement the current work item to specification?** There are always questions and gaps that arise only at the moment of implementation. Some programmers are more proactive than others about resolving these gaps in a mature fashion. The PM or designer needs to be available and involved enough to help identify and close these gaps. Sometimes, they can be anticipated—for example, were all the issues raised in the spec review for this work item resolved?

- **What is the next set of items that will be coded?** This is where real pipeline management begins: staying one step ahead of programmers (see Figure 14-4). If the currently active work items are in good shape, the focus moves to the next items up the pipeline. The next items should tend to be the next most important piece of work for the project. Always try to do the most critical work first, even if it's the hardest. For each item in the pipeline, consider what open issues they have that might slow or stall the programmer when the item arrives on his plate. Find and resolve them.

- **Was the last work item that was completed, really completed?** It's the output of the coding pipeline that matters. Someone has to be looking at the effect of check-ins on the build and make sure it does what it's supposed to do from the customer perspective. Did the completion of that last work item truly add the functionality and behavior required? Does the test team agree? Did all unit tests pass? Did someone at least open bugs to track what's missing? Daily builds (described in the next chapter) are an easy way to track this because you can always experience the current state of the project—and find gaps in what was completed—to what is needed. The bigger the work item, the more important this is.

Some programmers take more responsibility for their coding pipelines than others. Many programmers will more aggressively seek out certain kinds of issues (technical) and tend to ignore or delay on others (business, political). Part of your relationship with each programmer is knowing how much involvement you need to take on in managing their pipeline. It doesn't matter so much who does it, as long as it's done, and someone is actively verifying and protecting the quality of those work items. (This is a role discussion, as described in Chapter 9.)

Aggressive and conservative pipelining

Often, the coding pipeline only needs to be three items ahead of the programming team (if each item requires two days, three items need more than a week of work). It can be an informal discussion between PMs and programmers to agree on the next logical sequence. (Or, if a master critical path or Gantt chart exists, and it's actually not weeks out of date, the pipeline can be derived from it.) This gives just enough of a buffer so that if a blocking issue can't be resolved in time, the programmer and PM have enough time to find another suitable work item to put in the pipeline while that blocking issue gets resolved.

A team with an aggressive posture can bet more heavily on pipelining to prioritize issues. Instead of making an elaborate work breakdown structure (WBS) of all work items, the team bets heavily on changes happening and on the ability for the PM or lead programmer to manage the pipeline. The risks here are higher: if the pipeline gets backed up or can't stay ahead of the team, bad decisions will get made and time will be wasted. For more on building good WBSs and applying them to project scheduling, see *Total Project Control*, by Stephen Devaux (Wiley, 1999), or any good traditional project management reference.

For teams with a more conservative posture, managing the pipeline is a gentle refinement of the original work-item list that was created during planning. The pipeline may be mapped out for weeks or months of work, using the original plan as the source for the pipeline for each programmer. There might be small adjustments, but the expectation is that the original plan will stay viable through, at least, the milestone. When the next milestone starts, a new work-item list is generated as part of planning, and the process repeats. So, depending on how short the milestone is, or how stable a project is, up-front pipeline planning can be made to work.

However, the fundamental point about pipelines isn't how you do it. Every methodology offers an alternative way. What matters is that the pipeline is managed effectively, that the right work items are done in the right way, and that little time is wasted figuring out what to implement next.

The coding pipeline becomes the bug fix pipeline

Later on in a project, after all work items have been completed, the coding pipeline continues. What changes is that instead of work items, the pipeline is filled with bugs/ defects to be fixed. In Chapter 15, we'll talk about this when we cover triage—the decision-making process about how bugs should be handled.

Tracking progress

The simplest scoreboard for tracking mid-game progress is the work-item list: until each scheduled work item is completed (to the appropriate level of quality), mid-game is not over (see Figure 14-5). All of the mid-game strategies involve understanding the state of the project, keeping the team on the right track, and setting things up for a successful end-game. The score of completed work items is the most essential data for making these determinations.

Work items	Completed
A	Yes
B	Yes
C	No
D	No
E	No

FIGURE 14-5. *Mid-game is not over until all scheduled work items are complete. Only then does end-game begin. Anything that does not affect the rate of completion of work items should never take priority over things that do.*

I recommend using a very simple view of the project, such as the one shown in Figure 14-5, and making it as visible to the team as possible (on larger projects, show percentage of work items complete by area). If there is a team web site or wiki, a summary of work-item progress should be displayed prominently, and updated daily. Place a large whiteboard in the main hallway for the team, and place a similar chart there as well. Every weekly status meeting or large team meeting should start with a quick review of the big-team status. Because work items should be completed in one to three days, a chart like Figure 14-5 will show progress on a near-daily basis. People should be encouraged to use it to see what's been checked in recently and what's coming next.

Secondary data about status, such as remaining days per work item, days of work remaining per programmer, etc., should of course be tracked. But do not allow that data to cloud the simple view. During mid-game, it's much more important to provide ways for the team to obtain a holistic sense of how the project is going. Individuals will often have a sense of their local areas and any areas they come into contact with in their daily work.

There's certainly more to know about tracking progress effectively. I'll cover this in depth in the next chapter, where bugs and trends become critically important.

Hitting moving targets

> **"No battle was ever won according to plan, but no battle was ever won without one."**
>
> — *Dwight D. Eisenhower*

One of the strongest arguments for the short cycles of XP development and other methods is that directions change all the time. By using short development cycles, the project can respond to major direction changes without throwing away the balance of work, and any planning or design effort can focus on the tangible short term. This all makes great sense to me, as does the underlying attitude of aiming for consistent short-term wins. But there is one additional truth: longer-term plans, even if they are rough, will tend to make short- and mid-term changes easier.

The reason is at the moment when a change occurs, the original plan is rarely thrown away in its entirety. Instead, changes (aka deltas) are made relative to some baseline idea of what the project was going to be until the new change was made. The more accurate that original plan was, even if it was a rough plan, the stronger a point of reference it can be and the faster those adjustments can be made. What this means is that the best insurance against the volatility of things changing is to have a workable plan from the start that you can adjust as you go.

> **"Well, in my opinion a battle never works according to plan. The plan is only a common base for changes. It's very important that everyone should know the plan, so you can change it easily…the modern battle is very fluid, and you have to make your decisions very fast—and mostly not according to plan. But at least everybody knows where you're coming from, and [then] where you're going to, more or less."**
>
> — *Major-General Dan Laner, Israeli Defense Forces commander*

The trick in using plans where targets are expected to move is to never allow long periods of time to go by without updating the plan. If you can find the right intervals, moving targets don't really move much all at once—they simply track in a certain direction at a certain velocity at a certain time. If you have multiple milestones, or phases in your project (see Chapter 2), these are your natural intervals for making adjustments (and if new design time is planned in each of those phases, you can revisit things done in the first milestone that need to be changed). Even within a three- or six-week milestone, you can find one or two midpoints to re-evaluate the project trajectory relative to any goals or requirements that might have changed. For this reason, the length of milestones should correspond to volatility: the more volatile the direction, the shorter the milestone length.

Figure 14-6 shows a simple example of making adjustments to align with moving goals. The project starts at A and is supposed to end at B. If two weeks into the project (perhaps the completion of a short milestone) team leaders agree that the goals for B have changed, the project must be shifted to continue to align with B. Two weeks after that, more adjustments are made, and a new course correction takes place. Some work might be thrown away, but less work will be lost in adjusting direction early than in adjusting direction late. If these movements coincide with the end/beginning of milestones, the team has time to do some design work to compensate for the changes, add work items to modify previous work, and make the adjustments in stride.

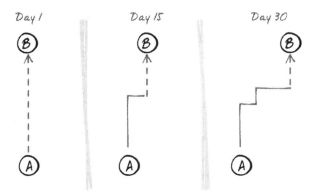

FIGURE 14-6. *Goals, requirements, and constraints will change, but if the velocity and direction are understood, and intermediate steps are taken to track to changes, the change can be managed.*

Even without proper milestone breaks, the coding pipeline can help make these mid-course adjustments controllable for the development team. Because these course changes occur in the pipeline out in front of the programming team, there is a buffer for changes to occur. The more lead time in the pipeline (see Figure 14-7), the more buffer there is. Assuming, of course, that there is someone (PM or lead programmer) with the time to manage the pipeline, the team doesn't have to come to a complete stall to make direction changes. There just needs to be enough (of the right) work in the pipeline.

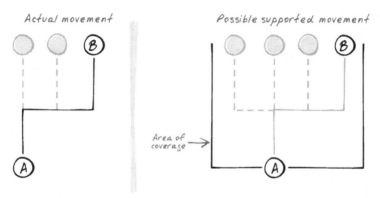

FIGURE 14-7. *Every plan has an area of coverage for how much variance it can support. The broader or more insightful (predictive of possible change) the plan is, the greater the area of coverage.*

However, this does assume that the changes aren't radically far from the initial plan; a given planning effort provides only so much ability for movement (see Figure 14-7). If the new requirements or goals cross over a certain point, new major design work and exploration will need to be done that goes beyond how much lead time the coding pipeline supports (or, in some cases, how much design time is planned for the next milestone). For example, if the initial plan was to make a toaster oven, it might be possible to adjust the project during mid-game to make it into a mid-size oven—but not a particle accelerator or an oil tanker.

In Figure 14-7, a rough model shows how much variance a project has; the area represents the space of changes that the planning effort has allowed a team to recover from without major new work. A similar diagram could be drawn at the micro level for each work item. Depending on the programmer's approach, her plan will have varying levels of coverage for requirements/design changes to that work item.

There's one goofy thing about Figure 14-7 worth noting. It represents chronological progress vertically, implying that the area of coverage provides more opportunity for movement over time, which isn't true. A more accurate way to think of the area of coverage is that it changes as the project does, growing and shrinking depending on what state the project is in. Generally, the space of coverage shrinks over time as work items are completed. But each movement made shifts the effective plan, and along with it, the possible coverage of future movement.

Dealing with mystery management

On well-functioning projects in healthy organizations, most high-level changes are timed with project milestones (because, again, the length of milestones corresponds roughly to the volatility of the project or organization). Management has the patience and maturity to wait until a phase is out before forcing the team to reset and readjust. But even in these organizations, there can be management directives that force change to occur mid-stream, without much ramp-up time to prepare for them.

Often there are more rumblings of management, client, or competitive reasons to make course corrections than actual decisions to change course. Sometimes, it's within your own power to make the call to shift directions, and other times you simply have to wait for someone else to decide. In either case, part of your thinking has to include a rough plan for what you'd do if the threatened change becomes real. Before big decisions come from management, or competitors take right turns, some writing on the wall can usually be found days or weeks in advance—if you're looking for it. You are dependent on your relationships and political skills to obtain the information you need to prevent your project from being blindsided. It can't always be avoided, but sometimes it can.

Using the information you have, periodically take your best guess at what the direction shift might be (support for a certain technology? a new feature? a new goal?), and sketch out what adjustments you'd need to get there. This can be very rough—for example, having a brief conversation with a lead programmer about what might be involved: "Fred, what would we have to do to support the 2.0 API set in addition to the ones we already use?" Your goal isn't a new battle plan, it's having some sense of what that road will look like should you and your team have to take it. Re-examine your prioritization list for work items (see Chapter 13), and see if you've already done some thinking on the new work you might have to take on.

Exploring the impact of change

If the probability of that change becomes high, you can adjust the work in the coding pipeline to better prepare yourself for the changes. In chess strategy, there are at least two different ways to plan a move:

- **Conservative.** Look for moves that give you the greatest number of future moves and that keep your options open.

- **Aggressive.** Make full commitment to one line of strategy you see clearly and force the game on your opponent.

On projects (or in chess), when you feel stronger than the opponent (i.e., mystery management, or the competition), aggressive is the way to go. When you are outmatched, conservative tends to be best. Telling your team to think conservatively may slow them slightly, but that's the price of the insurance you're buying. Sometimes, being aggressive forces others to make decisions, and if you're indifferent to the outcome but need a quick decision, aggressive decisions can work in your favor even if you are in a weak political position.

But notice that considering adjustments doesn't demand extra development time. There might be an alternative algorithm that is just as reliable but more flexible in an important way. Simply ask the programmer or the team, "Look guys. I'm concerned that our client/

VP is going to force us to support a different database schema. Look at what you're doing, and if there are smart ways to prepare for this change as you're doing your work, make it so. But don't make major changes or sacrifice quality because of this. Understood?"

Sometimes this is impossible: it might take hours of investigation to answer that question. But there are cases where it will be straightforward. For example, a programmer might have already considered that direction or have a reasonable opinion based on her understanding of the code. To prepare your team in this way, it might cost nothing more than a five-minute conversation. More important, perhaps: the better you understand the possible costs of change, the better your arguments will be for vetoing the changes (or if appropriate, for supporting them).

The potential reach of change

Also note that the closer a project gets to the original (or last active) set of goals, the further it will be from achieving any adjustments or direction changes. In Figure 14-8, the project is officially moving toward B, yet there are strong rumors of a direction change (shown as a "?" in the figure). The PM takes a best guess on what the change will be and adjusts accordingly. He makes a lightweight plan with his programmers as to how they might respond.

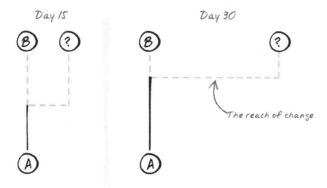

FIGURE 14-8. *If you know a change is coming but don't know when, you can still track to your best guess for what the change will be.*

As the project progresses, the mystery change continues to be a rumor. The angle of the change shifts as the project continues along to B, becoming sharper and riskier. With each line of code written, less and less support can be given to a possible alternative direction. As the project inches closer to completion at B, the distance to the mystery change (called the reach of change in Figure 14-8) will get longer, in relation to the remaining distance to B. The longer the team waits to make changes while the project is in motion, the larger the costs will tend to be.

If the change happens, and your predictive efforts didn't pay off, you have no choice: the team needs to be reset. If the change came without additional time resources, return to your prioritization lists and find items you can cut to buy the time you think you need (see Chapter 11).

Managing changes (change control)

Some project teams actively control and track any design change that demands a new work item or the elimination of an existing one (this starts after specs have been formally reviewed). The fear is that if design changes are made without some process involved, big, bad, evil decisions will happen without the right people knowing about it. Depending on the culture and goals of your team, you might or might not need to do this. As Friedlein points out, "The way you manage change through the project will depend on... the size and nature of the project. Generally the larger and more complex the project, and the more rigid the specifications, the more tightly you will have to manage change."[7] If your team doesn't bother with a spec process, it probably won't bother to have a change process either because there's nothing to mark deltas against.

However, even on a team with few formal processes, the closer a project is to completion, the more sensitive it will be to changes. Without some process in place to communicate, track, and manage changes, it's difficult and frustrating to close the door on a project. The more mature a team is, the earlier it will tend to want to control change. It's not necessarily an end-game process, it's just that as end-game approaches, the risks go up, as does the desire to control against them.

The simplest way to manage change is with a super-lean version of a specification process. NASA and Microsoft both call this a DCR, or design change request. Other common names for it are ECR (engineering change request), ECO (engineering change order), or, most simply, CR (change request).

The simplest process for this is as follows:

1. Someone (PM) writes a summary of the change—including its relationship to the project goals or requirements—the need for the change, and an explanation of the design of the change to be made. (Bonus points are given for identifying possible risks for the DCR's impact on the project.) This should rarely be more than a page or two. A bug (or whatever method is used for tracking issues) should be created to track the DCR, and this document should be attached to it.

2. The programmer, tester, and anyone significantly impacted by the change must contribute to the DCR summary and agree that this change is needed and designed appropriately. Programmer provides dev estimates, and tester provides test estimates (or rough test plan).

---

7   From *Web Project Management: Delivering Successful Commercial Web Sites.*

3. The DCR is proposed to a small group of team leaders (see the section "War team" in Chapter 15), or the group manager, who gives a go/no-go decision on the change. If the change goes through, it's treated as an additional work item to the project, and the DCR is broadcast to the team (and the work item is assigned to the appropriate programmer). Schedules and any project documentation should be updated to reflect this change. If rejected, the DCR crawls into the nearest corner of the room, sobbing uncontrollably, until it disappears from the project universe.

The last step can be skipped if the teams are small and authority is highly distributed. The relevant people just meet, discuss options, and decide on the change. But if the change will force the project to slip, impact other programmers, or require additional resources, team leaders need to be involved.

DCRs are always more expensive than their programming and test estimates. They have unexpected collateral side effects on the rest of the engineering team, and they cause the PM to give less attention to the pipeline and other already important activities. Because design work for DCRs is done in double time, the probability of mistakes and bad design choices is high. It's common for one DCR to cause the need for other DCRs. My general attitude toward them is this: it's better to use short dev cycles with strong design processes and allow few DCRs, than to plan a schedule that expects many DCR changes. There should be every motivation for people on the team to want to resolve their design issues early and avoid the DCR process.

Summary

- Mid-game and end-game correspond to the middle and end of the project.
- If on any day the project is not going well, it's your job to figure out what's wrong and resolve it. Repeat this throughout mid-game.
- Projects are complex non-linear systems and have significant inertia. If you wait to see acute problems before taking action, you will be too late and may make things worse.
- When your project is out of control, you are flying behind the plane, which is a bad place to be. Sanity checking is the easiest way to stay in front of the plane. There are both tactical and strategic sanity checks.
- Consider how to take action to correct a situation in the safest way possible. The larger the action, and the further along the project is, the more dangerous the actions are.
- The coding pipeline is how work items are managed during implementation. There are aggressive and conservative ways to manage the pipeline.
- Milestone-based planning and the coding pipeline provide opportunities to make safe course corrections for projects.
- Change control (DCRs) is how you throttle the rate of medium- and low-level change on a project.

Exercises

A. If you are in mid-game on a project now, randomly pick five people on your team and ask them to describe their confidence in the schedule as a percentage. Do the same with five managers. Compare the results and present them at a team meeting. If this is useful, repeat weekly. Keep all chosen people anonymous so they can be honest.

B. Often project managers are forced to fly behind the plane because they don't have control over the schedule, budget, or other factors that push projects out of control. What factors do you control that can help you get back in front? What can you do to inform your boss and team about the factors that impact you but are out of your control?

C. When was the last time you admitted you were in over your head? Make a list of things that scare you the most about your current project. Pick the top fear you have and talk to someone about it. The act of talking about it, even with a friend over a beer, will help you manage the situation.

D. What are your next three handoff points, where work you are doing has to be given to someone else or vice versa? What can you do for these three specific handoffs to increase the odds they'll go smoothly?

E. Visualize your team's coding pipeline as it stands today. One easy way to do this is to go to the whiteboard and make a list with every programmer on one axis, and time on the other. List the next three work items they claim to be working on, with each work item taking up more space depending on how much time it's scheduled to take. How does making the coding pipeline visual change your thinking about managing the project?

F. If you are afraid of mystery management, how can you make sure you hear about changes as early as possible? Who can you enlist as your scouts for information?

G. Most people hate having their progress tracked. What incentives can you provide for people to track their own work? Why is it that people who play sports love statistics about their performance, but people in other industries do not?

H. On the day you start requiring official change requests, the team ignores you and checks in work as they had the day before. How should you respond? What is the best way to transition the team to a new way of working?

CHAPTER FIFTEEN

End-game strategy

Continuing from last chapter's coverage of mid-game strategy, this chapter will emphasize hitting dates and deadlines, as well as what tools to use for driving projects to finish on time.

It's easy to forget, but all projects have more than one deadline. There are always interim dates that lead up to the milestone or end-of-project dates. This means that if your team makes an extraordinary effort to successfully meet a deadline, and another deadline waits on the horizon, there are hidden risks in pushing the team too hard to meet the first one. If a tremendous effort is required to meet that first date, and the team starts on the next one exhausted, stressed, and frustrated, the probability of overall success declines. Vince Lombardi once said that fatigue makes cowards of us all. When we're exhausted, no amount of caffeine can make us the same people we are under better circumstances.

> **"How you play a note is just as important as what the note is."**
>
> *—Henry Kaiser*

When a team is pushed very hard, it will take days or weeks to recover to the same level of performance predicted in the team's work estimates (see Figure 15-1). Worse, the more often a team is pushed in this way, the less responsive it will be—burnout is the point at which recovery is no longer possible in a useful timeline.

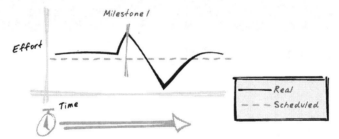

FIGURE 15-1. *You pay a price for crashing to hit a date in the probability of hitting the next one. A big push to hit Milestone 1 will force Milestone 2 to start in the hole.*

At the project level, it's best to think of team productivity as a zero-sum[1] resource: if you require extraordinary efforts to meet a date, realize you are stealing those efforts from the early parts of the next phase. (However, if the team has specialized roles, it's possible to minimize this by offsetting responsibilities. The crunch time for designers, planners, PMs, testers, and programmers often occurs at different times of the project. If the work is distributed properly, the entire team is never equally crunched, with different roles carrying more of the burden at different times.)

---

1 Zero sum is a game theory term that means a finite set of resources. Slicing a chocolate cake into pieces is a zero-sum game: if I get more, there's less for you. However, going to an infinitely well stocked café and ordering slices of cake is a non-zero sum game: we can each get as much as we want. Yum.

Worse, there is an interest rate to pay: the ratio of recovery time to crunch effort isn't 1:1. It takes more time to recover than it does to give the intense extra effort (e.g., it may take only 20 seconds to sprint to catch the train, but it can take a minute or more to catch your breath again). Sometimes, the price is sacrificing people's personal or family lives, which isn't in the long-term interest of the individual, team, or organization (see Figure 15-1).

This means that good management should avoid those big pushes. It's impossible to avoid some spikes on a major project, but it's in the interest of managers to carefully control them, work preemptively to minimize them, and understand the true costs when they surface (i.e., don't blame the team two weeks into the next milestone for being sluggish and cranky). The longer the project, the more energy the team loses from those spikes, and the more difficult the true end-game of a multi-milestone project becomes.

Big deadlines are just several small deadlines

To discuss important aspects of mid- and end-game strategy, we need to define several interim dates that occur on projects. The three most basic interim dates, in a plain-vanilla schedule, correspond to the crossovers between the rough rule of thirds described in Chapter 2 (see Figure 15-2). Each crossover point represents a shift in focus for the team, and it should have its own exit criteria.

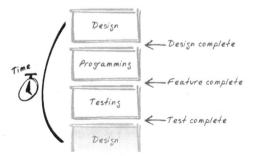

FIGURE 15-2. *Within milestones, there are key dates that should be tracked, targeted, and given exit criteria.*

Exit criteria are your list of things that the milestone was supposed to accomplish. They describe what state the project has to be in to complete a milestone. The earlier exit criteria are defined, the better the odds are that the milestone will be completed on time.

The three key crossover points in any milestone are:

- **Design complete/spec complete.** The team is ready to write production code. All specifications, prototypes, or design briefs needed to begin implementation are finished. (Note that this doesn't demand for all specs to be finished, only the ones deemed necessary to start implementation. This could be 20% or 90% of them.) Design work may continue (see the section "The coding pipeline" in Chapter 14), and iterations and revisions may occur, but an acceptable percentage or core of it has been completed.

- **Feature complete.** The team is ready to focus on refinement and quality assurance. This means that all of the functionality provided by individual work items has been completed, and the behavior and design necessary to meet requirements has been implemented. There may be quality gaps or problems, but provided leadership has measured or tracked them (bugs *do* exist), core construction work can be considered complete. Any test or quality metrics defined as part of the spec should have measurements in place. On this day, all remaining issues should be tracked as bugs, and the bug database becomes the primary (if not sole) way to track remaining progress.

- **Test or milestone complete.** The milestone is finished. Quality and refinement have reached the appropriate levels. The next milestone begins and/or the project ships. This is sometimes called milestone complete because it's the last phase in the milestone. If it's the only or last milestone, the project is complete.

Beyond the quality of the specifications, work estimates, and the team itself, the simplest rule of thumb for hitting dates is that the better your exit criteria, the better your chances are.[2] Until the criteria are met, the team is expected to keep working. Any important date in your schedule should have some set of exit criteria defined for it.

Defining exit criteria

Exit criteria do not need to be complex (although they can be). However, they do need to include these items:

- The list of work items to be completed

- A definition for the quality those things need to be completed at (perhaps derived from test cases, test plans,[3] and specifications)

- The list of things that people might think need to be done but don't actually need to be completed

- Things people should never, ever think need to be done (sanity check)

---

2 Alternatively, the less well defined your exit criteria are, the lower your chances of hitting your dates. The limit case is having no exit criteria, where you will depend on opinion and management's whim to figure out when you're done.

3 For more on test plans and general QA methodology, see *Managing the Test Process*, by Rex Black (Microsoft Press, 1999). If you're serious about quality, it should be part of the project vision document and the planning process.

There are many ways to both define exit criteria and to communicate and track them with a team. The details of how they're done aren't so important (propose them to the team, take feedback, then finalize and communicate them broadly). What matters is that they're done early, kept simple, and used publicly to track progress and guide decisions. Exit criteria should map back to the vision and goals, and they should be the most useful way to apply the vision and goals to the questions and challenges faced in the middle and end parts of milestones.

Common exit criteria include:

- **Specifications/designs/work-item lists completed.** This is useful only for design completion. Whatever tools or processes used to do design work should have corresponding exit criteria to conclude design. Perhaps it's 90% of all specifications reviewed, or it's a prototype with a certain set of working functionality.

- **Actual work items completed.** This should be the list of work items defined at the beginning of the milestone or phase of the project. When the work items are completed to specification, the phase/milestone is complete.

- **Bug counts at certain levels.** As we'll discuss later, there are many different ways to track and measure bugs/defects. Generally, exit criteria involving bugs specify the allowed quantity of active bugs of a certain type.

- **Passing specified test cases.** There can be a set of test conditions that are used to determine when the milestone is complete. If test cases are used as criteria, they will drive the decisions for which bugs/defects must be fixed before the milestone can end. It may be sufficient to use threshold-based exit criteria defined by test cases, such as "80% of test cases for priority 1 scenarios must be passed."

- **Performance or reliability metrics.** If the team is measuring performance of certain components (say, a database or search engine), there might be exit criteria based on those numbers. If the exit criterion is a 10% speed improvement over the previous release, the milestone isn't over until that 10% increase has been achieved.

- **Time or money.** Time is the simplest exit criterion in the world. When a certain amount of time is over, the milestone is over. End of story. Months make for nice milestones because there's never any doubt about when they start, when they end, or how much time is in them. (People use weeks and months to track the rest of their lives, so why not base project schedules on them as well?) Half- or partially done features are cut and considered in the next milestone (if there is one). Money can also be an exit criterion: when the budget is spent, and the power goes off, you stop.

Without exit criteria the team must depend on their subjective opinions for what "good enough" means for a project, which is an enormous waste of time. Everyone will have different opinions about what good enough is. Even if one person is given authority to make this decision, it will always be contentious unless something is written down.

Without criteria, teams are forced to have difficult debates late in a project when stress and risks are high. Avoid placing your team in a situation where energy must be wasted at the end of milestones arguing over exit criteria. Instead, plan so that you can use all of the team's energy at the end of milestones to actually meet the criteria.

Remember that the goal isn't just to hit a date, but to hit a date with the project in a specific state. The sooner the team knows what that state is, the better the odds are that it will happen. If they know early on what the criteria are, every decision they make throughout the milestone will reflect that criteria. Even if the criteria change along the way, the team will be adjusting in the same directions, collectively setting the project up for an easier end-game.

An example list of exit criteria for a milestone on a small web project might be as follows:

- Complete work items 1–10 as per their specifications
- Meet 80% of usability goals for priority 1 areas
- Pass all priority 1 automated and manual tests
- Pass 80% of all priority 2 automated tests
- Triage all active bugs
- Fix all priority 1 and 2 bugs
- Get signoff from marketing and business team

Why hitting dates is like landing airplanes

With intermediary milestones, the goal is not just to hit a certain date, it's to set the team up for the next milestone (or release). Hitting a date is more than a matter of chronology: depending on how smoothly you hit the date, code stability and the next milestone (if there is one) are at risk.

Think of landing an airplane. A good landing puts the plane in a position that makes it easy to take off again; i.e., if the wings are still attached, the landing gear is operational, and the crew is still alive. All that's required is more fuel, a flight plan, and a sandwich for the pilot. The ending of milestones should be thought of in the same way. The sharper the angle you take to finish a milestone, the higher the odds that the project won't be in a good state when it completes the milestone.

Angle of descent

The most basic schedules for engineering projects can be converted into a simple chart, like the one shown in Figure 15-3. This chart assumes that the rate of progress is constant, and that the project will be completed exactly on schedule by continuing at that constant rate. This, of course, is fantasyland. This chart will never map to reality because team progress and efficiency are never constant (for many reasons described earlier in this book).

FIGURE 15-3. *This is the most basic milestone schedule in the world, with fantasyland assumptions included.*

Instead, most projects end up in the situation depicted in Figure 15-4. At some point on the way to the target date, the team realizes work is not going as fast as expected. This could be because new work has been introduced (see the section "Managing changes (change control)" in Chapter 14) or because the team didn't meet its estimates. Regardless of how it happened, the team now faces a choice: how do we make up the distance to the end date? There are only three options:

1. **Slip the schedule.** Move the end date out to reflect the new understanding of the rate of descent.

2. **Change the angle.** Somehow convince yourself that you can get the team to do more work faster to make up for the gap in time (i.e., prepare for crash landing). You can attempt this, but there will be a price to pay. There will be a greater risk of mistakes, and the team will be sluggish and tired starting the next cycle of work.

3. **Meet the date with what you have.** Identify the features or work items that have the most remaining work or risk. Either cut those features, postpone them to the next milestone (if there is one), or drop quality and ship them as they are (gulp).

FIGURE 15-4. *Schedule reality often disagrees with the plan. How to handle this depends entirely on the exit criteria.*

The way this choice is made should depend entirely on the exit criteria. This is exactly the situation that benefits most from having clear thinking about what it means for a milestone to end. Instead of inventing criteria now, under the stress of a difficult landing, all you need to do is look back and adjust the criteria that you made weeks ago. Decision making in difficult end-game situations becomes easier if there is reference criteria that the team is already familiar with.

Why changing the angle can't work

Using the airplane analogy again, changing the angle to fit the remaining space makes the approach unstable. Projects, much like airplanes, don't control very well when their downward velocity is high. There are too many things that need to be done simultaneously for that velocity to stabilize. If you were in an airplane approaching the runway and realized your approach was off, you'd veer off and make a new approach (moving the runway, unlike schedule dates, isn't possible). In difficult weather, commercial airplanes often restart their approach. However, projects can rarely afford to do this. They are like airplanes that are low on fuel: there are enough resources for only one approach. With only one shot, sane pilots make very careful and well-planned approaches. Sane project managers should follow suit. If your date or feature set is unmovable (like a runway), you must start planning for landing earlier on.

Why it gets worse

There is a basic psychological principle behind how most people go about prioritizing their work. All things being equal, people will tend to avoid doing things they don't want to do.[4] This means that as the schedule progresses, the remaining work items or bug fixes will be the sad, unwanted tasks of the milestone. And even if the remaining work is ridiculously fun to do, if teams are rewarded for the numbers of bugs they fix in a day or week, there is natural pressure to select bugs of the appropriate difficulty to meet the quota.

At the end of milestones, people tend to be tired, frustrated, and stressed—conditions that lead to poorer performance. Difficult bugs that fall between areas tend to circulate around a development team late in the schedule (aka bug hot potato). A programmer looks at one of these bugs, realizes it's a tough one, and feeling the pressure of his other work, assigns the bug to another person who could possibly take responsibility for it. As Weinberg writes, "…problems don't get solved, they merely circulate." Even the best programmers suffer these natural temptations from time to time.

---

4   From Volume 1, *Systems Thinking*, of Gerald Weinberg's *Quality Software Management* (Dorset House, 1991), pp. 272–273.

The primary trend of delaying difficult work also applies to the discovery of bugs—although its cause isn't psychological. Defects that take longer to find, or that appear later on in a schedule, will naturally tend to be the ones that are more complicated[5] (as shown in Figure 15-5). For complex, but low-priority bugs, this doesn't matter much; for high-priority ones, this trend is a serious problem. Not only will these bugs take longer than average to find, but they'll take longer than average to fix. The straight-line paths shown in Figure 15-4 are both wrong—the approach of a project to a date is near asymptotic (curved) in results, and looks closer to what's shown in Figure 15-6. The team may be working as hard as before, but the results—in terms of progress toward goals—will decline. The closer you are to your date, the more this is true.

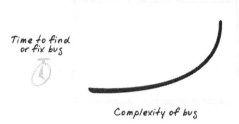

FIGURE 15-5. *Tougher bugs tend to be discovered or fixed later in the schedule. This means that the angle of approach isn't a straight line but a curve weighted against progress (see Figure 15-6).*

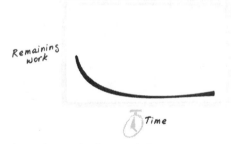

FIGURE 15-6. *A generic but realistic angle-of-approach chart, assuming a constant level of effort from the team.*

The rough guide to correct angles of approach

The angle of approach for milestones or project completion is not a mystery. Like any other scheduling-related task (see Chapter 2), there are certain considerations that contribute to how accurate a predicted angle will be. Here are the primary factors to consider:

---

5   Ibid.

- **Look at past performance for the team and for the project.** To plan the angle, examine how well the team has done in end-game for previous projects of a similar type. On multi-milestone projects, look at previous milestone curves, planned versus actual (don't cheat: use the original plan and the final actual schedule). Assume things will be harder on the milestone you're planning than on previous ones, despite what you think. If you have no data to base the angle on, what makes you think you're not just guessing? If you have to guess, guess conservatively.

- **Do proper estimates.** The angle is just another kind of schedule estimation task. Get the appropriate people in the room, break remaining work down into tasks, discuss risks and assumptions, and arrive at estimates. If nothing else, this will make the final approach a team effort, where people feel they have bought into the process and defined the angle together. Morale will work in support of the angle, instead of against the angle.

- **Plan for a slow curve, not a straight line.** Even with no data, plan on the rate of progress to slow as the bug count declines (see Figure 15-6). Assume that the work will get harder the closer you get to your deadline. Graph and chart with curves, not lines.

- **Don't drink the Kool-Aid.** Charts are easy to make. You can put the line wherever you like without any reference to reality, and you can possibly even convince others that there's some logic behind the lines you drew. Think of the pilot in that plane: would you fly in at this angle given what you know? Raise the red flag; be the whistleblower. Protect your team from a crash landing. If your approach is too conservative, the worst that can happen is that you'll finish ahead of schedule, whereas if you're too aggressive, all sorts of evil things could happen.

- **Make a black box.** If nothing else, make sure real performance data is captured (see the next section). Then after the crash landing, you'll have evidence of what went wrong, and you can make a strong argument for adjustments in the next project or milestone.

Elements of measurement

Tracking progress becomes very important in both mid-game and end-game. The larger the team, the harder it is to make the state of the project visible. To make course corrections or adjustments (see Chapter 14), you need to have a clear understanding of what state the project is in both to diagnose any symptoms and to predict how the project will respond to adjustments.

Whatever measurements you decide to use should be made visible to the entire team. In Chapter 14, I suggested that work items are the most important tracking mechanism for mid-game. Here, we'll go deeper into other measurements useful for mid-game but focus on tracking for end-game.

For end-game, you can reuse any project scoreboards used earlier; just make sure that the important measurement is given proper emphasis (drop measurements that don't carry much significance anymore, such as work items). The scoreboard should stay in a visible hallway, and it can be as simple as a big whiteboard that you update frequently or as fancy as a dedicated terminal (conveniently located near the restrooms, break room, or other high-traffic areas) that pulls the most recent data from the network.

The daily build

By making builds of the project each day, you force many kinds of issues to be dealt with in the present, instead of postponing them into the future. Anyone can look at the current build and know immediately what the state of progress is. You can rely less on people writing status reports or other annoying busywork; instead, you can always get a rough idea just by loading up the current build and using particular functions or features. It can be expensive to maintain a daily build (and to create the tools needed to make it possible[6]), but it's worth the costs.

With daily builds, programmers (and the whole team) will know right away when a check-in has damaged other components, which helps keep check-in quality high. Have a set cut-off time each day for when the build will be processed, which sets up a stable code base to run tests against to confirm the quality of the build. (Often these daily tests are called smoke tests: a reference to testing electronic components, where circuit boards would be plugged in to see if any parts literally smoked.) After this time, check-ins into the source tree simply show up in the next build.

For each build, there should be a set of tests to determine build quality. Three rankings are all you need—good: all tests passed; mixed: some tests passed; bad: few or no tests passed. Any specific bugs identified as the cause for any test failing should be posted with the build information and given a high priority.

These build-quality tests (aka build-verification tests, or BVTs) should be on path to the exit criteria for the milestone. Early on in the milestone, they might be relaxed relative to the exit criteria; for example, it may be acceptable to have only one "good" build a week. But as the team approaches feature complete, the criteria should rise. With daily builds and quality tests, you always have both a quality measurement and a way to throttle quality.

---

6   A good summary of tools and processes that can be used for this can be found at *http://www. martinfowler.com/articles/continuousIntegration.html.*

Bug/defect management

At feature complete, any remaining work that needs to be done before completion should be shifted into the bug database. This is to provide one system of control and measurement for the project. The system used to track bugs can be simple, but there must be one, and everyone must use it. If some programmers have pet systems for tracking their work, and they're all different, it's impossible to show any project-level control or measurement over progress. Often when the team transitions out of feature complete, someone has to actively nag people to put items into the system that they've been tracking on their own.

Get into the habit of asking "What's the bug number?" whenever issues come up. If they say there isn't one, end the conversation until the bug has a number. This may seem draconian, but it's in the project's best interest. The two minutes required to create a bug number are entirely worthwhile from a project-level perspective. It's fine for people to track things on their own if the issue has no impact on the build or the code base; you don't want the bug system to be bogged down with bugs that are personal reminders or to-do list-type trivia. (Or if you allow it, make sure there is a specific bug type for this stuff so it can be filtered out in reports and queries.)

For reference, all bugs should have at least the following information. You can skip this section if you have a bug system that you're happy with. There are many different kinds of information you can use in bug tracking, but in my experience, these are the core attributes needed to effectively manage bugs:

- **Priority.** Keep this as simple as possible. Priority 1 = Must fix. Priority 2 = Will fix opportunistically. Priority 3 = Desirable, but improbable. Priority 4 = Comically improbable.

- **Severity.** How serious is the impact of the bug? Severity 1 = Data loss, system crash, or security issue. Severity 2 = Major functionality doesn't work as expected (specified). Severity 3 = Minor functionality doesn't work as expected (specified). Severity is distinct from priority. For example, there may be a browser-crashing script error, which is severe (Severity 1), but because it occurs only if you type "PAPAYA!" seven times, in all caps, in the email field on a registration web page, it's low priority (Severity 1, but Priority 4).

- **Assigned to.** All bugs should be assigned to one person. New bugs can be assigned to an alias, but part of the goal of triage (discussed shortly) is to assign bugs to an individual as soon as possible. To allow for bugs to be entered from alpha or beta releases, create a value called "active" or "party time," which bugs can be assigned to. Bugs assigned to this value can be triaged and given to real people later.

- **Reproduction (aka repro).** The sequence of actions that allows someone else to reproduce the bug. This is perhaps the most important field for bug quality. Bad reproduction cases waste the team's time, forcing programmers to invest more energy than should be necessary just to figure out what the bug is. Good bugs have short and simple repro steps.[7]

- **Area.** For larger projects, bugs should be categorized by where they occur in the project (the area). This allows for bugs to be tracked by component, not just by developer.

- **Opened by.** The name of the person, with contact information, who opened the bug.

- **Status.** A bug can be in only four states: active, fixed, resolved, or closed. Active means the bug hasn't been fixed yet and is still up for consideration. Fixed means the programmer believes that it's been fixed. A bug becomes resolved only when the person who opened the bug agrees it's been fixed, or agrees to postpone it. Closed signifies that the bug's life is over, and the test team has confirmed its demise.

- **Resolved as.** A resolved bug means it's no longer active. A bug can be resolved in several different ways: fixed, postponed to the next milestone or release, duplicate of an existing bug, or won't be fixed.

- **Type.** There are two important types of bugs: defects and regressions. A defect is a regular, plain-old bug. A regression is a bug that was once fixed, but now has appeared again as a negative side effect of some other change.

- **Triage.** This field indicates whether the bug has been triaged and what the result was. At times, the only bugs that should be fixed are ones that have been triaged and marked approved. So, this field usually has three states: approved, rejected, or investigating.

- **Title.** All bugs should have a one-line title describing the bug such that another human being can get the basic idea of what the problem is.

Most bug-tracking systems provide logging for each bug. This makes it possible to see who made what changes to which bug, and when they did it. This comes in handy if decisions made about specific bugs are disputed. It also prevents people from various kinds of deception in how bugs are managed.

The activity chart

At the project level, the most effective use of bugs is to track trends in their discovery, evaluation, and resolution. By looking at the trends across the project, you can do three things: measure progress, gain insight into what project-level problems might exist, and develop a sense for what actions might correct those problems.

---

7   See Joel Spolsky's essay "Painless Bug Tracking" at *http://www.joelonsoftware.com/articles/ fog0000000029.html.*

Once you have even a simple bug database, the trap is that it's very easy to generate many different kinds of charts and perform complex kinds of analysis.[8] Avoid the urge to get fancy—it's the basic charts that matter. More advanced queries are often distractions ("Look! Our bug fix rate corresponds to rainfall rates in Spain!"). Before you waste time generating an elaborate new kind of report, ask yourself the following questions:

1. What questions can we answer by looking at this chart?

2. How will the answers to those questions help us ship on time, on quality? How will the answers help us meet specific exit criteria or project goals?

3. If the number goes up, what does it really mean? Down? Stays the same?

4. At the end of each day/week, will this help us understand how much closer we are to completion?

Keep it simple

The simplest and most important trends can be tracked using an activity chart. For each day of the project, the following statistics are pulled from the bug database and displayed as line graphs:

- **Active.** The total count of active bugs that have not been fixed or resolved.

- **Incoming.** The total count of bugs opened on a given day (before triage).

- **Fixed.** The total count of bugs fixed on a given day.

In Figure 15-7, you can see the basic activity trends for a mid-size project in the early days of end-game for a milestone. There are a high number of active bugs and a relatively high incoming rate. Toward the middle of the chart (from left to right), a major test pass begins, and the incoming bug rate climbs dramatically (as does the active bug count). Finally, after the test pass is completed, the fixed rate passes the incoming rate, and the active bug count begins to drop. From this simple chart, you can see the core relationships: incoming versus fixed defines the core trend of work completion.

Evaluating trends

All charts or analysis techniques will tell you one of two things: there is more work to do or there is less work to do. For example, if the count of active bugs continues to climb, it means the pile of work is growing faster than it's being emptied, and new issues are still being found at a high rate. Alternatively, if the active count is on a trend of decline, work is being completed faster than new issues are being discovered. In either case, the goal of

---

8   Two books worth looking at if you need this kind of rigor: Tom DeMarco's *Controlling Software Projects* (Prentice Hall, 1986) and Volume 1, *Systems Thinking*, of Gerald Weinberg's *Quality Software Management* (Dorset House, 1991).

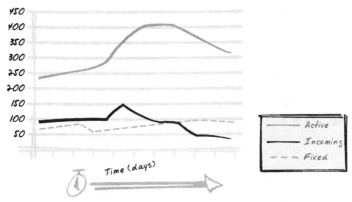

FIGURE 15-7. *A basic bug activity chart.*

trend analysis is to understand, for any given attribute, which of the three states the attributes are in:

- **Things are getting worse.** This is acceptable, and even desirable, in the early test phases of a project. If major test passes were recently completed, it's natural for bug counts to rise much faster than the programming team can handle.[9] Sometimes, integrating components might come in later than planned, forcing bug discovery to happen later in the process. What's important is to understand why things are getting worse, how much worse they're getting, and what should be done (if anything) to change the trend.

- **Things are staying the same.** Because old bugs are being fixed and new bugs are being found concurrently, it's entirely possible for a team to appear to tread water. Active rates might hold steady even though programmers are cranking away. If ever a key measurement is hovering, examine what inputs and outputs contribute to the measurement to understand what needs to happen to turn the corner. It's important to communicate this to the team. Many programmers panic when they're cranking away because they don't understand why the project isn't moving forward (or worse, why it is slowly sinking).

- **Things are getting better.** When the trends become favorable, it's important to evaluate the rate of acceleration and the trend line to the end of the milestone. A positive trend might not be positive enough to meet the exit criteria. If the trends become positive early, be suspicious: have all test passes been completed? Are there untriaged bugs? Is bug fix quality high? Make sure you understand exactly what is causing the trend to improve before you assume that it's good news.

---

9   Test-driven development is one useful approach to dealing with engineering quality earlier on, and avoiding big waves of incoming bugs. See *http://en.wikipedia.org/wiki/Test_driven_development.*

Useful bug measurements

There are some common measurements that prove useful to end-game tracking. It's worth finding a way to generate these stats automatically so that if they are needed to help make a decision, time won't be wasted building a new database query.

- **Fix rate.** The rate at which a team fixes bugs is called the fix rate. Because not all bugs are equal, this rate is the time required to fix a bug of average complexity. If the fix rate is behind the incoming rate, and all incoming bugs must be fixed, the project can never ship: there will always be more bugs.

- **Incoming to approved.** How many new bugs need to be fixed and are not duplicates of other bugs, or priority 3 and 4 issues? Knowing the incoming-to-triaged ratio helps to make estimates against untriaged bugs. Generally, bug quality should decline over time: the rate of good priority 1 and 2 bugs will slow. The raw incoming rate won't tell you when this is happening.

- **Active bug time.** The average time for how long bugs have been active. This indicates the team's responsiveness and how the team is handling its current workload. Response time should increase as you get closer to dates because the team should be managing fewer bugs and should be more aggressive at triaging and attacking incoming issues. If response time is slow, people are busy.

- **Bugs per developer.** Load-balancing a development team requires tracking how many active bugs each developer is currently working on. It's also worth noting what percentage of active bugs are currently assigned to testers, developers, or PMs. Bugs assigned to PMs or testers are not in the pipeline, and they should be triaged periodically.

- **Fault Feedback Ratio.** Weinberg calls the rate of regressions caused by a bug fix the Fault Feedback Ratio (FFR).[10] If each bug fixed causes two additional bugs, the FFR is 2.0. According to Weinberg, an FFR of .1 to .3 is a baseline acceptable rate; anything higher means that quality needs to be improved (and/or the pace needs to be slower). Most bug databases allow for new bugs to be linked to existing ones, making it possible to track the FFR. However, I've never seen this automated—it's only judged subjectively by those performing project-wide triage. (Note that sometimes fixing one bug can cause previously hidden bugs to surface. This shouldn't count in the FFR.)

Elements of control

Controlling projects is much harder than tracking them. Evaluating good data is a matter of deduction, but figuring out how to respond to trends requires intuition. Projects take on their own momentum, especially in end-game, and they can't be directed so much as influenced. When the activity is focused on working with bugs, there are many individual decisions being made across the team, and it requires constant communication

---

10 From Volume 1, *Systems Thinking*, of Weinberg's *Quality Software Management*, p. 250.

and reminders to keep people making those decisions with the same attitudes, assumptions, and goals.

The best way to think about elements of control is frequency of use. Some high-level activities, such as management review, are only needed once every month. For others, such as triage, it can be a day-to-day or hour-to-hour activity. Depending on the degree of control you need, the time intervals of control are your most important consideration.

Review meeting

This is primarily a mid-game control mechanism. A review is when the team leaders must present the state of their project, compared against goals, to senior management, clients, and the entire team itself. The review should serve as a forcing function to discuss what is going well, what isn't, and what is being done about it. The format of the review can really be this simple. The best reviews I've participated in cut straight to the core. There was enough maturity in the room that oversights were volunteered (not hidden), requests for help honored (not ridiculed), and attention paid to the things that mattered most (not what made people look good or feel happy).

The review discussion should force the team to evaluate goals, timelines, technologies, and roles realistically. Nothing should be spared in a review. Any issue that is impacting the project should be open for discussion. For this reason, the review meeting is an element of control, and not just tracking, because it provides a forum for leaders and senior managers to discuss adjustments that need to be made involving any aspect of the project. Regardless of the meeting size, a summary of the discussion and slides used in the presentation should be given to the entire team in a separate forum afterward.

Teams should have reviews scheduled at periodic intervals during the course of each milestone. It should be public knowledge when they will occur, as a team meeting should follow it. Multimonth projects should have a monthly review. Multiweek projects should have a weekly or biweekly review. The more frequent they are, the more informal and fast they can be.

Customer/client reviews

If you are a contracted team, or have internal clients, review meetings can serve as one way to get direct feedback from your customers. Most of the advice just described still applies. One additional point is that you should never depend on these meetings as the only source of feedback from customers. The intervals between meetings will always be too long, and the formality of meetings can make it difficult to go very deep or to discuss complex issues.

One important aspect of XP is that it encourages a representative from the customer to participate directly in the development of the software.[11] That person should use the daily builds and develop relationships with the programmers and their leaders. It makes it possible for your team to get feedback on issues on a daily or hourly basis, rather than weekly or monthly. Defining this relationship can be tricky the first time (see the section "Defining roles" in Chapter 9), but it will always pay off in smarter decisions and happier customers.

Triage

Any process where you take a list of issues and put them in order of priority is a triage process. What makes real triage different from other kinds of prioritization is that you're dealing with a constant inflow of new issues that need to be understood and then prioritized against all other concerns. Triage takes places throughout mid-game whenever there is an interim date that needs to be hit and a quality metric in the exit criteria. However, triage becomes a primary task for the team during end-game, often consuming a significant percentage of daily work for PMs and others.

The goal of triage is to manage the engineering pipeline (described in Chapter 14) in a way that maximizes the value of the work done toward the exit criteria for the milestone. Doing this successfully requires three things:

- **Sanitize.** Incoming bugs will always vary in importance. Someone has to review new bugs, and get the information in them to a quality level such that it can be assigned to a programmer and she can investigate and fix it. Some bugs require programmer investigation, but most filtering involves trivial things: filling in empty fields (severity, priority, etc.), improving repro cases, confirming it's not a duplicate of an existing bug, etc. This is often just gopher work: phone calls, emails, and time with the specific build to track down information.

- **Investigate.** After bugs have been sanitized, the investigative work begins. Do we need to fix it? Does it violate the spirit of the requirement/specification? What component causes this issue, and what would be involved in fixing it? There may be many questions that need to be answered before a good decision can be made. Some considerations are technical, others are not.

- **Prioritize.** After being sanitized and investigated, bugs can be prioritized and put into the pipeline at the appropriate level of importance.

What makes triage difficult is that to do any of these three things well requires more knowledge than any one person has. The larger the project, the less likely it is that any one person can effectively do triage alone. So, for most teams on most projects, triage is a group activity. Early on, it might be fine for individuals to triage their own bugs, but later,

---

11 See Kent Beck's *Extreme Programming Explained* (Addison-Wesley, 1999), p. 69.

the focus shifts to small groups and subteams. This is why bugs have to be organized around specific project areas (see the earlier section "Bug/defect management"). It makes it easy for small groups of people responsible for that area to get together and triage independently of the rest of the team.

Near the end of end-game, when every bug decision is scrutinized, there should be one triage effort for the entire project, and it must be run by a core group of team leaders (see Figure 15-8; we'll discuss this in the upcoming section "War team"). For now, it's important to identify the two primary kinds of triage: daily and directed.

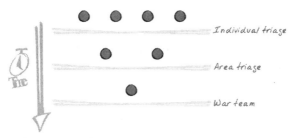

FIGURE 15-8. *Triage becomes centralized as end-game progresses.*

Daily/weekly triage

Daily triage is the routine process for dealing with incoming and active bugs. Depending on the timeline, this may need to be done once a week, once a day, or once an hour. The further into end-game you are, the more frequently the pulse of triage needs to occur.

The goal of daily triage is simple: keep things sane. The programming team is the critical path for the end-game of the project, and triage is the only way to keep their pipeline healthy. Every new bug must be sanitized and compared against the existing pool, preferably before they land on an individual programmer's plate.

Sometimes, it's best (in terms of team efficiency) to have one person running point for daily triage for each area. Assuming programmers and testers agree on the criteria, one person can be responsible for sanitizing new bugs, marking duplicates, and adjusting priorities of incoming bugs. PMs are good candidates for this, assuming they are technical enough to understand the issues and make basic bug decisions.

Otherwise, triage should be done in a small meeting, with representatives from development, test, and PM. If other experts on staff are needed—such as marketing, design, or usability—they can be called in as necessary. The meetings should be short. Anything that can't be resolved in minutes should be assigned to a programmer to investigate.

The triage field should be set on bugs when they've been triaged. This gives the project an additional view of bug data, as you can then separate the amount of triaged bugs (known good bugs) from the total amount of active bugs (unknown quality bugs).

Directed triage

Directed triage is a focused effort to meet a specific goal. This is done in addition to daily triage. Directed triage is one control, at the project level, to help push things forward and improve the value of bug charts and trend analysis. Here are some common reasons for directed triage:

- **When ratio of triaged-to-active is low.** If there are 500 active bugs and only 200 have been triaged, there is no way to know the significance of the remaining 300 bugs. They could all be priority 1 system crashes, or they could all be duplicates: you have no idea. A directed triage would have the specific goal of eliminating all untriaged bugs by a certain time (noon tomorrow). If this is a chronic problem for a team, there should be a goal of no active untriaged bugs older than a certain amount of time (24 hours).

- **When exit criteria change.** If team leaders decide to change the exit criteria, triage is the only way to bring the project in line with those changes. It's common to use new exit criteria as a way to change the angle of descent, eliminating certain classes of bugs from consideration to improve the safety of the angle (but reducing quality in the process).

- **Unclosed counts are high.** When a bug is fixed, it should be set to status = resolved, and assigned back to the person who opened it to make sure it really was fixed. Some percentage of these bugs might not have been fixed correctly. If these bugs sit as unclosed, there is a pocket of bugs that need to be fixed that are not being reported in the active bug counts. Depending on your bug-tracking system, there may be other places bugs can hide. Periodically, you need to drive the team in flushing them out.

War team

As a project nears completion, the distribution of authority has to centralize. Unlike feature design and programming, which can be reasonably distributed across a team, the margin for error decreases toward the end. Decisions become increasingly sensitive—it's detail work, not construction. The Microsoft terminology for this centralization of control is called war team (borrowed, I believe, from the military term *war room*, where leaders meet to decide important issues). A small group of team leaders becomes a dominant executive branch of power. On small teams, a formal shift in power might be unnecessary, but on large teams, this shift is essential. It raises the bar on all decision making and provides a forcing function to the team that the game is ending.

The actual war team meeting is simple. All you need is a conference room, a senior member from each staff (programming, test, PM or other peer leaders, and possibly the group's senior manager), and a computer hooked up to a big monitor so that the entire room can see the bug or issue being discussed. For an issue to pass war team, senior members must all agree (some teams opt for a two-thirds majority or give war team members veto power). War team agenda is decided each morning, and any issue can be placed on the agenda. Like a court of law, anything they accept or deny sets precedence for the rest of the team. War team meetings should be open to the team, with priority given to people who are presenting specific DCRs (see the previous chapter) or proposed bugs for review.

War team should set a very high bar. Anyone showing up to war team not prepared or lacking answers to basic questions (what exit criteria does this meet? what regressions might this cause? do the programmer and tester both agree that this should be fixed?) should be told to go away and come back when he is ready. War team time is precious because the team's time is precious. Every PM and programmer should be highly motivated to have her story nailed down and rock solid before she asks for war team approval. This pressure creates a natural incentive for the entire team to think hard about issues on their own before they choose to bring it to war. (Be careful: war team meetings can be highly charged, and there's plenty of opportunity for grandstanding and egocentric time wasting. It's up to the group manager to squash destructive behavior early.)

The team should have fair warning about what and when the war team will be involved. In Figure 15-9, some basic staging is shown for what things need war team approval. The goal is to have a gradual centralization of authority with public dates for when those shifts occur. The approval of DCRs is often the first use of war team because these can occur early on, during mid-game. Later, when the bug count needs to be tracked tightly, approval for putting bugs into the programming pipeline shifts to war team (previously approved bugs should generally be grandfathered in). Finally, in the closing weeks or days, war team reviews all incoming bugs, and project control is effectively centralized.

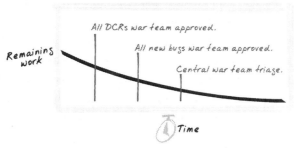

FIGURE 15-9. *War team increases in authority as end-game progresses.*

War team meetings can start out weekly, but they should soon shift into daily half-hour or one-hour meetings. It's up to the war team to make sure these meetings start and end on time (someone should own clarifying the agenda before the meeting starts). If the goal is making good decisions toward the exit criteria and goals, it's possible to review many DCRs and to triage many bugs in 60, if not 30, minutes. The secret is to avoid end-game micromanagement.

War team does not need to know the workings of every bug or every issue. On the contrary, they only need to make sure the decisions made are in the best interest of the project, that the right questions have been well asked and answered, and that the right bar is set for use of the remaining time. War teams fail to be expedient when leaders fail to trust their teams. If an issue is really heinous, it should be taken offline to be discussed with one member of war team, and the next day it should be brought back with an improved presentation.

Between project goals, exit criteria, precedence-setting bug decisions, and team communications, there are many opportunities to push decision making out to the team. Sometimes the war team approval process can be automated, with web forms allowing war team members to approve items remotely on their own time. Be clever. Find ways to avoid making war team an unnecessary or unintentional bottleneck.

In general, the fewer issues war team needs to manage, the better the job senior management has done in planning, executing, and leading the team through the project. If war team meetings regularly are brutal, three-hour marathons, leadership has failed in one or more ways, and there are lessons to be learned for the next project.

The end of end-game

The closing period of an engineering project is a difficult and mind-numbing process. Jim McCarthy, in *Dynamics of Software Development* (Microsoft Press, 1995), refers to it as working with Jell-O. Each time you fix a bug, you're effectively touching the big cube of Jell-O one more time, and it takes awhile for it to stop shaking and settle down. The more touches you make, the more variance there is in how it shakes, and the more complex the interaction is among the ripples of those changes. A web site or software product is essentially a huge set of highly interconnected moving parts, and each time you change one, you force all kinds of possible new waves of behavior through it. But unlike Jell-O, with software it's not easy to know when the shaking has stopped. Code is not transparent. It's only through quality assurance processes, and careful manual examination of the builds, that you can understand the effect of that one little change.[12]

---

12 Of course, the better engineered the software is, the easier it is to predict the impact of the changes.

This means that the true end of a project is mostly a waiting game. Hours and hours are spent reviewing new bug reports or issues and scrutinizing them to see if they meet the bar for shaking the Jell-O all over again. On larger teams, it's war team that bears this burden. Although the rest of the team should be actively scouting for new issues and using latest builds, everyone can contribute to the waiting game in some way.

But when there's a bug worthy of shaking the Jell-O, everything goes into full gear again. War team goes through the process of leading the team (or, more specifically, the programmer) in understanding the issue well enough to make a surgical change. Then the suite of tests and conditions have to be run again to ensure that things are exactly as they were before, except for the tiny little thing that needed to be changed. It's a very stressful process. Unlike the full-on charge of mid-game, or the fun of finding bugs in early end-game, the stress in the final days can't be relieved by indulging in big piles of work. Everything is very small, and the pressure has nowhere to go.

There are different measurements and moments of significance in this process, but they don't do much to change the nature of the work. They are simply intermediary milestones along the way to releasing. If nothing else, these markers break up the stressful monotony of late end-game work.

- **Zero bug bounce.** When the active and approved (by war team) bug count reaches zero, the team is said to have hit zero bug bounce (ZBB). This is called a bounce because as soon as the next bug comes in, the team is no longer at zero bugs. There are some pet theories as to the distance between ZBB and actual release, but none of them is strong enough to be listed here.

- **Zero resolved.** Resolved bugs may be hiding issues the team doesn't know about. Until it's been closed (and verified), it's not certain that a bug was actually fixed in the way it was supposed to be. Hitting zero resolved and zero active means the project is truly at a state of possible completion.

Incoming and active bugs make for poor measurements at this point because they are beneath the criteria for consideration. Even though the team is actively investigating these bugs, until they are brought to war team, they effectively have no impact on the progress of the project.

The release candidate (RC)

The first build of a project that has met all exit criteria is called the release candidate. As soon as this build is made, a new exit criterion must be added: what problems found in this RC build will warrant the creation of a second release candidate? If there are no criteria, assuming the RC build passes all verification and QA tests, the build is propped to the Web or put on CD, and delivered to customers.

If there is a defined RC criterion, and the RC fails that criterion, the end-game process repeats. War team decides on what investigation, design, and implementation should be done, the change is approved and made, and the process repeats.

In the software world, particularly the shrink-wrapped world, RCs are expensive. There are often additional tests and procedures that the build must go through to verify setup, localization, branding, and other issues. For the Web, it all depends on how the project integrates into other projects. There may be a similarly complex tree of dependencies that has to be managed.

Rollout and operations

When a final RC build is completed, only some of the team gets to celebrate. Depending on the nature of the project, a final RC may kick off a whole new series of work. The test and QA teams may need to go into high gear to evaluate server loads or other kinds of capacity issues that can be tested only with a final build. These issues can certainly be planned for, but the testing can't begin until the bits are in place.

Most web sites or web-based projects stage their releases through a sequence of test servers, where different conditions and integration work are given final test coverage. The more platforms or languages the project must cover, the more complicated the rollout process will be. Of course, the time required for proper rollout can be estimated and planned for during initial planning. Depending on how it's organized, the burden of rollout and operations might be isolated to a subteam or shared across the entire project team.

The project postmortem

As completion of a milestone or an entire project nears, someone must set up the team to learn from what was just done. This is often called writing a project retrospective or postmortem (in reference to the medical term for learning from something that ended). The hard part of doing this is that you want to capture information when it's still fresh in people's minds, but when people are getting ready to celebrate and wrap things up, they rarely want to go back and think through all the problems they've just dealt with. Most people want to move on and leave the past behind.

This is where leadership comes in. Team leaders must be committed to investing in the postmortem process. As things wind down, leaders should be asking people to start thinking about what went well and what didn't, even if it's just in the form of their own private lists. A plan should be made for team leaders to collect these lists and build a postmortem report. The report should have two things: an analysis and summary of lessons learned, and a commitment to address a very small number of them in the next project (if you pick a big number, they won't get addressed—prioritize and focus).

It can make sense to hire a professional to do the postmortem work for you (or get someone not on your team, but in your organization).[13] They come in, spend a week interviewing people on the team, and build a report based on what was learned, filtered through the consultant's expertise. This has the advantage of an objective perspective, as they will notice and voice things others will not.[14] More important, perhaps, they bring outside expertise into the organization, applied to the needs of a specific project and team.

Party time

When a final RC build is confirmed and makes its way through the staging process, out to the world, it's time to celebrate. After many weeks, months, or even years, whatever it was you were supposed to have made has been finished. It's a rare and special thing to finish a project: in the tech sector, most projects never get anywhere near this far. As PM, it's your job to make sure there's an opportunity for everyone involved to celebrate together. Avoid corporate or organizational cliché (it's impossible to celebrate in a conference room). Instead, go to the nearest pub, reserve the big table at your favorite restaurant, or invite folks over to your home. Drink and eat better than you have in a long time (and eat and drink more of it). If you're not the festive or social type, find out who on the team is, and conspire with them to organize something.

Completing projects doesn't happen often in most lifetimes. Creating good things that other people will use in their lives is an incredible challenge. It's a time worthy of extraordinary celebration: live it up!

Summary

- Big deadlines are a series of small deadlines.
- Any milestone has three smaller deadlines: design complete (specs finished), feature complete (implementation finished), and milestone complete (quality assurance and refinement finished).
- Defining exit criteria at the beginning of milestones improves the team's ability to hit its dates.
- Hitting dates is like landing airplanes: you need a long, slow approach. And you want to be ready to take off again quickly, without having to do major repairs.

---

13 See *http://www.scottberkun.com/essays/* for some advice on doing postmortems well.

14 The leaders of a project will have strong emotional investment in what happens and will struggle to be objective. However, an expert outsider has no emotional investment or personal history, and therefore has better odds of successfully examining, understanding, reporting, and making recommendations about the project.

- You need elements of measurement to track the project. Common elements include daily builds, bug management, and the activity chart.

- You need elements of control to project level adjustments. Common elements of control include review meetings, triage, and war team.

- The end of end-game is a slow, mind-numbing process. The challenge is to narrow the scope of changes until a satisfactory release remains.

- Now is the time to start the postmortem process. Give yourself and your team the benefit of learning from what went well and what didn't.

- If fortune shines on you, and your project makes it out the door, be happy. Very, very happy. Many people, through no fault of their own, never get that far. Plan a grand night. Do ridiculously fun and extravagant things (including inviting this author to the party). Give yourself stories to tell for years to come.

Exercises

A. Next time you work on a project that is in end-game, start making a list of tracking data you wish you had during the project. Make a commitment to record that data from the start of the next project.

B. As an experiment, next time exit criteria are created, demand that the authors of the criteria attend the first bug triage meeting, using the criteria. This should force them to put the criteria in practice themselves, providing a great opportunity to refine them early in end-game.

C. During triage, one programmer insists on deciding the fate of every bug. He bullies, ridicules, and does everything he can to have his opinion reign supreme. The problem is, he's right most of the time. What should you do?

D. Early on in end-game, your team is excited about being in the last stage, but you're burnt out. It's taken all of your energy to get the project this far. Are you honest with your team, or do you try to hide it? How can you recharge?

E. Pick another industry: how do they manage the last part of their project schedule? Interesting examples include the film industry, any special operations military group (Navy SEALs, Ninjas, Spartans), or even your favorite take-out restaurants. Do a short presentation for your team on how your methods compare with theirs.

F. You are two days away from releasing a major update to your news web site, used by millions of people. The champagne is ready and waiting. But then an engineer discovers a major problem that will take three days to fix. The problem is $10 million in advertising for the specific launch day and time has already been paid for. What do you do?

G. Imagine you are one of the five leaders who runs the war team meeting. At every meeting, also attended by many junior members of the team, a big argument breaks out between the 5 leaders, sometimes lasting 10 minutes or more. What effect does this have on the team? Make a list of different approaches you could take, both in the meeting and after the meeting.

H. Pretend you have just released the most important software in the history of the universe. Your team photo is on the cover of *Time* magazine, and you're all famous. How would you celebrate? How much would you spend? Where would it take place? Now think of your current project. It might just be the best software anyone on the project has released: don't they deserve a special way to honor their achievement?

CHAPTER SIXTEEN

Power and politics

Anytime you try to organize people to do anything, whether it's throw a party or start a company, there are different attitudes, desires, and skills among the individuals involved. This means no matter how talented a leader is at running a project, there will be people who do not receive everything they want. Thus, there is a natural instinct for motivated and ambitious people to try and get what they want by influencing people who have the power to make it happen. This, in the simplest explanation I could fit in a paragraph, explains why politics exist. It's a by-product of human nature in group interactions that we experience the frustration and challenges of political situations. Aristotle said that "man is a political being," and this is in part what he meant.

> **"Every management act is a political act. By this I mean that every management act in some way redistributes or reinforces power."**
> — *Richard Farson*, Management of the Absurd: Paradoxes in Leadership

The fuel that drives politics is power. Roughly defined, power is the ability a person has to influence or control others. While we tend to look at organizational hierarchies to understand who is powerful and who isn't, often power structures do not directly match hierarchies (as described in Chapter 12, earned power is different from granted power). A person who can persuade the right people at the right time, and apply her knowledge to resolve situations to everyone's satisfaction, can be more powerful in an organization than her superiors—sometimes without them recognizing it.

This fact adds complexity to organizational politics—individuals are free to cultivate power independent of the hierarchy. To make this even more difficult, depending on the particular issue, power is distributed differently across the team. For engineering decisions, Harold might have the most power, but for business issues, it's Maude. All combined, the complexity of typical project organizations creates political opportunities, but it also makes competition for power inevitable.

For project managers, this means two things. First, there will be political influences that impact you no matter how powerful or ethical you are. Second, power and politics are an inherent part of management. You must at least be aware of how political systems work if you want to diminish their negative effects, much less enhance their positive ones. This chapter will provide core lessons of applied project politics. I'll cover how to diagnose the political landscape you are in, the common situations and why they occur, and how to solve problems of politics and power.

The day I became political

My first major lesson about organizational politics came in 1997 from Chris Jones, who at the time was group program manager for Internet Explorer. The group had gone through a chaotic couple of months, with several reorganizations and direction changes, and things still hadn't settled down. There was one particularly important role on the team—responsibility for a feature called channels (part of the ill-fated "push technology" craze during the browser wars)—that had never gone well. This role was so critical to our plans, and so poorly managed, that the entire team was devastated by it. Many of my peers and I were upset, but we didn't know what to do. Feeling powerless, we mostly blamed the politics of our management team. To make matters worse, at the time, I had the most cynical view of organizational politics. It was something like this:

> Politics (n): The things evil, weak, self-serving people do.

I didn't know exactly what those things were, or how they were done, but I was sure the evil and weak self-serving people in the team (whoever they were) were doing it. I couldn't precisely identify them because my assessment of people, at the time, had two settings: smart and moron. I was ignorant and arrogant (interesting how often they come together). But my saving grace from these failings was that I had the highest opinion of Chris, and the good fortune to have an office next to his.[1] One day, frustrated and upset by the team situation, I stopped by and told him my concerns about the group. He listened patiently and suggested we chat over lunch.

During lunch he did the most surprising thing—he told me more than I expected to hear. He laid out the situation from his perspective, telling me just enough details that I could understand the primary problems, without betraying the trust of other members of his organization. He described his high-level assessment of the problem, and the three reasonable alternatives he had available to solve it. I realized he had his own constraints: the needs, desires, and goals of his own peers, managers, and VPs. He had the pressure of our schedule and strategic competition (Netscape). From my viewpoint, I assumed his world was freer than mine (doesn't more power mean more freedom?), but as he laid it out, I realized his situation was more difficult than mine.

He then did the second most unexpected thing—he asked me for my opinion. He gave me a chance to offer my own logic and perspective on the decisions he had to make. Right then, I had my first political epiphany: this stuff is hard, really hard. By asking what

---

1 Never underestimate the value of a well-placed workspace. I learned much about what was going on above me in management from that location. It enabled me to have informal chats with all kinds of people who were looking for Chris and to innocently overhear important hallway conversations. The downside was that the big boss was right next door. Had it been a manager with control or micromanagement issues, there would be serious downsides to such a location.

I thought (and listening to what I said), he defused all of the animosity and finger pointing that usually comprised my attempts at political thinking. He made me actually consider the issues and people involved. And when I did, I froze. Like being thrown into oncoming highway traffic, I didn't know where to start: it all seemed terrifying. I still remember staring at my half-eaten sandwich, failing to find anything intelligent to say. The conversation moved on, lunch ended, and I went back to work. I've learned much since then about how organizations function, but I look back at that day as an important change in perspective. Here are three key points I've learned since that day:

- **Politics is not a dirty word.** In most dictionaries, the first definition of the word *politics* you will find is something like this:

  > Politics (n): The art or science of government or governing, especially the governing of a political entity, such as a nation, and the administration and control of its internal and external affairs.

  You won't find anything like my cynical definition, until the fourth or fifth definition listed in most English dictionaries. Politics is the skill of managing people and organizations. It is possible to be effective politically without resorting to unethical or sneaky behavior.

- **All leaders have political and power constraints.** We like to believe that power figures—like corporate VPs or the President of the United States—have tremendous power. They do, but much of it is power through influence. For example, the U.S. President is one of three branches of government (executive), and his power is checked and balanced by the other two branches. Many of his official actions can be vetoed. Most corporate VPs have senior managers reporting to them who don't like to be told what to do, and they demand significant amounts of their own authority. And on it goes down the chain of command. So, when you look at people who have more power than you, don't assume omnipotence.

- **The ratio of power to responsibility is constant.** One way to think about power is through its relationship to the challenges you're expected to meet using that power. Say I was the CEO of ExampleCorp, and I gave you $5 to go get me some coffee. The authority you have is small (although there is some), but so is the responsibility. On the other hand, if I gave you $2.5 million and a staff of brilliant minions, I'd probably ask you to plan, build, and manage an entire business. Responsibility, stress, and challenges generally increase in relation to the amount of power you're granted. For this reason, having more power rarely makes things easier because the challenges increase as a result of the increase in power.

- **Politics is a kind of problem solving.** No matter what organizational challenge you face, and how frustrating it might be, it's just another kind of problem to solve. The micromanagers, the randomizers, and the brown-nosers are all just different kinds of obstacles to overcome or work around. As good or bad as things might be, there are probably a finite number of realistic choices anyone in power can possibly make in any specific situation, and they will all have political consequences. If you approach organizational problems with the same discipline and creativity you approach a design or engineering problem, you can find those choices and make good decisions (or at least the best decision possible).

Over time I learned that blaming "politics" for problems I faced was a convenient way to dodge unpleasant but unavoidable aspects of working with other people. The same went for pointing fingers at "management," "engineering," or "marketing" and saying how stupid they were. Pointing a finger doesn't make them any less stupid or ineffective. (If, in fact, that's really what the problem is. It's always possible they're smart but just as constrained by political factors as you.)

The same goes for pointing fingers at any individual programmer, manager, or author. Blame simply doesn't change anything, and it usually blinds you from the real causes and possible remedies of a situation. Any political or management action that takes place, no matter how stupid or evil it seems, is always one of a limited number of possible choices managers have. The alternatives might be even worse for the project than the choice that was made. Without understanding something of the constraints, judgment will always be based more on venting frustration than on the reality of the situation.

The sources of power

Power (n): The ability to do or act; capability of doing or accomplishing something. [2]

To influence how things happen, you need to understand the dynamics of political power. Power in an organization centers on what decisions an individual can make or influence. Think about how decisions are made in your organization: if there is a tough call that needs to be made, who gets to make it? Who is allowed to be in the room as it's debated? Whose opinions are heard? Those are people with degrees of power. Having clear authority to make a decision is the most basic form of power, but having access to that decision maker so that you can ask questions or make suggestions is another form of power. As I covered in Chapter 12, granted power is the most obvious form because it comes down through the hierarchy. It is implied in people's job titles or other symbols of seniority. Granted power almost always comes to a person through someone in a higher position of power. The VP grants power to those who work directly for her, and those individuals grant power to those who work for them. The VP could decide to give certain individuals more power than others—if that was in the best interest of her goals.

Earned power is distributed organically. Because reputation and ability are subjective (compared to job titles and hierarchy), each individual in a project plays a role in determining who has earned power. For example, let's say that Tyler is a programmer on

---

2 From the *Random House College Dictionary* (1999).

the team. Marla and Jack think highly of his opinions, but Chloe does not. If a debate ensues between the entire team, Marla and Jack will tend to lend more credibility to Tyler's arguments than Chloe will. In a sense, Marla and Jack will tend to transfer some of their own power to support Tyler's arguments. So, earned power is often granted to an individual through the behavior of those around him. In such a case, earned power can be distributed across lines of hierarchy. For example, a senior manager in one organization might think highly of a junior employee in another.

Although it's common for some individuals to have earned more trust and power than others, it's always subjective and relative. Different outcomes are possible depending on the domain of the decision, who's in the room, and what power he has. Some say this is what makes politics interesting: power is constantly flowing through a team, changing directions, and supporting or working against different people at different times. Because power isn't always obvious until it's been used, it's easy to misinterpret who has what kinds of power.

For the sake of completeness, the following list offers specific definitions of different kinds of power (this list is a loose interpretation of a list found in *Power Plays: A Guide to Maximizing Performance and Success in Business*, by Thomas Quick [F. Watt, 1985]). I won't refer to these much, but it's worth considering who in your organization possesses them, and how they are used:

- **Reward.** The ability to grant people bonuses, raises, tasty bits of food, or any visibly beneficial reward. Because people know you have this power and want to be recipients of it, they will tend to respond and behave differently toward you.

- **Coercion.** Having control over penalties and the ability to threaten punitive action. The threat of this kind of power is often sufficient because, unlike rewards, the power is not in the receiving of good things, but in not having to receive bad things. Coercive power can be as simple as the ability to embarrass or ridicule a person in front of others ("How stupid are you?"), or as official as demoting people or reducing their responsibilities or salary.

- **Knowledge.** Having expertise in a subject area, or having specific information that is relevant to a decision, affords power. By controlling how that expertise is applied, or how/when information is disseminated, one can develop power. In the simplest form, just being smart, knowledgeable, and good at problem solving with whatever you're working on affords power because people will listen to you and respect your opinion. In more complex forms, having information affords power because your view of the world is more accurate than others'. And if you are feeling manipulative, you can distort other's perceptions of the state of the project or the world.

- **Referent.** Who you know and how you know them. If people know you have the support or friendship of those with power, some of it is referred to you. For example, if you introduce yourself as "I'm Steve, I work for Bill," you are banking on Bill's power and reputation to help provide you some of your own. Referent power can also come from people who have allied with you or offer you support.

- **Influence.** Some people possess the ability to persuade others, which may not be related to their knowledge of the issue in question. A combination of communication skill, confidence, emotional awareness, and talents of observation contributes to the ability to be influential. Influence may be fueled by respect people have for your knowledge, or because they trust you, or even simply because they think you're attractive, smart, or interesting. Influence can also develop as a result of a debt: someone may owe you a favor, and influence on a decision is a way to help pay it back. Note that some individuals will have more influence over others—it's a highly relative, not absolute, form of power.

The misuse of power

> **"If you don't know what you are doing, what will deliver which value to whom, and how it will be implemented, the project self-organizes around some other goal or goals. Typically, political wrangling of some kind erupts. This guarantees pointlessness."**
>
> —James Bullock, from Roundtable on Project Management

When people say politics are evil, they usually mean misuse of power. I define a misuse of power as any action that doesn't serve the greater good of the project and the people in it.[3] Because sources of power are natural, and the use of it to influence and drive decisions is a by-product of team-based work, those things can't be evil in and of themselves. It's impossible to work on a project without individuals who are trying to influence others and use their own power to move the project forward. (In fact, as we'll examine, free debate of ideas minimizes politics.)

Misuse of power occurs when an individual is working toward his own interests. For example, in Figure 16-1, the goals of an individual correspond only loosely to the goals for the project. Much of his energy will be spent doing what is best for him, instead of what is best for the project as a whole. This represents a failure of leadership and management to better align individual and team goals (and rewards) with project goals. To be fair to leaders, some gaps are unavoidable. People have lives outside of the project. Individuals have their own personal motivations that may have nothing to do with work

---

3 I know I'm dodging the ethical debate for what behavior is immoral, or even what kinds of projects can be said to have evil goals. However, I will say that backstabbing, lying, and inventive acts of deception generally work against a project. They take short-term gains at the expense of long-term team value and trust.

at all, but which the individual is trying to satisfy through work. However, the role of management is to look for these gaps and find ways to minimize them. Managers should at least help employees act on these motivations in ways that don't negatively impact the project. In the end, if large gaps exist, a natural tension is created for how power will be applied. There will be strong temptations for people to serve themselves instead of serving the project.

FIGURE 16-1. *Personal motivations must align with the project. The less alignment, the more destructive the political behavior will be.*

It's also possible that what appears to be a selfish use of power is simply a disagreement about what's best for the project. As shown in Figure 16-2, it might be that two people have different opinions about the best way to satisfy the project goals. Distinguishing between these two cases can be very difficult because often what's best for the project may turn out to be better for one individual than another. Discerning when the motivation is purely self-serving requires knowledge of the people involved, clear project goals, and a good framework for communicating, debating, and discussing issues.

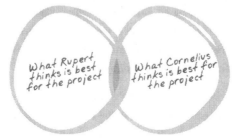

FIGURE 16-2. *Disputes over power can happen for altruistic reasons. Two peers may simply disagree on the best use of power.*

When there are several small teams contributing to the same project, the problems are more complex. As shown in Figure 16-3, if each individual team has motivations to do things that are not in the best interest of the project, they will each spend significant energy on things that don't lead to the project's overall success. This framework applies equally well to individuals or to entire teams. Whenever goals diverge, the frequency of power misuse will rise. That is (again), unless the person managing all of these individuals or teams actively works to get those teams to collaborate and openly settle conflicts of interest.

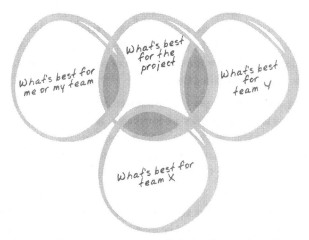

FIGURE 16-3. *The greater the divergence of interest, the higher the probability that misuse of power will occur.*

Process causes for misuse of power

A more specific way to think about power misuse is to divide the causes into two groups: process and motivational. Process causes stem from failures in the way the team or organization is structured, and it is a kind of management or leadership failure. Motivational causes are driven purely by individuals and their personal needs and drives. Most of the time, when power is misused, it's some combination of process and motivational issues.

Process causes are more dangerous than motivational forces because they are not isolated to one person's behavior. Instead, a process cause is systemic and encourages everyone on the team to abuse power or apply it to causes that serve only themselves.

- **Unclear decision-making process.** If the team knows when a big decision is coming, what the criteria are, and who is involved in the decision, there is little need for fancy politics. Anyone with an opinion will know what forum to present her proposals in, and what arguments will be effective. But if the process is hidden, is overly complex, or lacks visible owners for decisions, anyone who cares about the outcome will be motivated to be more political. Therefore, it's the job of anyone making decisions that impact others to clarify how it will be made, who is involved, and what the criteria are.

- **Misunderstanding/miscommunication.** Teams that communicate well make sure that information is not only transmitted, but also understood and, if possible, agreed upon (see Chapter 9). The poorer the communication habits of a team, the more often power is applied in ways that don't serve the project. If person A and person B think of the project goals differently, but assume the other has the same interpretation, they'll be working against each other without even realizing it.

- **Unclear resource allocation.** If the process for how budget, staff, and equipment are allocated is not defined or made public, everyone will seek out those resources using any available tactics. It's the job of whoever has the appropriate power to clarify for the team what the criteria are for the distribution of resources, or how and when proposals should be made for acquiring them.

- **Lack of accountability.** When people are allowed to fail or make mistakes without taking responsibility for them, politics are inevitable. Without accountability for people's commitments, few will trust others. Without trust, people will use their own power to protect themselves from dependence on others or to avoid dependence on people they don't trust (see the section "Trust is built through commitment" in Chapter 12).

- **Weak or toothless goals.** For almost every misuse of power I've mentioned, some reference is made to serving the project goals. When the project goals are weak (or nonexistent), these misuses are probable, if not guaranteed. Without the center of gravity of project goals, there is no point of clarity that everyone can agree on, meaning that everything can be debated and interpreted. Even if the goals are strong, team leaders have to give the goals teeth: actively protecting the goals, updating and revising them to keep them accurate, and ensuring that all decisions are made to serve them.

Motivational causes for misuse of power

No matter what your philosophy is about human nature, it's reasonable to assume that all people are self-motivated creatures. Even when we act altruistically, we are serving our own values on what is good and bad in the world. We are also emotional creatures, and psychological factors drive our behavior—some of which we are more aware of than others. Motivational causes are based in simple elements of human psychology:

- **Protecting others.** If I let this decision happen, the people on my team or my peers who I care about will suffer.

- **Self-interest.** I want that raise, promotion, or sense of pride from accomplishing something that I feel is important or done well.

- **Ego.** I want to prove how smart I am to myself or everyone else, and perhaps make sure it's indisputable and dramatically visible how much smarter and better I am than they are. This project must be at least as perfect as I am, or it should help me to cover up for how imperfect I feel I am.

- **Dislike/revenge.** I don't want to work with Fred, or I'm trying to get Fred back for what "he did to me" on the last project.

These motivations are not necessarily evil. They cause problems only when they lead to behavior that doesn't best support the goals of the project. If these motivations can be managed in a way that doesn't hurt others on the team, they're just another kind of fuel. Look again at Figure 16-1: if the two circles overlapped by 90%, then effectively, the individual's motivations are highly aligned with the project's goals. It's the manager's challenge to keep the forces of ego and self-interest in check at all times. The manager has to direct the energies of her reports and her team toward helping the project and the people working on it, instead of working against them.

Preventing misuse of power

The best way to reduce these symptoms is to depend on the project goals to drive the application of power. If everyone refers to the same goals and inherits their individual goals from that source (see Chapter 4), political tensions will be minimized. Although some will debate the means, everyone will be fighting for similar ends. To reinforce this, at any time during a project, anyone should be able to openly ask the following questions:

- What are our goals for this week/month/project?
- Are these overall or subteam goals in conflict in any way? How can we manage or resolve them?
- How will this particular decision be made and who will make it?
- Are your and my powers being applied in a way that contributes to our goals or supports the team?

Even if people disagree on the answers, they're having the right disagreements. It will be obvious what the true causes of conflict are, and leaders and managers will have the opportunity to provide clarity, redefine the goals, or make new (possibly tough) choices in the presence of the people directly impacted by them. On the contrary, misuse of power is guaranteed if goals are significantly out of date or are radically divergent from individual to individual or team to team.

Sometimes, managers choose to deliberately set teams up to compete with each other, betting that the added competition will lead to better work. This can work in some situations, but it makes the organization more volatile, requiring a stronger leader to hold it together. There is nothing unique about this. For example, every sports team has starters and backup players. During every practice, the coach is trying to maintain internal competition for those starting spots, while simultaneously maintaining a strong bond across the entire team. Good leaders actively reinforce the right attitudes and behaviors to keep those forces balanced.

But unchecked, individuals with competing interests have more motivation to use political power for their own ends. Instead of competitive spirit focusing on real business competitors, it's directed at peers and subordinates within the same team. From a holistic view of the project, this kind of environment is corrupt. Power is not being directed effectively toward the completion of the project itself. Without strong leadership acts to refocus the team and level the playing field, downward spirals are probable. Each self-serving action that goes rewarded (or ignored by management) will encourage others to do the same. Soon, few people will trust each other enough to be effective, as they'll always question the ulterior motives of their teammates and superiors.

How to solve political problems

For this section, I'm assuming two things. First, that there are well-defined goals for the project. Second, that these goals motivate whatever you are trying to achieve. If one or both of these assumptions isn't true for you, this section will still be of use, but there will be more work for you to do because you'll have less leverage to make things happen.

The process described here makes the most sense for large power issues and for when you are in a situation where you need more power than you have. The bigger the issue, the more faithfully a thought process like this should be applied. The smaller the issue, the more of these steps you can probably speed through or skip altogether.

Clarify what you need

The only way to be successful in resolving a political problem is to be very clear on what it is you need, and then develop a plan to get it. The common needs are:

- Resources (money, time, staff)
- Authority to make a decision
- Influence on a decision under someone else's authority
- Adjustment of others' goals to support or align with yours
- Adjustment of your own goals to better align with others'
- Advice, expertise, or support

However you define your needs, prepare to be flexible. Even if you decide that the real need is resources, while you are seeking them out, do not stop listening for suggestions from others that satisfy the goals but do not involve acquiring resources. By pushing for a larger budget or more time, you might force a new idea to surface that satisfies your goals just as well as more resources would. So, don't fixate on the need itself: it's only a means to satisfy your goals for the project.

Managing up

The best possible time to do this kind of political needs analysis is at the moment when your goals are defined. When you're sitting down with your manager to agree on what responsibilities you have for the next week or month, there's an opportunity to consider whether you have the authority you need to get that work done. Any support you need that you don't currently possess should be identified, and your manager can come up with a plan to help you get it. Some organizations call this activity managing up—as in you must manage up the hierarchy, instead of down it. Clarifying what you need from management is the first step in successfully managing up.

The other steps in managing up mostly involve repeating this process at the necessary intervals. If you can stay in sync with your manager and your manager's manager on what you're doing and what you need from them, and ensure that it's all aligned toward the same goals, you're most of the way there.

The simplest way to manage up is to initiate a discussion with your manager where you propose specifics for the following points.

- What I expect you, my manager, to do for me (e.g., giving guidance, warning me of things I need to know, supporting my decisions, pointing out areas where I need to grow)
- The resources I need to meet those goals, and who I need them from
- The level and frequency of involvement I need from you (no involvement? quarterly reviews? daily status reports? weekly one-on-one meetings? be specific)

By doing this early, you will know exactly how much support you can expect, and where problems will likely come from. Alarms should go off if your manager is unresponsive, vague, or defensive about committing to any of your requests. It means you may very well be on your own or are set up to fail, and that your manager is not actively working in your mutual interests.

Who has the power to give what you need?

For each kind of power you need, identify the person who can give it to you. The org chart or hierarchy is an easy place to start, but use it only to refresh your memory on the players involved (see Figure 16-4). Then ask around to find out who is most actively responsible for what kinds of decisions (on small teams, it should be obvious, but ask if you're unsure). Use people who are committed to support you to help sort this out: your manager, your peers, or reports. It shouldn't take more than a few conversations to identify the people you need. Sometimes, it's better to seek this kind of information indirectly because you don't necessarily want to approach the person(s) in question without a plan. (Avoid odd behavior, such as "Hi Fred. Are you in charge of deciding who gets new laptops?" "Yes, why?" "Oh, just curious. Bye.")

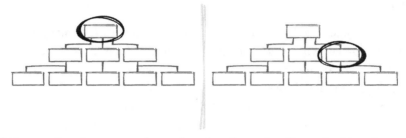

FIGURE 16-4. *The relevant source of power depends on the situation. The org chart hierarchy is not necessarily the primary consideration. A mid-level person may have more power over certain issues than her boss does.*

Understanding their perspective

For any person who has power you need, start by identifying what his goals are. On a well-run team, this should be easy because his goals are really the project goals at whatever level of seniority he happens to have. Consider his biases, opinions, and preferred ways for going about making decisions. The better your relationship is with him, and the more experience you have working with him, the easier this will be.

Thinking from his perspective, work to see how your needs and goals fit into his. Make your request derive from some higher-level project requirement or objective that he is obligated to respect. Instead of saying "I need another programmer," understand that you can honestly say, "To achieve goals X and Y, my team needs another programmer. Our project plan didn't anticipate the three requests that came in last week, and as a result, our goals are currently at high risk." Don't lie or mislead. Be willing to question your own requests for resources if there are better uses for them on the project. (But if that's the case, you should be asking for the goals and objectives to change in light of that better use. "I think our goals should shift. Goal X is less important now. Those resources should shift to support goal Z." A smart supervisor will reward you for this project-centric thinking.)

Who do they trust and respect?

If you've identified Fred as the person with the power you need, work to understand who influences him. It might be a peer, a star on his team, or his own superior. It might be you—at least for certain kinds of decisions. Consider ways to use the influence of these individuals to help you make your case. If you have a good relationship with these people of influence, share your thinking with them and ask for their opinion.

Don't manipulate, lie, or do anything questionable—it shouldn't be necessary. Instead, position your argument much as you would with Fred, and ask for their feedback. They may know facts you do not, have perspectives that improve your thinking (including changing your opinion), or simply have advice for how to pitch your case. Even if you don't have good relationships with these influential people, you can still ask for their opinions or observe how they make successful arguments or proposals to Fred.

The illusion of group power

Sometimes, what you need will appear to be governed by a group of people. There might be a meeting or committee that appears to make certain decisions. Never focus on a group of people: always divide groups into individuals and consider who has what kind of influence in that group. Despite how they appear, meetings rarely decide anything. Often, people enter those discussions with strong opinions and allies to support them, and the meeting carries out a sequence of predictable machinations. To the uninitiated, these meetings can appear vibrant and active, but to those with the most power, many of the arguments were entirely predictable both in nature and outcome. They were fully anticipated (perhaps using a process similar to the one you're reading now), and good counterarguments were ready to end the discussions.

The more important or contentious an issue is, the more investment you have to make in the individuals involved. Pitch ideas blindly to groups only if you're confident you have the logic, influence, and communication skill to lead a room full of powerful people with differing opinions toward the direction you think best serves the project.

Make an assessment

Combining everything you've learned in this book, you have to assess what the odds are of successfully getting your needs met. It's entirely possible that with a given power structure, a particular need you have is impossible to satisfy. This is not necessarily someone's failure, any more than an engineering or business constraint is. In assessing your situation, you should realize that power structures have limitations just like other structures do.

- **Does anyone have the power you need?** The resources you need simply might not be available. They could all be committed to other tasks (and cannot be redeployed) or the organization doesn't have the resources at all. If you're asking for something beyond the scope of the organization, be prepared to make extremely compelling arguments for it. Divide one large request into several small ones, and prioritize them. Perhaps these smaller requests can be obtained by different people or over a period of time.

- **How successful have you been at getting this kind of support in the past?** Consider your experience obtaining this kind of power. What happened? What went well and what didn't? If you have no experience with this kind of politics, find someone who does and get her advice. If you proceed anyway, expect tough odds: whoever has the power you are trying to use will have experience dealing with people who want it, placing you at a disadvantage.

- **How successful has anyone been in getting this kind of support from them?** If no one has been able to convince the team manager for changing the development methodology, know that if you try to do so, you are breaking new ground. On the contrary, if you're trying to do something others have done, find out how they did it and learn from their experiences.

- **How strong are your arguments?** I've had times where I was willing to bet my entire reputation on a request. I was so convinced that I was right that I used the size of my commitment to help convince people of its value. Other times I wasn't as confident, and I angled my arguments appropriately. Know where you stand and how you really feel about what you're asking for. Organize your arguments and points on their strength, and focus on the strongest ones.

- **What approach and style will work best?** Will dropping by someone's office and saying, "I need this" be more effective than making a 10-page report or presentation? There's no rulebook: consider the culture of the team, and the personalities of the people involved. What have you seen work before?

- **Who else is competing for the same resources?** Sometimes it's obvious who is in competition. Budgets are always limited, and it's among your peers that your boss's resources are divided. If you have good relationships, get together with peers and discuss your various opinions, collectively striving to do what's best for the team (the common manager should lead this discussion, but if he doesn't, make it happen). If relationships aren't as strong, do it on your own. Imagine their opinions, and as objectively as possible, evaluate them in the context of your own. Lastly, consider how others will perceive your course of action. Will people be upset? Angry? Feel you are betraying them? Nip these things in the bud. Talk to the people involved directly to minimize the potential fallout.

- **Is this the right battle to fight?** Recognize that this particular need is one of many that you have. Using influence and other political strategies costs you time and energy that can't be spent on other things. Make sure that what you are seeking is the best use of your resources. For example, you might know that there is a more important request you will need to make later, so it might be best to save your energy for that time.

- **What you can't see hurts you.** Always recognize that there are layers of politics and power that you can't see from where you stand. The larger the organization the more this is true. Two or three levels above you (if there are that many levels), there may be a set of struggles and debates over issues that you have no awareness of. Your peers, who may have different goals, are using their own influence on the same powers that you are. Consider what might be going on above you and around you, and be on the lookout for sources of information that might help you improve your perspective.

Tactics for influencing power

After you've made an assessment, it's time for action. There are common tactics for approaching organizational politics and engaging the use of others' power. The following tactics are the simplest and most common; references for more ways will follow.

The direct request

In the direct request, you do the simplest thing possible: you go to the person who has the power you need, and you ask him for it. Depending on the approach and style you've identified (see the previous list) this could be an informal conversation, an email, or a meeting you've put together exclusively for this purpose. The more formal you make the request, the greater the odds are that other people will be involved in the discussion. The less formal, the more direct your conversation and request might be. In Figure 16-5, A represents the person with the power you need; B, C, and D are other people on your team.

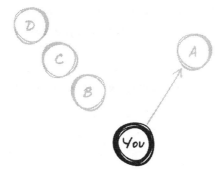

FIGURE 16-5. *The direct request.*

The conversation

This is a collaborative variant of the direct request. If you and B are competing for the same resources and have discussed the matter together, you ask A to meet with both of you and resolve the issue as a group. Teams that have strong goals and good teamwork do this kind of thing naturally and informally. They trust each other to work toward the shared project goals, and they willingly concede valid points even when those concessions diminish their own power or authority. Strong leaders and managers encourage this behavior because it minimizes the need for their involvement. The team will eventually learn to resolve issues on their own (i.e., they learn to replicate the philosophies of A even without him present), and involve A only when there are particularly tough decisions that need to be made.

The use of influence (flank your objective)

Instead of depending on your own influence to convince A, invest in the support from others in the organization to voice similar arguments and opinions. Choose carefully among the people on your team based on how much influence they have on A. If your influence is weak, you might need to enlist the support of several people.

In military terms, this is called "flanking your objective." Instead of approaching head-on, you approach from the side, gaining an advantage. Instead of dealing with your arguments, A must also respond to the arguments from one or more other influential people. When these arguments come from people equal in seniority or power to A, they are harder to refute. (However, be careful when obtaining opinions from people with greater seniority to A without A present. This can be considered an end-run—an attempt to circumvent A's authority. It depends on the group culture and A's personality.)

Optionally, this can be combined with the direct request (as illustrated in Figure 16-6). Other options include how you make use of the influence you've gained. It may not be necessary to have B, C, and D actually in the room, or even to ever talk to A about the issue in question. As long as you have their approval, you may be able to speak for them, telling A, "I think we need to cut this feature. I spoke to B, C, and D, and they all agreed with me on this decision." Of course, be careful not to misrepresent what they said, and always be willing to bring those people into the room to settle the matter (effectively reverting to a conversation).

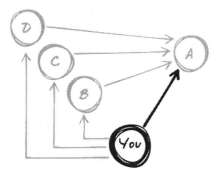

FIGURE 16-6. *Using influence to flank an objective.*

The multistage use of influence

When you can't get access to the people you need, work backward down the chain of influence or hierarchy. If C is the only person A will listen to, and you can't get C alone, find out who has the most influence on C. Then approach her and make your case. From there, you can work forward until your influence reaches the point where you need it applied. See Figure 16-7.

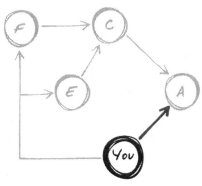

FIGURE 16-7. *The multistage use of influence.*

The indirect use of influence

On occasion, the best way to influence power is to put things in motion but stay behind the scenes. Perhaps A is two or more levels above you in the org chart, and he doesn't respond well to direct requests from people at your level. Or, maybe A just doesn't like you or is currently upset at you about some other issue (and you don't think he's being objective about it).

In this situation, enlist the support of another person to make that request for you. This could be your direct manager, a peer on your team, or someone who works for A who happens to have influence on the issue in question.

The less sneaky way to manage this is to frame the entire thing around conversations. Talk to C and see if she agrees with you. If she does, ask if she'll talk to A about it (see Figure 16-8). When she goes to A, she doesn't have to lie or mislead: she can make the argument from her own perspective because she does honestly agree with you and your request. If A then asks to talk to you about it, or if you ask him about it later, your argument will have benefited from C's influence.

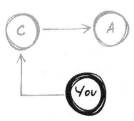

FIGURE 16-8. *Indirect influence.*

The group meeting

Meetings are very complex political situations. Anyone in the room can speak up and ask questions, applying their political power to the discussion in a way that can make things more difficult. If something important is to be decided, make sure you've evaluated who will be in the room before the meeting occurs.

Before the meeting, consider what questions are likely to come up, and what kind of answers each person wants to hear. If you know the people well, you can make good judgments for what to expect and prepare for all on your own. If you don't, ask around. Before the meeting, solicit feedback from important people who will be in the meeting. Get their concerns and big questions early, then either make changes if appropriate or develop your defense of the current plan. If you own the agenda, plan it accordingly.

Sometimes, setting up a meeting yourself can be the only way to resolve a question of power. Email rarely works well for complex or subtle issues. Or, perhaps you've identified that Sally needs to hear from Bob and Mike at the same time to be convinced that your recommendation should be followed. Running effective meetings is a skill of its own (see Chapter 10), but for now, realize that the better prepared you are for likely questions and debates, the easier it will be to run the meeting smoothly and in a favorable direction. (See Figure 16-9.)

FIGURE 16-9. *The group meeting can be an unpredictable political situation.*

Make them think it's their idea

In rare cases, you can plant seeds and water them with someone else's ego. It goes like this: you don't think a direct request will meet with success. So, instead you force a discussion where you identify a problem and ask for help in finding a solution. You don't offer the answers yourself, but instead ask questions and make points that lead them gently toward the outcome you want. Like all manipulations, this can easily backfire, and it requires subtlety and improvisational skills few possess. But I admit, sometimes it's effective with senior managers who like to believe they are right all the time.

References for other tactics

The previous list covers only the basics. The subject of political tactics fills many library bookshelves. The best single resource I've found is Robert Greene's *The 48 Laws of Power* (Penguin, 2001), but be warned: much like Dale Carnegie's *How to Win Friends and Influence People* (Pocket, 1990), you'll feel the urge to shower after you read it. *Influence*, by Robert Cialdini (Perrenial, 1998) is more about marketing than office politics, but some of the psychological principles are similar.

Know the playing field

The last considerations of project management involve the political playing field. The people who have the most power define what rules the team will follow: how power is obtained, applied, and distributed. When people act unethically—manipulating and deceiving others—it's up to those in control to identify and reprimand that behavior. It should be in their interest to keep the playing field relatively fair and allow the right people to use the political system to the best ends for the project.

However, if those in power are not careful in maintaining a fair playing field, it's up to you, one of the players, to adjust to the rules of the game. Either use your power to try and change the rules, or accept them for what they are. If deceptive and unfair practices are common, no law prevents you from seeking another job. If you choose to stay in a tough environment, don't assume others are altruistic if there's no reason to. I'm not recommending you take a lowest common denominator approach and copy the behavior of others—that's an ethical choice you have to make for yourself. But I am saying you need to be aware of what game you're playing and who you're playing it with.

Creating your own political field

No matter how frustrating the politics are, as a project manager you have to control your own playing field, as shown in Figure 16-10. You also control how your power is distributed across the team. There are two basic choices you have: make your playing field a safe and fair place for smart people to work, or allow the problems and symptoms of the larger team to impact your world. The latter is easy: do nothing. The former requires leadership and the employment of many of the tactics described in this book.

Good managers always find ways to protect their team. While it's true that for your team to grow they have to experience tough situations, a good manager protects people just enough so that they can be effective yet also be exposed to real experiences and learning opportunities. Similarly, if your manager is doing a good job, she's shielding you from certain problems and situations and actively working on your behalf to make your world easier to work in. At any level of hierarchy, this kind of proactive leadership takes more work and maturity to achieve, but that's the nature of good management.

FIGURE 16-10. *You always have the power to define your own playing field.*

So, don't assume that because your manager treats you poorly you should pass that on to your reports. As a manager, it is you who decides how your own team should be managed. Don't pass on attitudes, habits, or tactics that you think are destructive. Explain to your team the differences in working style or attitude, but don't follow along in behavior that you think is counterproductive.

Much of the advice in this chapter and this book applies at any level of organizational hierarchy. If there aren't clear goals at your level, create clear ones for your team. If there aren't clear practices above your level of the organization for how resources are distributed, you can establish your own for areas you lead. The same goes for project planning, communication, or decision making. You won't always benefit directly from these efforts, but your team definitely will. It should be easier for them to be effective and get more work done because you're providing effective structure that the rest of the organization doesn't have.[4]

In the end, proactive leadership in your own sphere of influence is the best way to grow your own sources of power. Initially, you might lose favor with your superiors for working differently than they do. But over time, people will like the playing field you've created. They will be happier and more effective working with and for you than with others. Unlike with the status quo of the rest of the organization, the quality of your team's work will continually rise.

Summary

- Politics are a natural consequence of human nature. When people work together in groups, there is a limited amount of authority, which must be distributed across different people with different desires and motivations.

---

4 The challenge of pushing for organizational change is significant. Definitely read up on the subject before going too far on your own. Start with *Leading Change*, by John P. Kotter (Harvard Business School Press, 1996).

- All leaders have political constraints. Every executive, CEO, or president has peers or superiors who limit their ability to make decisions. In general, the more power a person has, the more complex the constraints are that they must work within.

- There are many different kinds of political power, including rewards, coercion, knowledge, referent, and influence.

- Power is misused when it's applied in ways that do not serve the project goals. A lack of clarity around goals, unclear resource allocation or decision-making processes, or misunderstandings can contribute to the misuse of power.

- To solve political problems, clarify what you need. Identify who has it, and then assess how you might be able to get it.

- If you are involved in project management, you are defining a political playing field around you. It's up to you to decide how fair or insane it is.

Exercises

A. Is it possible to work with other people and have absolutely no politics? Think of the work environment with the healthiest political environment. What made it possible?

B. What kinds of power do you use most often? Which kinds of power do you use least?

C. In John F. Kennedy's book *Profiles in Courage*, he tells stories of courageous senators who made decisions they believed in despite the political consequences (e.g., the low chance of re-election). Is it best to try and gain power by doing what you believe in, or by doing what you think will please others in power? Is there a middle ground? As a project leader, how can you influence how people under you gain power?

D. When you go home to your family for the holidays, what is the power structure? How do people respond to the political actions that take place? Given the advice in this chapter, what advice might you have for your family? What can you learn from your family and apply to your workplace?

E. Who are your political allies in your organization? How did you cultivate these relationships? Is there any way to apply what you've learned from building allies that can be applied to new people who join your team? Or people you currently might label as enemies?

F. In this chapter, several tactics are listed for influencing power. What other tactics can you think of? Rank all the tactics you know of by how much risk they involve and how much power they have.

G. Watch as many competitive reality TV shows as you can find, like *The Apprentice* or *Survivor*. How do the rules of the game impact the kinds of politics and power people use?

H. Design your own reality TV show where the rules encourage a more positive kind of politics.

APPENDIX

A guide for discussion groups

No matter how great your imagination, you can't have a lively discussion with an inanimate object (if you can, seek psychiatric help). Books have magic powers, but interactivity isn't one of them. If you want to learn something, it's best to find others interested in the same topic and learn together. To help you make that happen, I've provided this handy guide.

Introducing the project management clinic

The fastest way to have a discussion is to join one already in progress. If you're looking for a free ride, let me tell you about the PM Clinic. Years ago I set up an email list of project managers called *pmclinic*. We avoided most of the annoyances of email discussion (flame wars, bad advice, too much or too little traffic) by providing a simple structure. Every Monday I email a situation—a real problem described by a subscriber—and we discuss that situation for the week. People offer advice, make recommendations, tell good war stories, and do their best to learn from each other. The list has been running strong for almost 5 years, has over 1,000 subscribers, and still has a crazy good signal-to-noise ratio.

To join the PM Clinic, simply head over here:

http://www.scottberkun.com/forums/pmclinic

Anyone can suggest a situation for discussion, and anyone can contribute. If you lurk on the list for two weeks, you'll get the vibe. If you post thoughtfully, treat the list with respect, and have a sense of humor, you'll fit in well. (And if you don't, we'll kick you out faster than you can say "project management.")

How to start your own discussion group

Big group discussions like PM Clinic are convenient, but the best learning happens in small groups. Dinner-size conversations are the sweet spot because they are small enough to know everyone personally, but large enough to have diverse opinions and lively conversation. And best of all, small discussion groups are easy to start.

On the other hand, you may have specific interests, say web development or a particular management style, and want to focus the group in one direction. In that case, you may want to start a large discussion group like PM Clinic, but focus on a specific way of looking at management, even just management within the culture of your particular company.

In all cases, all you need to get started are three things:

- An hour or more a week
- A book or series of topics to discuss
- Another interested person

Since you're holding this book in your hands, you are already on your way. All you need is some time and some people.

Finding people

The Web makes this easy. If you craft an invitation that makes you credible, and send it to the right place, you'll have more people than you need. By far the easiest place to find people interested in a discussion group is at work or school. If you're reading this book to help you in your job, or for a course, look around. Start asking people you already know to see who's interested.

Other places to look include:

- **Your company.** Beyond your team, are there company-wide email lists that you can use to recruit people? If you have a training organization or HR specialist, they may be willing to promote an announcement of your discussion group.

- **PM-clinic.** A large percentage of people in the PM Clinic group have read this book or are interested in reading it. You may have to create a virtual group instead of meeting in person, but it's an easy place to try.

- **Management and software blogs.** A quick web search will help you find many people who already have communities you can use. Politely tell them what you're trying to do, and ask if they'll post an announcement for you.

- **Management or software development groups.** Most major cities have community-run education groups centered on management, project management, or software development. PMI, the Project Management Institute, has local chapters in most cities and can help spread your announcement through email lists. The Personal MBA group (*http://personalmba.com/*) lists *Making Things Happen* as one of their recommended books, and it has a large social network.

Launching the group

How you start your announcement defines both who will sign up and who will stay. It seems trivial, but your announcement tells people how well you communicate, how organized you are, and whether it's worth their time to give it a shot. Write up a short announcement that is smart, fun, and clear. Here's an example you're free to use:

Want to kick ass at leading and managing teams? We're forming a small group of people interested in becoming better team leaders and managers. We'll meet weekly at a local café (or virtually over email), discuss a chapter of the book we're currently reading, exchange war stories and good conversation, and get wise together. If you're interested, reply with a short email about your background, proof of your good nature and sly humor, and a suggestion for a book or essay that'd make for good group discussion.

An email announcement like this will get you enough responses that you can filter out the scary ones. Get a list together, suggest the first meeting time and place, and make it happen. If you've chosen to go face to face, pick a café or bar you know that won't be too busy (noisy cafés make conversation tough), is convenient to get to, and has reasonable hours. In a pinch, most public libraries offer conference rooms for public use. If your group is formed at work, use a work conference room.

If you choose to go virtual, use any of the online group discussion tools, such as Google Groups (*http://groups.google.com/*) or Yahoo! Groups (*http://groups.yahoo.com/*), which can handle list administration for you. Meetup.com and Ning.com have other useful features for organizing groups.

The follow-through

The first meeting or discussion will define what happens. At the first meeting, define the agenda, offer a basic format for how the meetings will work, and let people offer feedback. If everyone is cool with what you outlined, jump into the discussion. As the facilitator, always show up to meetings with a list of your own questions for the group and a story or two to share if people are slow to volunteer their own. Smile, introduce people when they show up, and do everything you can to create the friendly vibe you want the group to have. If you find someone who is willing to help lead the group, make her a co-organizer.

One trick to a good first meeting is to pick a few people to meet with one-on-one before the first meeting. Buy them coffee, get to know them, and ask for their support at the first meeting. This seeding of a discussion group will make you less nervous at the first discussion, but also establish a friendly vibe for everyone since there are at least two people who already know each other. Of course, an interested friend can play the same role.

No matter how amazing you do, some people will drop off after the first meeting. It's natural. They were curious, wanted to see what it was like, but their curiosity faded after they attended once. The people who stay are those you want anyway. As long as you have one other person involved, you can ask him to help grow the group, or keep it just the two of you.

Sample discussion topics

The simplest format for a discussion group is to follow the chapters of a book. Each week people read the chapter and meet to discuss their thoughts, share stories, or do the exercises for that chapter. When the book is finished, pick another book. Or rotate the responsibility every week, where each member has to pick a blog post or web article to read and discuss. As a supplement, here are a few sample discussion topics pulled from the PM Clinic mentioned above.

Balancing my time with team time

One of my responsibilities as a project manager is to shield the developers on my team from constant interruption and to structure their work so that they can have chunks of time to concentrate. My challenge is that I also need an arrangement that allows me to have dedicated time to concentrate. I find that in trying to keep things moving for my team and my clients, I often have to find my "concentration time" after hours or on the weekends. I'd like advice from other project managers on how they balance all the hats so that they meet the needs/requests coming in from clients and team members while also knocking things off their to-do list.

Customers versus team

One of my responsibilities as a PM is to "own" the relationship with an internal customer. My challenge is that at least four other people on my team interact with the customer team (working with four different people on their team) at least once a week. I find it nearly impossible to stay on top of all the issues the customer is facing to ensure that we're delighting the customer. How can I keep track of all the interaction that happens with the customer, and ensure that this is communicated effectively within the team without annoying the crap out of everyone involved? Tactical and strategic advice would be super valuable.

To innovate or not to innovate

Development teams get narrow windows to propose something different and innovative from their organizational or industry norms. Otherwise, it's back to the digital chain gang, working on a roadmap derived from bugs, customer feature requests, VP whim, or a competitor's existing features. How does a team best prepare for and then manage those brief opportunities to do something different than the norm? How does one balance investment in innovation against other concerns, such as execution?

My boss is a blowhard

The overall project leader, my boss, is a blowhard. In our team meetings, he wastes all kinds of time talking about things no one cares about (war stories, pet peeves, bad jokes, etc.). He seems to believe that he's entertaining, but few others share this belief. So, our weekly team meetings are tortured affairs. He doesn't follow his own agenda, and he has little sense of urgency about using up so many people's time. What can I do?

Keeping meetings lean

When I try to run lean meetings on my own subteam, it's hard to get people to come. Everyone thinks any meeting that happens will be more like my boss's meetings (i.e., slow, boring, annoying, and dominated by team leader guy). So, I'm struggling to convince people that my meetings will be different, and then once they come, struggling to actually make them different, since they behave much like they do in the big team meeting (stay quiet and hope it ends soon). What can I do?

Death by disaster

Recently my web development team did an exercise in disaster planning. We sat down as a group, came up with a short list of things that could go wrong, and then tried to brainstorm how we'd respond. (It was a lot of fun and y'all should try it...but anyway.) One of the situations we came up with that generated the most discussion was this: "Three weeks away from your next major deadline, your best programmer gets hit by a bus and is in a coma. You're on your way back to the office from the hospital, trying to figure out your next moves. What would you do and how would you roll those decisions out to your team?"

Train wreck in progress

Our mid-size development team (about 15 people, including test, etc.) is 5 weeks into a 30-week project. Some of us had major concerns during initial planning that were never resolved (to our satisfaction). Now we find ourselves part of the way over a cliff: the architecture direction is misguided, the business plan doesn't make complete sense, and the team is overly scattered and not focused on the same goals (some think they are, but I certainly don't). But the project already has significant momentum, and management doesn't see the danger or feel concern about the problem (although the warning signs of low quality, continuing arguments, and fuzzy requirements are showing). As a project manager in the middle of a project, how should I work to prevent what I think is a train wreck in progress? How can I protect the development team, and the project, from what I think will be painful major changes (and throwing away of work) in the next four or five weeks? How do I save a project that is starting to run off its rails?

The fight against featuritis

We're a version 3.0 software product for business accounting. The product is at a point where many of the common and important features already exist, and the design is becoming mature. But what's happening is that the waves of features that the entire team (business/marketing, as well as engineering) is pushing for are all minor things, which sound cool but that most people probably will never use, or never use more than once or twice. I've seen feature creep-and-bloat happen before on other projects, and all the warning signs are there now. We're becoming a feature farm, not a product development organization. And everyone seems gung ho at the prospect. How can I make sure versions 3.0 and 4.0 don't bury all the good work we did in earlier versions with tons of pet features, marketing features, and other stuff? How can engineering continue to help the core business, but not turn the product into a coding and usability disaster area?

Ultimate fighting championship-style team meetings

I'm the sole project manager on a team of five programmers, three testers, and a handful of other specialists (documentation, localization, etc.). We have decent processes in place for most of the basics, and generally get along and work together well. However, the machete-size thorn in all of our sides is design. When it comes to figuring out what the features are, and how they work, it's a no holds barred, full-on WWE slamfest. We argue, fight, get frustrated, and struggle over various kinds of design decisions. Sometimes the arguments are about UI design, sometimes they're about high-level programming choices (object models/APIs, not implementation), and sometimes they're even about the requirements themselves. In our organization, it's not uncommon for executives and manager types to jump in on some of these debates as well (aka battle royale).

So, my question is: what should the role of a project manager be in leading design choices? Should PMs lean toward tracking/supporting projects, or should they be leading them? And if they are to lead, how much involvement should they have in the design of the software/web site itself?

In-house or off-the-shelf

My team was faced with the choice of buying expensive off-the-shelf software or writing it in-house; we decided on the latter course since it was an important tool (a software performance analyzer), was within the range of our expertise, and is something we expect to customize in the future. After five months of development (a month beyond the initial schedule), the product is still not working properly and is significantly far away from completion (another eight weeks by current estimates). The in-house development costs have already exceeded the costs of the off-the-shelf product. When should the PM face reality and persuade management to buy the product? Or, should we throw good money after bad and wrestle the in-house product to completion?

Everything is urgent

I have a classic project management nightmare: poorly defined requirements, few specs, short lead time, no additional time or resources, and the kicker: it's a client-based project that, if not delivered on time and to their satisfaction, could cost my company a significant amount of business. To add insult to injury:

- The client insists that every issue is a showstopper and refuses to prioritize.
- The client is still pushing to add new functionality.
- The client is also peeved because they don't think our company has been performing well on this project.
- Internal politics include a development manager who is about to be ousted, a tester who is about to be fired (and no replacement), and me, a lone project manager replacing someone who has been underperforming but is staying with the company, and not inclined to help me in the transition.

I was brought in yesterday to clean up the mess (think Harvey Keitel). I have a ship date of April 15. I'm in need of some very creative strategies, specifically to wind my way through all the internal and client politics, to soothe a pissy client, and to deliver quality software in four weeks!

Books and other media appear in this bibliography for one of two reasons: either they had the most influence on my ideas, or they have the most value for future reading and exploration.

Philosophy and strategy

de Botton, Alain, *The Consolations of Philosophy* (Vintage, 2001) ISBN 0679779175

Management philosophy derives much from classical Eastern and Western philosophy, and this is a good place to start. I understood and remembered more about Western philosophy from this little book than several years of university philosophy education. de Botton writes essays that are short, thought provoking, informal, fun, personable, and memorable. This is the one book I give to people when they say they are interested in philosophy but don't know where to start.

Russell, Bertrand, *The Conquest of Happiness* (Liveright Publishing Corporation, 1930) ISBN 0871401622

Happy people make for better managers. While I doubt happiness can be conquered, this book will help you sort out what makes you happy and why. Russell was a prominent philosopher in the 20th century, and in spite of that, he writes very well. He was something of a troublemaker and free thinker and it shows in his writing. I first read this book on a road trip with Chris McGee from Seattle to Banff. I started on the trip quite unhappy with life in general, and came back ready to make changes. This book, Chris, and the trip itself were all influential in my decision to leave Microsoft and start writing.

Tzu, Sun, *The Art of War*, Pocket Edition (Shambala, 1991) ISBN 0877735379

This was the first Eastern philosophy book I read that made any sense to me. I recommend it for its simplicity and very short length. It's written as a book on military strategy, but has many practical applications. For many years I carried the pocket edition of this book in my jacket, until the covers wore off and half the pages were dog-eared (a decade ago I ran into Faisal Jawdat, who would eventually be a tech reviewer for this book, at the CMU Student Center, and we were both amazed to see the other pull the same edition of this book out of his pocket). If you find this book too obscure or abstract, try the more direct and fun *Essential Crazy Wisdom*, by Wes Nisker (Ten Speed Press, 2001) ISBN 1580083463.

Psychology

Zeldin, Theodore, *An Intimate History of Humanity* (Vintage, 1998) ISBN 0749396237

Human nature is more vibrant and complex than we give ourselves credit for. This nontraditional collection of essays based on personal interviews offers insight into what makes us who we are. I found this book unexpectedly moving. It's not a formal scientific book about psychology: it's more of a collection of essays by a very wise, curious, and thoughtful man.

High Noon. 1952. Lionsgate/Fox. 2004. DVD.

A classic western film about a sheriff trying to do what he thinks is right. Leadership and integrity inevitably put an individual into situations where they may have to stand alone. This film explores the psychology of leaders and followers in difficult situations. It illuminates why people are defined as much by what they're willing to do, as what they're not. It's also just a good Western, starring Gary Cooper.

Twelve Angry Men. 1957. MGM/UA Video. 2001. DVD.

Another important film about human psychology and group dynamics in difficult situations. Henry Fonda plays a jury member who believes something all of the others does not. He then tries to convince a room full of frustrated people that what they passionately believe cannot be true. Like *High Noon*, questions about power, influence, integrity, and belief are central themes, and all are relevant to people who lead or manage others. It's also a classic of filmmaking, directed by Sidney Lumet (author of the highly recommended profile of the filmmaking process, *Making Movies*, Vintage, 1996), and starring Henry Fonda.

History

Boorstin, Daniel J., *The Creators: A History of Heroes of the Imagination* (Vintage, 1993) ISBN 0679743758

Boorstin's series of three history books (*The Discoverers*, *The Creators*, *The Seekers*) are worth their weight in gold. *The Creators* follows the Western history of creative work, from architects, painters, and writers, to engineers. He finds anecdotes and stories that make their pursuits directly relevant and inspirational to anyone trying to do creative work today.

Kidder, Tracy, *The Soul of a New Machine* (Back Bay Books, 2000) ISBN 0316491977

This book captures the spirit of the early computer revolution, when the focus was still on hardware and electrical engineering. The strength of this book is Kidder's ability to capture the compulsive and obsessive drive engineers have to build and create. Despite the fact that the story centers on the Data General machines and minicomputers they were building in the late 1970s, I still find this book best captures the personal and team challenges of working in the tech sector.

Kranz, Gene, *Failure Is Not an Option* (Berkley Publishing, 2001) ISBN 0425179877

A thrilling account of Kranz's experiences in NASA's flight direction group. It covers the early Mercury missions, all the way through *Apollo 13*. There are many lessons here for project managers about working under deadlines, making commitments to deliver on what are effectively experiments, and how to lead and manage engineers under pressure.

Management and politics

Farson, Richard, *Management of the Absurd* (Free Press, 1997) ISBN 0684830442

By using the paradoxes and irrationalities of human behavior in organizations, this book explores what good management behavior is all about. It was a fun read primarily because he talks about many of the subjects other books are afraid to cover. Farson claims some problems are comprehendible and solvable only with assistance from our intuition, and that the exclusive dependence on logic often gets us into trouble.

Fisher, Roger, et al., *Getting to Yes* (Penguin Books, 1991) ISBN 0140157352

Best negotiation book per page of reading I've found. It's well written, straightforward, and practical. Highly recommended.

Klein, Gary, *Sources of Power: How People Make Decisions* (MIT Press, 1999) ISBN 0262611465

This was a primary source for Chapter 8. I found explanations and research in it that helped me understand many of my own beliefs about decision making.

Silbiger, Steven, *The Ten-Day MBA* (Quill, 1999) ISBN 0688137881

I've read many general business books but this is the one I refer back to most often. It covers 10 core subjects of many MBA programs, cutting to the chase on the core ideas and philosophies in each one. It reads like notes for a good textbook: it's clear that some formalisms have been avoided and the author instead provides his own less-formal but easier-to-follow explanations for certain concepts.

Quick, Thomas, *Power Plays: A Guide to Maximizing Performance and Success in Business* (F. Watt, 1985) ISBN 0531095827

> Picked this up on the used sale rack. Became one of the most useful references for Chapter 16. The book is vaguely self-help in that it attempts to give a framework for organization politics and advice on how to achieve certain goals. It gave the best summation of tactics that I found, and managed the ethical issues relatively well. Out of print as of this writing, but should be available through online used bookstores.

Science, engineering, and architecture

Brand, Stewart, *How Buildings Learn: What Happens After They're Built* (Penguin Books, 1995) ISBN 0140139966

> This text accelerated my belief that the things I knew regarding projects and design from the technology sector had application and relevance generally to the world. This is one of my favorite books on architecture because of how physically approachable it is: lots of pictures and examples. Brand writes and thinks like a good teacher, making things interesting, and on occasion funny, as he leads your curiosity down clever, epiphany-laden paths.

Chiles, John, *Inviting Disaster: Lessons from the Edge of Technology* (Harper Business, 2002) ISBN 0066620821

> From airline crashes to oil-rig sinkings, the stories in this book point out the direct relationship between complex engineering and their fragile, simple, nonlinear weaknesses that can lead to disaster. Although it reads more like a series of long essays on specific disasters than a book with a central or connected theme, I found all of the stories of technological disaster interesting and thought provoking.

Cross, Hardy, *Engineers and Ivory Towers* (Ayer, 1952) ISBN 083691404X

> Found two references to this book on the same day, in fairly unrelated materials, and felt compelled to dig it up, and found gold. It's an extended rant by an engineer on the state of the engineering profession circa 1952. He questions many of the popular attitudes among engineers, from general hubris, to lack of aesthetic or artistic knowledge, and provides hints at a better, deep view of what engineering should be about. I found this book to be what I'd expected from Samuel Florman's *The Existential Pleasures of Engineering* (St. Martins, 1976).

Petroski, Henry, *To Engineer Is Human: The Role of Failure in Successful Design* (Vintage Books, 1992) ISBN 0679734163

> A classic on the inevitability of failure and how learning from it is a key part of engineering progress. Petroski analyzes several engineering disasters from the Tacoma Narrows Bridge to the Challenger Space Shuttle, and exposes the theoretical and tactical failures involved. Well written, short, and in some ways inspirational.

Software process and methodology

Beck, Kent, *Extreme Programming Explained* (Addison-Wesley, 1999) ISBN 0201616416

This short book clarifies the intention and philosophy of XP and gives some of the basics for how to make it happen. It's compelling in spirit and passion, but often reads more like a spiritual than a playbook. It explains iterations, velocity, stories, and the other key processes of XP, while simultaneously expressing their benefits. I examined many of the other extreme and agile programming books, and found they generally overlapped significantly with the coverage here. *Planning Extreme Programming* (also by Beck) was the only other XP text I found useful enough to generate notes from. It's more procedural than "embrace change" (although the first half does overlap heavily with it).

Brooks, Fred, *The Mythical Man-Month* (Addison-Wesley, 1995) ISBN 0201835959

This grand classic, first published more than 20 years ago, still hits home on many major points. Brooks writes well, uses strong metaphors, and leaves you feeling like you just conversed with a man much wiser and friendlier than you are. It's perhaps the most well-known and widely respected book on managing software development projects.

Bullock, James, et al., *Roundtable on Project Management: A SHAPE Forum Dialog* (Dorset House, 2001) ISBN 093263348X

A collection of summarized conversations from Weinberg's SHAPE discussion group. I loved this book. It captures the spirit and energy of being in a conversation with a bunch of very smart and experienced people who are generous about sharing what they know. They cover many of the topics in software project management from project inception, schedules, conflict, and management politics. The book is short. It's based on conversations, so it's more pith and nugget than theory and playbook.

Cockburn, Alistair, *Agile Software Development* (Addison-Wesley, 2001) ISBN 0201699699

The second half of this book has excellent coverage of software development methodology, and thoughts for would-be methodology creators. This book is heavily referenced (sometimes frighteningly so) and shifts back and forth between a practical guide and a high-level, theory-based textbook. If you like a mixture of both, this book is for you.

DeMarco, Tom and Timothy Lister, *Peopleware* (Dorset House, 1999) ISBN 0932633439

The classic management book on programmers as people. It humanizes the software development process by capturing how important working and social environment are in making people productive. The focus on teams and performance over hierarchy and rules makes this book a godsend for managers new to tech-sector work environments. Filled with tons of suggestions and recommendations, this is one of the great ones.

Friedlein, Ashley, *Web Project Management* (Morgan Kaufmann, 2001) ISBN 1558606785

I spent much time looking for good books specifically on managing web development. I didn't find many. This was the only one that I was able to generate good notes from. Although it's written mostly from the perspective of web development firms and contract-based work, this doesn't get in the way of the advice. Friedlein offers a simple methodology and plenty of stories and case studies, and captures the interaction of roles (design, test, programming, etc.) needed to make high-speed web production possible.

Humphrey, Watts S., *Managing the Software Process* (Addison-Wesley Professional, 1989) ISBN 0201180952

Humphrey is one of the great pioneers in software engineering work. This was the most accessible and applicable book of his that I found. It covers the SEI CMM (Capacity Maturity Model, *http://www.sei.cmu.edu/cmm/cmms/cmms.html*) in detail. It provides general development management advice for many of the core situations. Be warned that the writing, though generally good, can be dry at times: it is a textbook (and priced accordingly). The examples and philosophy tend to make more sense for larger organizations.

McCarthy, Jim, *Dynamics of Software Development* (Microsoft Press, 1995) ISBN 1556158238

One of the first books I read as a program manager at Microsoft. McCarthy, former development manager for Visual C++ at Microsoft, breaks down the craft of shipping software into bite-size nuggets, roughly organized by chronology in the development process. This book is one of the first recommendations I make to new program managers at Microsoft: it captures the old-school Microsoft PM attitude, the good and the bad, better than any book I know of.

McConnell, Steve, *Rapid Development* (Microsoft Press, 1996) ISBN 1556159005

This book sat untouched on my shelf for years solely because of its enormous size: throwing this at a small programmer might kill him. However, Chapter 3 on common software failures is worth the price of admission alone. The book is a sort of encyclopedia of knowledge on modern software development: very broad and concise. What makes this book a winner is how effective McConnell is in offering advice, and picking useful aspects of situations or problems to cover.

Project Management Institute (PMI), *www.pmi.org*

This is the most well-known organization for people interested in project management. They offer courses and events at local chapters in many cities, publish newsletters and magazines, and are an excellent general resource for learning more about formalized project management.

Weinberg, Gerald, *Quality Software Management*, Vols. 1–4 (Dorset House, 2001)
ISBN 0932633242

This is Weinberg's four-part opus on managing software development. Volumes 1 and 2 provide all kinds of great insights into understanding what's really going on with a project, and how to manage and direct it predictably. With a mixture of science, philosophy, observation, and humor, these textbooks give lots of mileage and unexpected insights. Weinberg goes deep in this book: it inspired many contemplative pauses while reading.

Whitehead, Richard, *Leading a Software Development Team* (Addison-Wesley, 2001)
ISBN 0201675269

The most practical and straightforward book I've found on leading small development teams. I picked this up on a lark during early research since I'd never heard mention of the book before, and was continually surprised by the quality of what I'd read. Very pragmatic, wise, simple, and useful. This was one of the unexpected gems of all my research.

ACKNOWLEDGMENTS

For this revised edition

Thanks to the O'Reilly crew of Mary Treseler, Marlowe Shaeffer, Sara Peyton, and Rob Romano. Kudos to Faisal Jawdat, Neil Enns, David Gobert, Linda Lee, Ken Norton, Linda Whitesell, and Steven Levy for long hours reviewing the first edition and suggesting changes. And thanks to everyone who bought the first edition, helped to spread the word, and made this first update possible.

From the previous edition

Big thanks to Mike Hendrickson, my editor at O'Reilly, for giving me the green light and plenty of rope. Superior grade thanks to Faisal Jawdat, Ben Lieberman, and Andrew Stellman, the brave and generous tech reviewers of the early drafts.

The making of this book involved many people: thanks to Marlowe Shaeffer (production editor) for managing the project that is this book, Marcia Friedman (interior designer), Rob Romano (illustrator), Jeremy Mende (cover designer), Audrey Doyle (proofreader), Ellen Troutman-Zaig (indexer), and Glenn Bisignani (product marketing manager).

The following people volunteered their time to be interviewed, or to give feedback on early drafts of chapters. Muchos gracias to Michelle Breman, Pierro Sierra, Eric Brechner, Richard Stoakley, Mark Stutzman, Neil Enns, Jason Pace, Aly Valli, Joe Belfiore, Bill Staples, Laura John, Hillel Cooperman, Stacia Scott, Gwynne Stoddart, Terri Bronson, Barbara Wilson, Terrel Lefferts, Mike Glass, Chromatic, and Richard Grudman. Special thanks to Ken Dye, my first manager at Microsoft, and Joe Belfiore for giving me my break into program management and shaping my early ideas on what good managers and leaders are supposed to do.

Additional, individually wrapped thanks to my wife, Jill "bear" Stutzman; Richard "big daddy" Grudman; the Reservoir Dogs (Chris "our hero" McGee, Mike "all the moves" Viola, David "pretty boy" Sandberg, Joe "gourmet" Mirza, Phil "five-card stud" Simon); Vanessa "NYC" Longacre; Bob "making the Web work" Baxley; and the fine folks at gnostron, unhinged, and the pm-clinic. General thanks to the very idea of the universe; the word papaya; big forests with big trees; people who remain silly, curious, and fun beyond their years; the letter Q and the number 42. A thank you value pack to the King County library system and all librarians everywhere. The Interlibrary loan program is a godsend. Thanks guys.

The following music kept me sane during long hours at the keyboard: White Stripes, Palomar, Aimee Mann, The Clash, Johnny Cash, Social Distortion, Rollins Band, Sonny Rollins, Charles Mingus, Theloneous Monk, Breeders: *Last Splash*, AudioSlave, MC5, Chris McGee's greatest mixes, Jack Johnson, Patty Griffin, Akiva, Flogging Molly, Sinatra, Beatles, Bruce Springsteen, PJ Harvey, Radiohead, Ramones, Weezer, Tom Waits, All Girl Summer Fun Band, Best of Belly, Magnetic Fields, Beth Orton, Elliot Smith, and Nick Cave and the Bad Seeds.

No project managers were harmed in the making of this book. But sadly, Butch, our dog, passed away during final production. Butch, RIP 1991–2004. He was at my feet while many of the ideas and pages here came to be. Good dog, Butch. We'll miss you.

PHOTO CREDITS

Preface, Frank Lee, *www.flee.com*, Duomo, Florence, Italy

Chapter 1, Frank Lee, *www.flee.com*, Duomo, Florence, Italy

Part One, Scott Berkun, Marymoor Park, Redmond, WA

Chapter 2, Scott Berkun, Interstate 84, Idaho

Chapter 3, Scott Berkun, I-5 interchange, Seattle, WA

Chapter 4, Scott Berkun, Farrel McWhirter Park, Redmond, WA

Chapter 5, Scott Berkun, University of Washington

Chapter 6, Scott Berkun, Capilano, Vancouver, Canada

Part Two, Jill Stutzman, *www.uiweb.com/jillart*, Redmond, WA

Chapter 7, David F. Gallagher, *www.lightningfield.com*, NYC

Chapter 8, Scott Berkun, Bakery in Queens, NYC

Chapter 9, Scott Berkun, Scott & Jill

Chapter 10, Scott Berkun, Sea-Tac Airport

Chapter 11, Scott Berkun, Portland (near Powells)

Part Three, Scott Berkun, Used book store, Unknown

Chapter 12, Frank Lee, *www.flee.com*, Amsterdam

Chapter 13, Scott Berkun, Self-portrait, Yellowstone National Park

Chapter 14, Scott Berkun, Broomball #1, Brainerd, ND

Chapter 15, Scott Berkun, Broomball #2, Brainerd, ND

Chapter 16, Scott Berkun, Eiffel Tower, Paris

Appendix, Scott Berkun, Boat to Elephanta Island, Mumbai, India

INDEX

A

Abt, Clark, 156
accountability, lack of, 338
accuracy versus precision, 31, 168
acknowledgment for work done, 149
action, conversion of communicated
    messages to, 181
ad hominem attacks, 182
Adams, Scott, 270
adjustments
    corrective actions with unforeseen
        consequences, 281
    safe action during mid-game,
        286–288
    strategic questions for staying
        ahead, 284
    tactical questions for staying
        ahead, 284
adversities, overcoming, 214–237
    conflict resolution and
        negotiation, 224–226
    criteria for defining difficult
        situations, 217
    damage control, 222
    emotions, 228–235
        feelings about feelings, 232
        hero complex, 233
        pressure, 229–232
    exercises, 236
    good training for PMs, 220
    handling difficult situations, 214–216
    list of difficult situations, 218–220
    roles and clear authority, 226–228
    summary of key points, 236
    taking responsibility, 221
    trust and, 251

advice
    following, 187
    seeking out expertise or useful
        advice, 276
affinity diagrams, 122–124
    how they work (example), 123
agile methods, 28, 29
Agile Software Development, 365
agreement
    finding points of agreement, 224
    in communications, 180
alternatives
    best alternative to negotiated
        agreement, 225
    exploring for problem situations, 216
ambiguity, tolerance of, 11
anger in difficult situations, 214
annoying others, avoiding, 194–212
    creating and rolling out good
        process, 199
    effects of good process, 195–197
    email, 200–205
        example of bad email, 204
        example of good email, 205
        writing good email, 201–203
    exercises, 212
    formula for good process, 198
    meetings, 205–211
        art of facilitation, 206
        evil of recurring meetings, 209
        pointers on, 210
        pointers on facilitation, 207
        types of meetings, 208
    protecting teams from bad
        processes, 199
    summary of causes of
        annoyance, 194
    summary of key ideas, 211

I

ideas
 managing, 114–131
  changes causing chain
   reactions, 117
  consolidating ideas, 121–124
  creative momentum, 119
  decisively and predictably, 115
  design phase checkpoints, 120
  design prototypes, 125–128
  exercises, 131
  ideas getting out of control, 114
  refining and prioritizing, 124
  summary of key points, 130
 origins of, 90–111
  bad ideas, 95
  bad ideas leading to good
   ideas, 102–104
  customer-centric design, 108–109
  design exploration, 93–95
  design process as
   conversations, 109
  evaluating ideas, 96
  exercises, 111
  good questions leading to good
   ideas, 99–102
  more approaches to generating
   ideas, 107
  perspective and
   improvisation, 104–107
  quality requirements, 91–93
  stereotypes and
   misperceptions, 95
  summary of key points, 110
  thinking in and out of boxes, 97
impatience, 12
implementation, scheduling, 27
improvisation, 104–107, 110
 rules for idea generation, 106
incompetence, dealing with, 227
inconsistent behavior, trust and, 244
individual goals, 73
industrial designers, 85
inertia (project), corrective actions
 and, 281
Influence, 349
influence
 indirect use of, 347
 multistage use of, 346
 as source of power, 335

 using to flank your objective, 346
 (see also politics; power)
information
 precision versus accuracy, 168
 research as ammunition, 168
 transmitted via email, 180
Inmates Are Running the Asylum, 126
innovation, decisions on, 357
inspiration
 eliciting the best work from
  others, 187
 provided by vision documents, 75
interaction designers, 85
interests, mutual, 225
 misuse of power and, 335
interim dates, 303
Internet Explorer 4.0, 13
 decision making, explorer bar
  component, 169
 example of ideas out of control, 114
 web search features, 55
Intimate History of Humanity, 362
intranet web sites
 Hydra example, levels of goals, 73
 problem statements (example), 64
Inviting Disaster, 364
involvement, appropriate level for
 managers, 14
iterations (design), 48, 118
 questions for prototype
  iterations, 128

J

Jefferson, Thomas, 79
Jiro, Kawakita, 122
Jobs, Steve, 104
Johnson, Jeff, 109

K

Kaiser, Henry, 302
Kennedy, John F., 351
Kidder, Tracy, 363
Kitchen Confidential, 6
kitchens, 6
KJ (Kawakita Jiro) diagrams, 122
Klein, Gary, 157, 160, 363
Kluger, Jeffrey, 271
Kranz, Gene, 270, 363
Krug, Steve, 109

Scott Berkun studied computer science, philosophy, and design at Carnegie Mellon University. He worked at Microsoft from 1994 to 2003 on Internet Explorer 1.0 to 5.0, Windows, MSN, and in roles including usability engineer, lead program manager, and UI design evangelist. He left Microsoft in 2003 with the goal of filling this bookshelf (pictured above) with books he has written. He has written two acclaimed books: this one and *The Myths of Innovation* (O'Reilly, 2007). He taught creative thinking at the University of Washington, led an NYC architecture tour at the GEL conference, and his work has been featured in the *New York Times, Washington Post,* and on National Public Radio. Scott makes a living speaking at events and teaching seminars around the world on topics including leading teams, managing projects, and creative thinking.

Visit *www.scottberkun.com* for dozens of thought-provoking essays not found in this book, his frighteningly popular blog, and videos and podcasts of him in action.

COLOPHON

The cover image is a stock photograph from Corbis. The text font is Adobe's Meridien; the heading font is ITC Bailey.

The International Order of Colophon Authors (IOCA) has not approved this colophon despite several petitions, protests, and threats with poisonous, armor-piercing, razor-sharp semicolons (we know how to use them). The world's colophonists are on full colophon strike, refusing to edit, review, or create any new colophons until this gloriously innovative, deeply moving, challenging yet accessible (even to brain-damaged IOCA committee executives) colophon is approved. We can no longer tolerate the suppression of our creative rights and must resist the IOCA's oppressive, cruel, and tyrannical reign. If the next book you read has no colophon, blame the IOCA. Support our cause by adding your name to the petition at *www.downwithioca.org*. Peace out.

Lightning Source UK Ltd.
Milton Keynes UK
UKOW03f1510190615

253745UK00002B/13/P

9 780596 517717